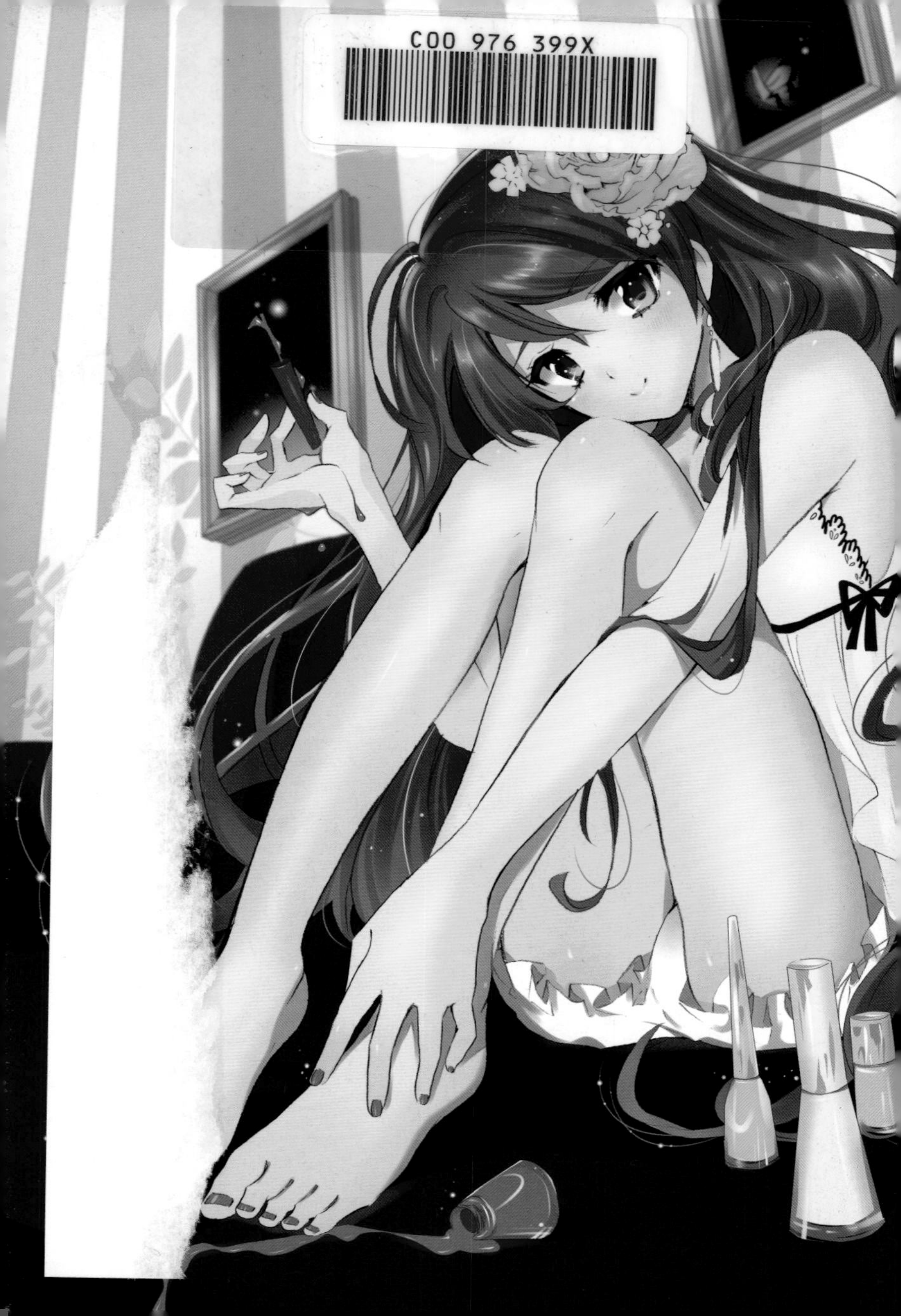

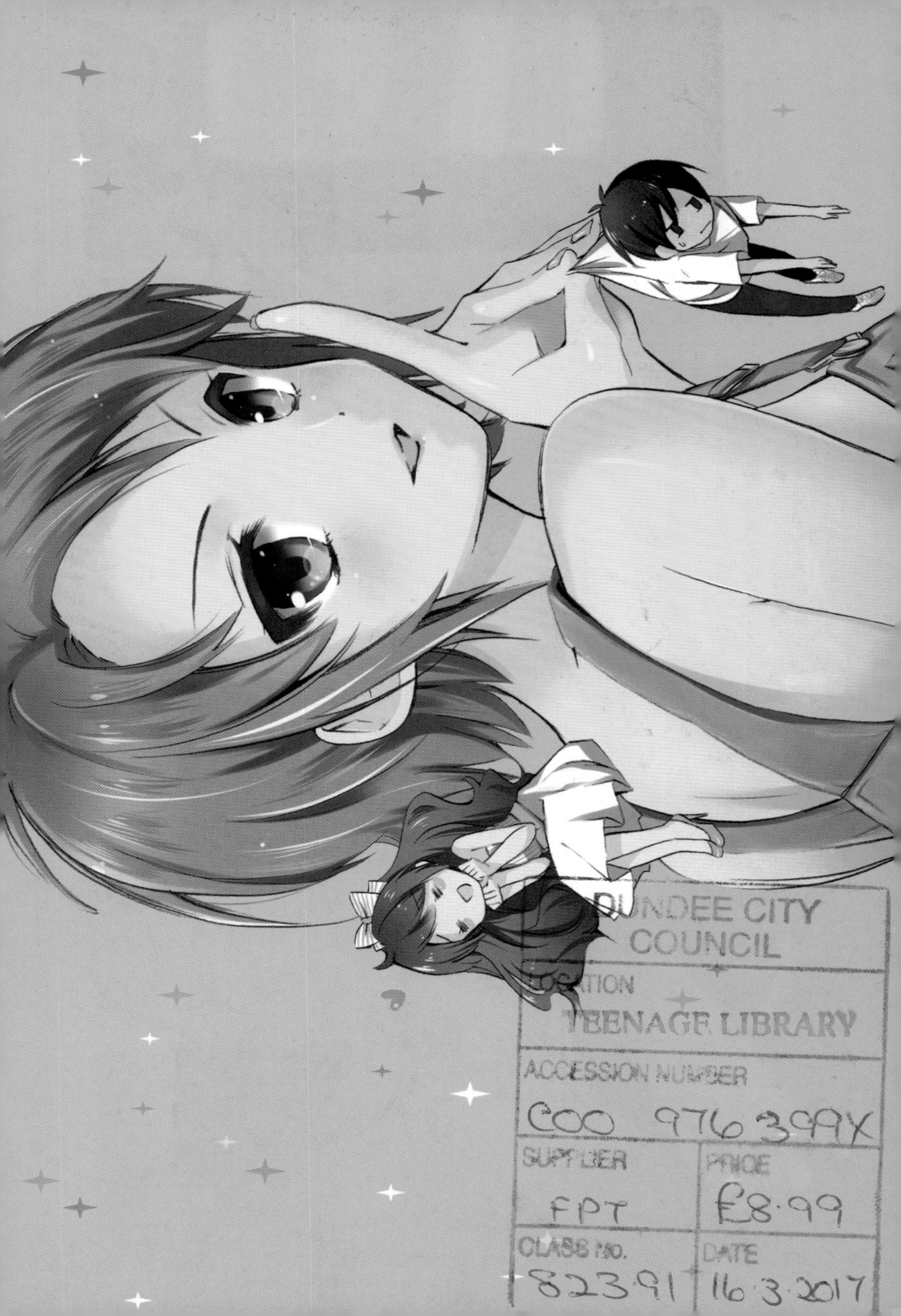

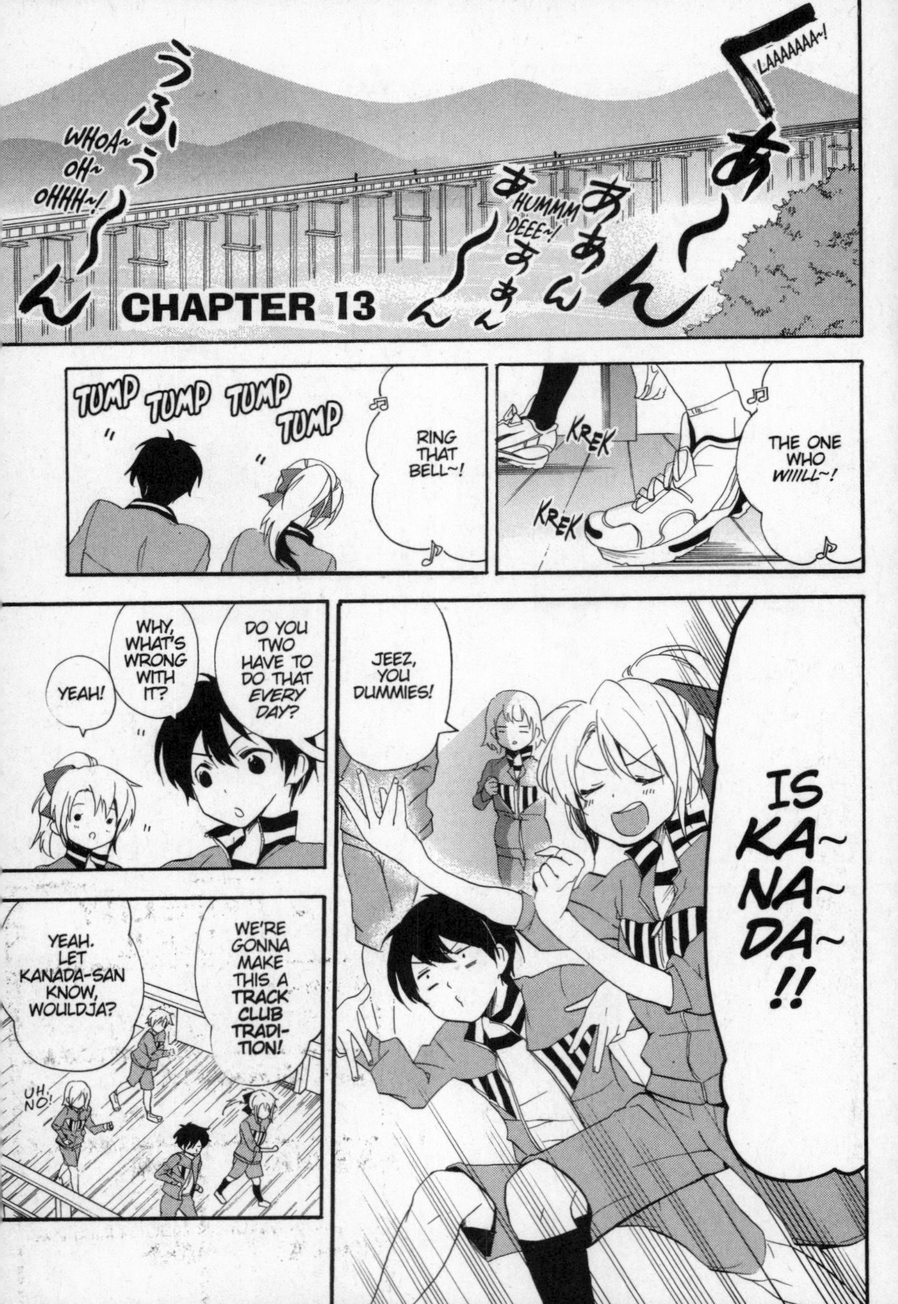
あ～ん
LAAAAAAA~!
あ あん あ あん～
HUMMM DEEE~!
うふう～ん
WHOA~ OH~ OHHH~!
CHAPTER 13
THE ONE WHO WIIILL~!
KREK
KREK
RING THAT BELL~!
TUMP TUMP TUMP TUMP
IS KA~ NA~ DA~!!
JEEZ, YOU DUMMIES!
DO YOU TWO HAVE TO DO THAT EVERY DAY?
WHY, WHAT'S WRONG WITH IT?
YEAH!
WE'RE GONNA MAKE THIS A TRACK CLUB TRADITION!
YEAH. LET KANADA-SAN KNOW, WOULDJA?
UH NO!

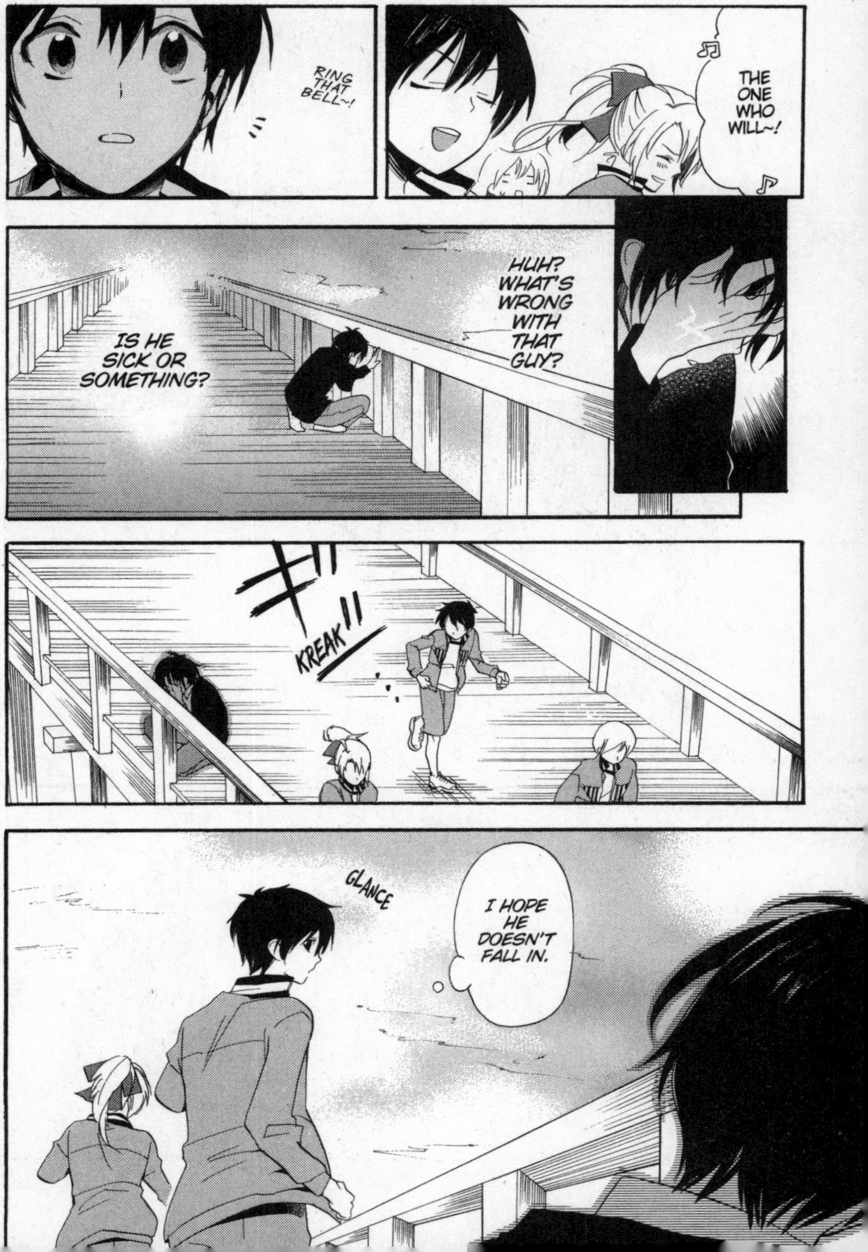
THE ONE WHO WILL~!
RING THAT BELL~!
HUH? WHAT'S WRONG WITH THAT GUY?
IS HE SICK OR SOMETHING?
KREAK
I HOPE HE DOESN'T FALL IN.
GLANCE

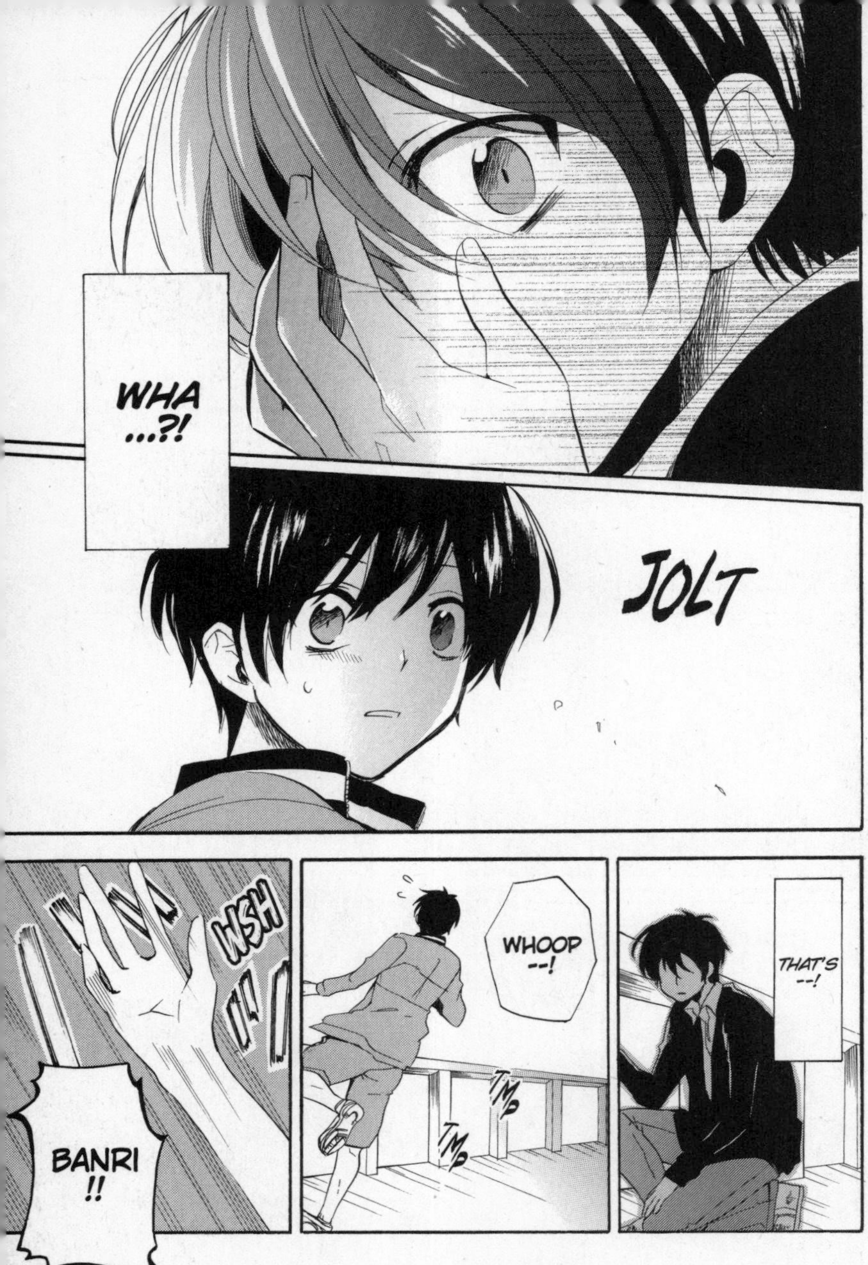
WHA ...?!
JOLT
THAT'S --!
WHOOP --!
TMP
TMP
WSH
BANRI !!

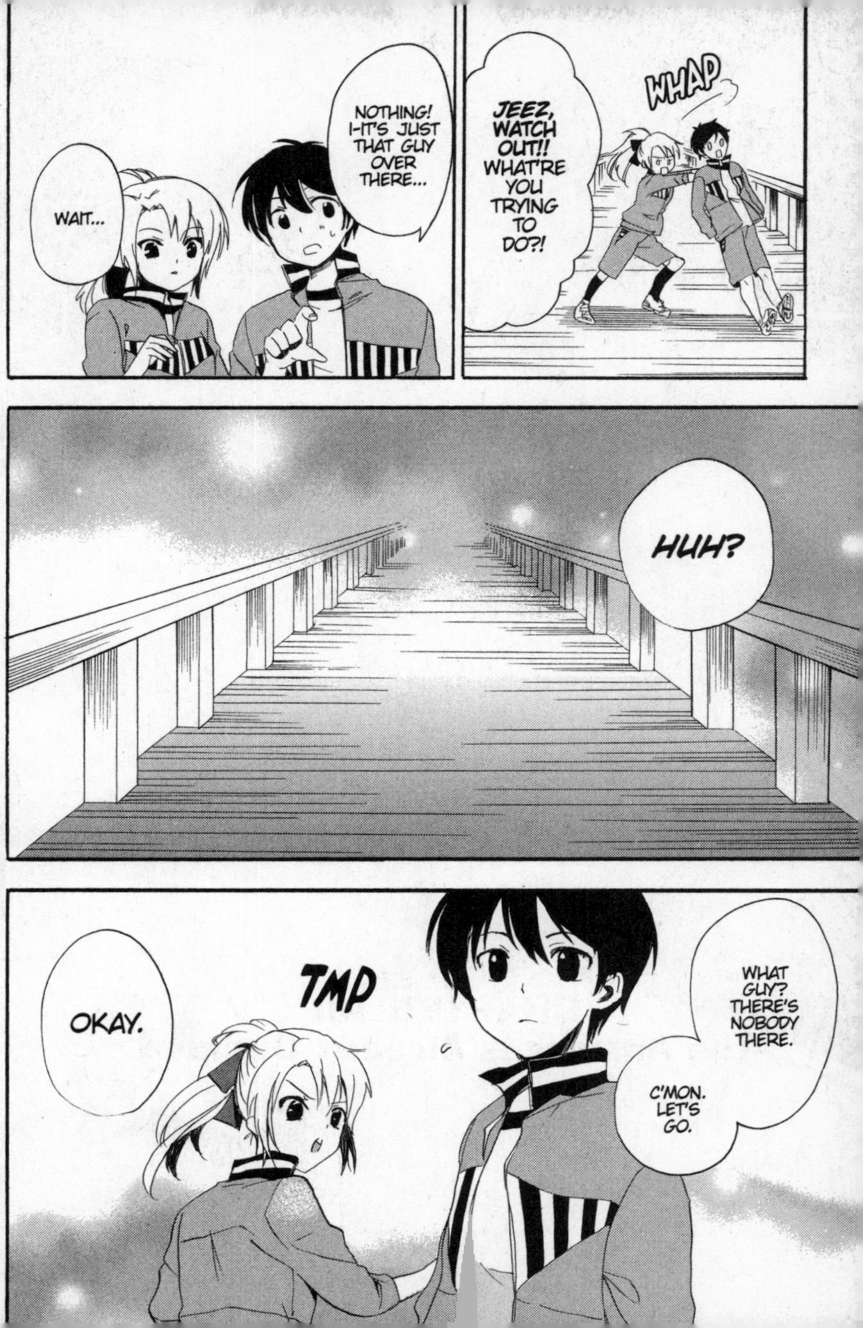
WHAP
JEEZ, WATCH OUT!! WHAT'RE YOU TRYING TO DO?!
NOTHING! I-IT'S JUST THAT GUY OVER THERE...
WAIT...
HUH?
WHAT GUY? THERE'S NOBODY THERE.
C'MON. LET'S GO.
TMP
OKAY.

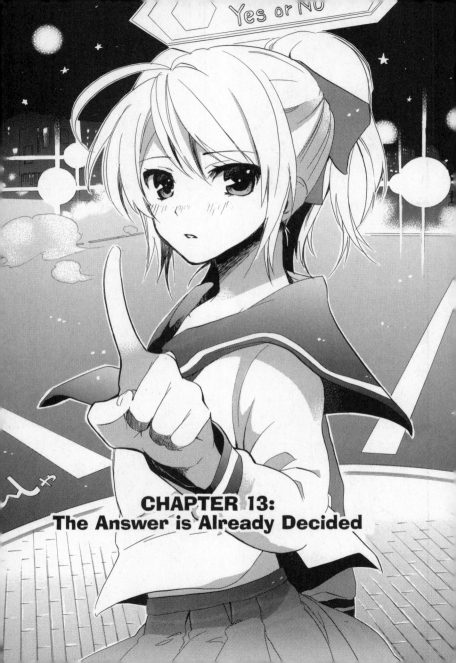

CHAPTER 13:
The Answer is Already Decided

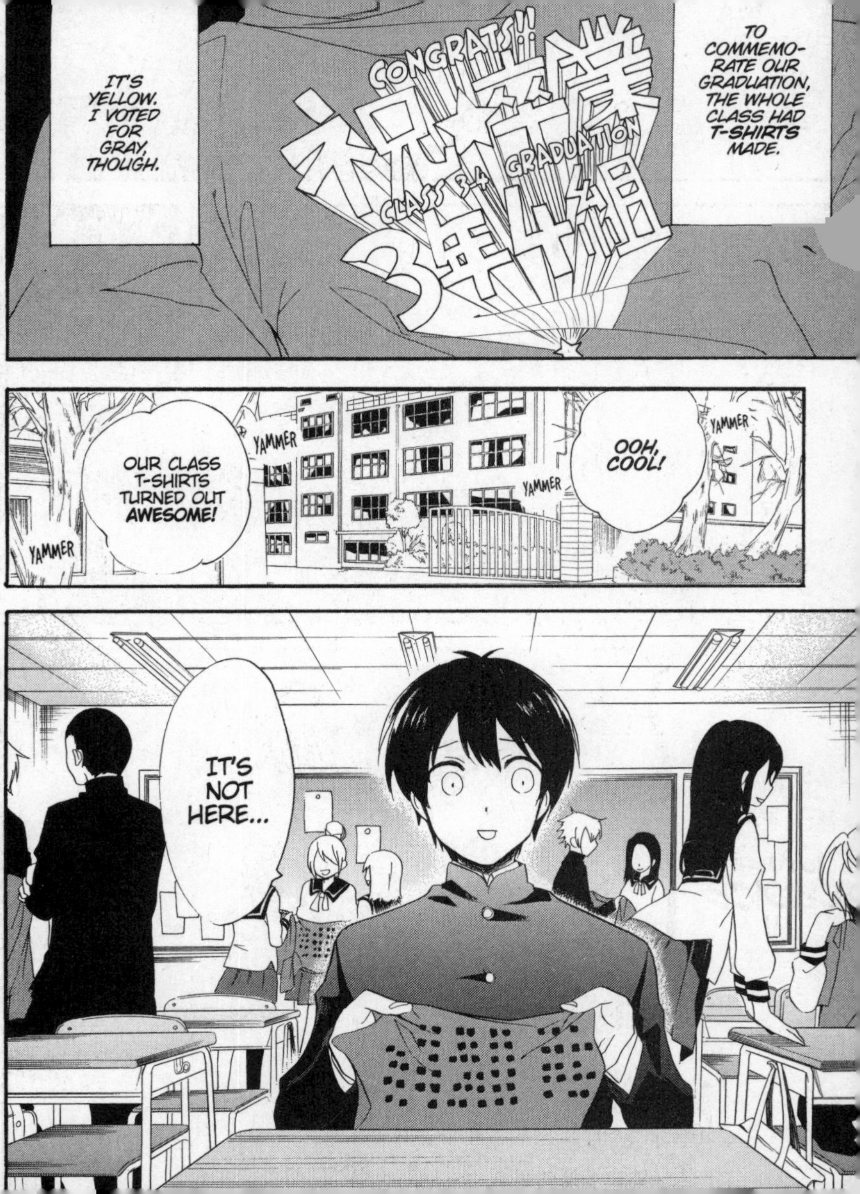
TO COMMEMORATE OUR GRADUATION, THE WHOLE CLASS HAD T-SHIRTS MADE.
CONGRATS!!
祝卒業
GRADUATION
CLASS 3-4
3年4組
IT'S YELLOW. I VOTED FOR GRAY, THOUGH.
YAMMER
OOH, COOL!
YAMMER
YAMMER
OUR CLASS T-SHIRTS TURNED OUT AWESOME!
YAMMER
IT'S NOT HERE...

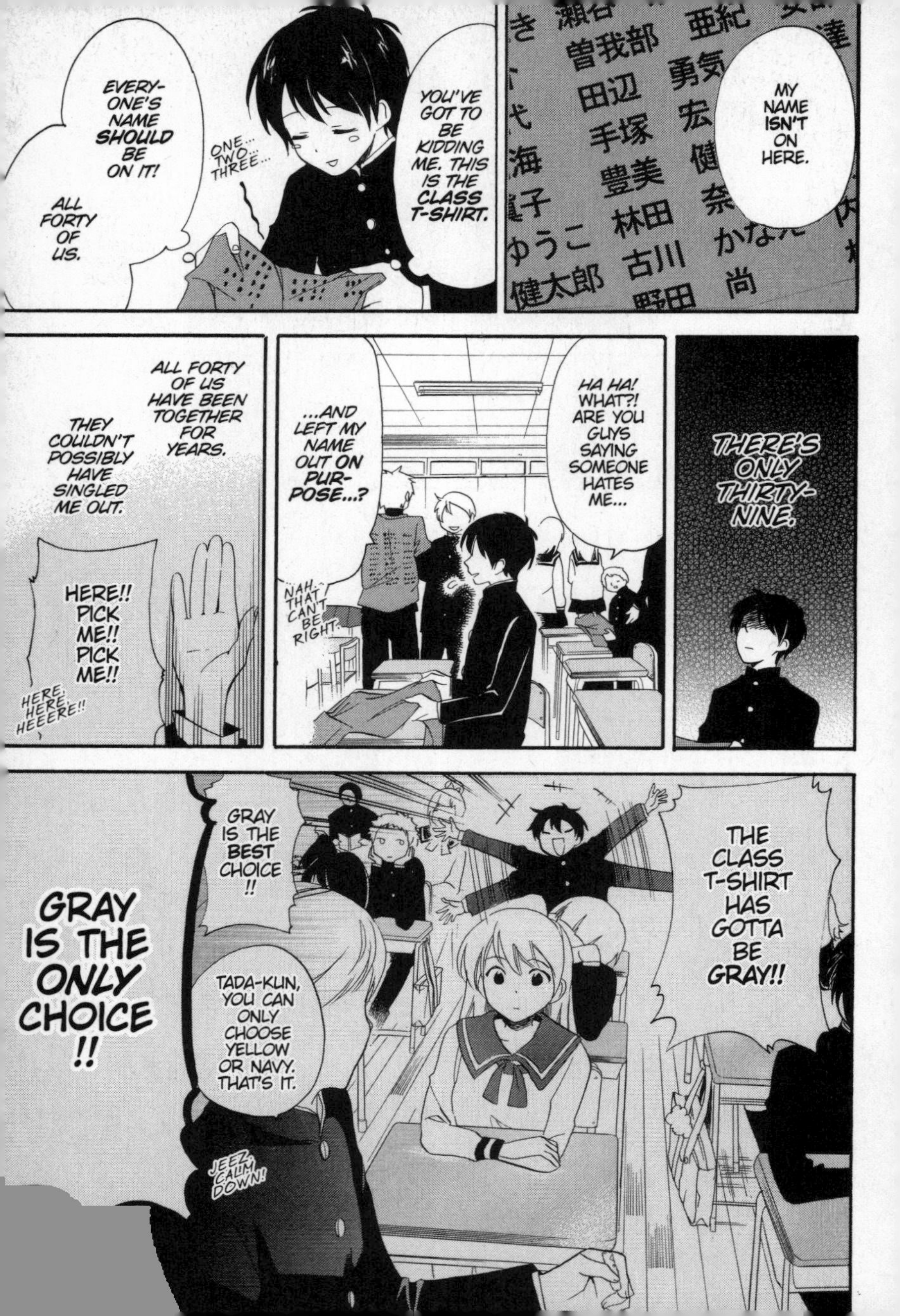

曽我部
亜紀
田辺
勇気
手塚
宏
豊美
林田
ゆうこ
古川
健太郎
尚
MY NAME ISN'T ON HERE.
YOU'VE GOT TO BE KIDDING ME. THIS IS THE CLASS T-SHIRT.
ONE... TWO... THREE...
EVERYONE'S NAME SHOULD BE ON IT!
ALL FORTY OF US.
THERE'S ONLY THIRTY-NINE.
HA HA! WHAT?! ARE YOU GUYS SAYING SOMEONE HATES ME...
...AND LEFT MY NAME OUT ON PURPOSE...?
...NAH... THAT CAN'T BE RIGHT.
ALL FORTY OF US HAVE BEEN TOGETHER FOR YEARS.
THEY COULDN'T POSSIBLY HAVE SINGLED ME OUT.
HERE!! PICK ME!! PICK ME!!
HERE, HERE, HEEERE!!
THE CLASS T-SHIRT HAS GOTTA BE GRAY!!
GRAY IS THE BEST CHOICE!!
TADA-KUN, YOU CAN ONLY CHOOSE YELLOW OR NAVY. THAT'S IT.
GRAY IS THE ONLY CHOICE!!
JEEZ, CALM DOWN!

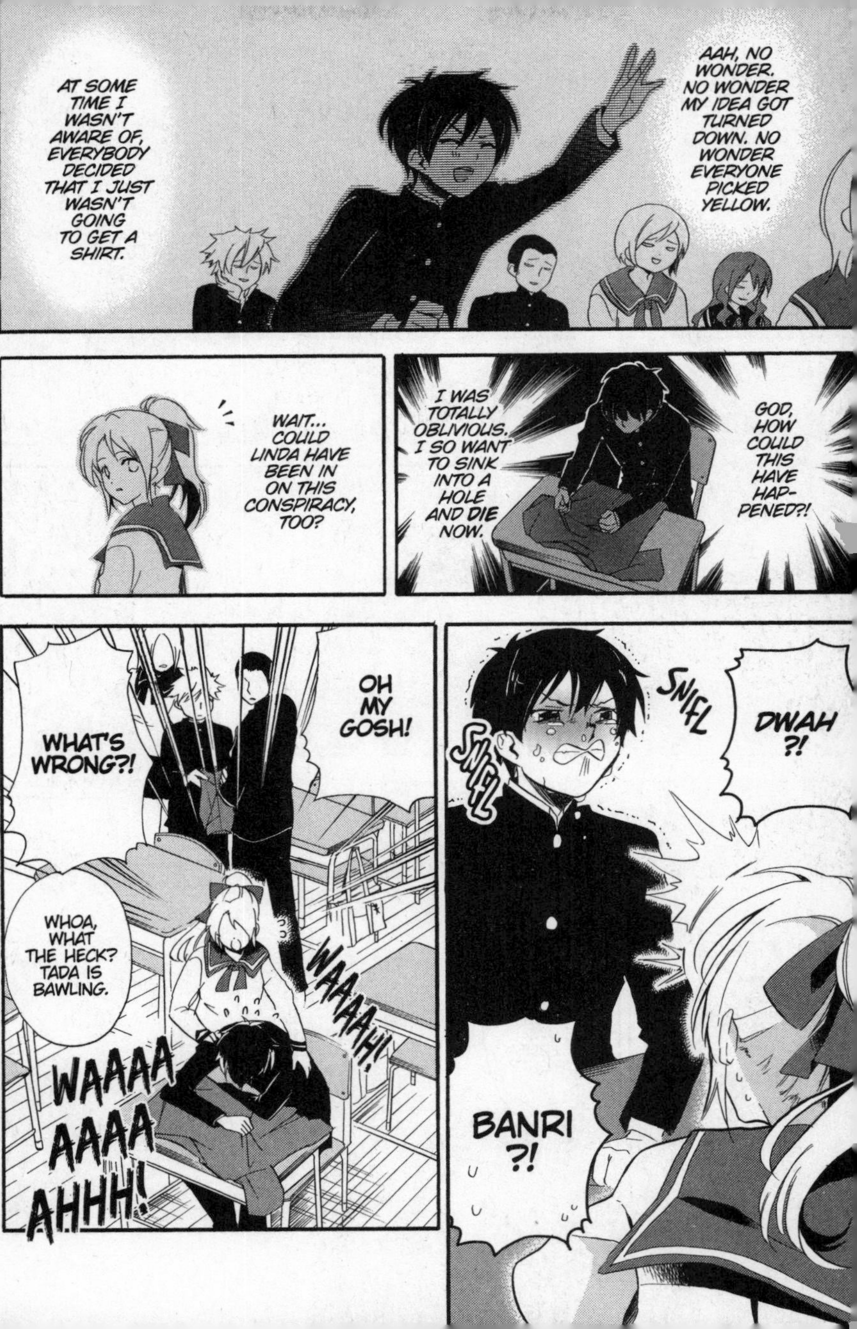
AAH, NO WONDER. NO WONDER MY IDEA GOT TURNED DOWN. NO WONDER EVERYONE PICKED YELLOW.
AT SOME TIME I WASN'T AWARE OF, EVERYBODY DECIDED THAT I JUST WASN'T GOING TO GET A SHIRT.
GOD, HOW COULD THIS HAVE HAP-PENED?!
I WAS TOTALLY OBLIVIOUS. I SO WANT TO SINK INTO A HOLE AND DIE NOW.
WAIT... COULD LINDA HAVE BEEN IN ON THIS CONSPIRACY, TOO?
DWAH ?!
SNIFL
SNIFL
BANRI ?!
OH MY GOSH!
WHAT'S WRONG?!
WHOA, WHAT THE HECK? TADA IS BAWLING.
WAAAAAH!
WAAAA AAAA AHHH!

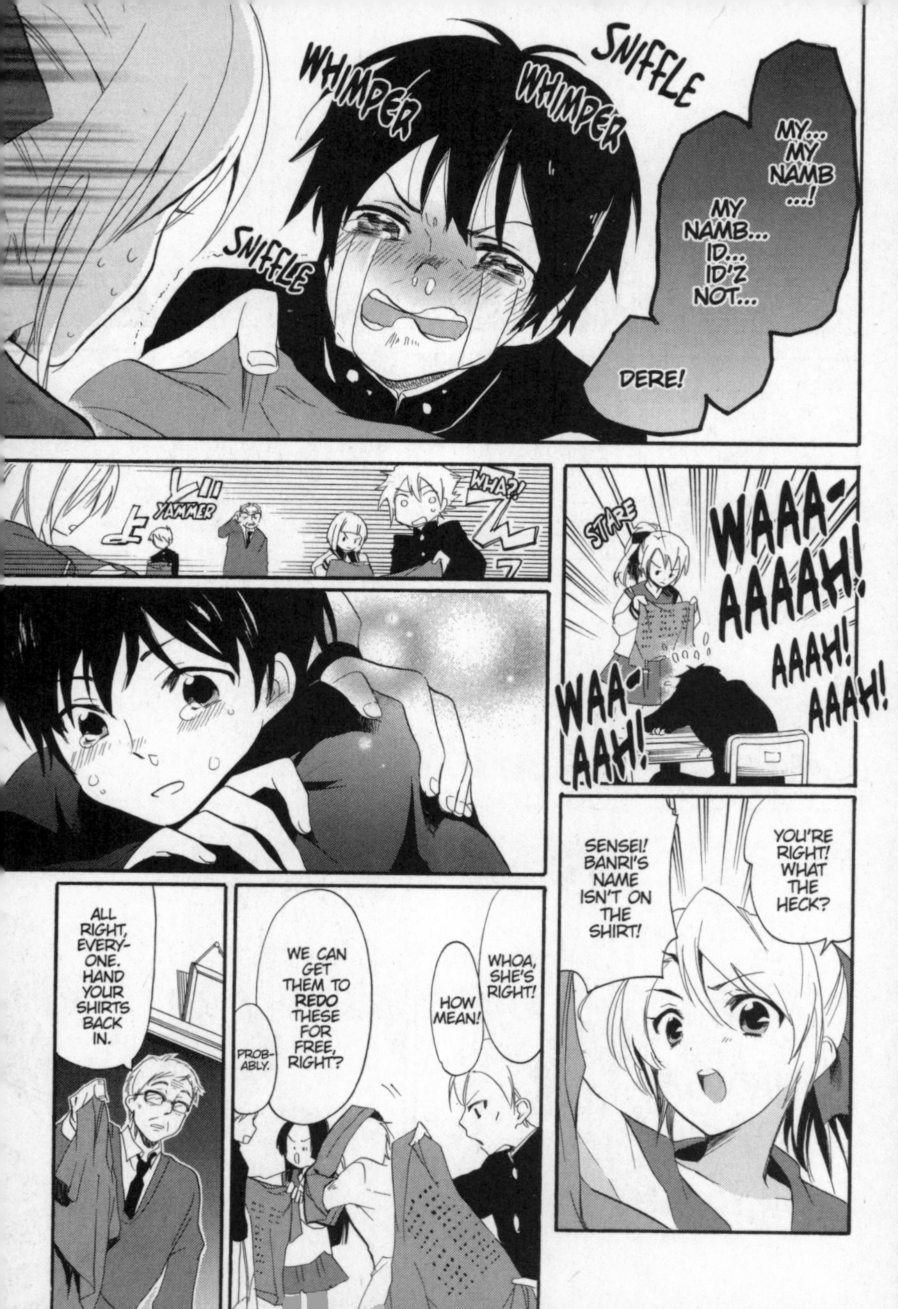
SNIFFLE
WHIMPER
WHIMPER
MY... MY NAMB ...!
MY NAMB... ID... ID'Z NOT...
DERE!
SNIFFLE
STARE
WAAA-AAAAH!
AAAH! AAAH!
WAA-AAH!
WHA?!
YAMMER
YOU'RE RIGHT! WHAT THE HECK?
SENSEI! BANRI'S NAME ISN'T ON THE SHIRT!
WHOA, SHE'S RIGHT!
HOW MEAN!
WE CAN GET THEM TO REDO THESE FOR FREE, RIGHT?
PROB-ABLY.
ALL RIGHT, EVERY-ONE. HAND YOUR SHIRTS BACK IN.

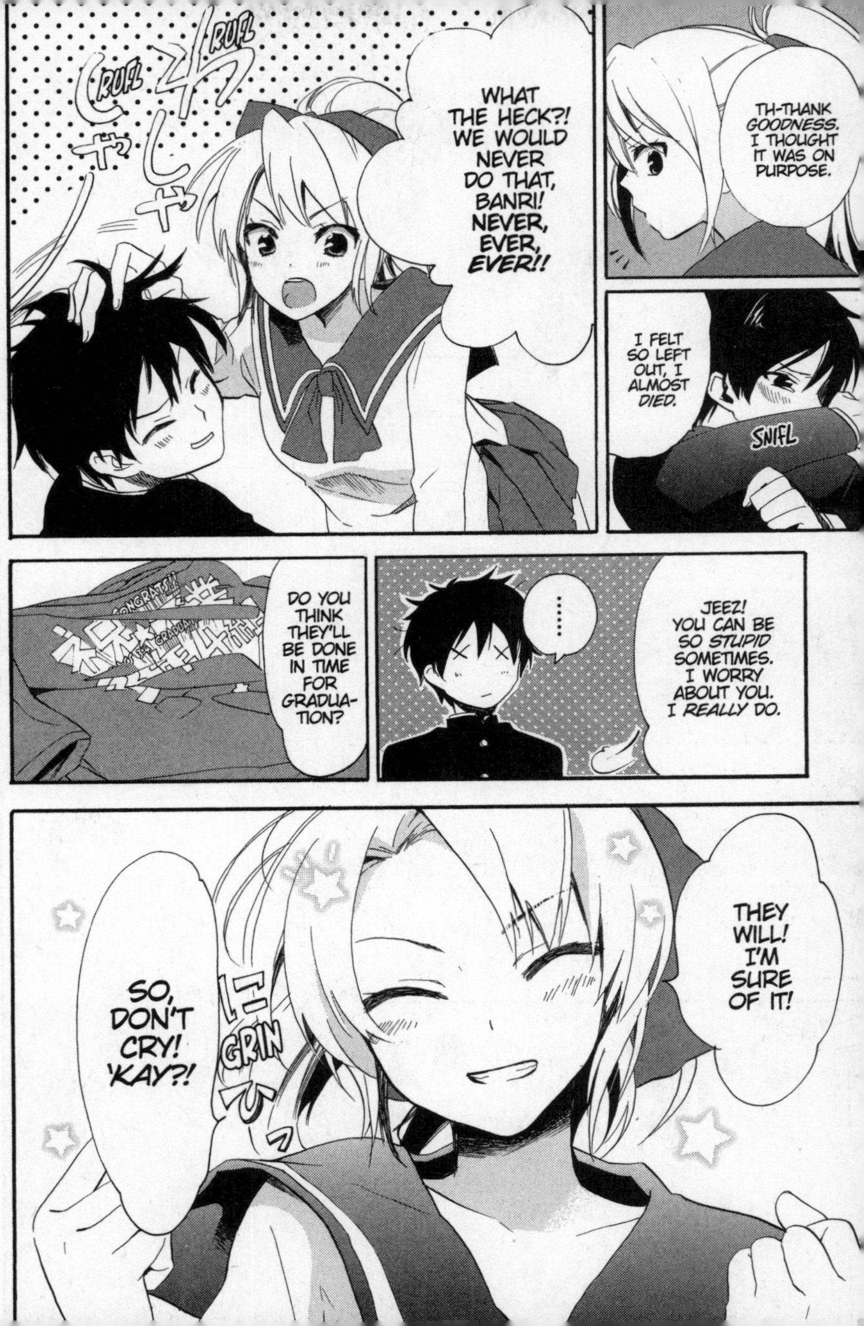
TH-THANK GOODNESS. I THOUGHT IT WAS ON PURPOSE.
I FELT SO LEFT OUT, I ALMOST *DIED*.
SNIFL
WHAT THE HECK?! WE WOULD NEVER DO THAT, BANRI! NEVER, EVER, *EVER*!!
RUFL
RUFL
JEEZ! YOU CAN BE SO *STUPID* SOMETIMES. I WORRY ABOUT YOU. I *REALLY* DO.
......
DO YOU THINK THEY'LL BE DONE IN TIME FOR GRADUATION?
CONGRATS!!
THEY WILL! I'M SURE OF IT!
GRIN
SO, DON'T CRY! 'KAY?!

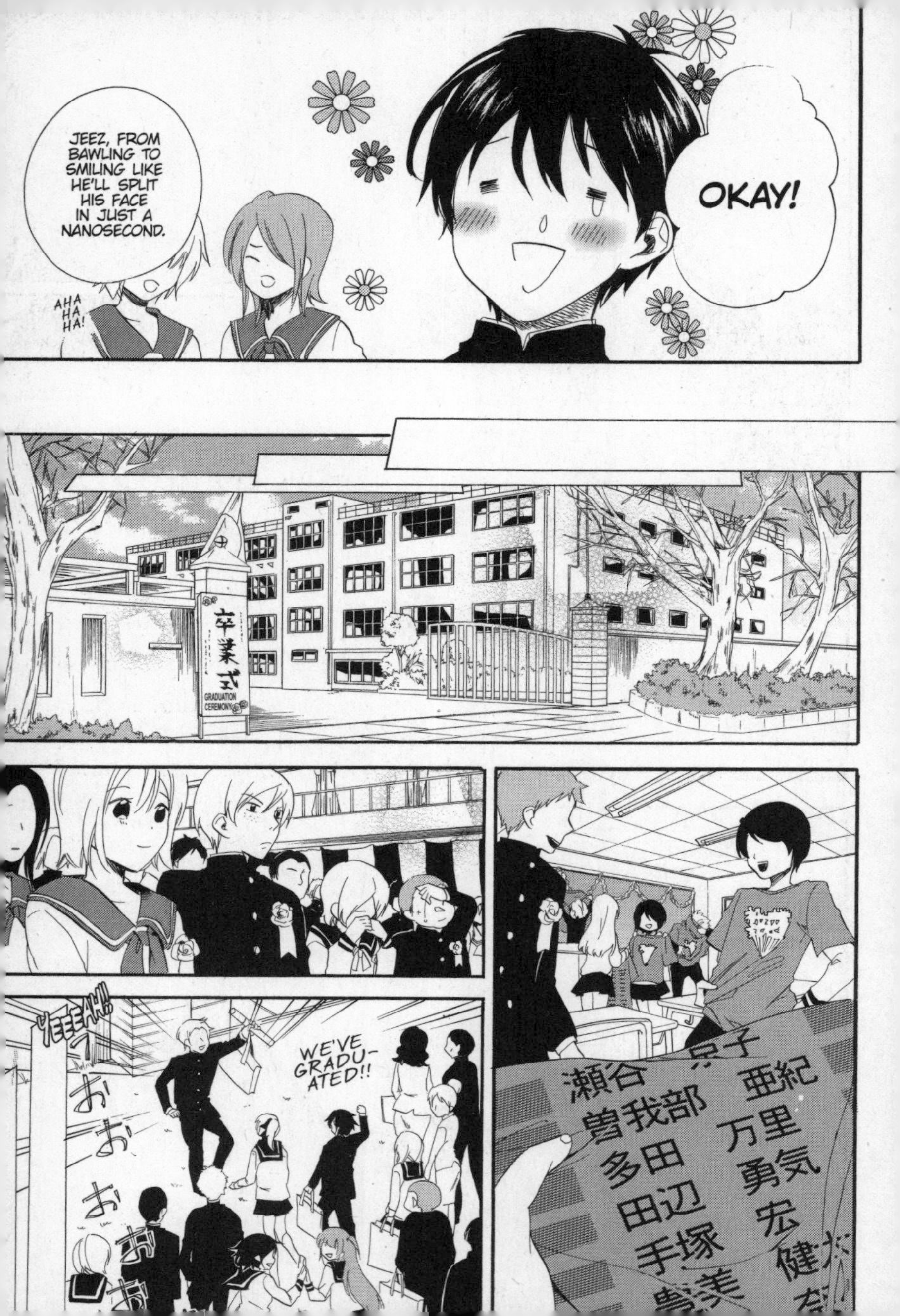
OKAY!
JEEZ, FROM BAWLING TO SMILING LIKE HE'LL SPLIT HIS FACE IN JUST A NANOSECOND.
AHA HA HA!
卒業式
GRADUATION CEREMONY
瀬谷 京子
曽我部 亜紀
多田 万里
田辺 勇気
手塚 宏
YEEEEAH!!
WE'VE GRADUATED!!
おおおお

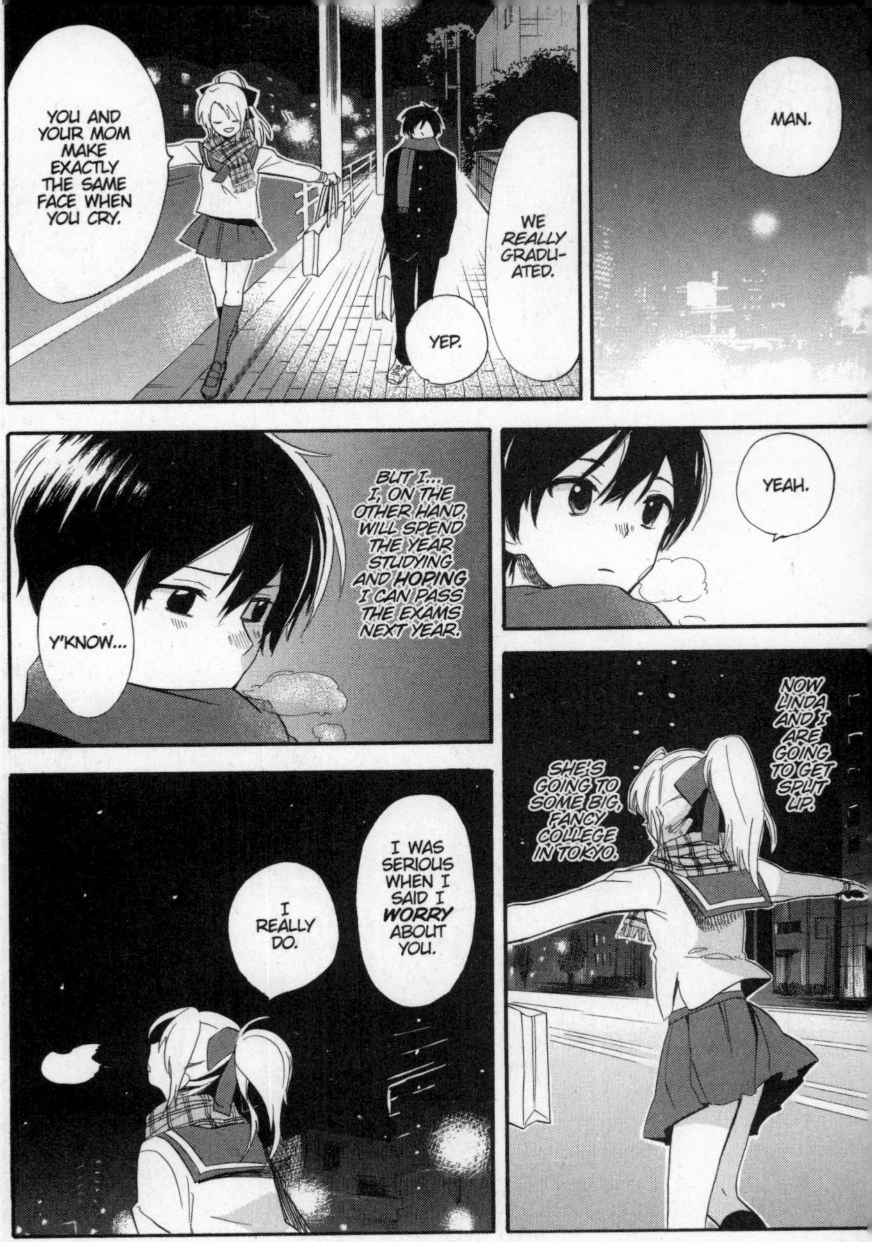
MAN.
WE REALLY GRADUATED.
YEP.
YOU AND YOUR MOM MAKE EXACTLY THE SAME FACE WHEN YOU CRY.
YEAH.
BUT I... I, ON THE OTHER HAND, WILL SPEND THE YEAR STUDYING AND HOPING I CAN PASS THE EXAMS NEXT YEAR.
Y'KNOW...
NOW LINDA AND I ARE GOING TO GET SPLIT UP.
SHE'S GOING TO SOME BIG, FANCY COLLEGE IN TOKYO.
I WAS SERIOUS WHEN I SAID I WORRY ABOUT YOU.
I REALLY DO.

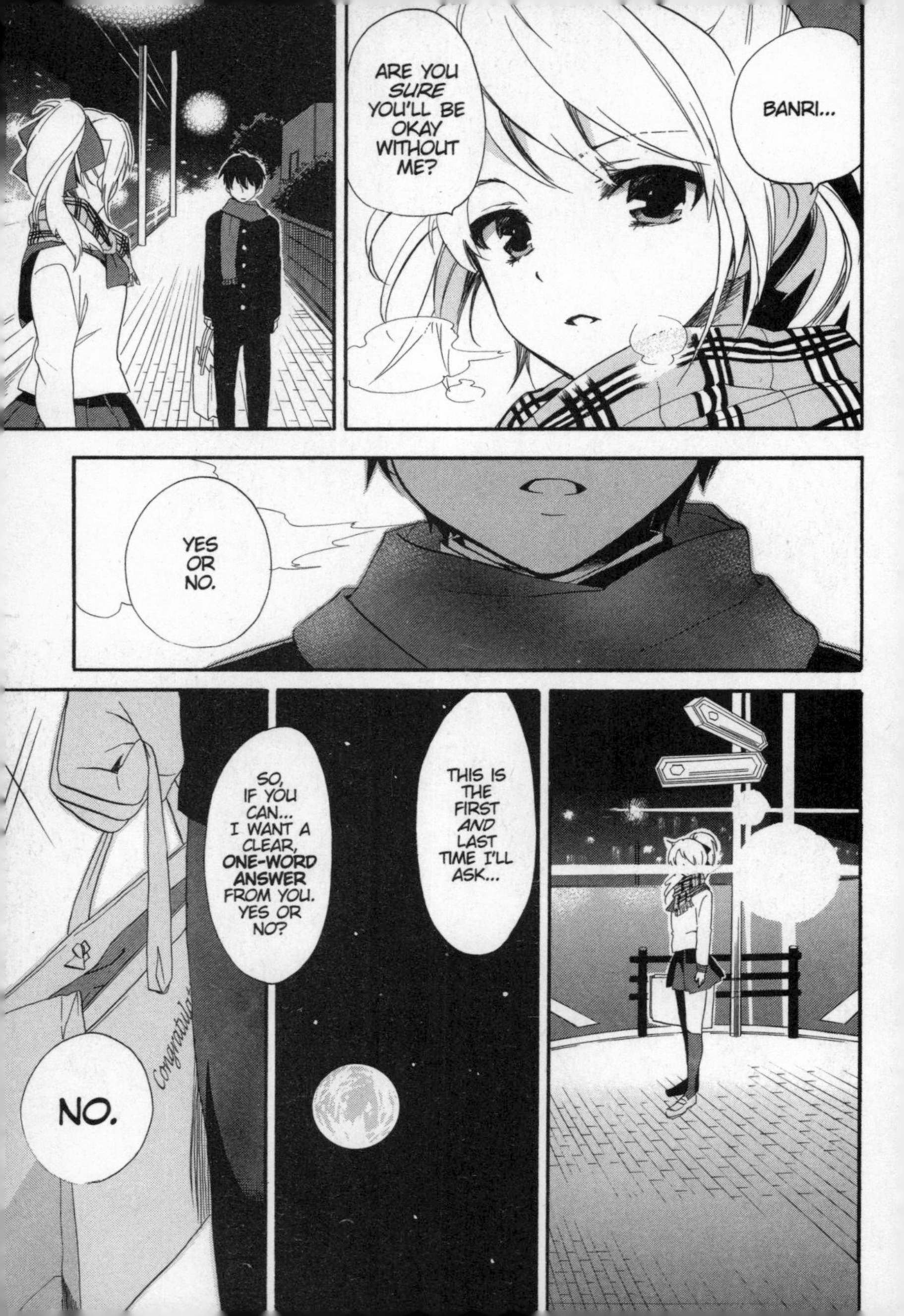
BANRI...
ARE YOU *SURE* YOU'LL BE OKAY WITHOUT ME?
YES OR NO.
THIS IS THE FIRST *AND* LAST TIME I'LL ASK...
SO, IF YOU CAN... I WANT A CLEAR, **ONE-WORD ANSWER** FROM YOU. YES OR NO?
NO.

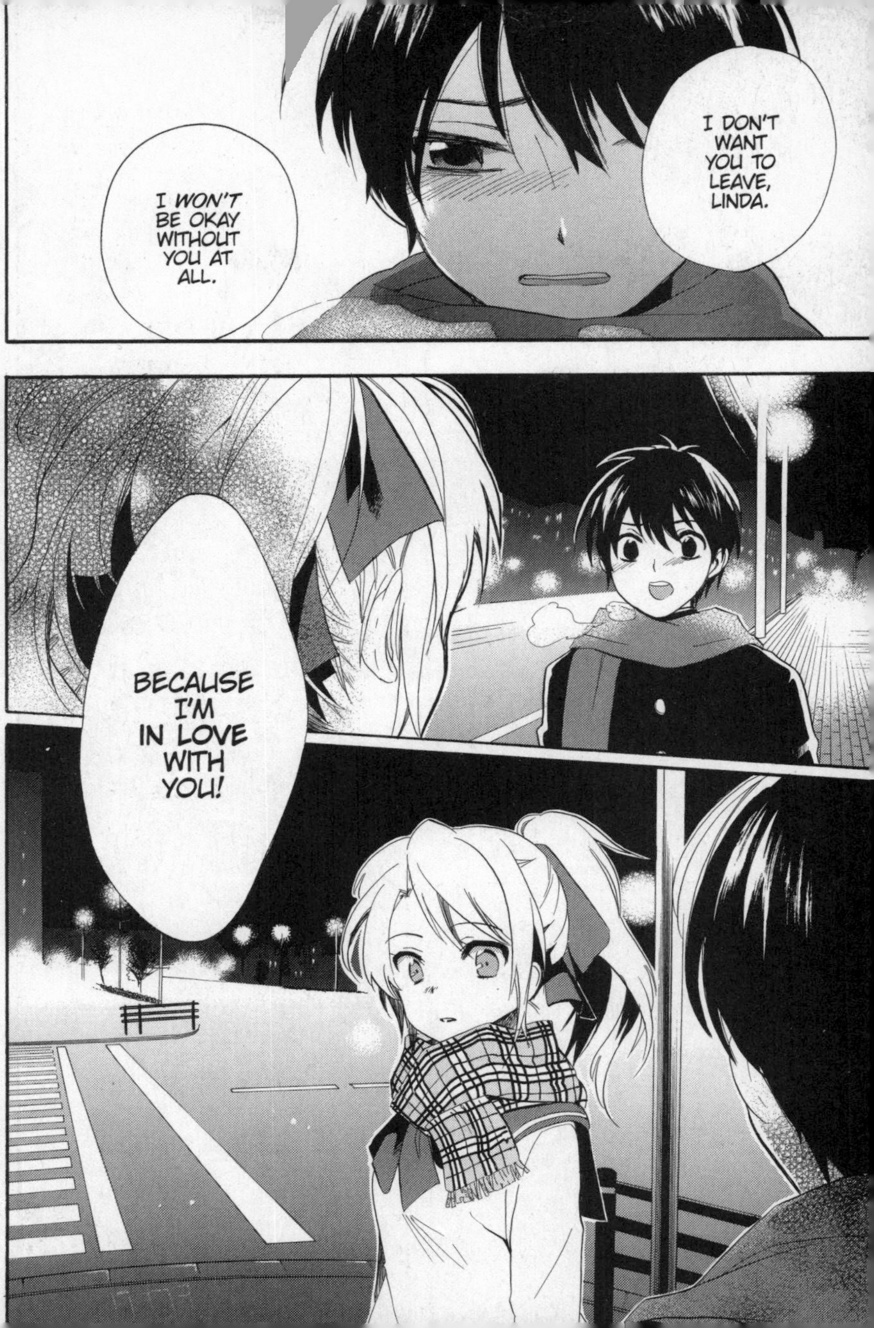
I DON'T WANT YOU TO LEAVE, LINDA.
I *WON'T* BE OKAY WITHOUT YOU AT ALL.
BECAUSE I'M IN LOVE WITH YOU!

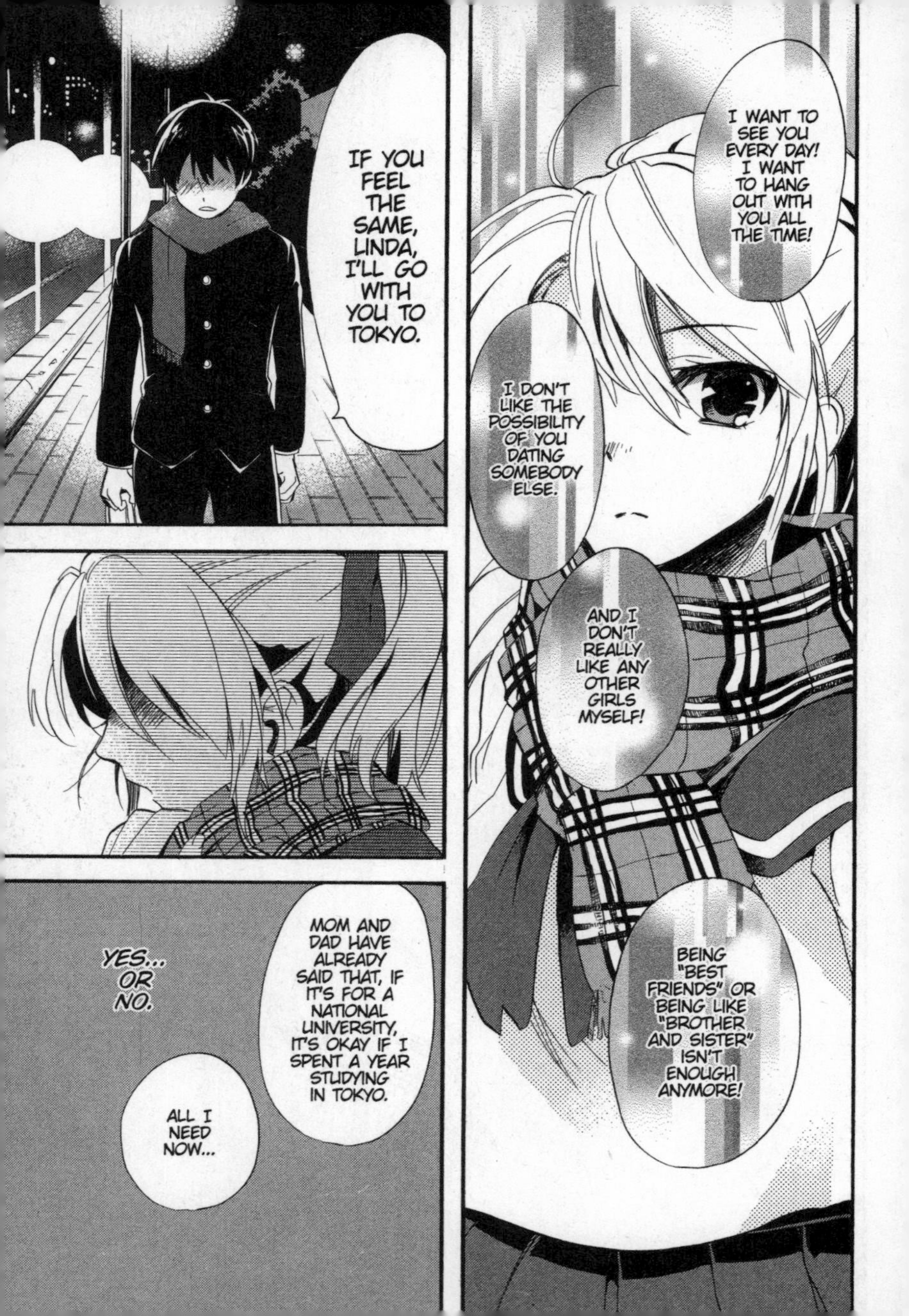
I WANT TO SEE YOU EVERY DAY! I WANT TO HANG OUT WITH YOU ALL THE TIME!
I DON'T LIKE THE POSSIBILITY OF YOU DATING SOMEBODY ELSE.
AND I DON'T REALLY LIKE ANY OTHER GIRLS MYSELF!
BEING "BEST FRIENDS" OR BEING LIKE "BROTHER AND SISTER" ISN'T ENOUGH ANYMORE!
IF YOU FEEL THE SAME, LINDA, I'LL GO WITH YOU TO TOKYO.
MOM AND DAD HAVE ALREADY SAID THAT, IF IT'S FOR A NATIONAL UNIVERSITY, IT'S OKAY IF I SPENT A YEAR STUDYING IN TOKYO.
YES... OR NO.
ALL I NEED NOW...

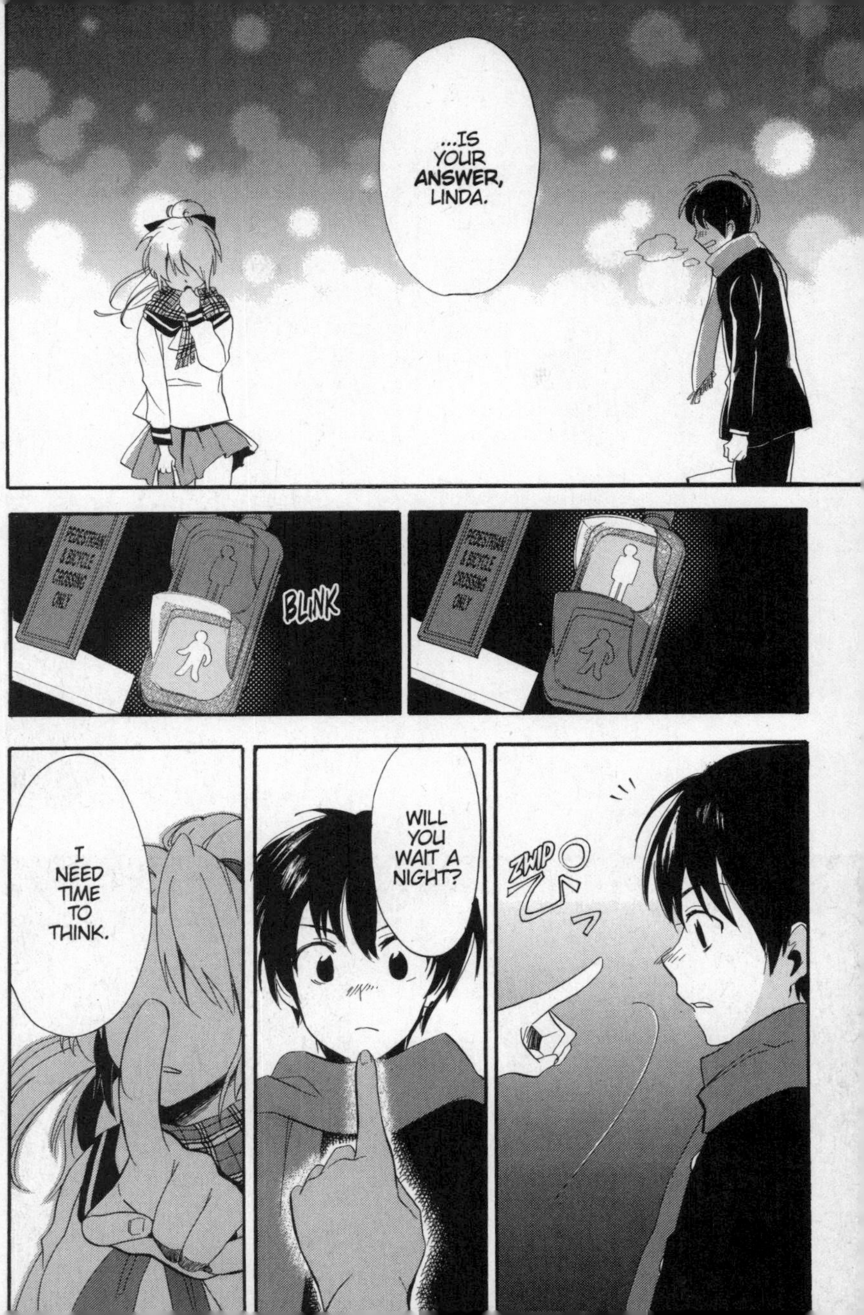
...IS YOUR ANSWER, LINDA.
PEDESTRIAN & BICYCLE CROSSING ONLY
PEDESTRIAN & BICYCLE CROSSING ONLY
BLINK
ZWIP
WILL YOU WAIT A NIGHT?
I NEED TIME TO THINK.

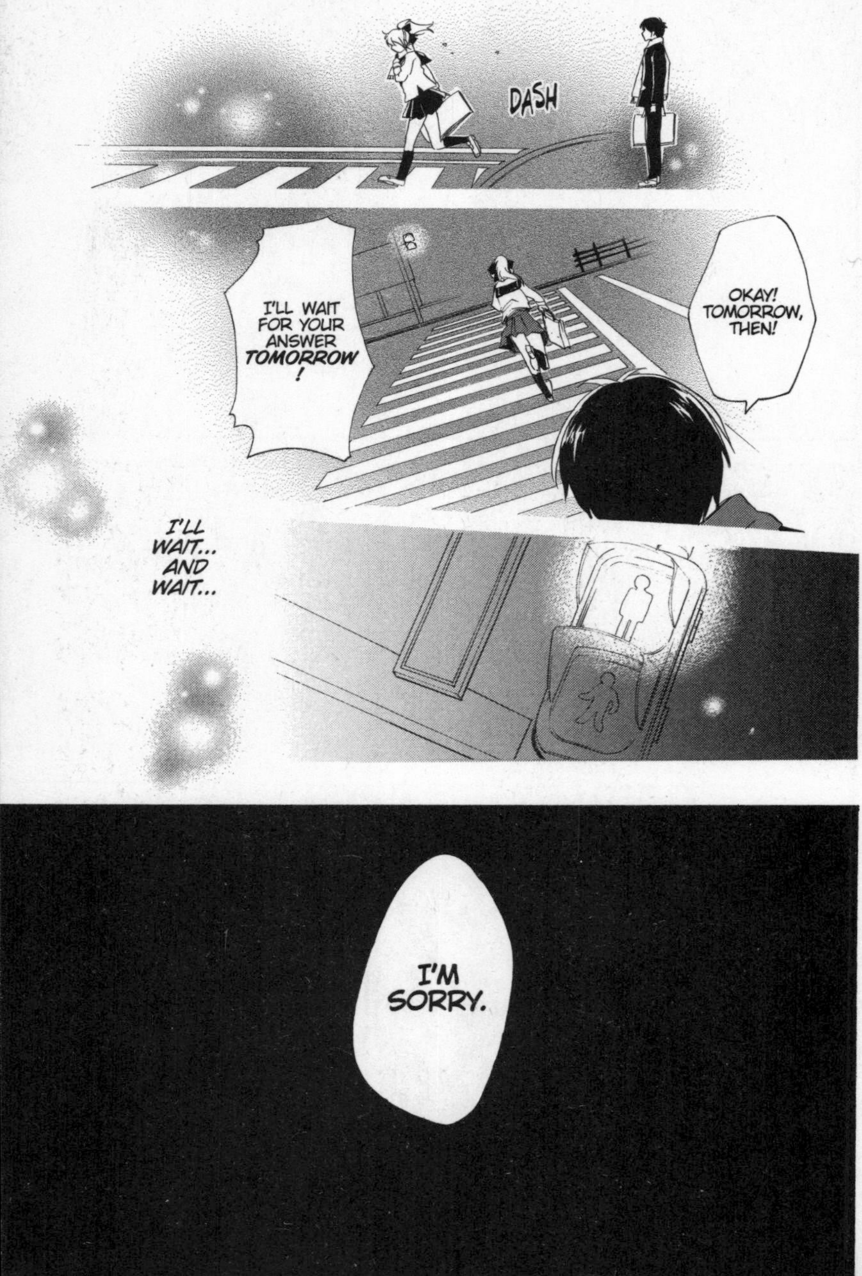
DASH
I'LL WAIT FOR YOUR ANSWER TOMORROW!
OKAY! TOMORROW, THEN!
I'LL WAIT... AND WAIT...
I'M SORRY.

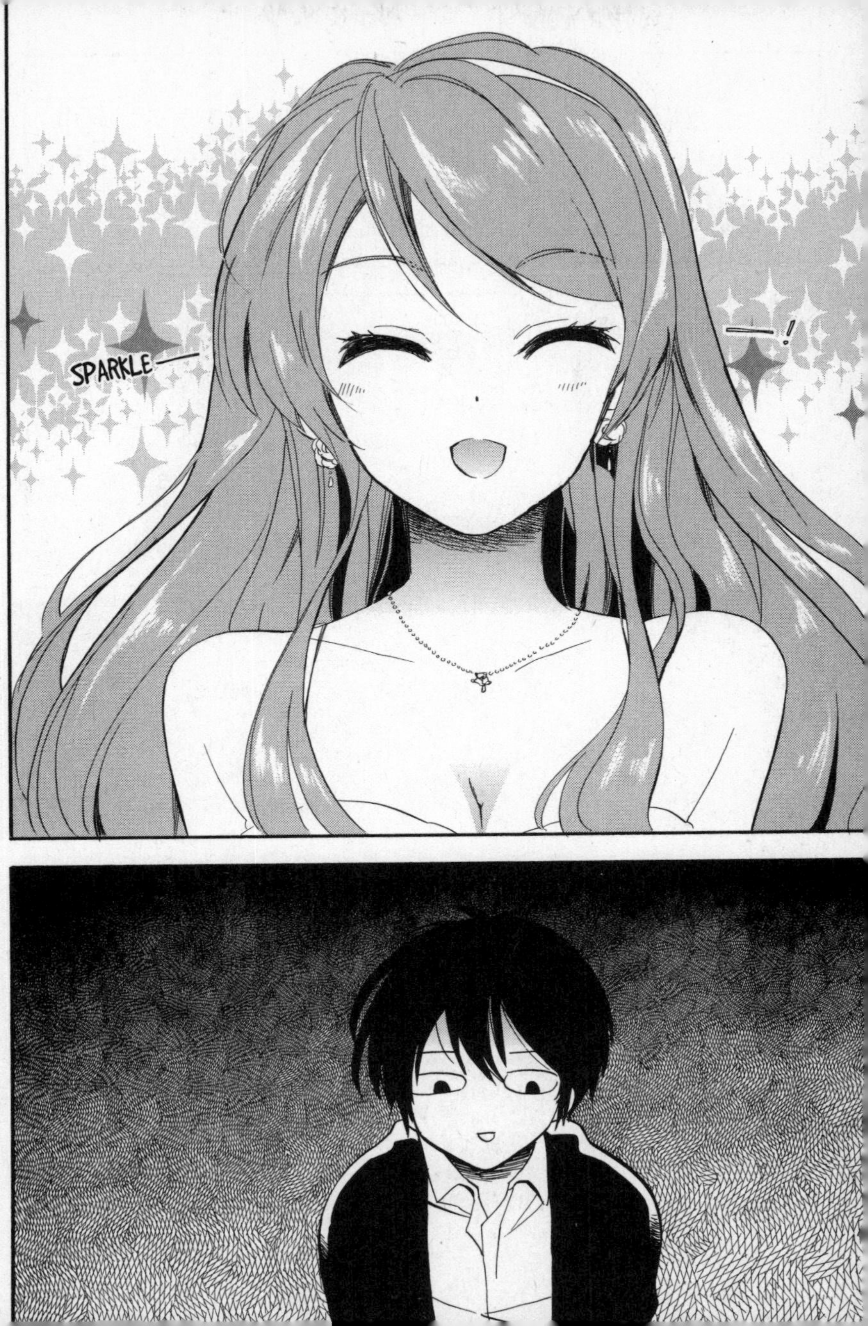
——!
SPARKLE——

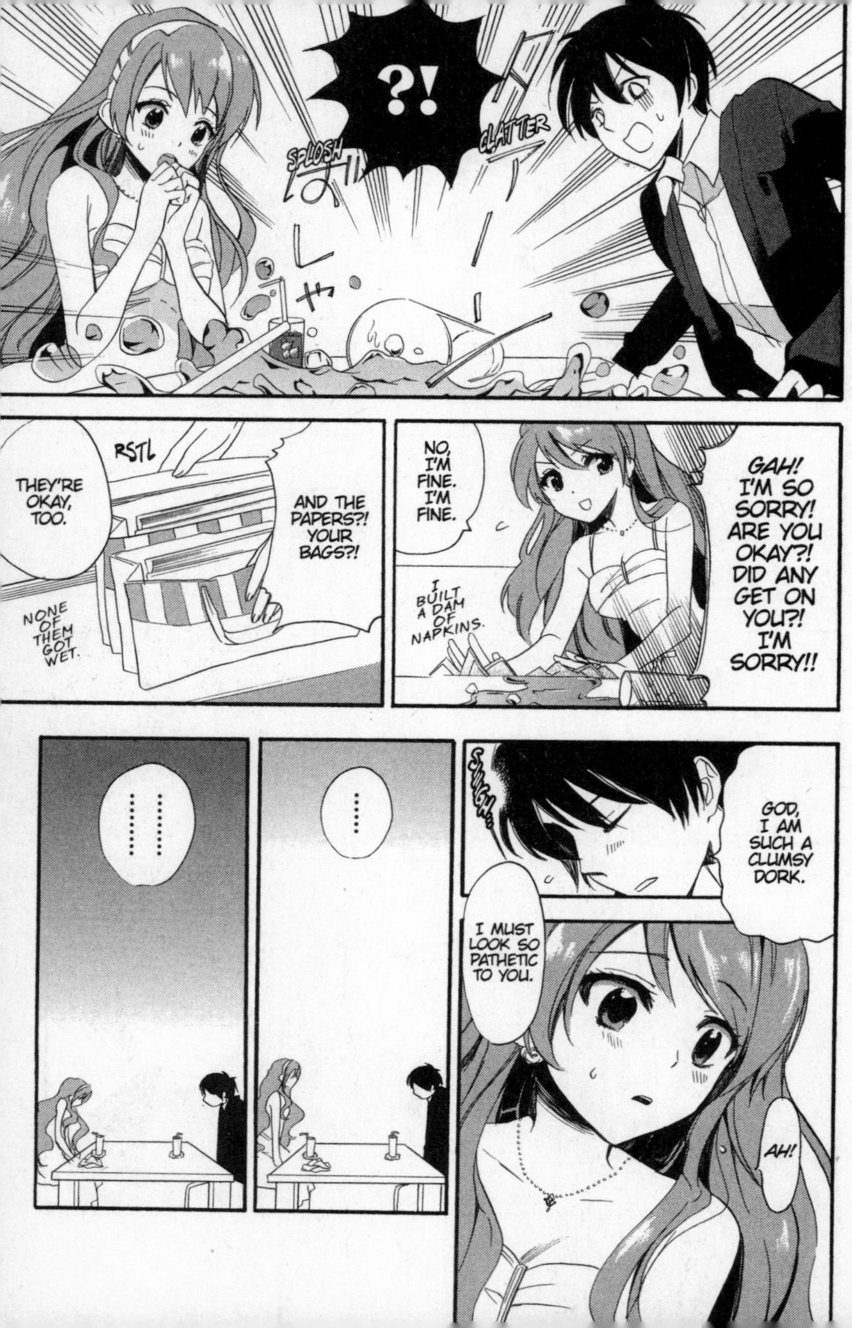
?!
CLATTER
SPLOSH
GAH! I'M SO SORRY! ARE YOU OKAY?! DID ANY GET ON YOU?! I'M SORRY!!
NO, I'M FINE. I'M FINE.
I BUILT A DAM OF NAPKINS.
AND THE PAPERS?! YOUR BAGS?!
RSTL
THEY'RE OKAY, TOO.
NONE OF THEM GOT WET.
SIIIGH...
GOD, I AM SUCH A CLUMSY DORK.
I MUST LOOK SO PATHETIC TO YOU.
AH!
......
....

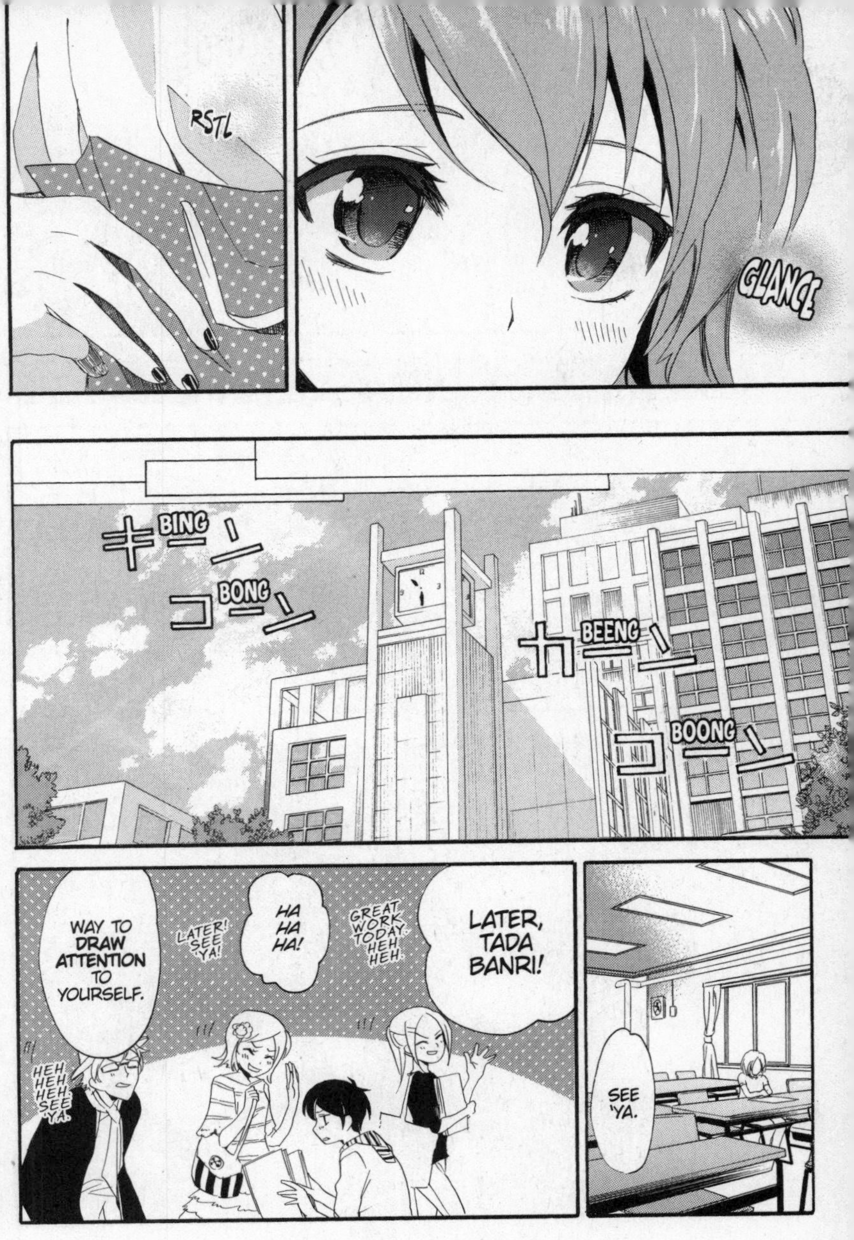
GLANCE
RSTL
BING
BONG
BEENG
BOONG
SEE 'YA.
LATER, TADA BANRI!
GREAT WORK TODAY. HEH HEH.
HA HA HA!
LATER! SEE 'YA!
WAY TO DRAW ATTENTION TO YOURSELF.
HEH HEH HEH. SEE 'YA.

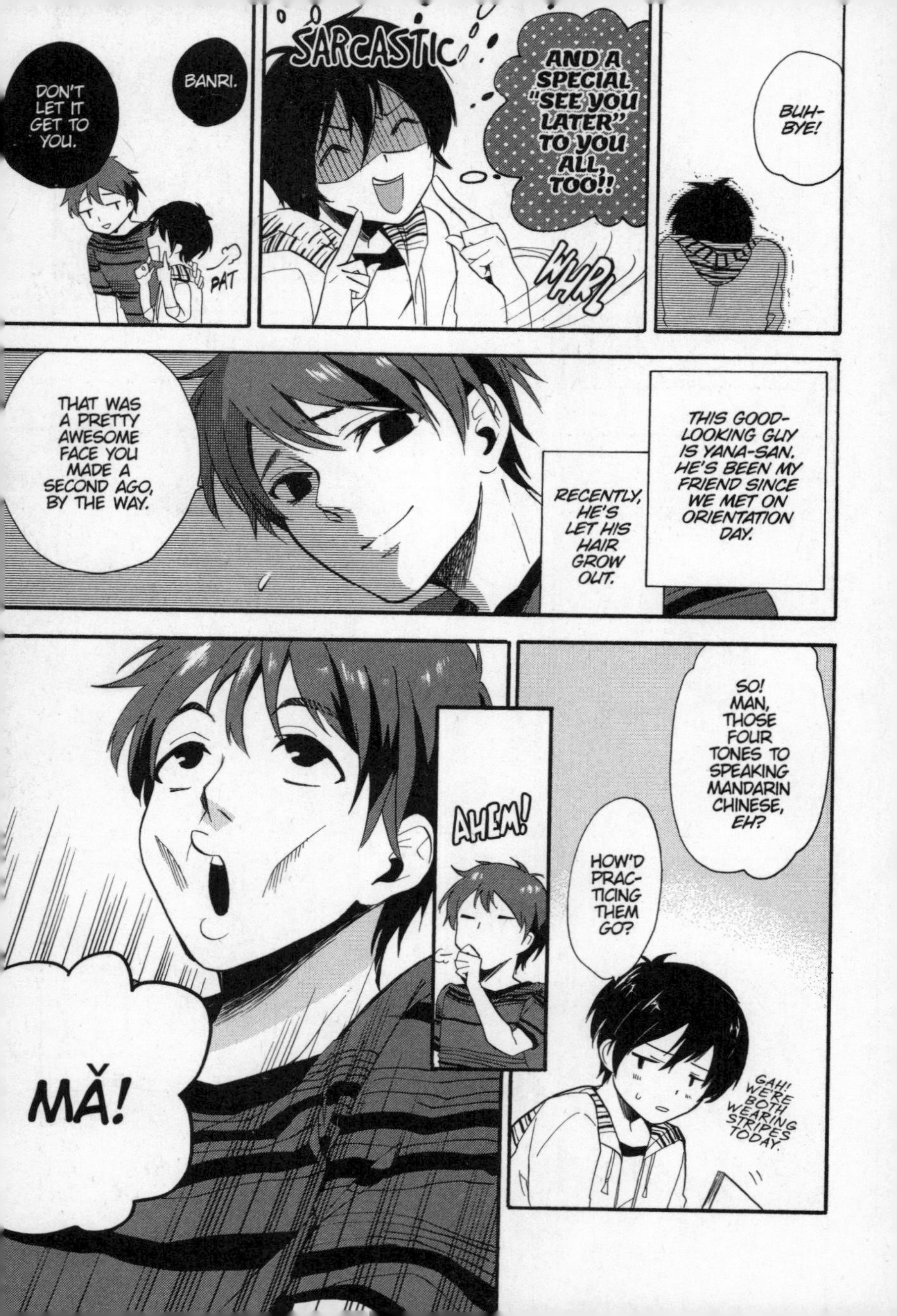
BUH-BYE!
SARCASTIC
AND A SPECIAL "SEE YOU LATER" TO YOU ALL, TOO!!
WHR!
BANRI.
DON'T LET IT GET TO YOU.
PAT
THIS GOOD-LOOKING GUY IS YANA-SAN. HE'S BEEN MY FRIEND SINCE WE MET ON ORIENTATION DAY.
RECENTLY, HE'S LET HIS HAIR GROW OUT.
THAT WAS A PRETTY AWESOME FACE YOU MADE A SECOND AGO, BY THE WAY.
SO! MAN, THOSE FOUR TONES TO SPEAKING MANDARIN CHINESE, EH?
HOW'D PRAC-TICING THEM GO?
GAH! WE'RE BOTH WEARING STRIPES TODAY.
AHEM!
MǍ!

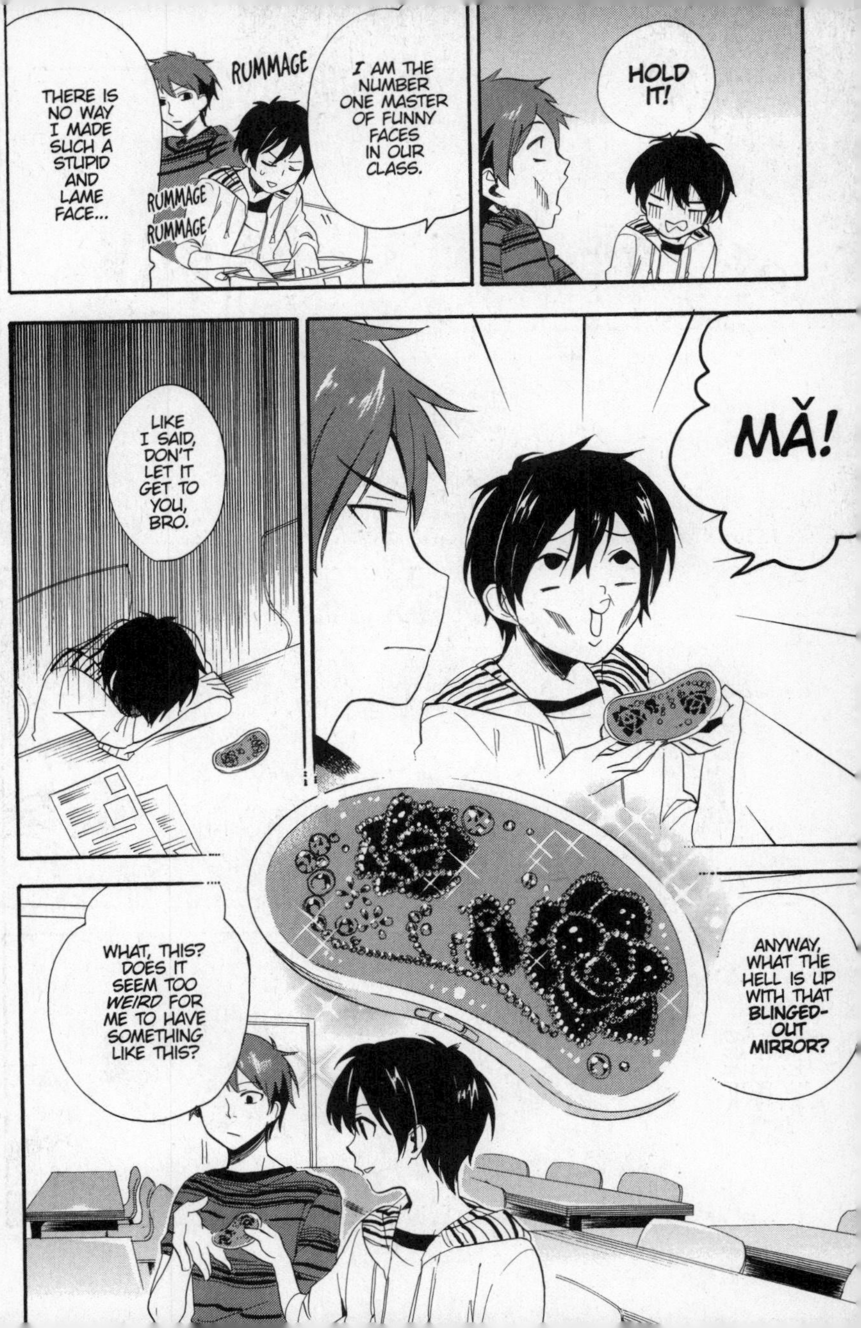
HOLD IT!
I AM THE NUMBER ONE MASTER OF FUNNY FACES IN OUR CLASS.
RUMMAGE
THERE IS NO WAY I MADE SUCH A STUPID AND LAME FACE...
RUMMAGE
RUMMAGE
MǍ!
LIKE I SAID, DON'T LET IT GET TO YOU, BRO.
ANYWAY, WHAT THE HELL IS UP WITH THAT BLINGED-OUT MIRROR?
WHAT, THIS? DOES IT SEEM TOO *WEIRD* FOR ME TO HAVE SOMETHING LIKE THIS?

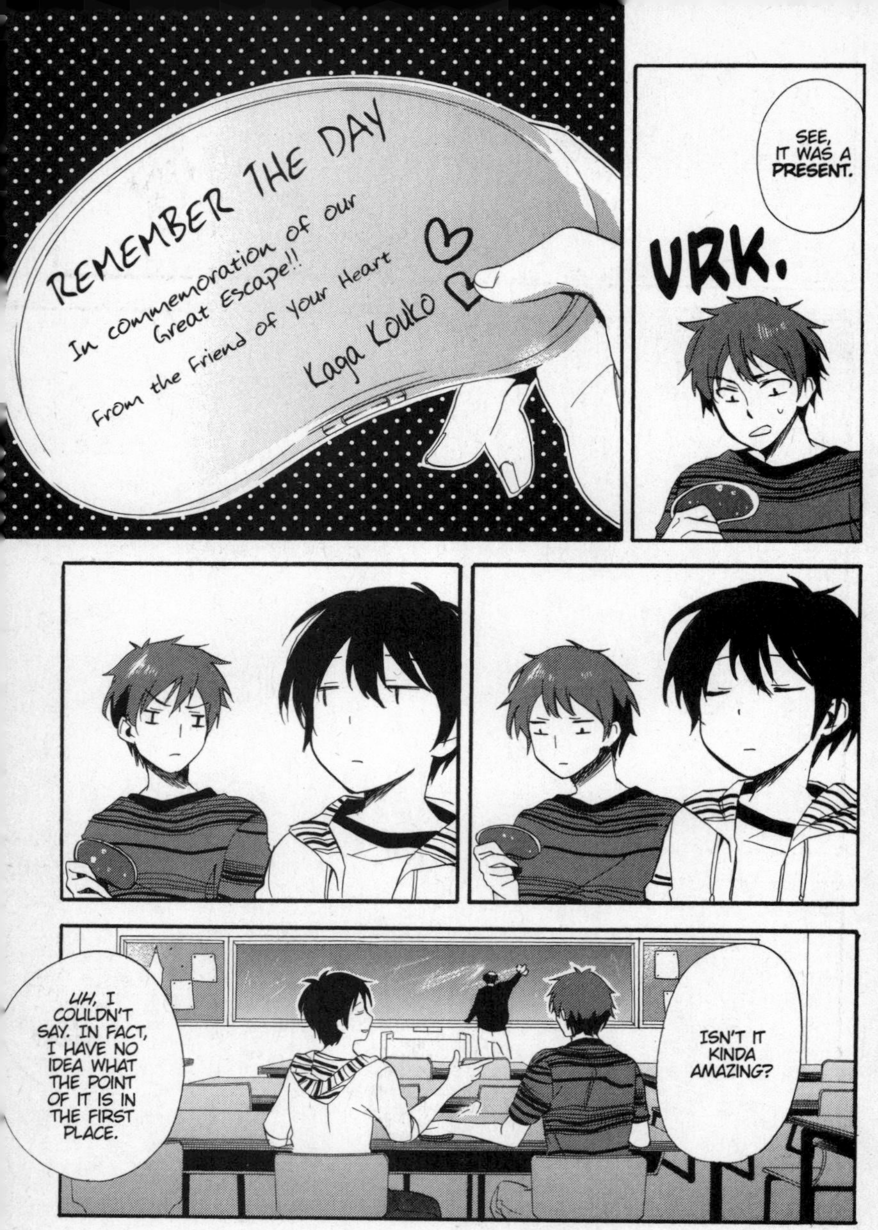
SEE, IT WAS A PRESENT.
URK.
REMEMBER THE DAY
In commemoration of our Great Escape!!
From the Friend of Your Heart
Kaga Kouko
ISN'T IT KINDA AMAZING?
UH, I COULDN'T SAY. IN FACT, I HAVE NO IDEA WHAT THE POINT OF IT IS IN THE FIRST PLACE.

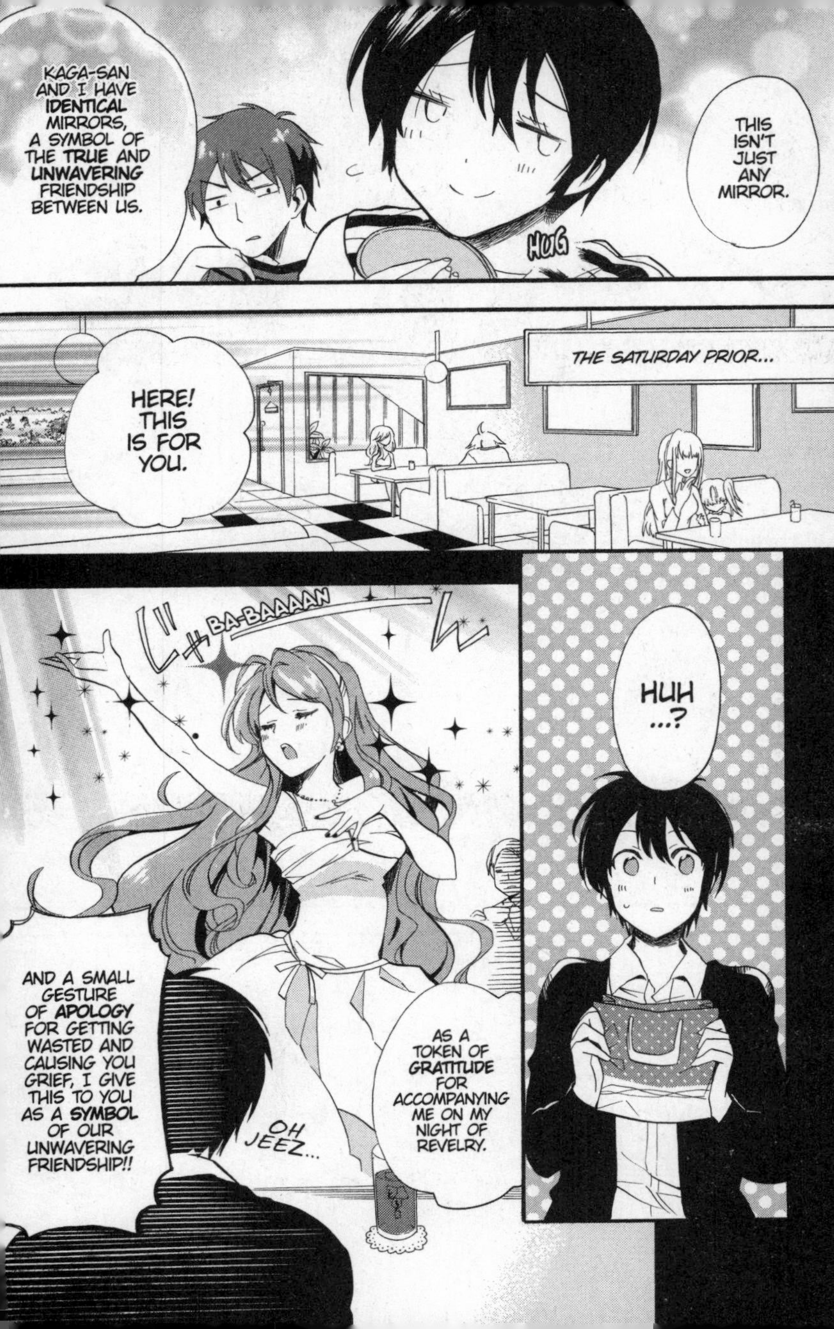
THIS ISN'T JUST ANY MIRROR.
HUG
KAGA-SAN AND I HAVE IDENTICAL MIRRORS, A SYMBOL OF THE TRUE AND UNWAVERING FRIENDSHIP BETWEEN US.
THE SATURDAY PRIOR...
HERE! THIS IS FOR YOU.
HUH ...?
BA-BAAAAN
AS A TOKEN OF GRATITUDE FOR ACCOMPANYING ME ON MY NIGHT OF REVELRY.
AND A SMALL GESTURE OF APOLOGY FOR GETTING WASTED AND CAUSING YOU GRIEF, I GIVE THIS TO YOU AS A SYMBOL OF OUR UNWAVERING FRIENDSHIP!!
OH JEEZ...

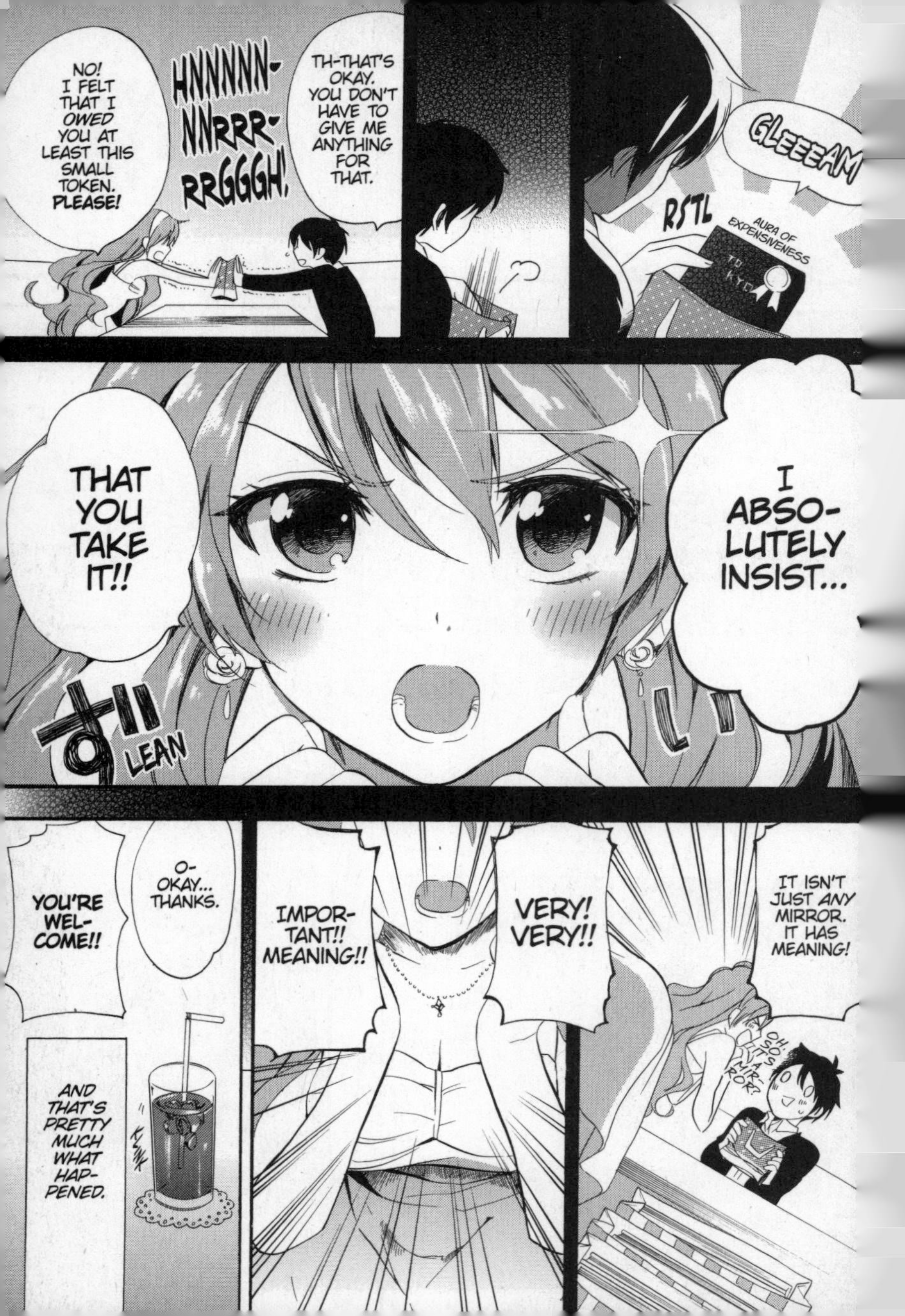
GLEEEAM
RSTL
AURA OF EXPENSIVENESS
TO KYO
TH-THAT'S OKAY. YOU DON'T HAVE TO GIVE ME ANYTHING FOR THAT.
HNNNNN-NNRRR-RRGGGH!
NO! I FELT THAT I OWED YOU AT LEAST THIS SMALL TOKEN. PLEASE!
I ABSOLUTELY INSIST...
THAT YOU TAKE IT!!
LEAN
IT ISN'T JUST ANY MIRROR. IT HAS MEANING!
OH. SO IT'S A MIRROR?
VERY! VERY!!
IMPORTANT!! MEANING!!
O-OKAY... THANKS.
YOU'RE WELCOME!!
AND THAT'S PRETTY MUCH WHAT HAPPENED.
KLINK

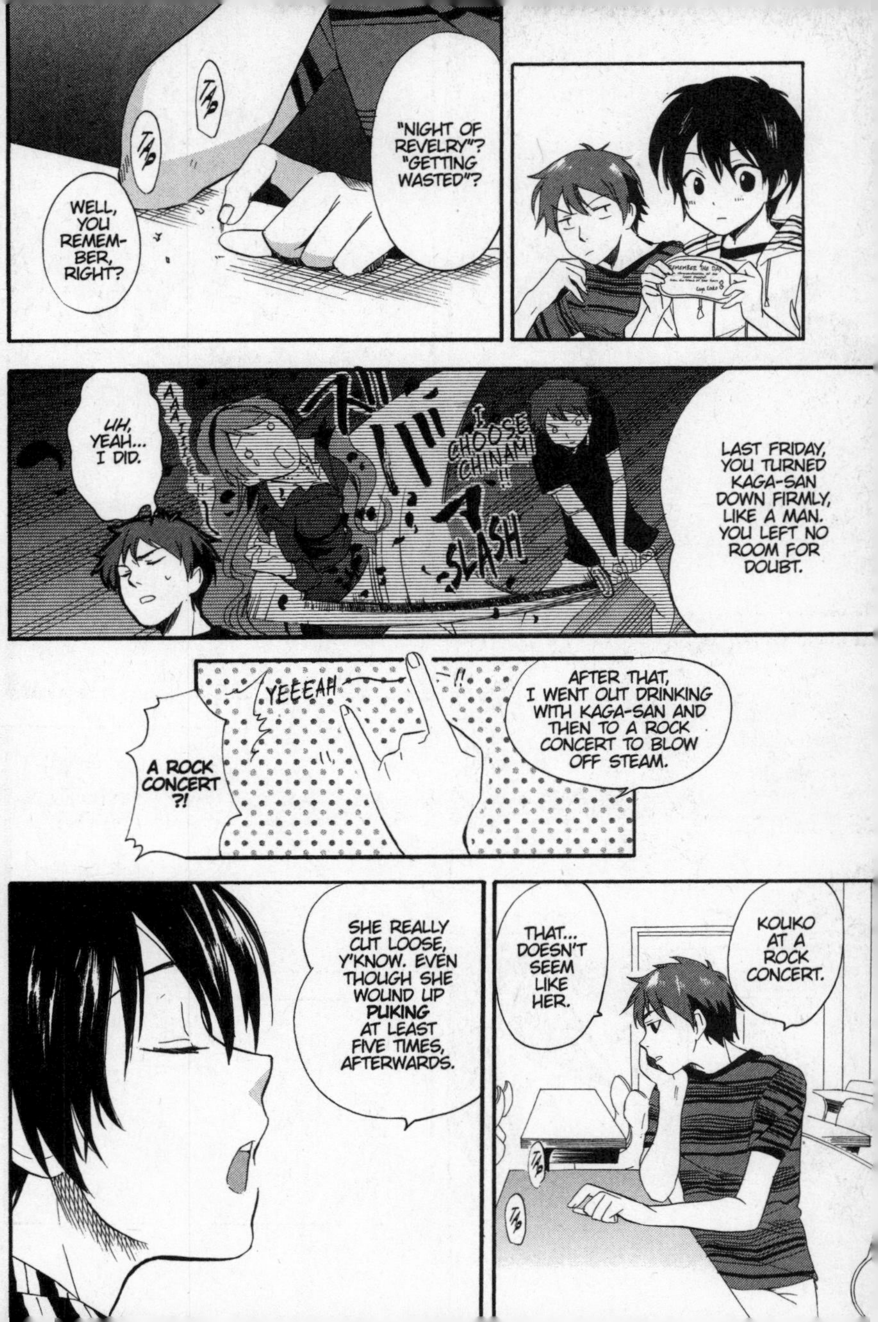
"NIGHT OF REVELRY"? "GETTING WASTED"?
TAP
TAP
WELL, YOU REMEMBER, RIGHT?
LAST FRIDAY, YOU TURNED KAGA-SAN DOWN FIRMLY, LIKE A MAN. YOU LEFT NO ROOM FOR DOUBT.
I CHOOSE CHINAMI!!
SLASH
AAAIII!!
UH, YEAH... I DID.
AFTER THAT, I WENT OUT DRINKING WITH KAGA-SAN AND THEN TO A ROCK CONCERT TO BLOW OFF STEAM.
!!
YEEEAH
A ROCK CONCERT?!
KOUKO AT A ROCK CONCERT.
THAT... DOESN'T SEEM LIKE HER.
TAP
TAP
SHE REALLY CUT LOOSE, Y'KNOW. EVEN THOUGH SHE WOUND UP **PUKING** AT LEAST FIVE TIMES, AFTERWARDS.

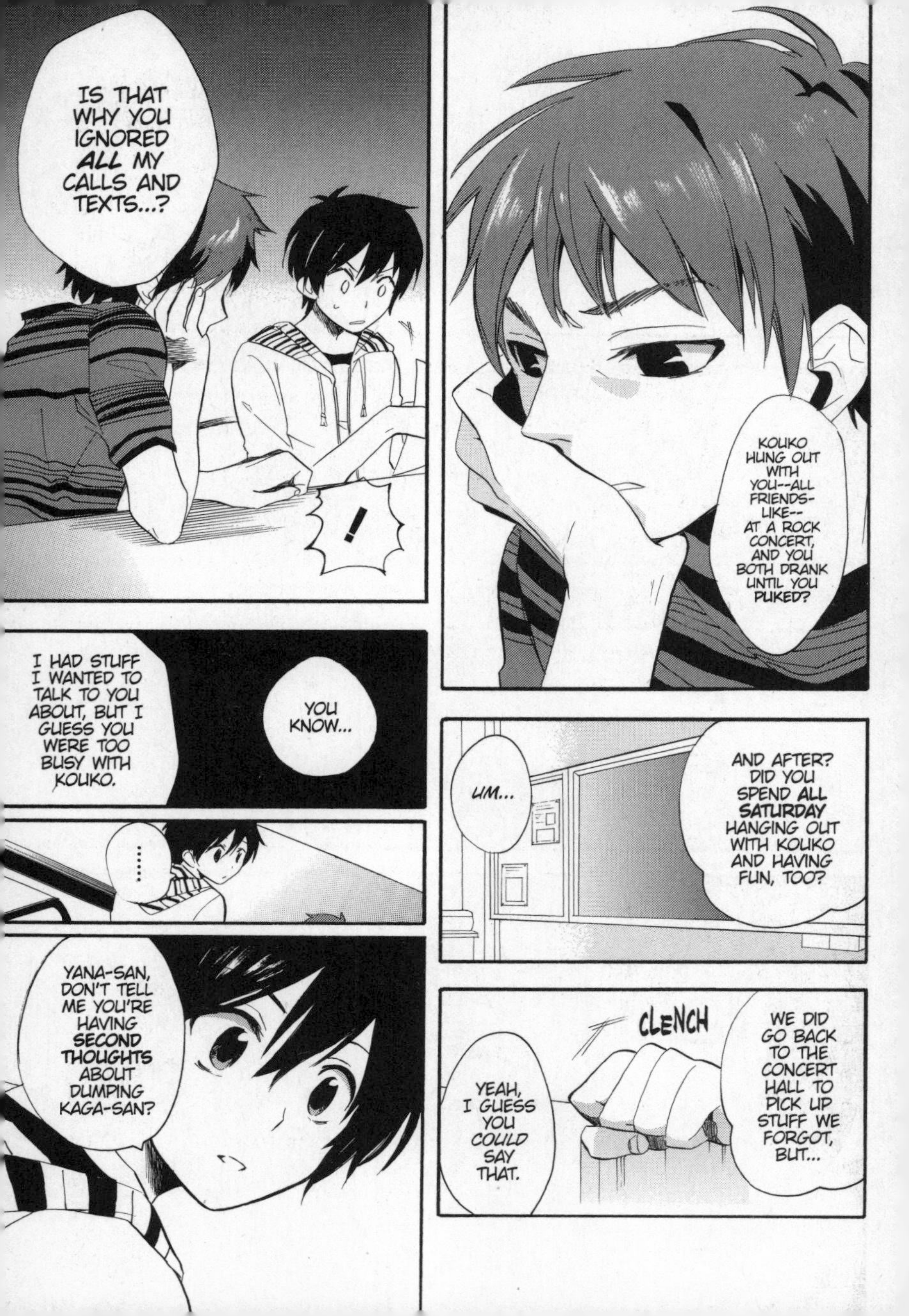
KOUKO HUNG OUT WITH YOU--ALL FRIENDS-LIKE--AT A ROCK CONCERT, AND YOU BOTH DRANK UNTIL YOU PUKED?
IS THAT WHY YOU IGNORED ALL MY CALLS AND TEXTS...?
!
YOU KNOW...
I HAD STUFF I WANTED TO TALK TO YOU ABOUT, BUT I GUESS YOU WERE TOO BUSY WITH KOUKO.
AND AFTER? DID YOU SPEND ALL SATURDAY HANGING OUT WITH KOUKO AND HAVING FUN, TOO?
UM...
......
WE DID GO BACK TO THE CONCERT HALL TO PICK UP STUFF WE FORGOT, BUT...
CLENCH
YEAH, I GUESS YOU COULD SAY THAT.
YANA-SAN, DON'T TELL ME YOU'RE HAVING SECOND THOUGHTS ABOUT DUMPING KAGA-SAN?

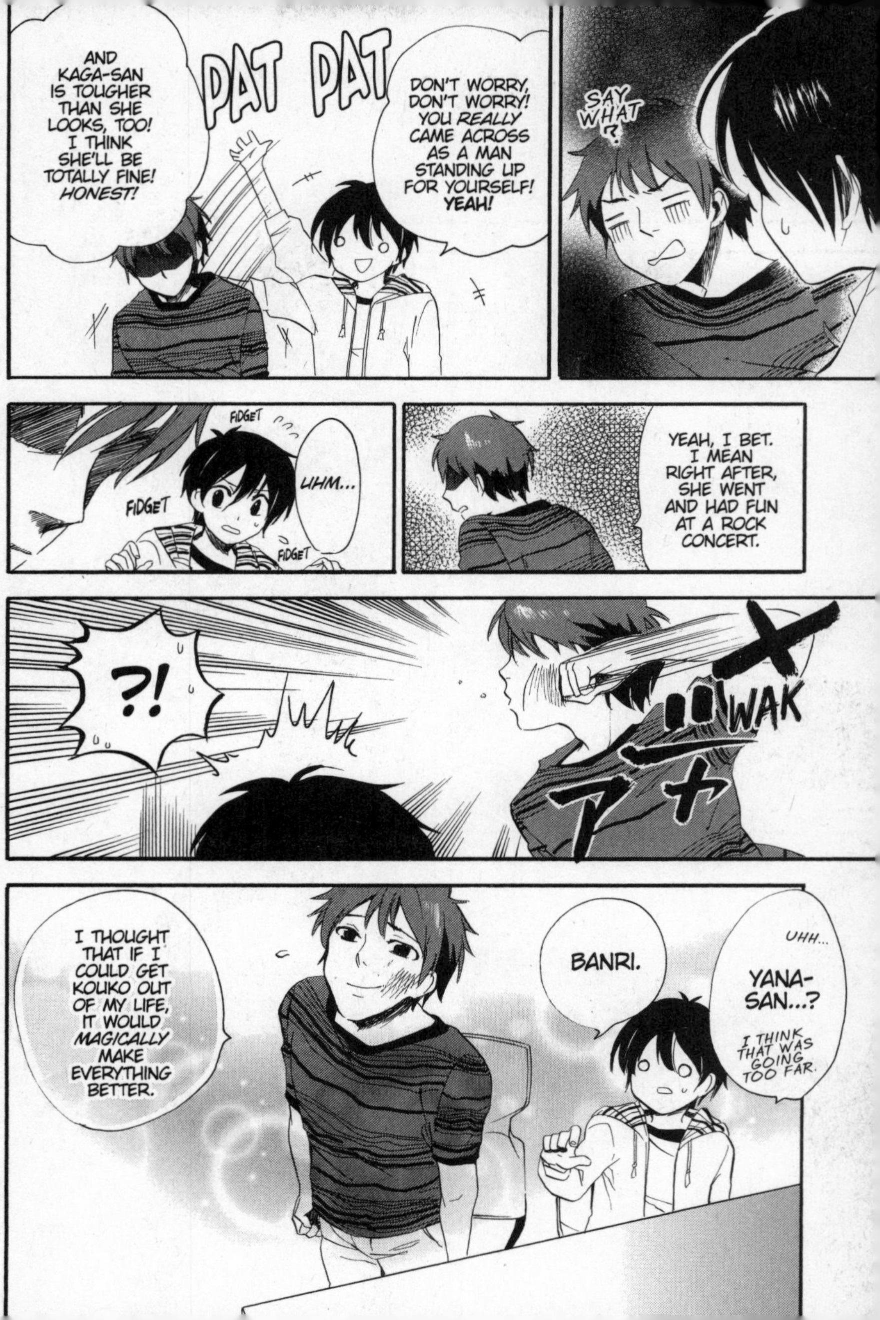
SAY WHAT!?
DON'T WORRY, DON'T WORRY! YOU REALLY CAME ACROSS AS A MAN STANDING UP FOR YOURSELF! YEAH!
PAT PAT
AND KAGA-SAN IS TOUGHER THAN SHE LOOKS, TOO! I THINK SHE'LL BE TOTALLY FINE! HONEST!
YEAH, I BET. I MEAN RIGHT AFTER, SHE WENT AND HAD FUN AT A ROCK CONCERT.
FIDGET
UHM...
FIDGET
FIDGET
WAK
?!
UHH...
YANA-SAN...?
I THINK THAT WAS GOING TOO FAR.
BANRI.
I THOUGHT THAT IF I COULD GET KOUKO OUT OF MY LIFE, IT WOULD MAGICALLY MAKE EVERYTHING BETTER.

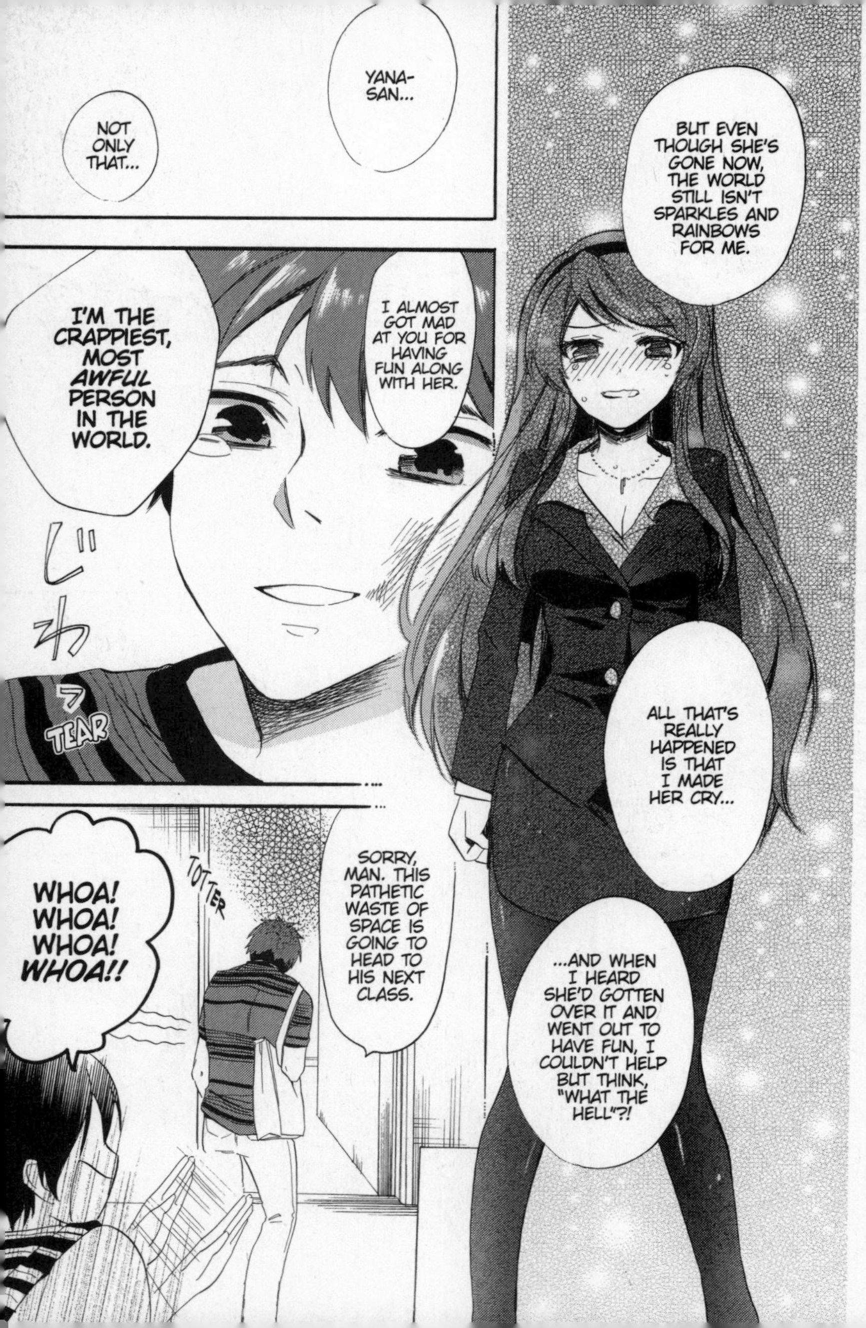
BUT EVEN THOUGH SHE'S GONE NOW, THE WORLD STILL ISN'T SPARKLES AND RAINBOWS FOR ME.
ALL THAT'S REALLY HAPPENED IS THAT I MADE HER CRY...
...AND WHEN I HEARD SHE'D GOTTEN OVER IT AND WENT OUT TO HAVE FUN, I COULDN'T HELP BUT THINK, "WHAT THE HELL"?!
YANA-SAN...
NOT ONLY THAT...
I ALMOST GOT MAD AT YOU FOR HAVING FUN ALONG WITH HER.
I'M THE CRAPPIEST, MOST AWFUL PERSON IN THE WORLD.
じわっ
TEAR
....
....
SORRY, MAN. THIS PATHETIC WASTE OF SPACE IS GOING TO HEAD TO HIS NEXT CLASS.
TOTTER
WHOA! WHOA! WHOA! WHOA!!

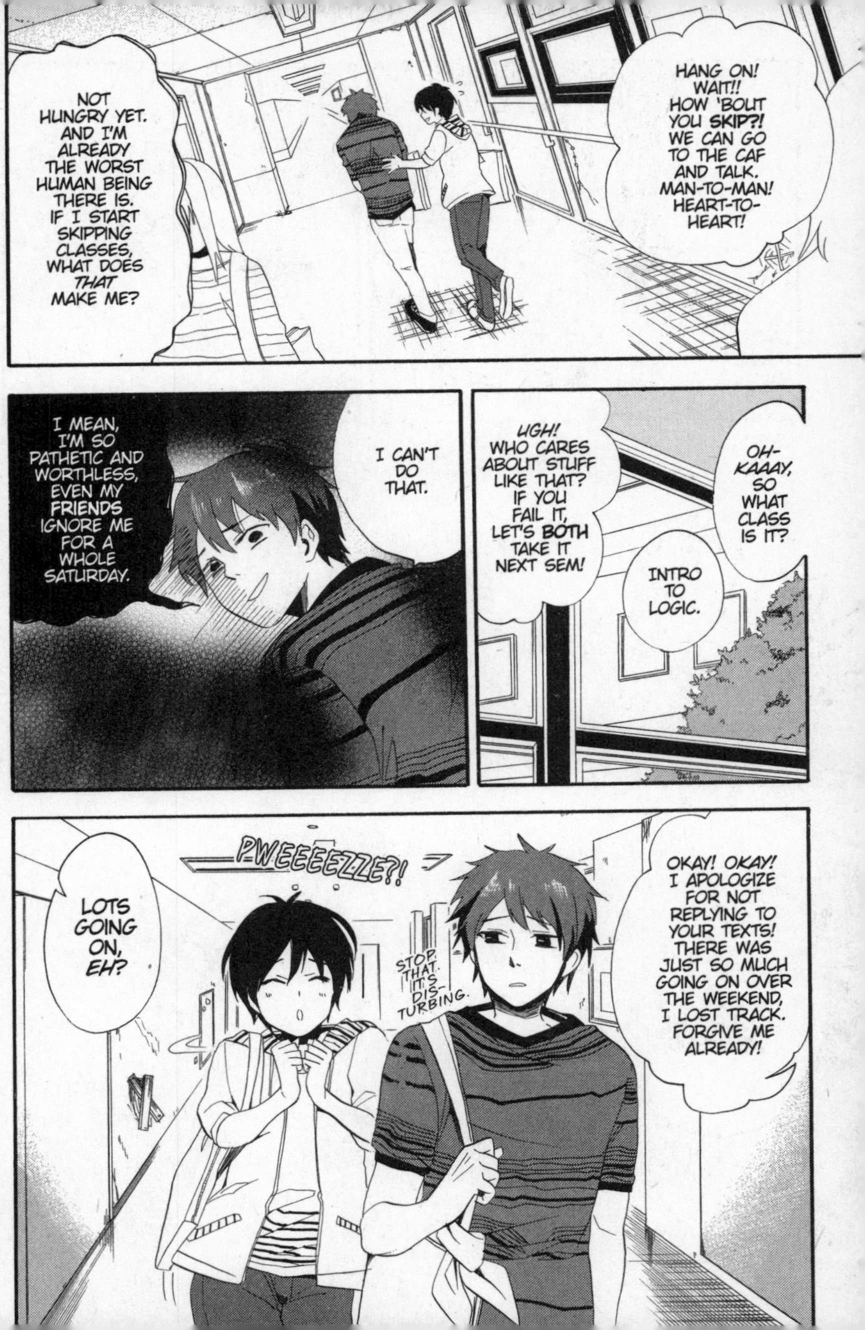
HANG ON! WAIT!! HOW 'BOUT YOU SKIP?! WE CAN GO TO THE CAF AND TALK. MAN-TO-MAN! HEART-TO-HEART!
NOT HUNGRY YET. AND I'M ALREADY THE WORST HUMAN BEING THERE IS. IF I START SKIPPING CLASSES, WHAT DOES THAT MAKE ME?
OH-KAAAY, SO WHAT CLASS IS IT?
INTRO TO LOGIC.
UGH! WHO CARES ABOUT STUFF LIKE THAT? IF YOU FAIL IT, LET'S BOTH TAKE IT NEXT SEM!
I CAN'T DO THAT.
I MEAN, I'M SO PATHETIC AND WORTHLESS, EVEN MY FRIENDS IGNORE ME FOR A WHOLE SATURDAY.
OKAY! OKAY! I APOLOGIZE FOR NOT REPLYING TO YOUR TEXTS! THERE WAS JUST SO MUCH GOING ON OVER THE WEEKEND, I LOST TRACK. FORGIVE ME ALREADY!
PWEEEEEZZE?!
STOP THAT. IT'S DISTURBING.
LOTS GOING ON, EH?

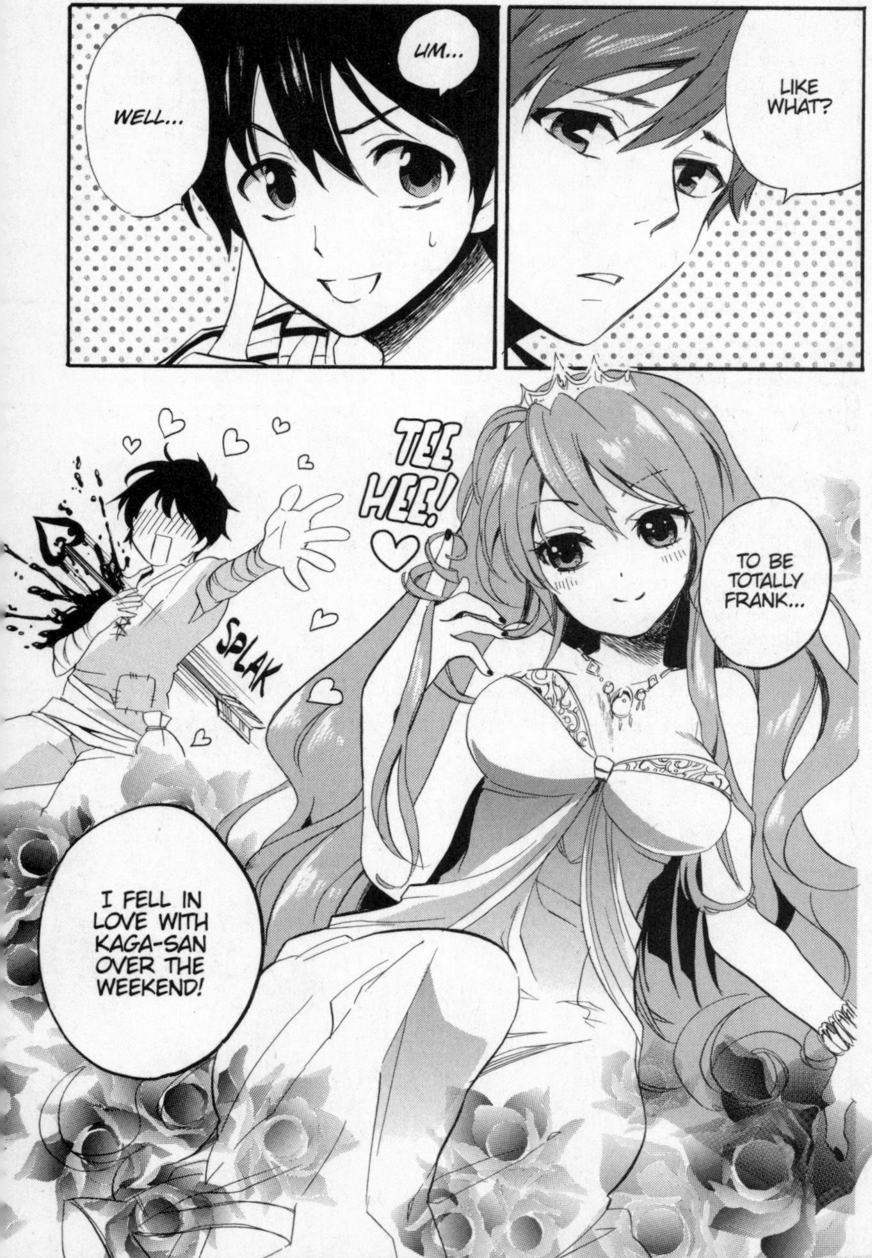
LIKE WHAT?
UM...
WELL...
TO BE TOTALLY FRANK...
TEE HEE!
SPLAK
I FELL IN LOVE WITH KAGA-SAN OVER THE WEEKEND!

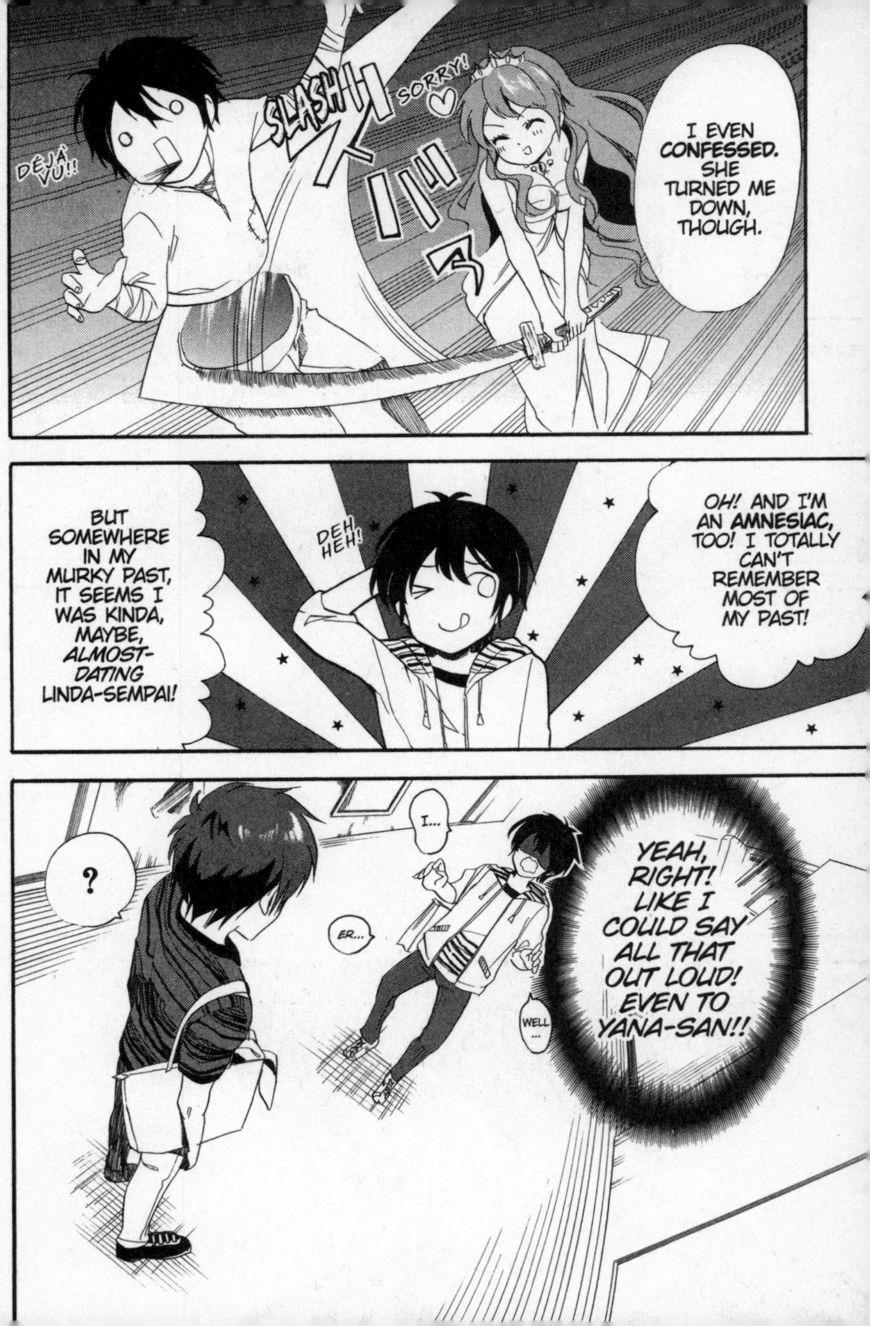
I EVEN CONFESSED. SHE TURNED ME DOWN, THOUGH.
SORRY! ♥
SLASH
DÉJÀ VU!!
OH! AND I'M AN AMNESIAC, TOO! I TOTALLY CAN'T REMEMBER MOST OF MY PAST!
DEH HEH!
BUT SOMEWHERE IN MY MURKY PAST, IT SEEMS I WAS KINDA, MAYBE, ALMOST-DATING LINDA-SEMPAI!
YEAH, RIGHT! LIKE I COULD SAY ALL THAT OUT LOUD! EVEN TO YANA-SAN!!
I...
ER...
WELL...
?

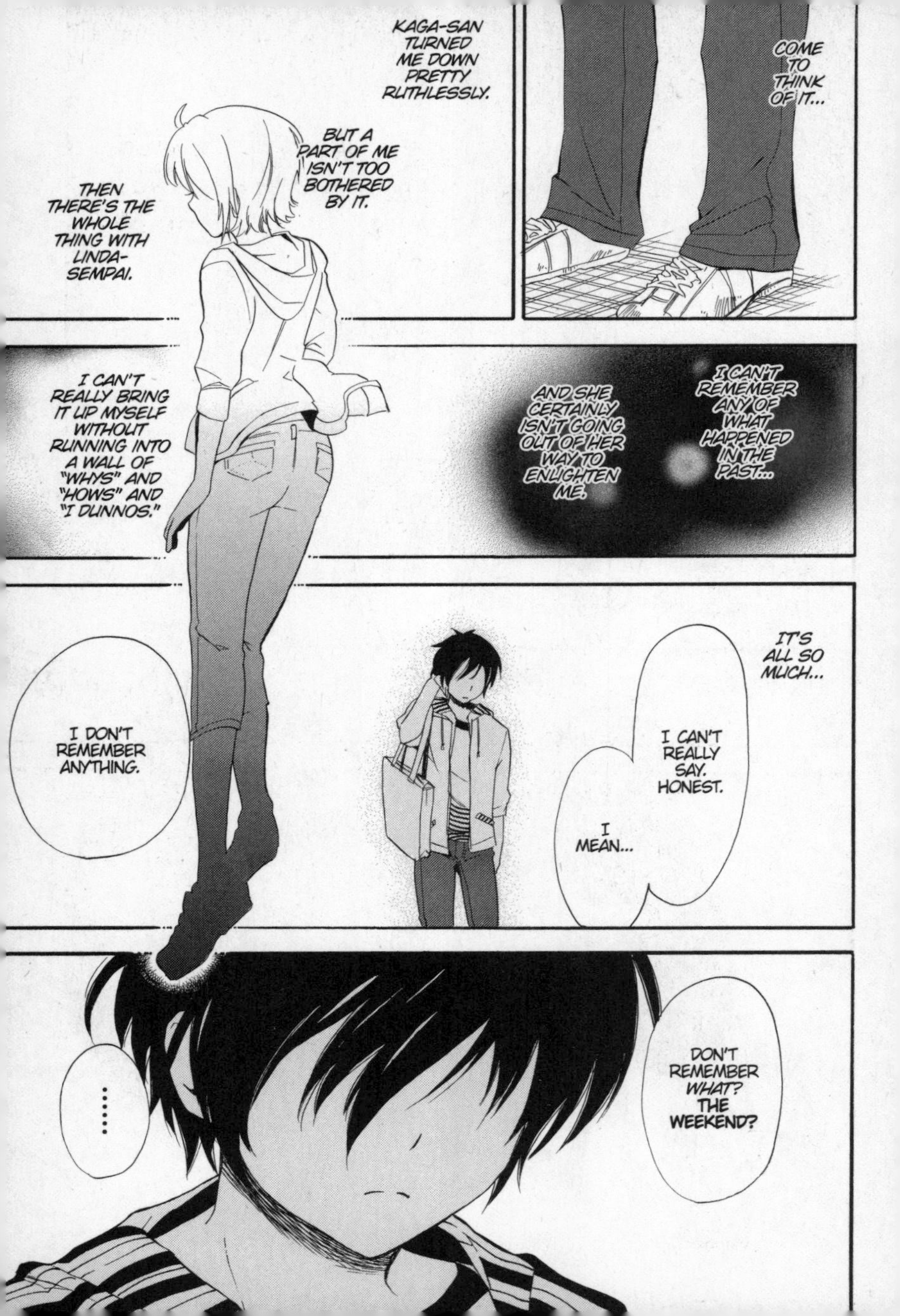
COME TO THINK OF IT...
KAGA-SAN TURNED ME DOWN PRETTY RUTHLESSLY.
BUT A PART OF ME ISN'T TOO BOTHERED BY IT.
THEN THERE'S THE WHOLE THING WITH LINDA-SEMPAI.
I CAN'T REMEMBER ANY OF WHAT HAPPENED IN THE PAST...
AND SHE CERTAINLY ISN'T GOING OUT OF HER WAY TO ENLIGHTEN ME.
I CAN'T REALLY BRING IT UP MYSELF WITHOUT RUNNING INTO A WALL OF "WHYS" AND "HOWS" AND "I DUNNOS."
IT'S ALL SO MUCH...
I CAN'T REALLY SAY. HONEST.
I MEAN...
I DON'T REMEMBER ANYTHING.
DON'T REMEMBER WHAT? THE WEEKEND?
......

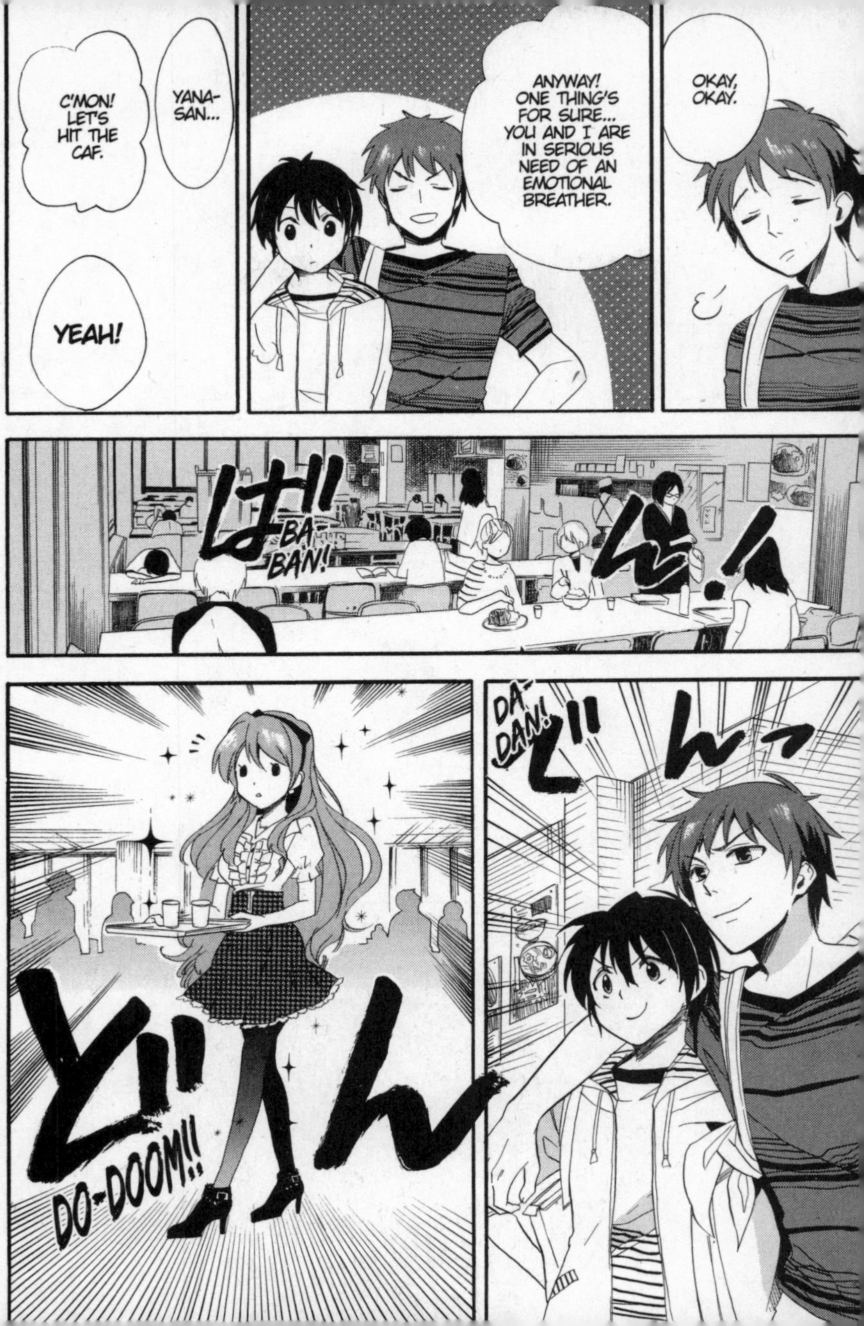
OKAY, OKAY.
ANYWAY! ONE THING'S FOR SURE... YOU AND I ARE IN SERIOUS NEED OF AN EMOTIONAL BREATHER.
YANA-SAN...
C'MON! LET'S HIT THE CAF.
YEAH!
BA-BAN!
DA-DAN!
DO-DOOM!!

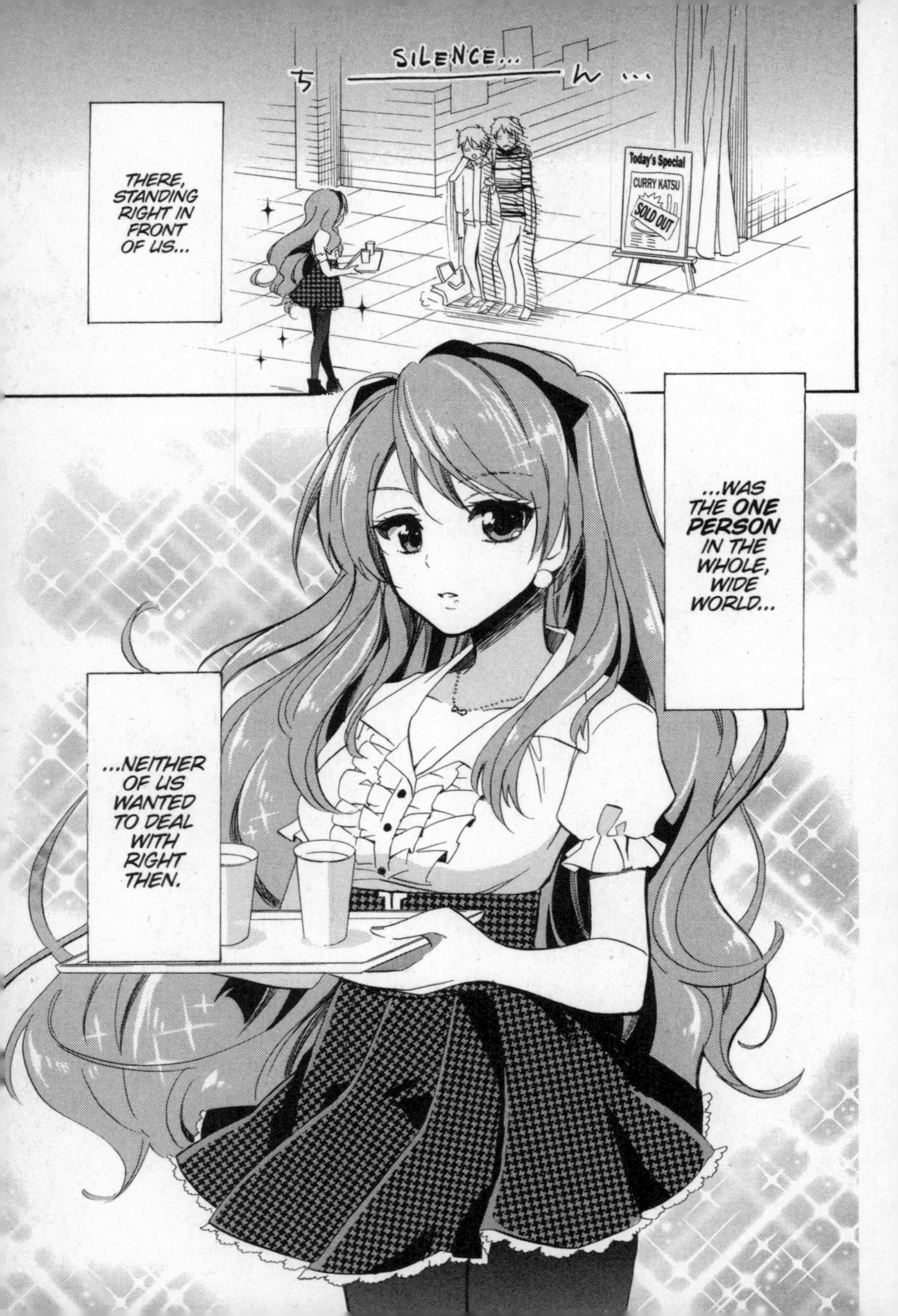
ち ん ...
SILENCE...
Today's Special
CURRY KATSU
SOLD OUT
THERE, STANDING RIGHT IN FRONT OF US...
...WAS THE ONE PERSON IN THE WHOLE, WIDE WORLD...
...NEITHER OF US WANTED TO DEAL WITH RIGHT THEN.

IN MANDARIN CHINESE (THE STANDARD CHINESE DIALECT), THE DEFINITION OF THE WORD "MA" VARIES DEPENDING ON THE FOUR DIFFERENT WAYS YOU PRONOUNCE IT.

THE ACCOMPANYING FUNNY FACES ARE NOT NECESSARY.

RISING PITCH.

HIGHER PITCH.

MĂ.

MÀ!

MÁ.

MÀ.

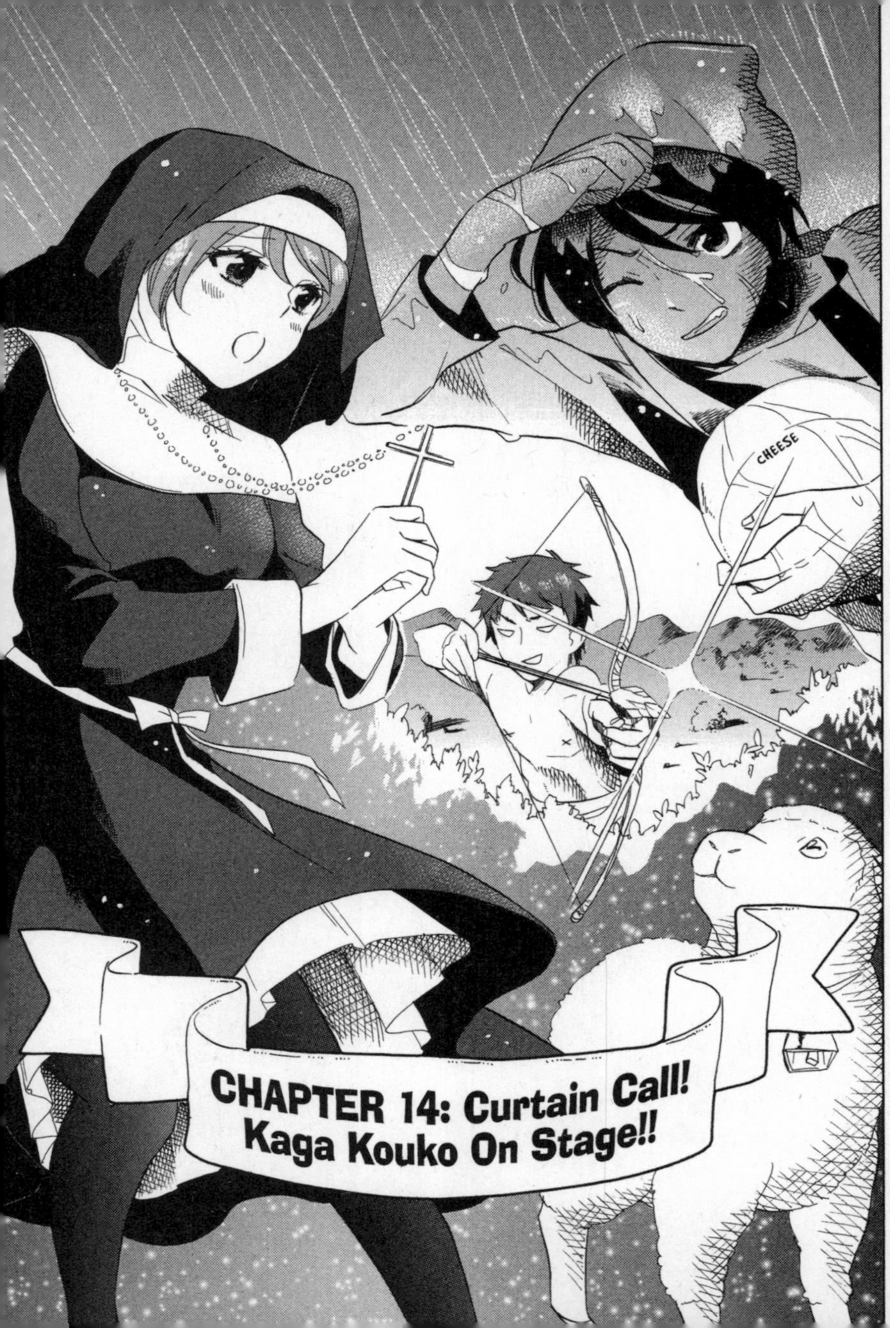
CHEESE
CHAPTER 14: Curtain Call!
Kaga Kouko On Stage!!

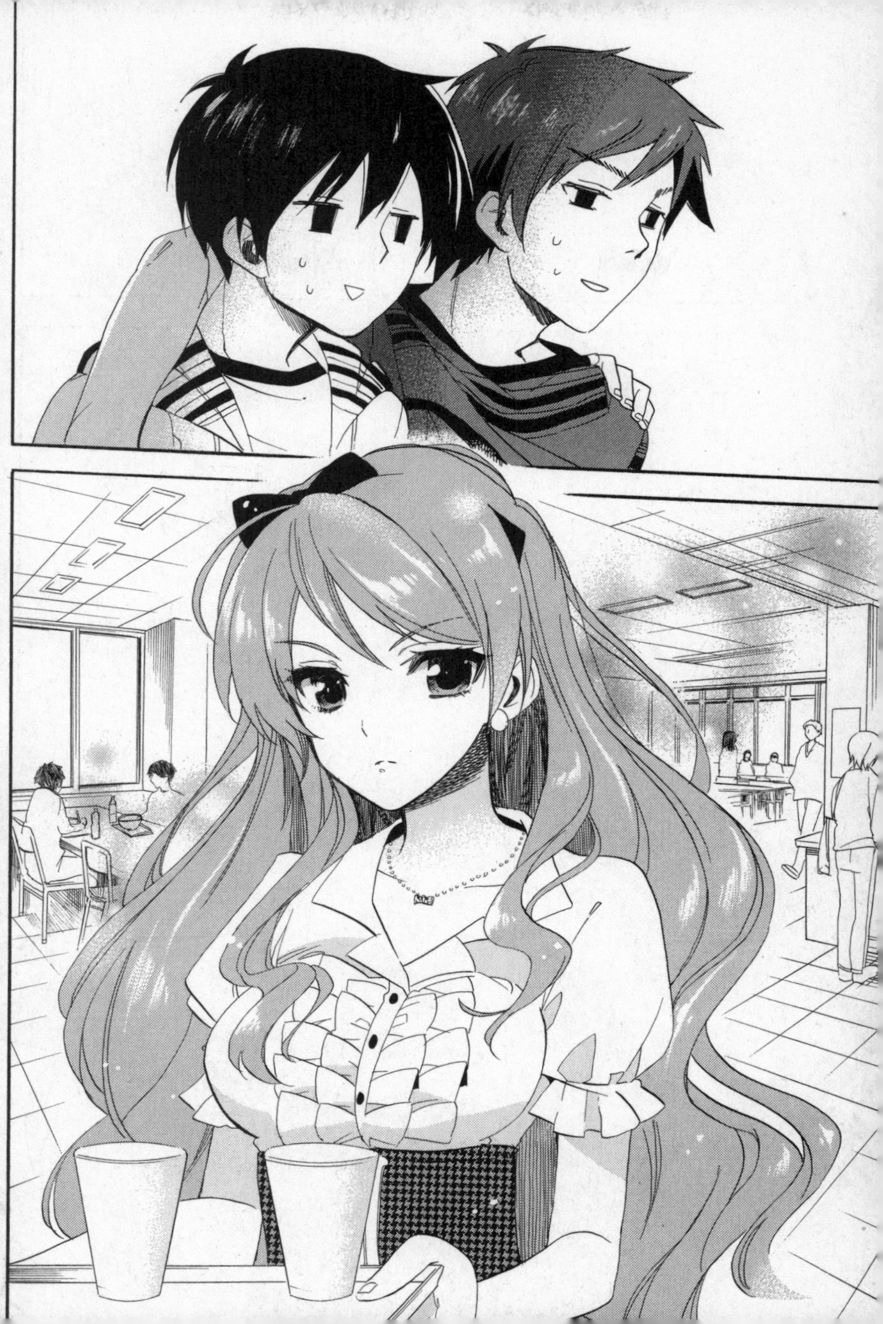

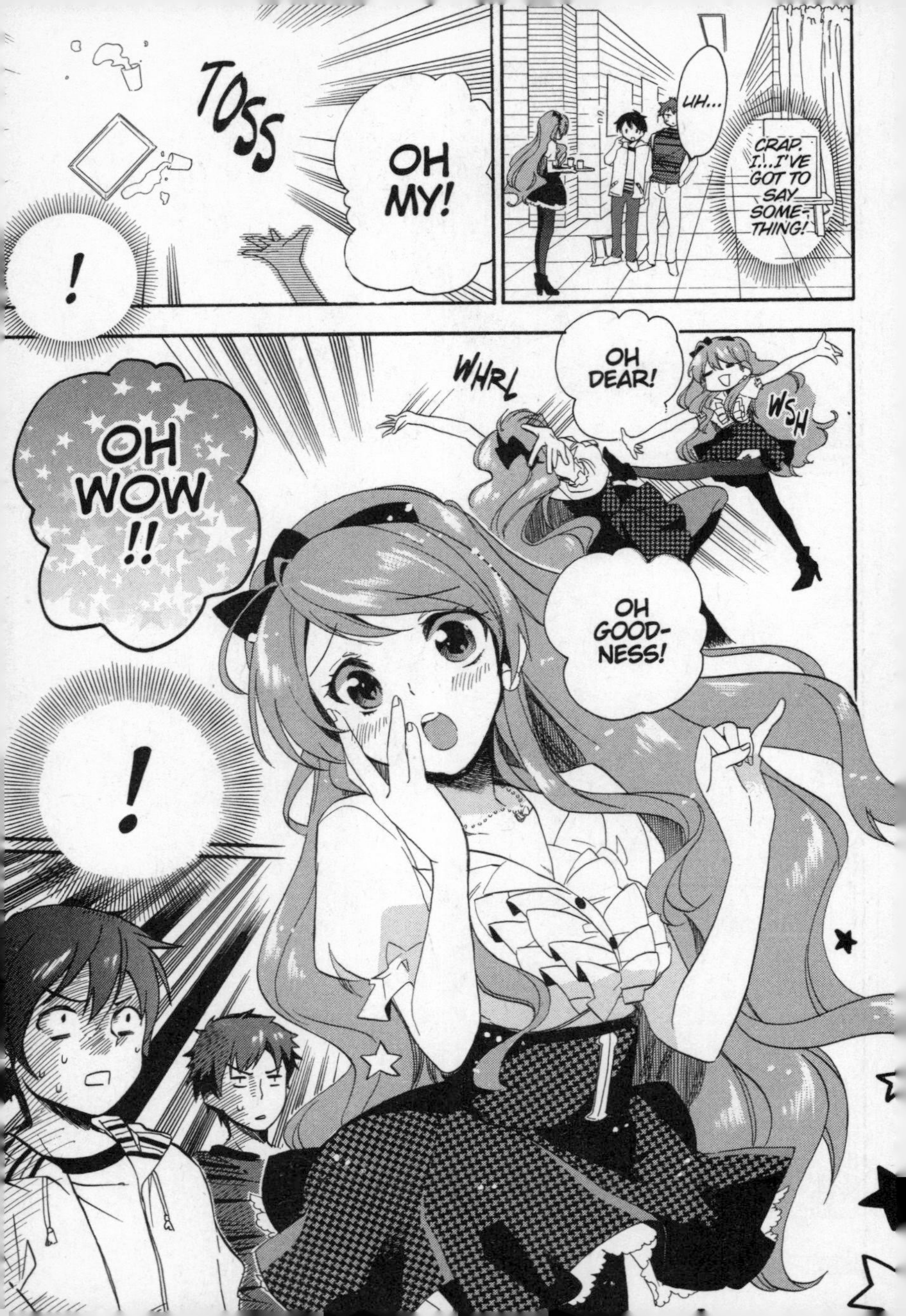
UH...
CRAP. I...I'VE GOT TO SAY SOME-THING!
TOSS
OH MY!
!
WSH
OH DEAR!
WHRL
OH GOODNESS!
OH WOW!!
!

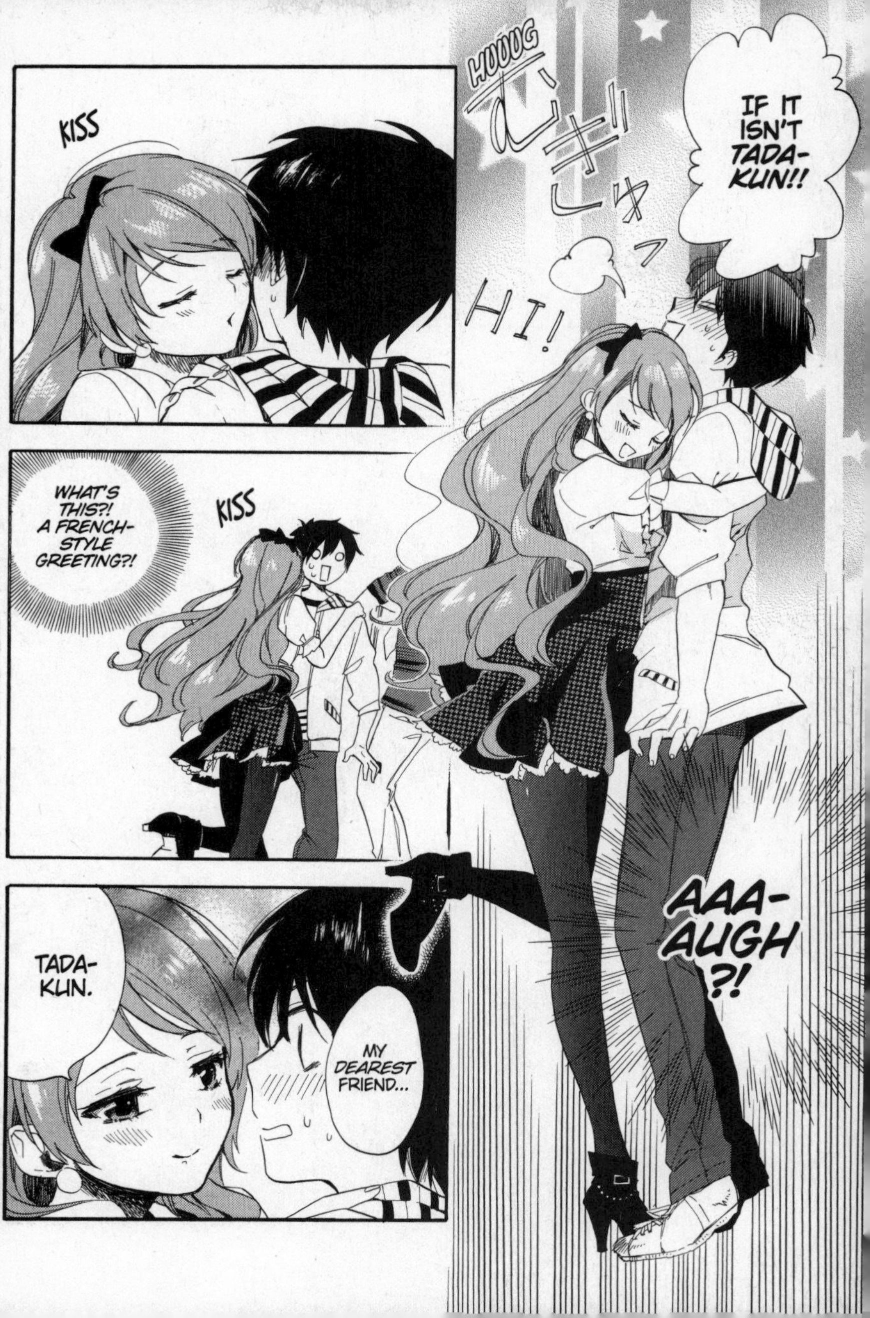
IF IT ISN'T TADA-KUN!!
HUUUG
むぎゅっ
HI!
AAA-AUGH?!
KISS
WHAT'S THIS?! A FRENCH-STYLE GREETING?!
KISS
TADA-KUN.
MY DEAREST FRIEND...

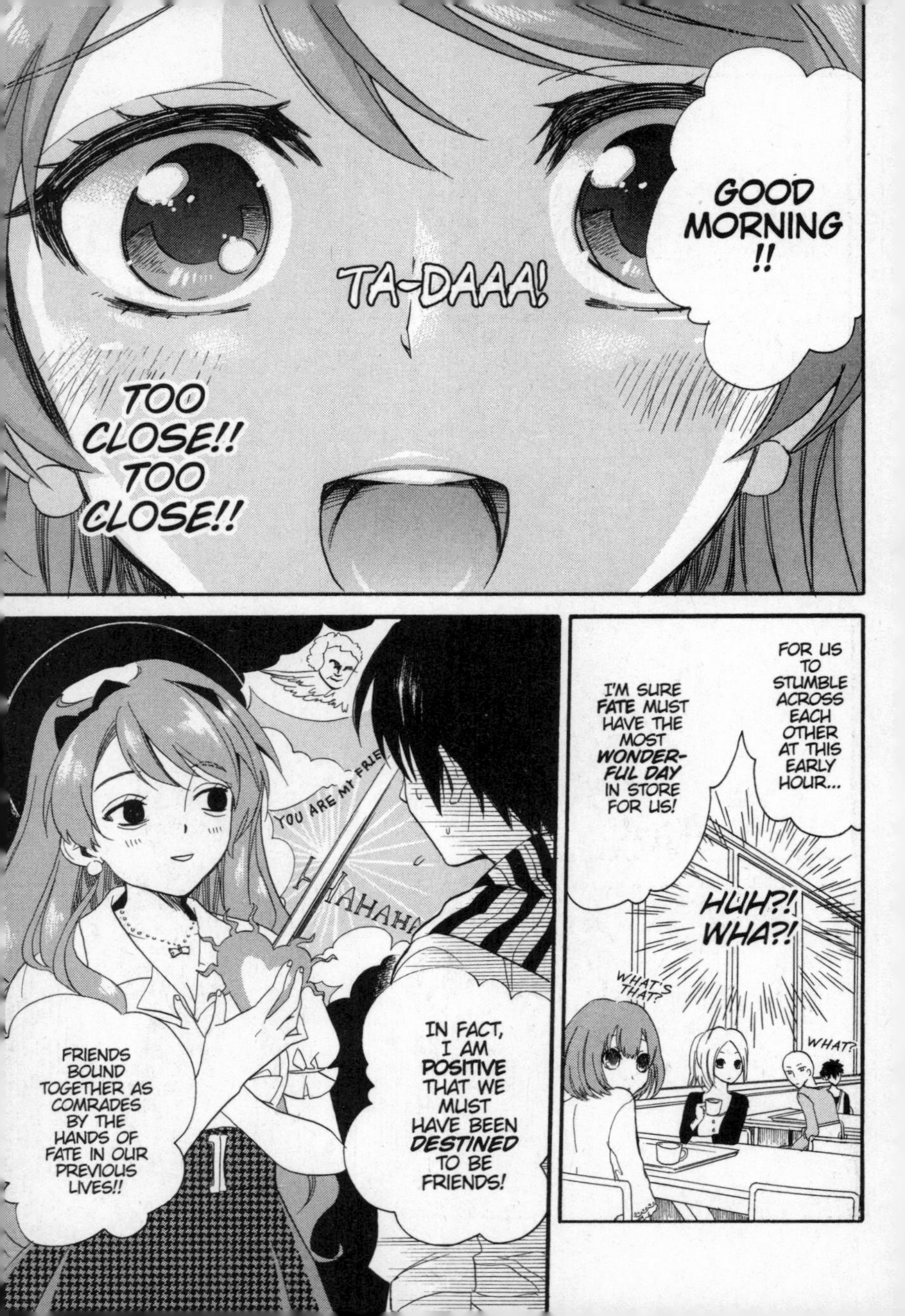
GOOD MORNING!!
TA-DAAA!
TOO CLOSE!! TOO CLOSE!!
FOR US TO STUMBLE ACROSS EACH OTHER AT THIS EARLY HOUR...
I'M SURE FATE MUST HAVE THE MOST **WONDERFUL DAY** IN STORE FOR US!
HUH?! WHA?!
WHAT?
WHAT'S THAT?
YOU ARE MY FRIE
HAHAHAHA
IN FACT, I AM **POSITIVE** THAT WE MUST HAVE BEEN **DESTINED** TO BE FRIENDS!
FRIENDS BOUND TOGETHER AS COMRADES BY THE HANDS OF FATE IN OUR PREVIOUS LIVES!!

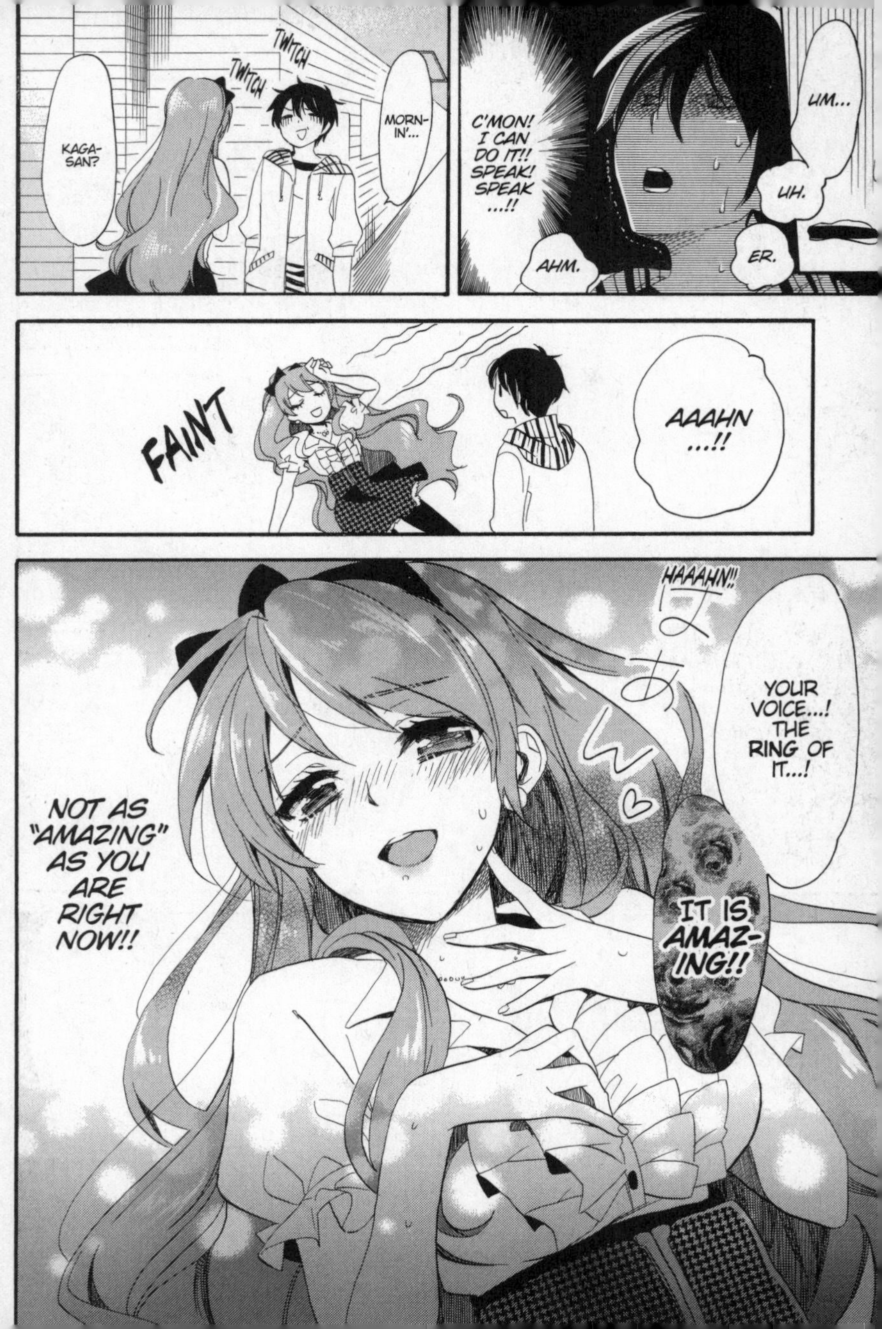
UM...
UH.
ER.
C'MON! I CAN DO IT!! SPEAK! SPEAK ...!!
AHM.
TWITCH
TWITCH
MORN-IN'...
KAGA-SAN?
AAAHN ...!!
FAINT
HAAAHN!!
YOUR VOICE...! THE RING OF IT...!
IT IS AMAZ-ING!!
NOT AS "AMAZING" AS YOU ARE RIGHT NOW!!

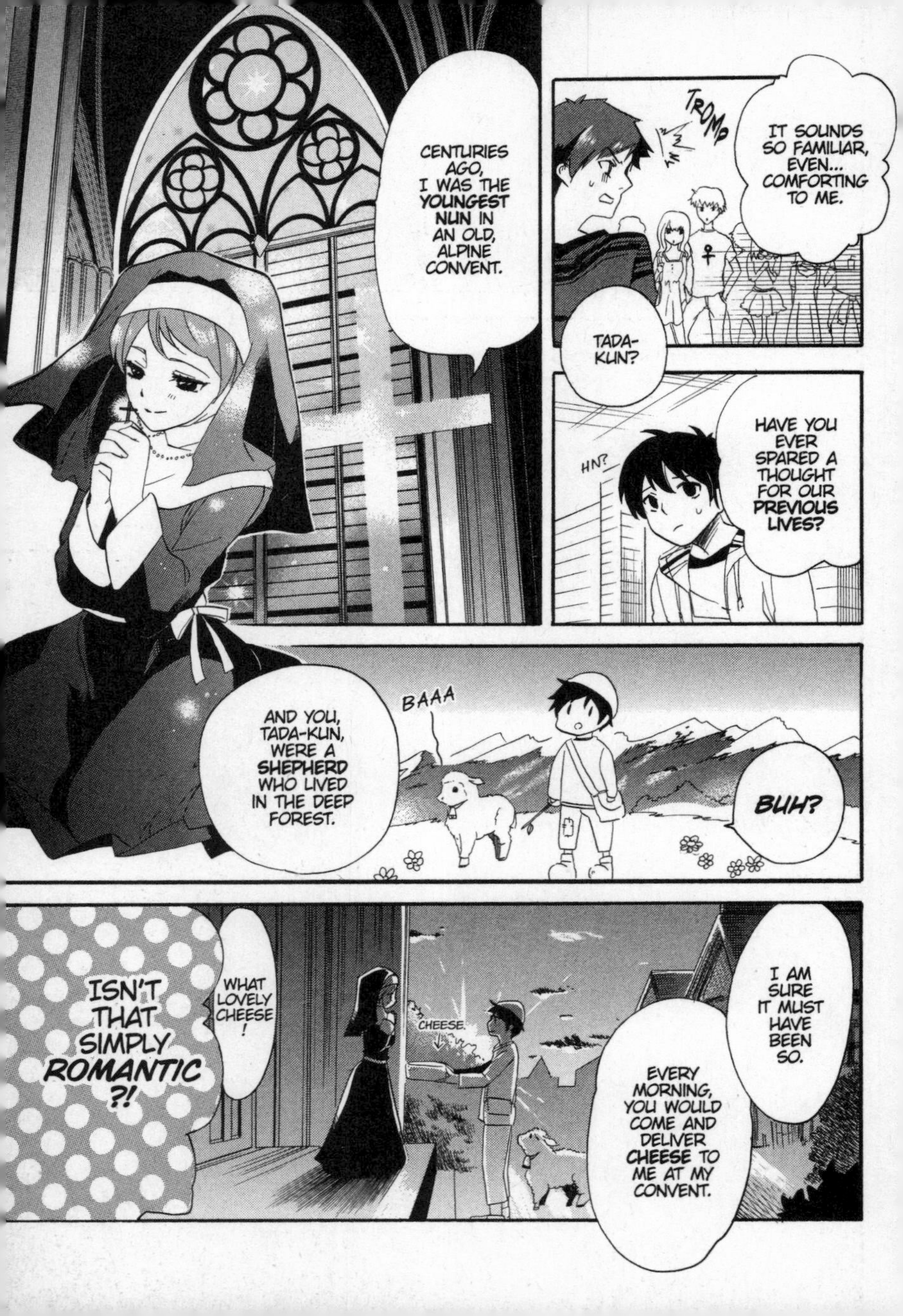
TROMP
IT SOUNDS SO FAMILIAR, EVEN... COMFORTING TO ME.
TADA-KUN?
HN?
HAVE YOU EVER SPARED A THOUGHT FOR OUR PREVIOUS LIVES?
CENTURIES AGO, I WAS THE YOUNGEST NUN IN AN OLD, ALPINE CONVENT.
AND YOU, TADA-KUN, WERE A SHEPHERD WHO LIVED IN THE DEEP FOREST.
BAAA
BUH?
I AM SURE IT MUST HAVE BEEN SO.
EVERY MORNING, YOU WOULD COME AND DELIVER CHEESE TO ME AT MY CONVENT.
CHEESE.
WHAT LOVELY CHEESE!
ISN'T THAT SIMPLY ROMANTIC?!

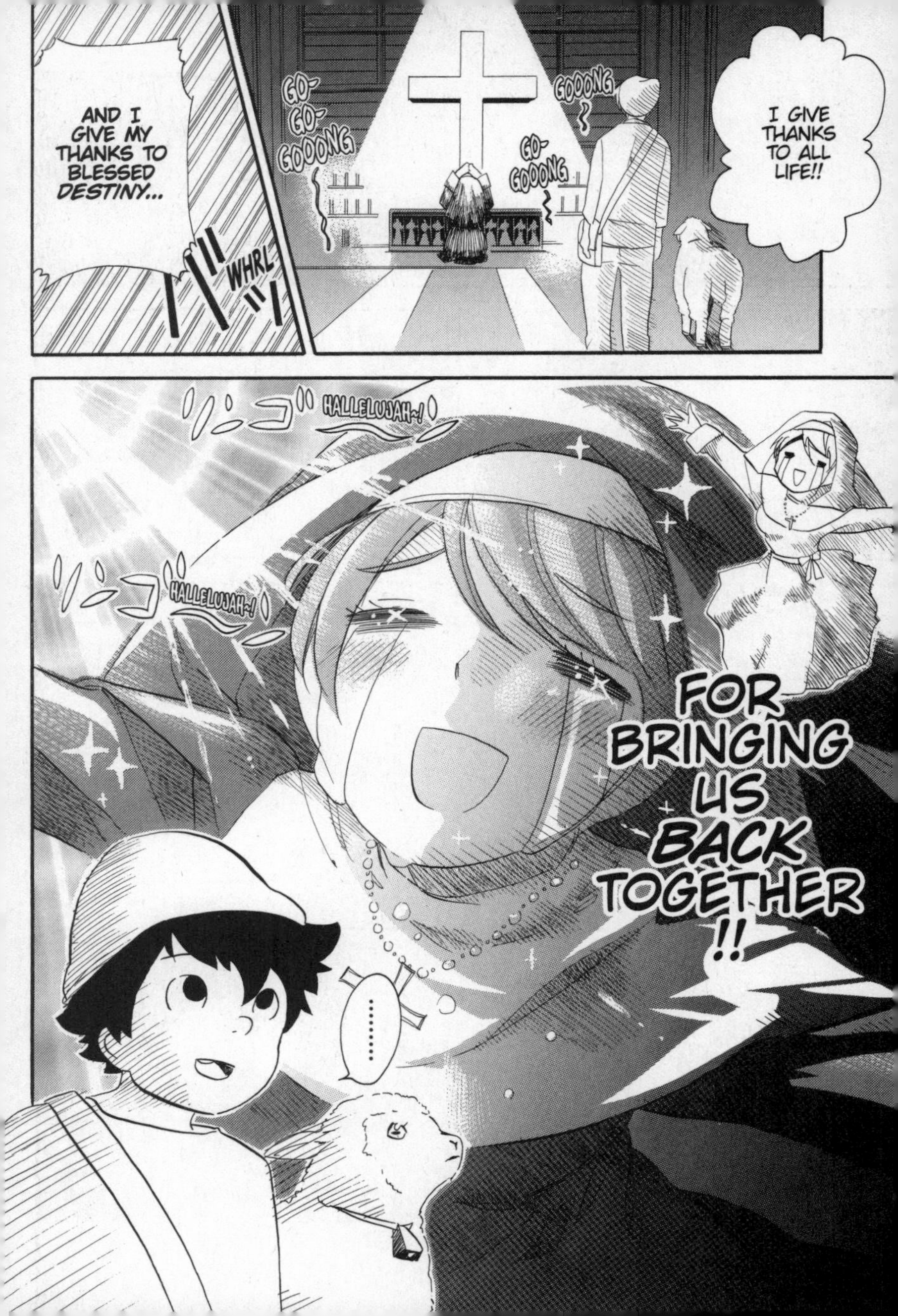
I GIVE THANKS TO ALL LIFE!!
GOOONG
GO-GOOONG
GO-GO-GOOONG
AND I GIVE MY THANKS TO BLESSED DESTINY...
WHRL
HALLELUJAH~!
HALLELUJAH~!
FOR BRINGING US BACK TOGETHER!!
......

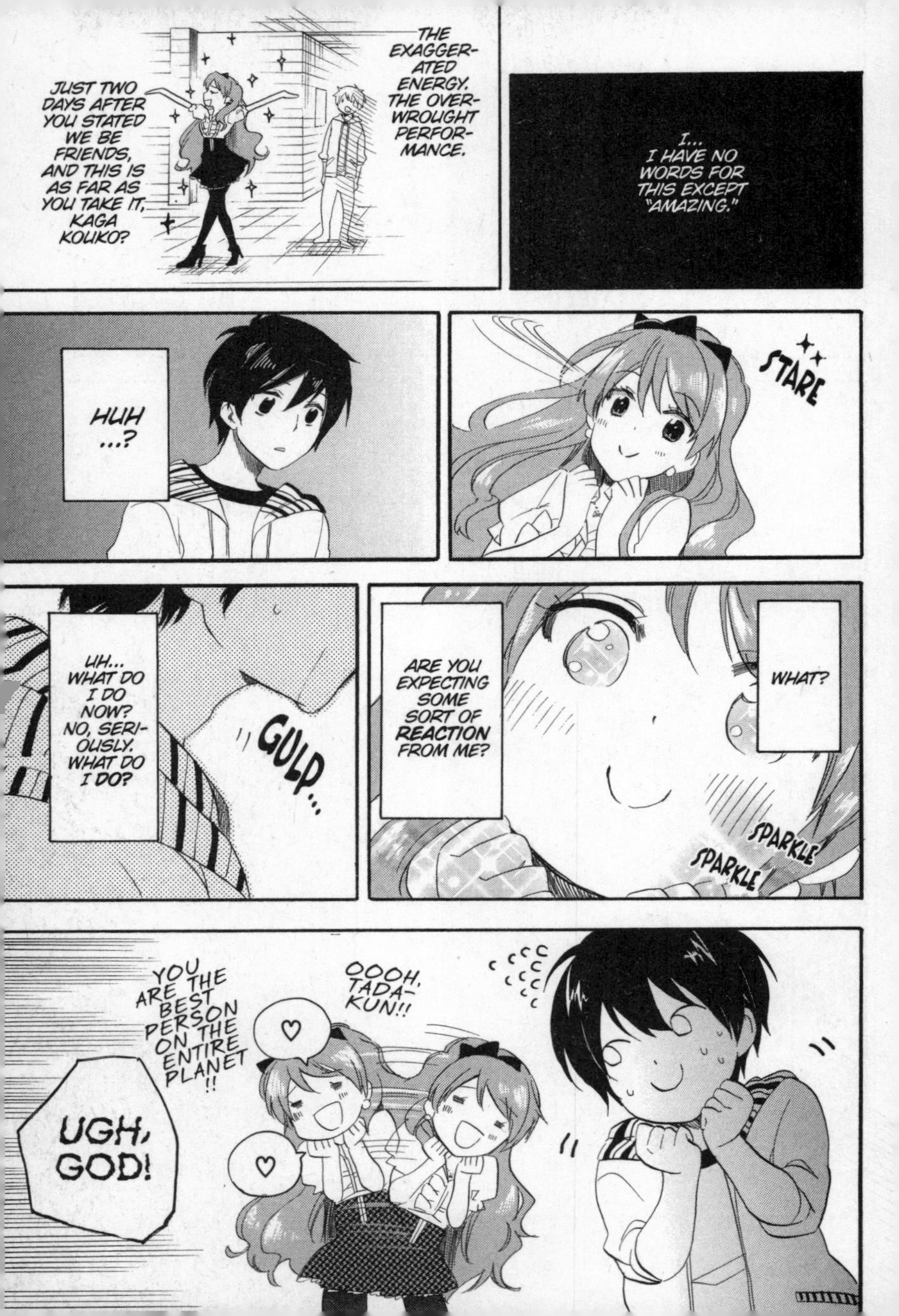
I... I HAVE NO WORDS FOR THIS EXCEPT "AMAZING."
THE EXAGGERATED ENERGY. THE OVERWROUGHT PERFORMANCE.
JUST TWO DAYS AFTER YOU STATED WE BE FRIENDS, AND THIS IS AS FAR AS YOU TAKE IT, KAGA KOUKO?
STARE
HUH ...?
WHAT?
ARE YOU EXPECTING SOME SORT OF REACTION FROM ME?
SPARKLE
SPARKLE
UH... WHAT DO I DO NOW? NO, SERIOUSLY. WHAT DO I DO?
GULP...
OOOH, TADA-KUN!!
YOU ARE THE BEST PERSON ON THE ENTIRE PLANET!!
UGH, GOD!

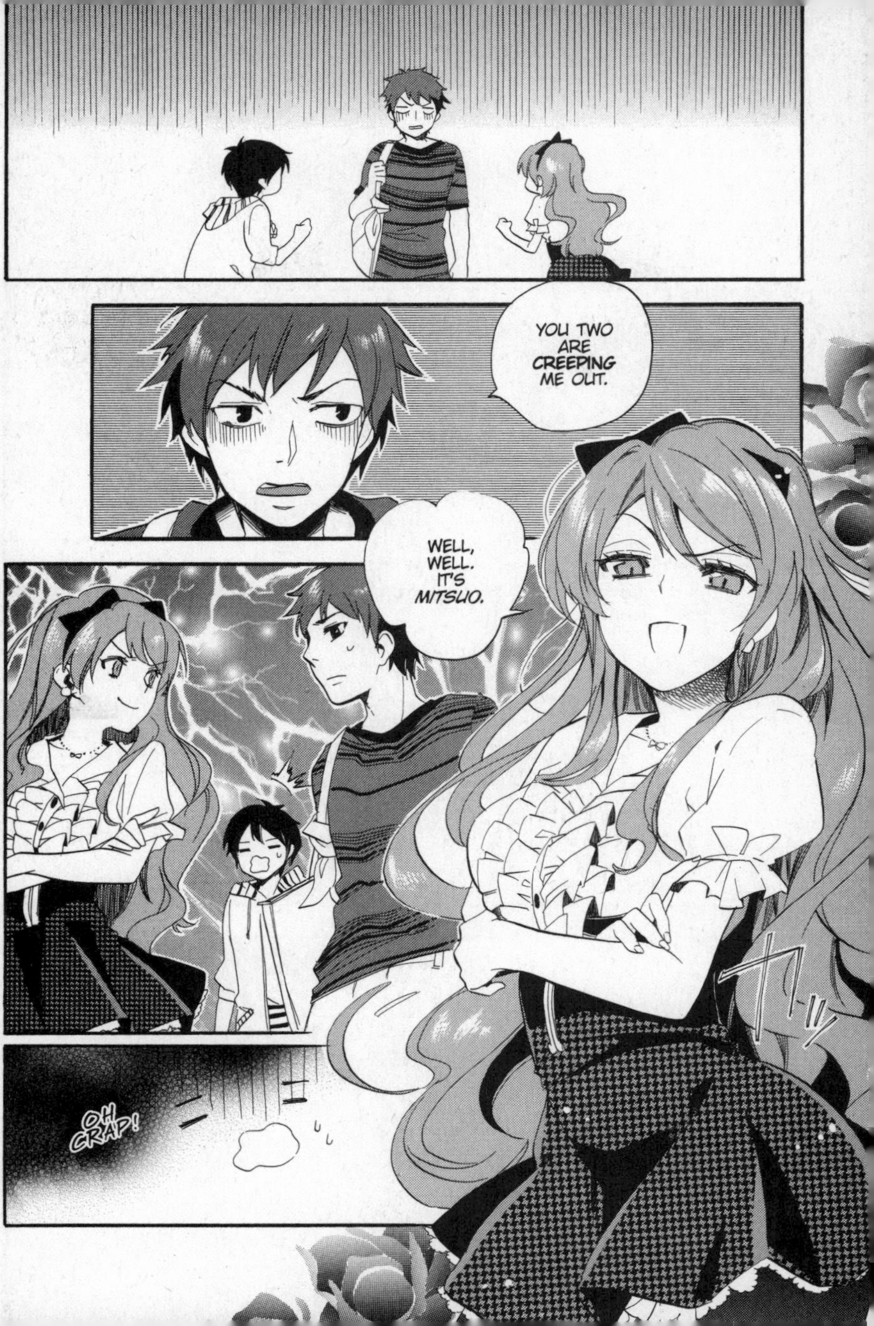
YOU TWO ARE CREEPING ME OUT.
WELL, WELL. IT'S MITSUO.
OH CRAP!

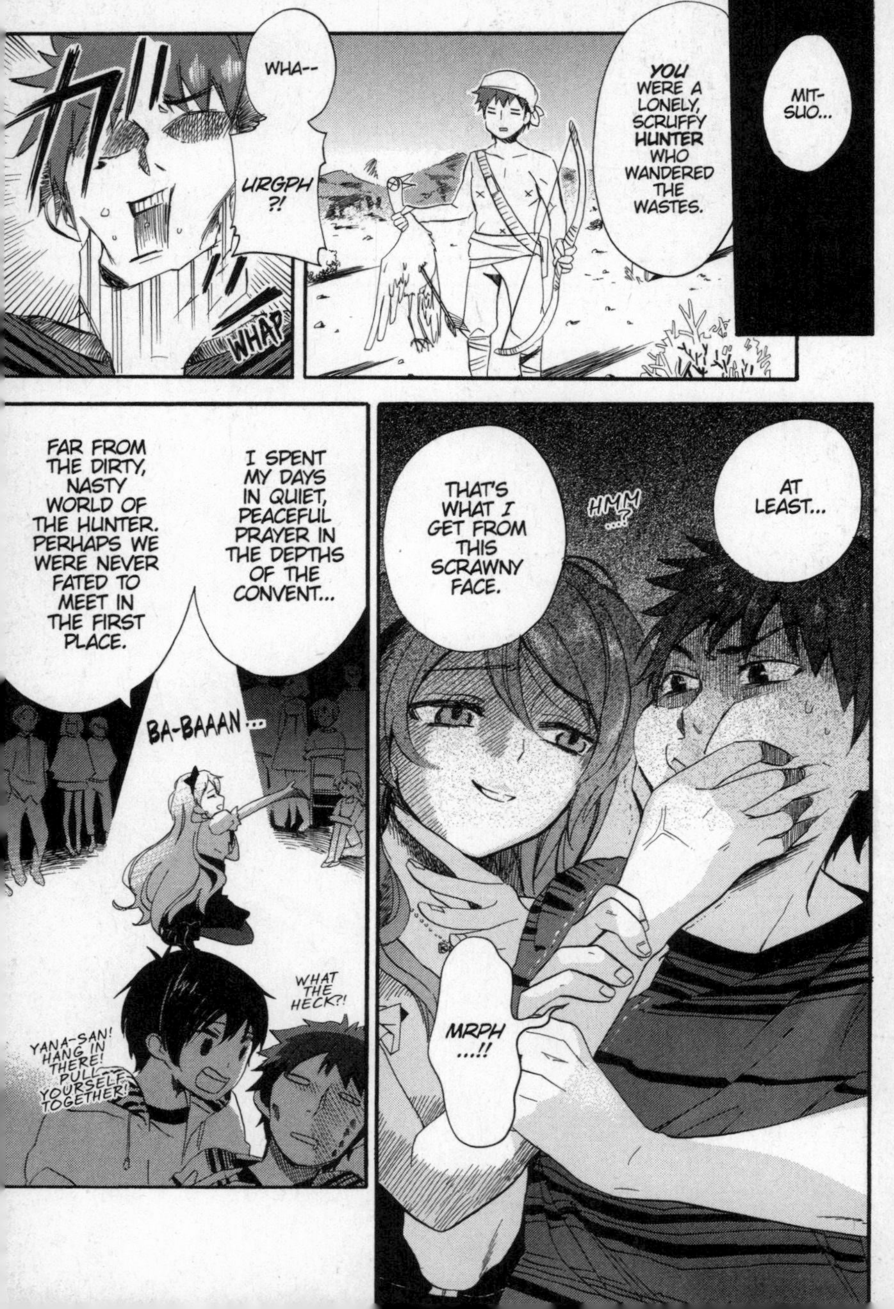
MIT-SUO...
YOU WERE A LONELY, SCRUFFY HUNTER WHO WANDERED THE WASTES.
WHA--
URGPH ?!
WHAP
AT LEAST...
THAT'S WHAT I GET FROM THIS SCRAWNY FACE.
HMM ...?
MRPH ...!!
I SPENT MY DAYS IN QUIET, PEACEFUL PRAYER IN THE DEPTHS OF THE CONVENT...
FAR FROM THE DIRTY, NASTY WORLD OF THE HUNTER. PERHAPS WE WERE NEVER FATED TO MEET IN THE FIRST PLACE.
BA-BAAAN...
WHAT THE HECK?!
YANA-SAN! HANG IN THERE! PULL YOURSELF TOGETHER!

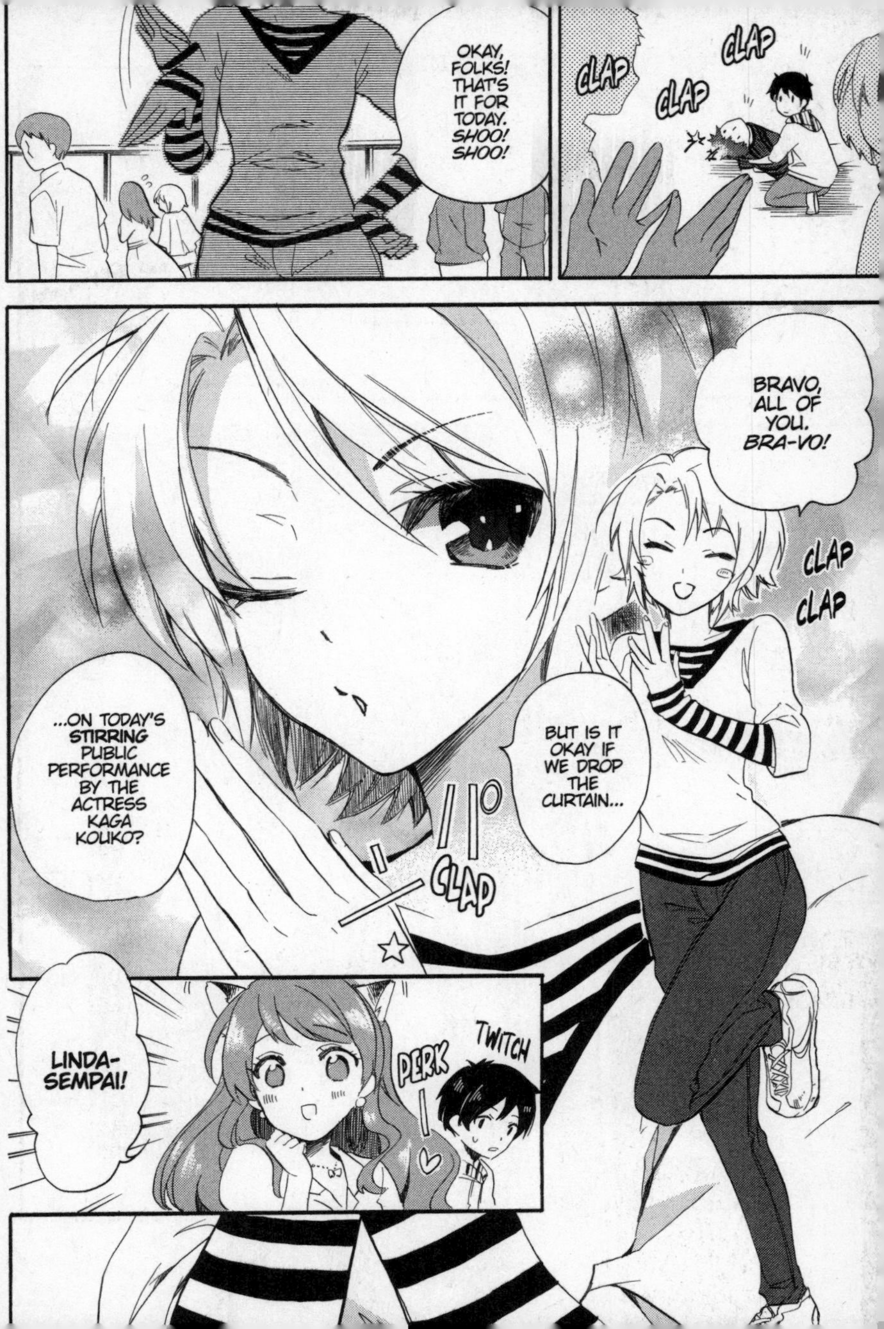
CLAP
CLAP
CLAP
OKAY, FOLKS! THAT'S IT FOR TODAY. SHOO! SHOO!
BRAVO, ALL OF YOU. BRA-VO!
CLAP
CLAP
BUT IS IT OKAY IF WE DROP THE CURTAIN...
...ON TODAY'S STIRRING PUBLIC PERFORMANCE BY THE ACTRESS KAGA KOUKO?
CLAP
TWITCH
PERK
LINDA-SEMPAI!

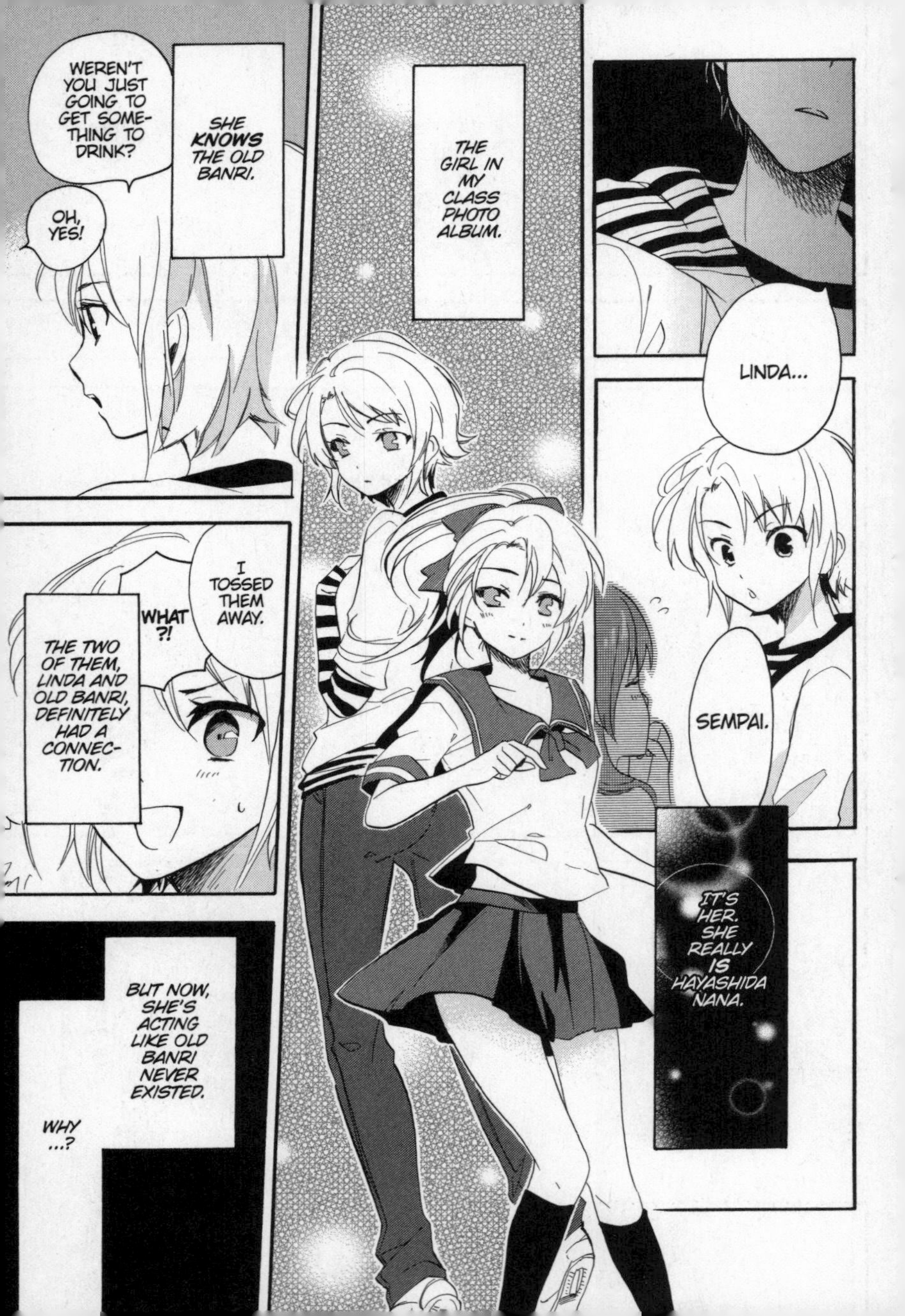
LINDA...
SEMPAI.
IT'S HER. SHE REALLY IS HAYASHIDA NANA.
THE GIRL IN MY CLASS PHOTO ALBUM.
SHE KNOWS THE OLD BANRI.
WEREN'T YOU JUST GOING TO GET SOME-THING TO DRINK?
OH, YES!
I TOSSED THEM AWAY.
WHAT?!
THE TWO OF THEM, LINDA AND OLD BANRI, DEFINITELY HAD A CONNEC-TION.
BUT NOW, SHE'S ACTING LIKE OLD BANRI NEVER EXISTED.
WHY ...?

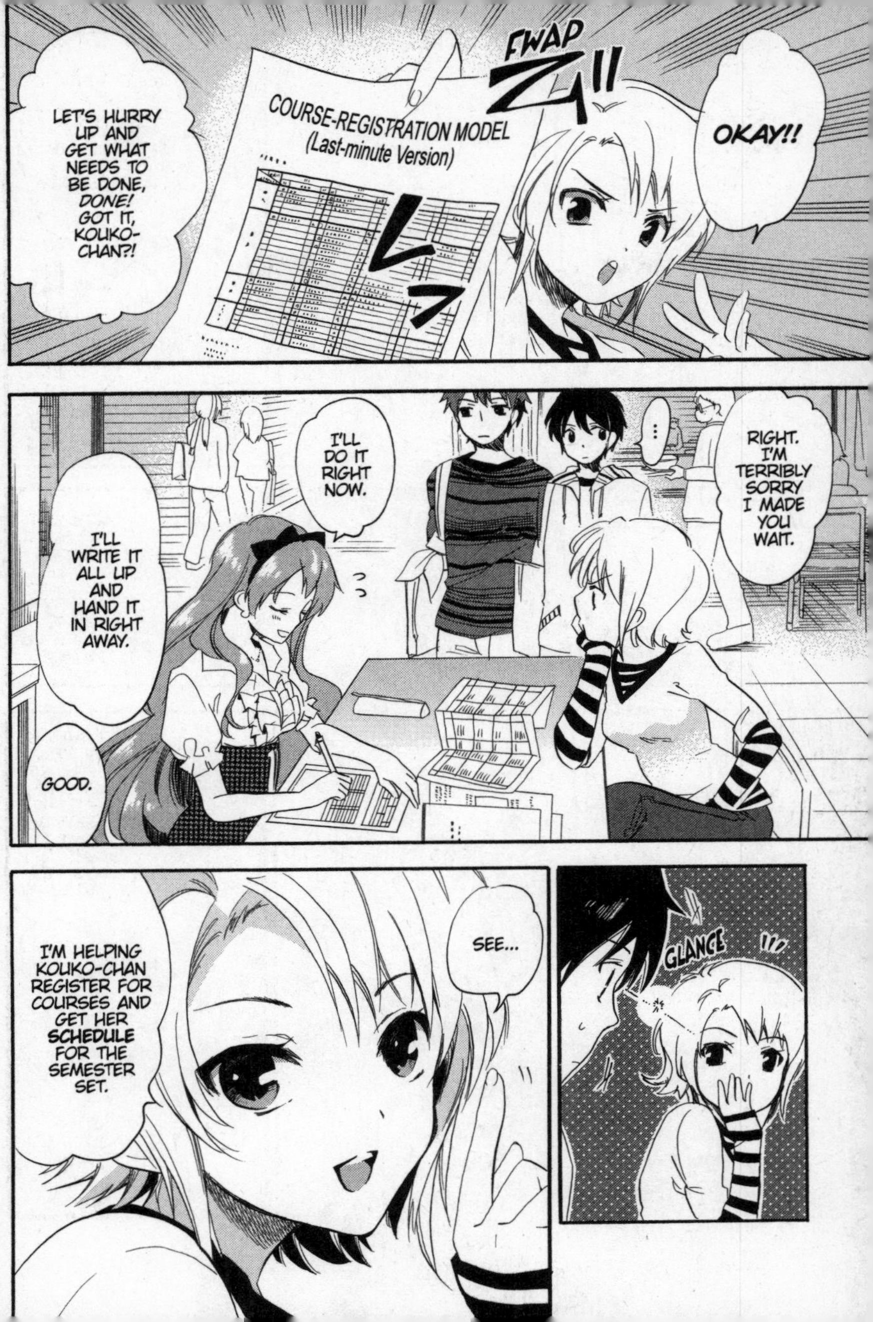
FWAP
OKAY!!
COURSE-REGISTRATION MODEL (Last-minute Version)
LET'S HURRY UP AND GET WHAT NEEDS TO BE DONE, DONE! GOT IT, KOUKO-CHAN?!
RIGHT. I'M TERRIBLY SORRY I MADE YOU WAIT.
...
I'LL DO IT RIGHT NOW.
I'LL WRITE IT ALL UP AND HAND IT IN RIGHT AWAY.
GOOD.
GLANCE
SEE...
I'M HELPING KOUKO-CHAN REGISTER FOR COURSES AND GET HER SCHEDULE FOR THE SEMESTER SET.

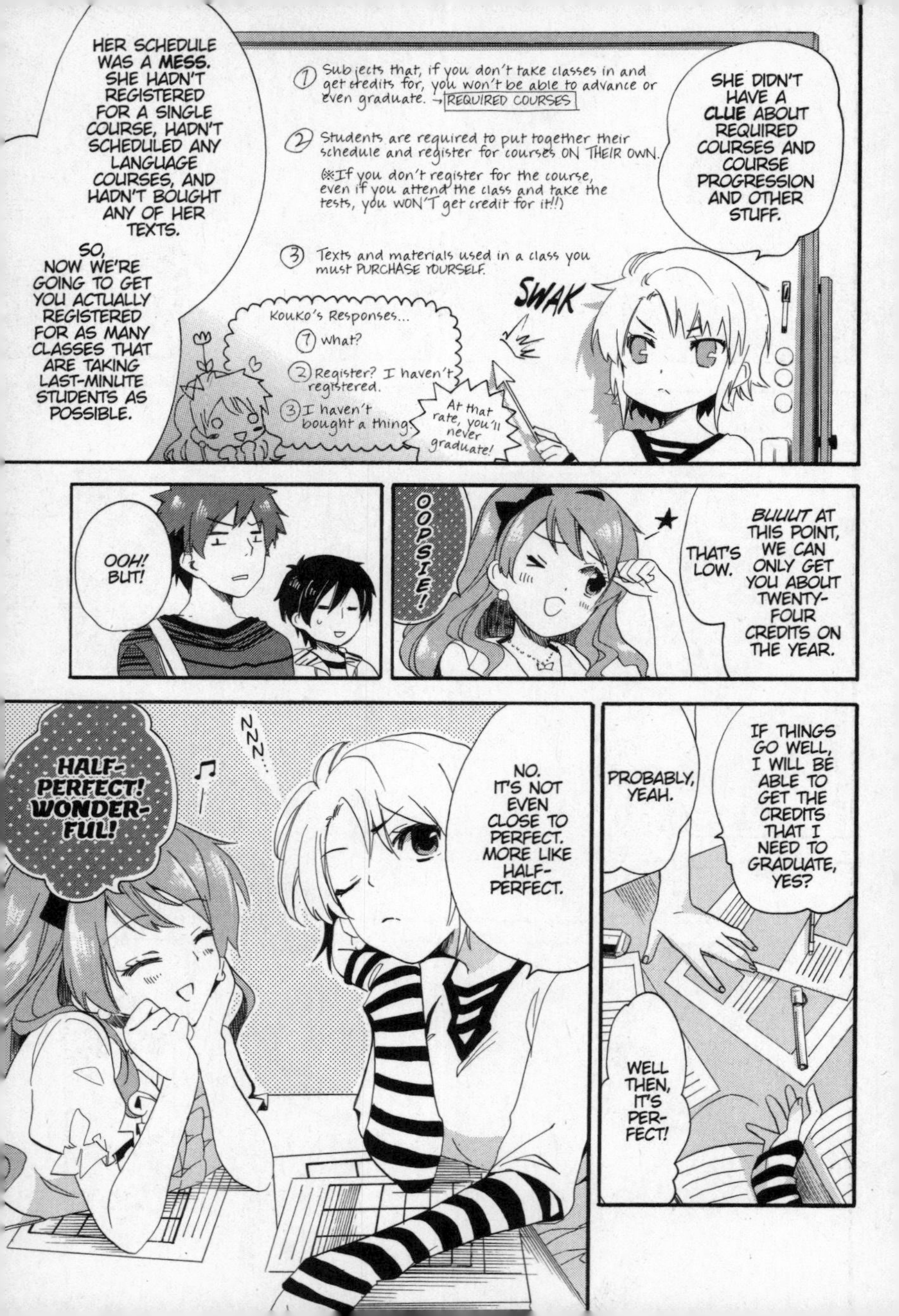
SHE DIDN'T HAVE A CLUE ABOUT REQUIRED COURSES AND COURSE PROGRESSION AND OTHER STUFF.
① Subjects that, if you don't take classes in and get credits for, you won't be able to advance or even graduate. → REQUIRED COURSES
② Students are required to put together their schedule and register for courses ON THEIR OWN.
(※If you don't register for the course, even if you attend the class and take the tests, you WON'T get credit for it!!)
③ Texts and materials used in a class you must PURCHASE YOURSELF.
HER SCHEDULE WAS A MESS. SHE HADN'T REGISTERED FOR A SINGLE COURSE, HADN'T SCHEDULED ANY LANGUAGE COURSES, AND HADN'T BOUGHT ANY OF HER TEXTS.
SO, NOW WE'RE GOING TO GET YOU ACTUALLY REGISTERED FOR AS MANY CLASSES THAT ARE TAKING LAST-MINUTE STUDENTS AS POSSIBLE.
SWAK
At that rate, you'll never graduate!
Kouko's Responses...
① what?
② Register? I haven't registered.
③ I haven't bought a thing.
BUUUT AT THIS POINT, WE CAN ONLY GET YOU ABOUT TWENTY-FOUR CREDITS ON THE YEAR.
THAT'S LOW.
OOPSIE!
OOH! BUT!
IF THINGS GO WELL, I WILL BE ABLE TO GET THE CREDITS THAT I NEED TO GRADUATE, YES?
PROBABLY, YEAH.
WELL THEN, IT'S PER-FECT!
NO. IT'S NOT EVEN CLOSE TO PERFECT. MORE LIKE HALF-PERFECT.
NNN...
HALF-PERFECT! WONDERFUL!

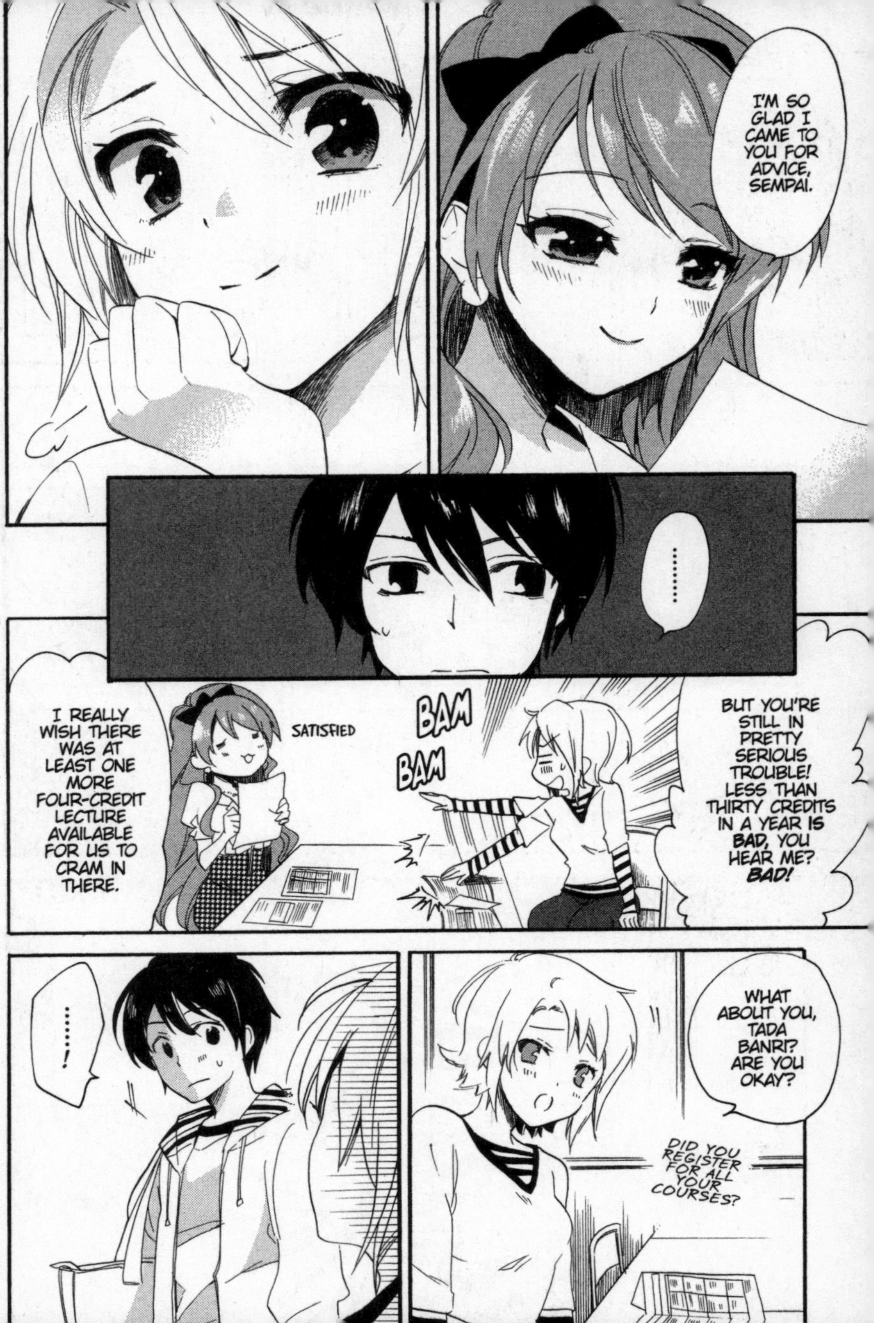
I'M SO GLAD I CAME TO YOU FOR ADVICE, SEMPAI.
......
BUT YOU'RE STILL IN PRETTY SERIOUS TROUBLE! LESS THAN THIRTY CREDITS IN A YEAR IS **BAD**, YOU HEAR ME? ***BAD!***
BAM
BAM
SATISFIED
I REALLY WISH THERE WAS AT LEAST ONE MORE FOUR-CREDIT LECTURE AVAILABLE FOR US TO CRAM IN THERE.
WHAT ABOUT YOU, TADA BANRI? ARE YOU OKAY?
DID YOU REGISTER FOR ALL YOUR COURSES?
......!

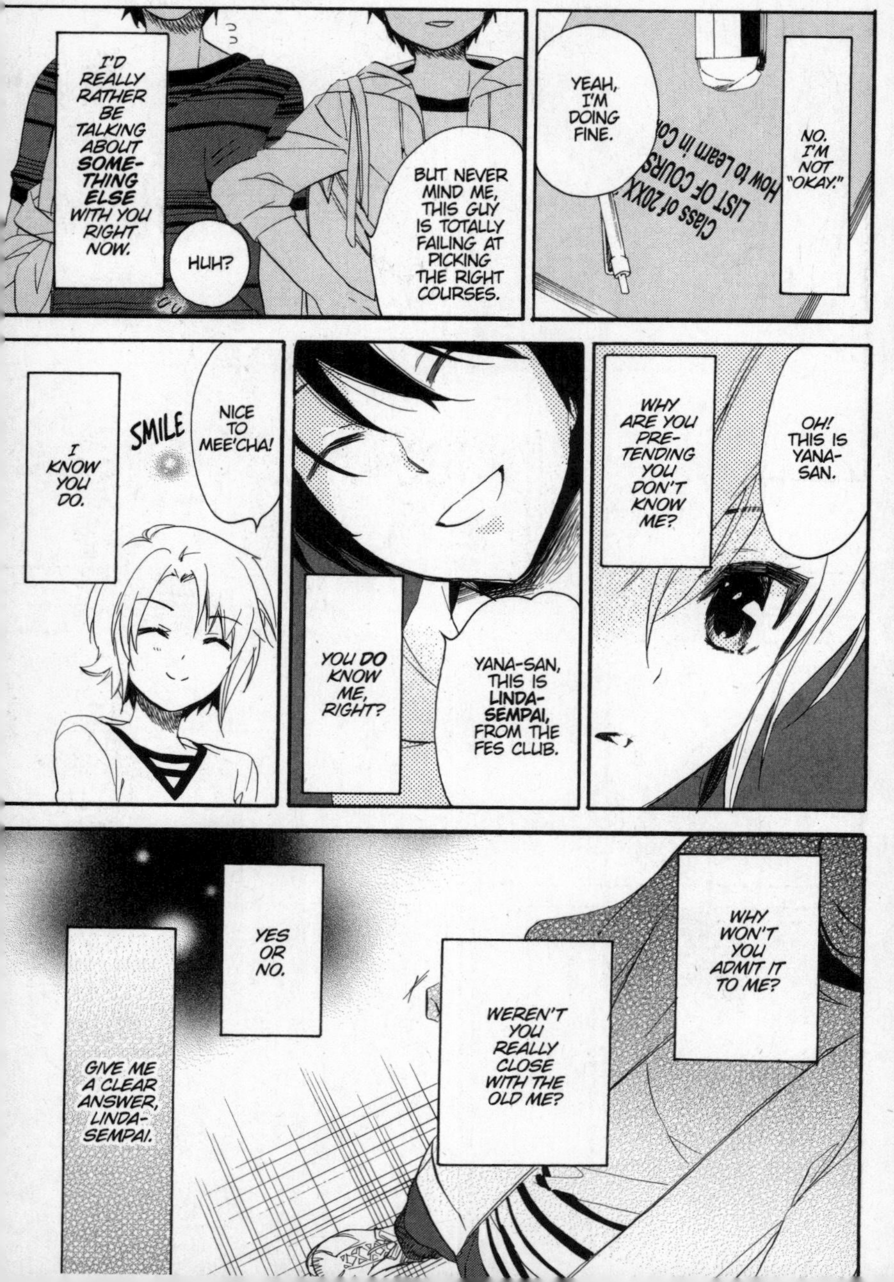

YEAH, I'M DOING FINE.
NO. I'M NOT "OKAY."
BUT NEVER MIND ME, THIS GUY IS TOTALLY FAILING AT PICKING THE RIGHT COURSES.
HUH?
I'D REALLY RATHER BE TALKING ABOUT SOMETHING ELSE WITH YOU RIGHT NOW.
OH! THIS IS YANA-SAN.
WHY ARE YOU PRETENDING YOU DON'T KNOW ME?
YANA-SAN, THIS IS LINDA-SEMPAI, FROM THE FES CLUB.
YOU DO KNOW ME, RIGHT?
NICE TO MEE'CHA!
SMILE
I KNOW YOU DO.
WHY WON'T YOU ADMIT IT TO ME?
WEREN'T YOU REALLY CLOSE WITH THE OLD ME?
YES OR NO.
GIVE ME A CLEAR ANSWER, LINDA-SEMPAI.

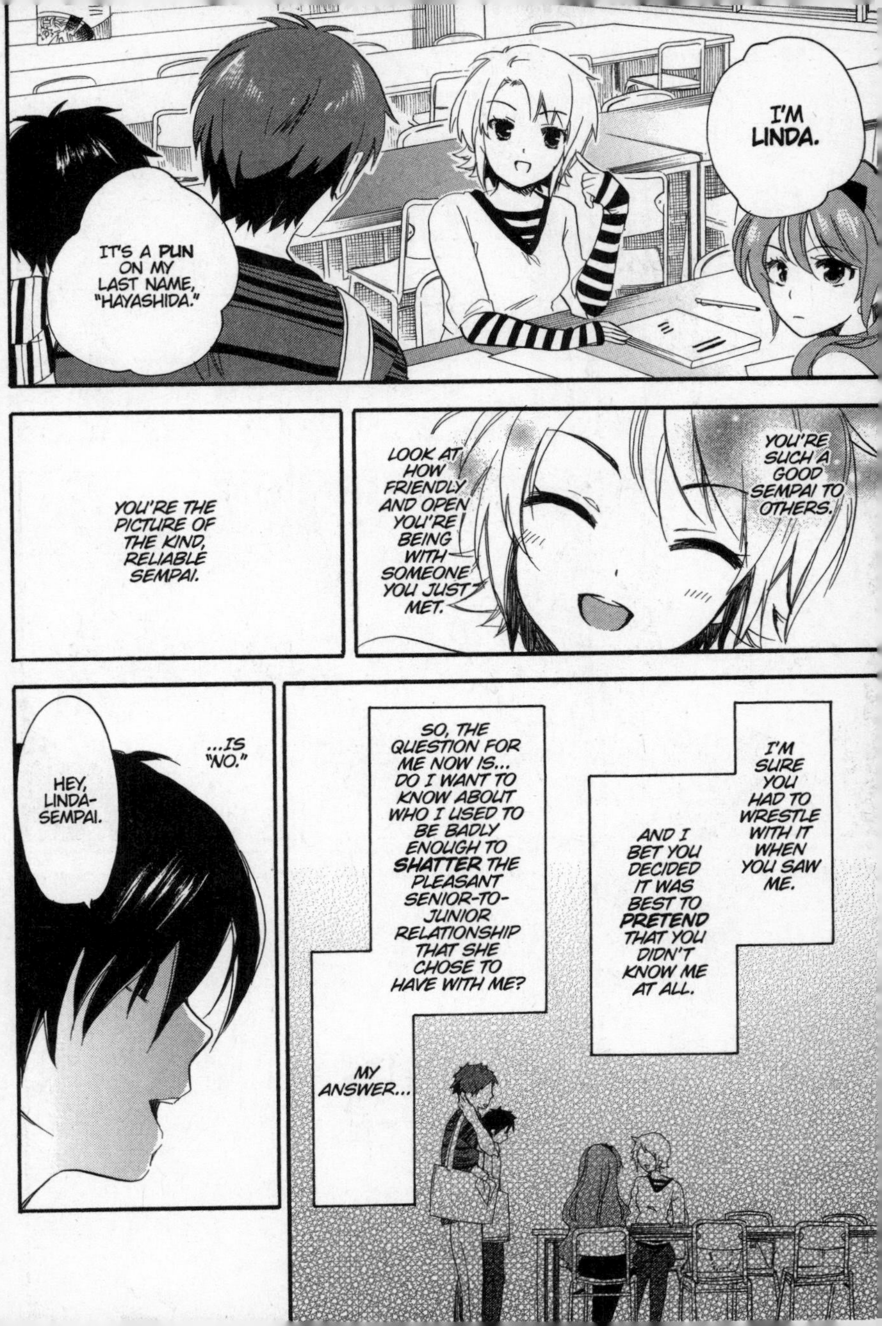
I'M LINDA.
IT'S A PUN ON MY LAST NAME, "HAYASHIDA."
YOU'RE SUCH A GOOD SEMPAI TO OTHERS.
LOOK AT HOW FRIENDLY AND OPEN YOU'RE BEING WITH SOMEONE YOU JUST MET.
YOU'RE THE PICTURE OF THE KIND, RELIABLE SEMPAI.
I'M SURE YOU HAD TO WRESTLE WITH IT WHEN YOU SAW ME.
AND I BET YOU DECIDED IT WAS BEST TO PRETEND THAT YOU DIDN'T KNOW ME AT ALL.
SO, THE QUESTION FOR ME NOW IS... DO I WANT TO KNOW ABOUT WHO I USED TO BE BADLY ENOUGH TO SHATTER THE PLEASANT SENIOR-TO-JUNIOR RELATIONSHIP THAT SHE CHOSE TO HAVE WITH ME?
MY ANSWER...
...IS "NO."
HEY, LINDA-SEMPAI.

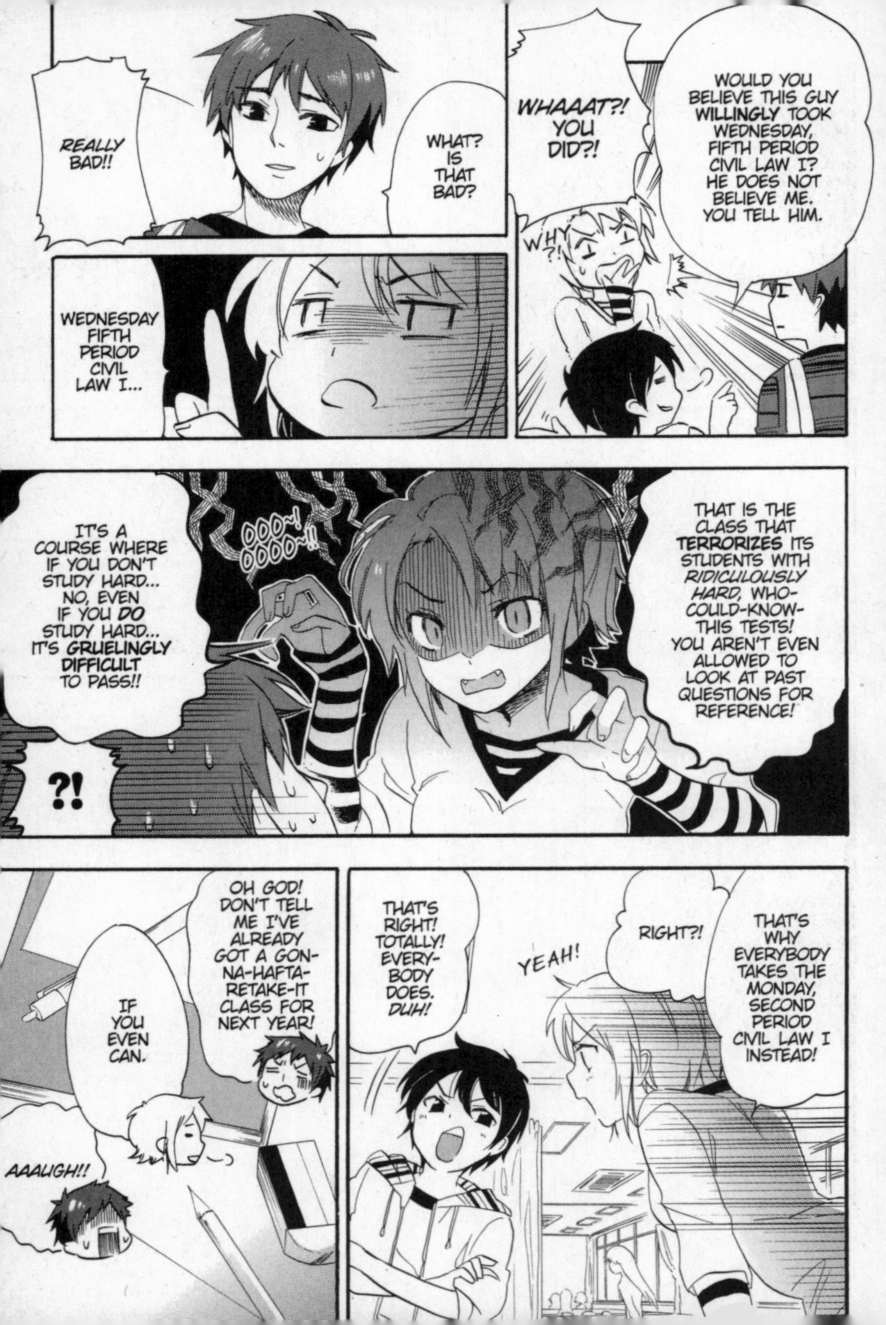

WOULD YOU BELIEVE THIS GUY WILLINGLY TOOK WEDNESDAY, FIFTH PERIOD CIVIL LAW I? HE DOES NOT BELIEVE ME. YOU TELL HIM.
WHAAAT?! YOU DID?!
WHY?!
WHAT? IS THAT BAD?
REALLY BAD!!
WEDNESDAY FIFTH PERIOD CIVIL LAW I...
THAT IS THE CLASS THAT TERRORIZES ITS STUDENTS WITH RIDICULOUSLY HARD, WHO-COULD-KNOW-THIS TESTS! YOU AREN'T EVEN ALLOWED TO LOOK AT PAST QUESTIONS FOR REFERENCE!
OOO~! OOOO~!!
IT'S A COURSE WHERE IF YOU DON'T STUDY HARD... NO, EVEN IF YOU DO STUDY HARD... IT'S GRUELINGLY DIFFICULT TO PASS!!
?!
THAT'S WHY EVERYBODY TAKES THE MONDAY, SECOND PERIOD CIVIL LAW I INSTEAD!
RIGHT?!
YEAH!
THAT'S RIGHT! TOTALLY! EVERY-BODY DOES. DUH!
OH GOD! DON'T TELL ME I'VE ALREADY GOT A GON-NA-HAFTA-RETAKE-IT CLASS FOR NEXT YEAR!
IF YOU EVEN CAN.
AAAUGH!!

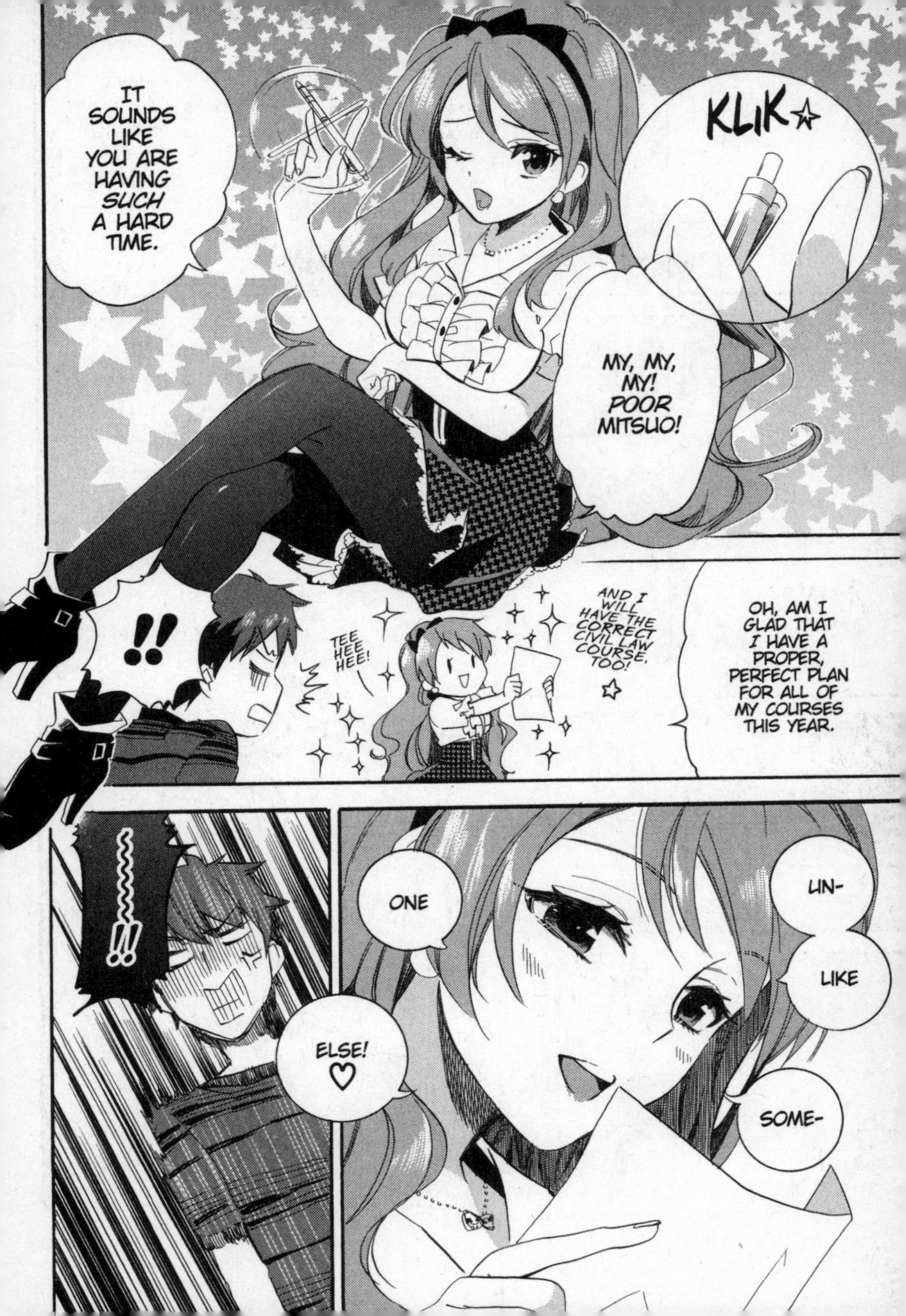
KLIK☆
MY, MY, MY! POOR MITSUO!
IT SOUNDS LIKE YOU ARE HAVING SUCH A HARD TIME.
OH, AM I GLAD THAT I HAVE A PROPER, PERFECT PLAN FOR ALL OF MY COURSES THIS YEAR.
AND I WILL HAVE THE CORRECT CIVIL LAW COURSE, TOO! ☆
TEE HEE HEE!
!!
UN-
LIKE
SOME-
ONE
ELSE! ♡
!!

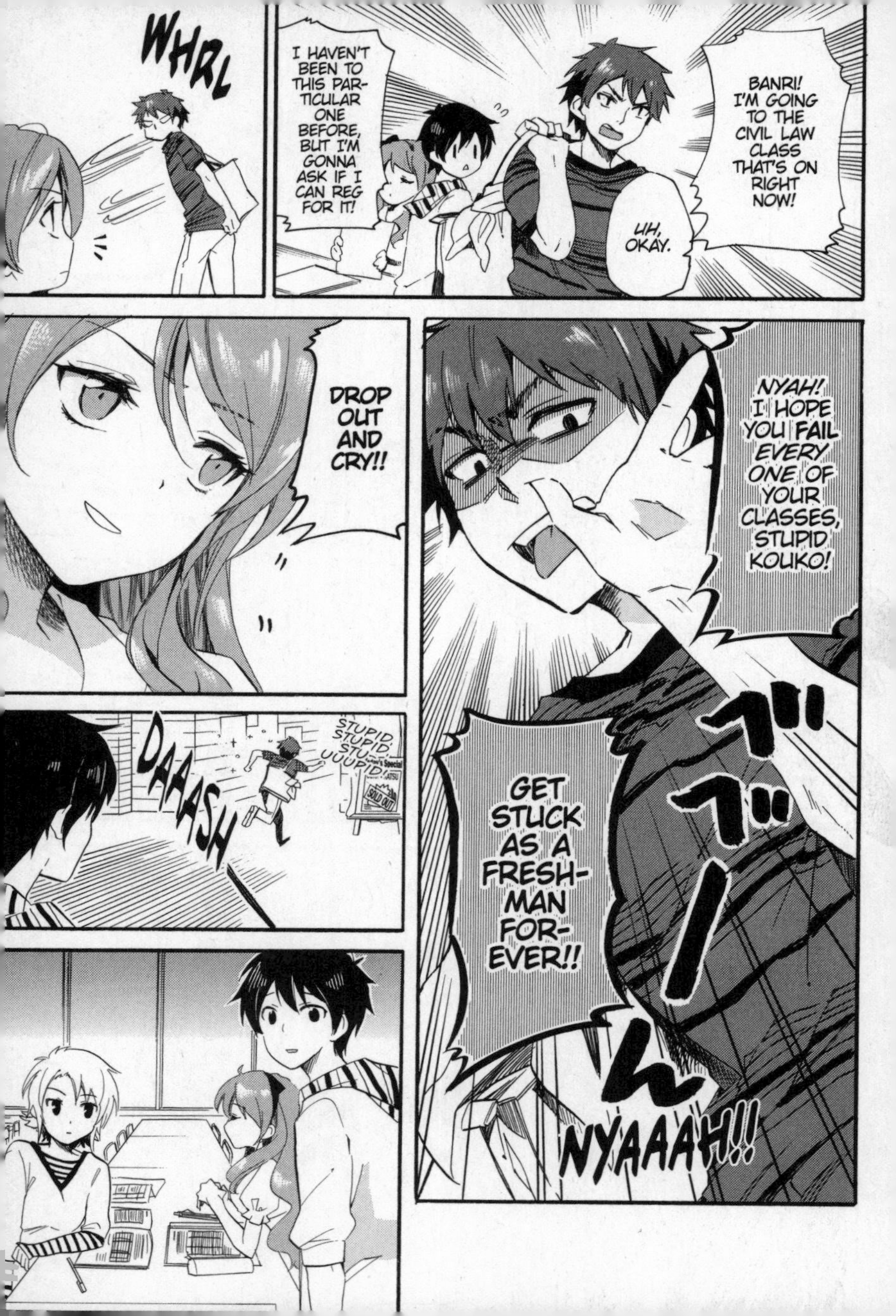
BANRI! I'M GOING TO THE CIVIL LAW CLASS THAT'S ON RIGHT NOW!
I HAVEN'T BEEN TO THIS PARTICULAR ONE BEFORE, BUT I'M GONNA ASK IF I CAN REG FOR IT!
UH, OKAY.
WHRL
NYAH! I HOPE YOU FAIL EVERY ONE OF YOUR CLASSES, STUPID KOUKO!
ブブーん
GET STUCK AS A FRESHMAN FOREVER!!
NYAAAH!!
DROP OUT AND CRY!!
DAAASH
STUPID, STUPID, STUUUUPID!
SOLD OUT

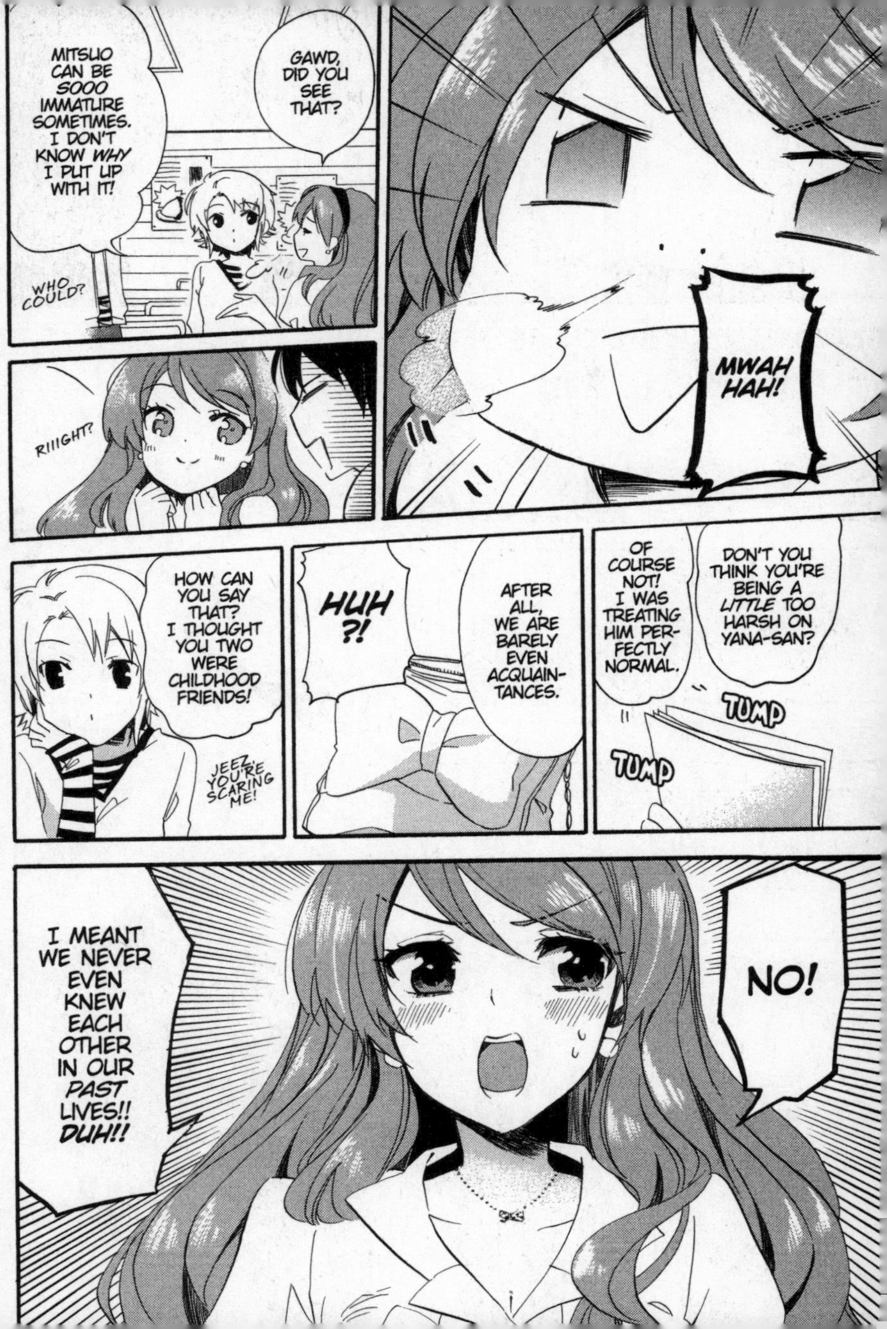
MWAH HAH!
GAWD, DID YOU SEE THAT?
MITSUO CAN BE *SOOO* IMMATURE SOMETIMES. I DON'T KNOW *WHY* I PUT UP WITH IT!
WHO COULD?
RIIIGHT?
DON'T YOU THINK YOU'RE BEING A *LITTLE* TOO HARSH ON YANA-SAN?
OF COURSE NOT! I WAS TREATING HIM PER-FECTLY NORMAL.
TUMP
TUMP
AFTER ALL, WE ARE BARELY EVEN ACQUAIN-TANCES.
HUH ?!
HOW CAN YOU SAY THAT? I THOUGHT YOU TWO WERE CHILDHOOD FRIENDS!
JEEZ, YOU'RE SCARING ME!
NO!
I MEANT WE NEVER EVEN KNEW EACH OTHER IN OUR *PAST* LIVES!! *DUH!!*

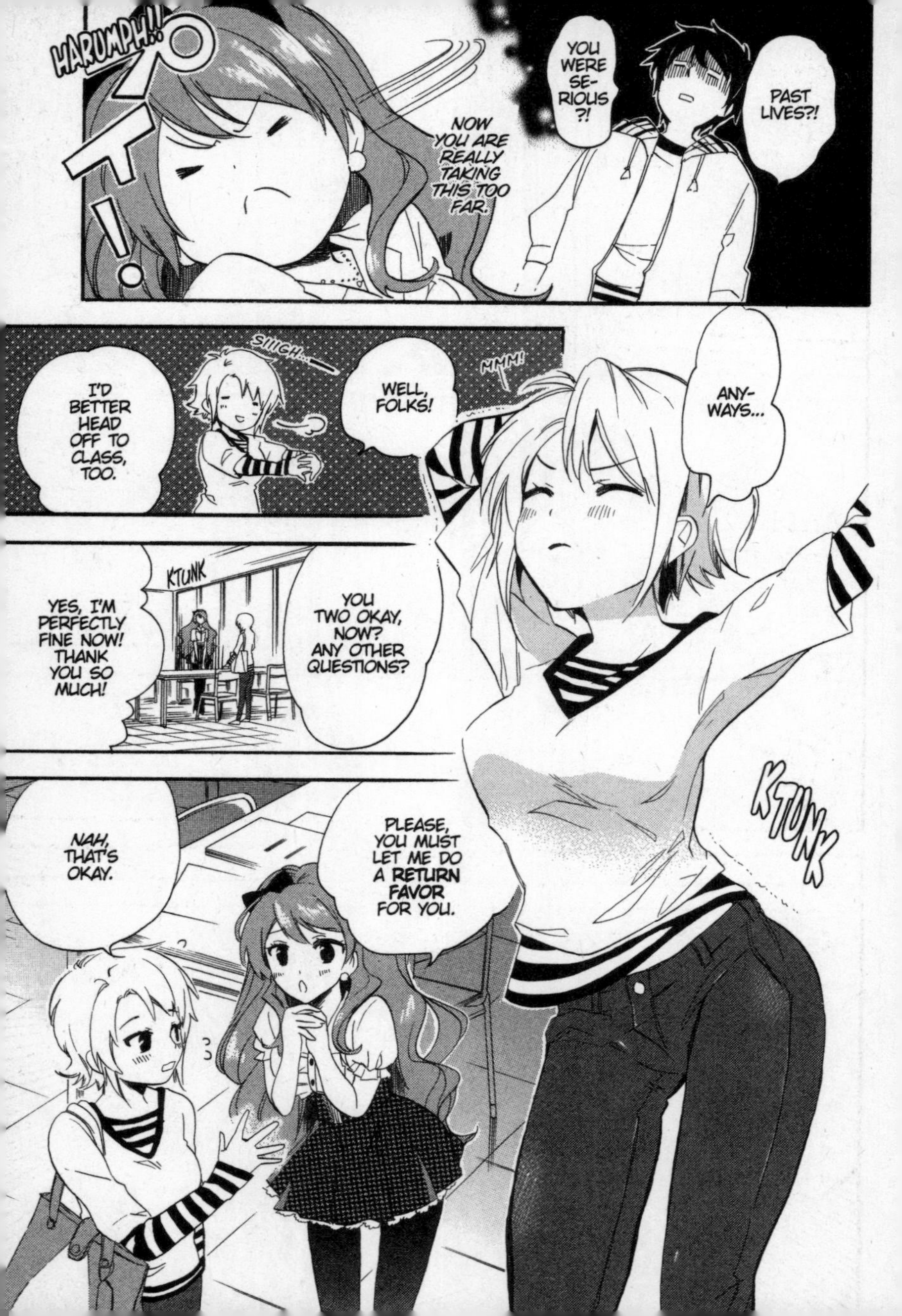
PAST LIVES?!
YOU WERE SE-RIOUS ?!
NOW YOU ARE REALLY TAKING THIS TOO FAR.
HARUMPH!!
ANY-WAYS...
KTUNK
MMM!
WELL, FOLKS!
SIIIGH...
I'D BETTER HEAD OFF TO CLASS, TOO.
YOU TWO OKAY, NOW? ANY OTHER QUESTIONS?
KTUNK
YES, I'M PERFECTLY FINE NOW! THANK YOU SO MUCH!
PLEASE, YOU MUST LET ME DO A RETURN FAVOR FOR YOU.
NAH, THAT'S OKAY.

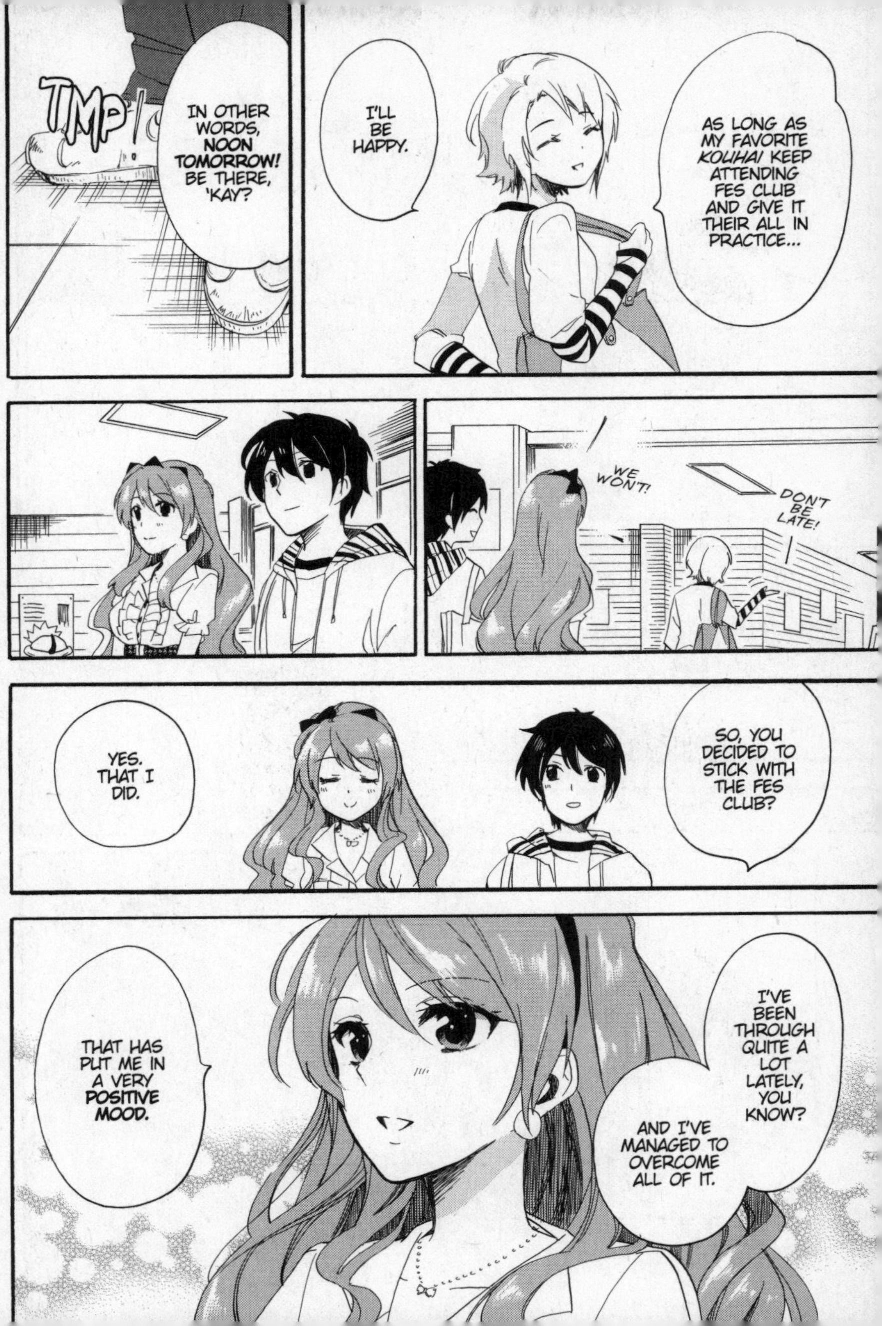
AS LONG AS MY FAVORITE *KOUHAI* KEEP ATTENDING FES CLUB AND GIVE IT THEIR ALL IN PRACTICE...
I'LL BE HAPPY.
TMP!
IN OTHER WORDS, **NOON TOMORROW!** BE THERE, 'KAY?
DON'T BE LATE!
WE WON'T!
SO, YOU DECIDED TO STICK WITH THE FES CLUB?
YES. THAT I DID.
I'VE BEEN THROUGH QUITE A LOT LATELY, YOU KNOW?
AND I'VE MANAGED TO OVERCOME ALL OF IT.
THAT HAS PUT ME IN A VERY **POSITIVE MOOD.**

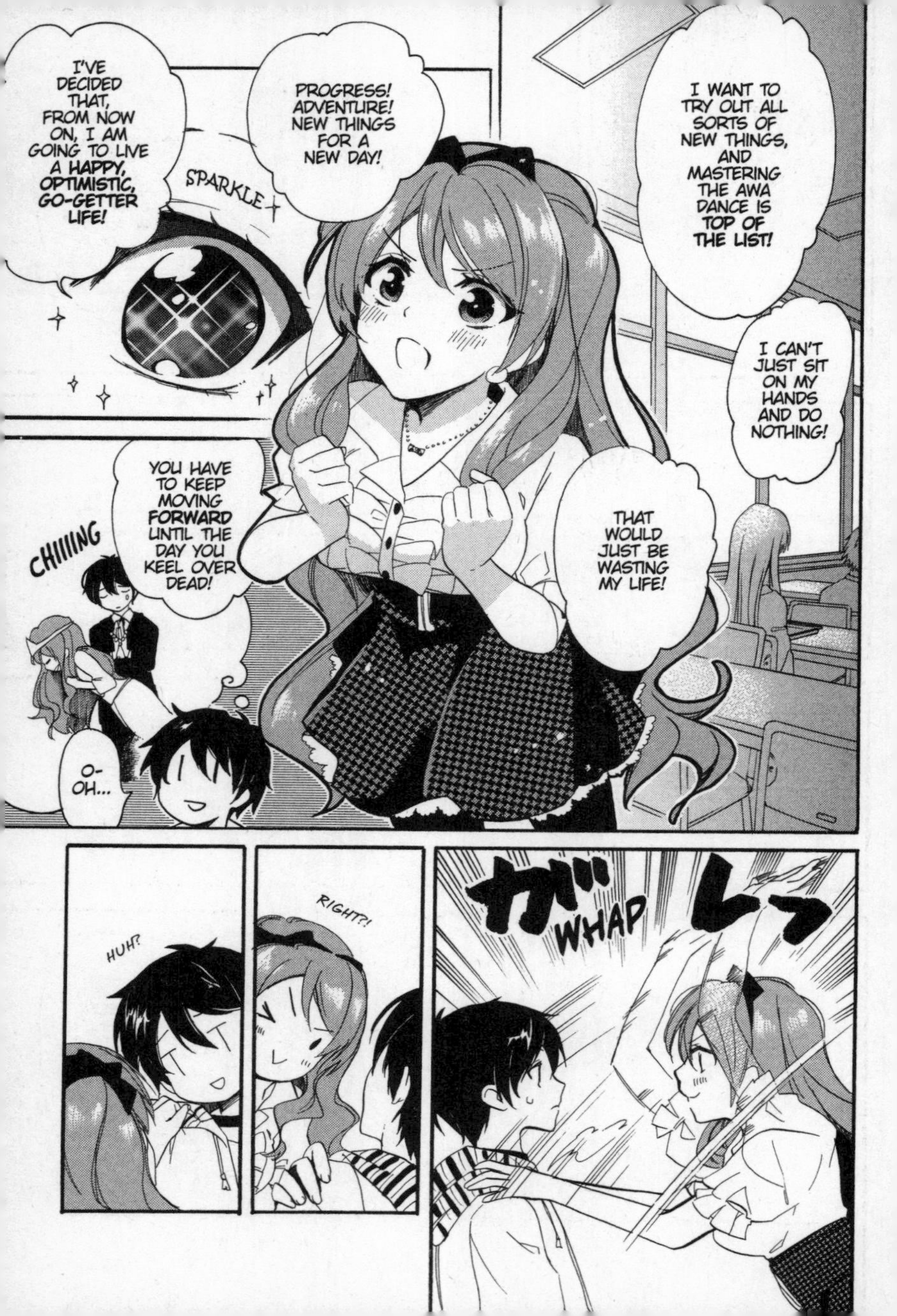
I WANT TO TRY OUT ALL SORTS OF NEW THINGS, AND MASTERING THE AWA DANCE IS TOP OF THE LIST!
I CAN'T JUST SIT ON MY HANDS AND DO NOTHING!
THAT WOULD JUST BE WASTING MY LIFE!
PROGRESS! ADVENTURE! NEW THINGS FOR A NEW DAY!
I'VE DECIDED THAT, FROM NOW ON, I AM GOING TO LIVE A HAPPY, OPTIMISTIC, GO-GETTER LIFE!
SPARKLE
YOU HAVE TO KEEP MOVING FORWARD UNTIL THE DAY YOU KEEL OVER DEAD!
CHIIIING
O-OH...
WHAP
RIGHT?!
HUH?

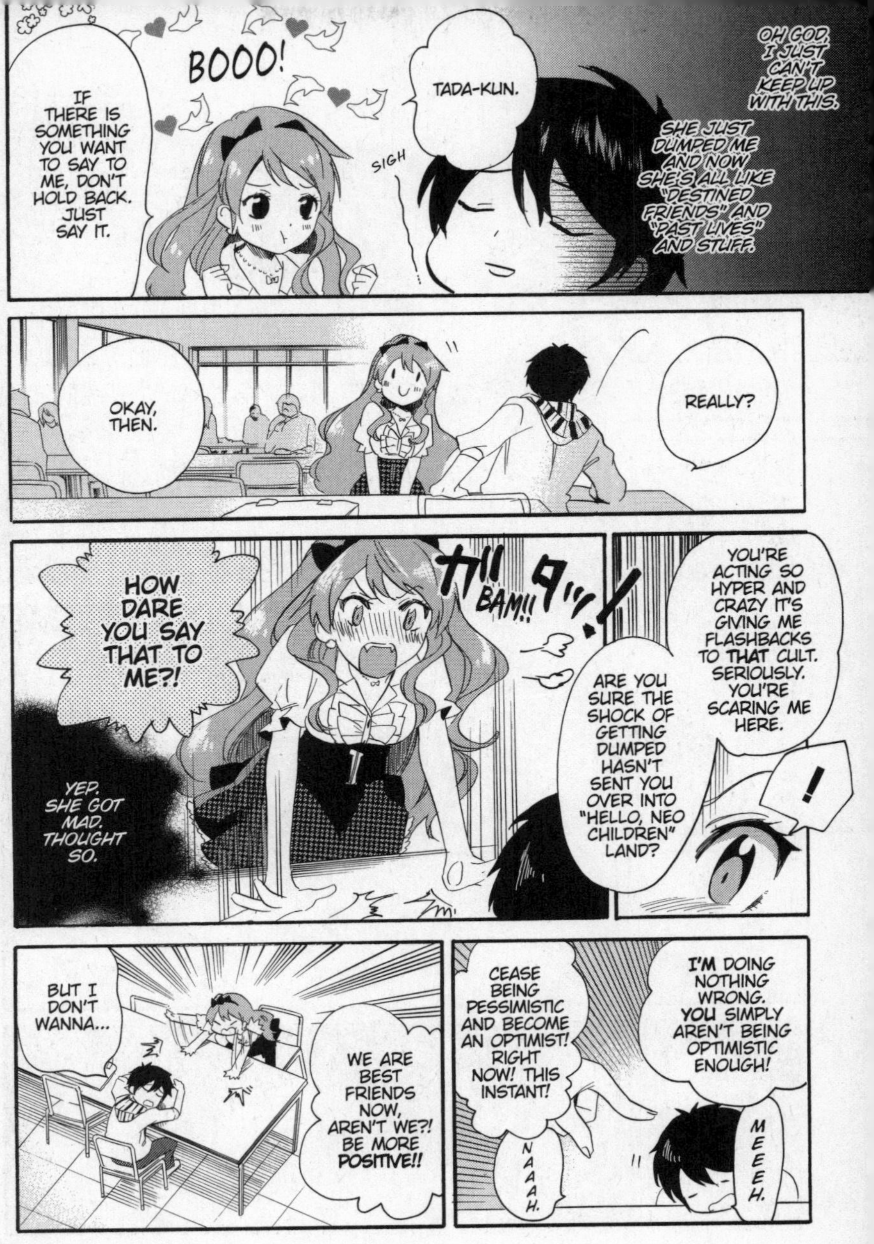
OH GOD, I JUST CAN'T KEEP UP WITH THIS.
SHE JUST DUMPED ME AND NOW SHE'S ALL LIKE "DESTINED FRIENDS" AND "PAST LIVES" AND STUFF.
TADA-KUN.
SIGH
BOOO!
IF THERE IS SOMETHING YOU WANT TO SAY TO ME, DON'T HOLD BACK. JUST SAY IT.
REALLY?
OKAY, THEN.
YOU'RE ACTING SO HYPER AND CRAZY IT'S GIVING ME FLASHBACKS TO THAT CULT. SERIOUSLY. YOU'RE SCARING ME HERE.
ARE YOU SURE THE SHOCK OF GETTING DUMPED HASN'T SENT YOU OVER INTO "HELLO, NEO CHILDREN" LAND?
!
BAM!!
HOW DARE YOU SAY THAT TO ME?!
YEP. SHE GOT MAD. THOUGHT SO.
I'M DOING NOTHING WRONG. YOU SIMPLY AREN'T BEING OPTIMISTIC ENOUGH!
MEEEH.
CEASE BEING PESSIMISTIC AND BECOME AN OPTIMIST! RIGHT NOW! THIS INSTANT!
NAAAAH.
WE ARE BEST FRIENDS NOW, AREN'T WE?! BE MORE POSITIVE!!
BUT I DON'T WANNA...

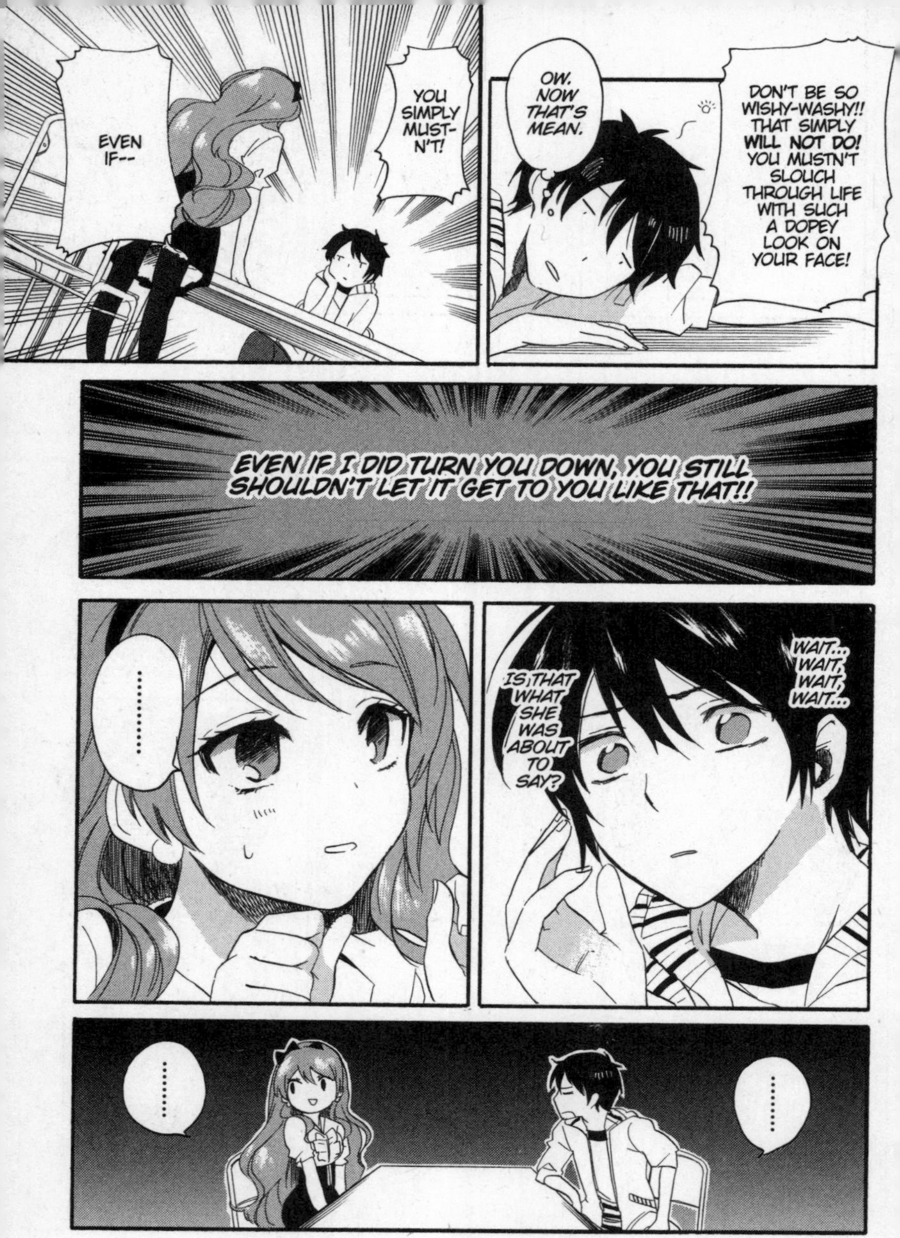
DON'T BE SO WISHY-WASHY!! THAT SIMPLY WILL NOT DO! YOU MUSTN'T SLOUCH THROUGH LIFE WITH SUCH A DOPEY LOOK ON YOUR FACE!
OW. NOW THAT'S MEAN.
YOU SIMPLY MUST-N'T!
EVEN IF--
EVEN IF I DID TURN YOU DOWN, YOU STILL SHOULDN'T LET IT GET TO YOU LIKE THAT!!
WAIT... WAIT, WAIT, WAIT...
IS THAT WHAT SHE WAS ABOUT TO SAY?
....
....
....

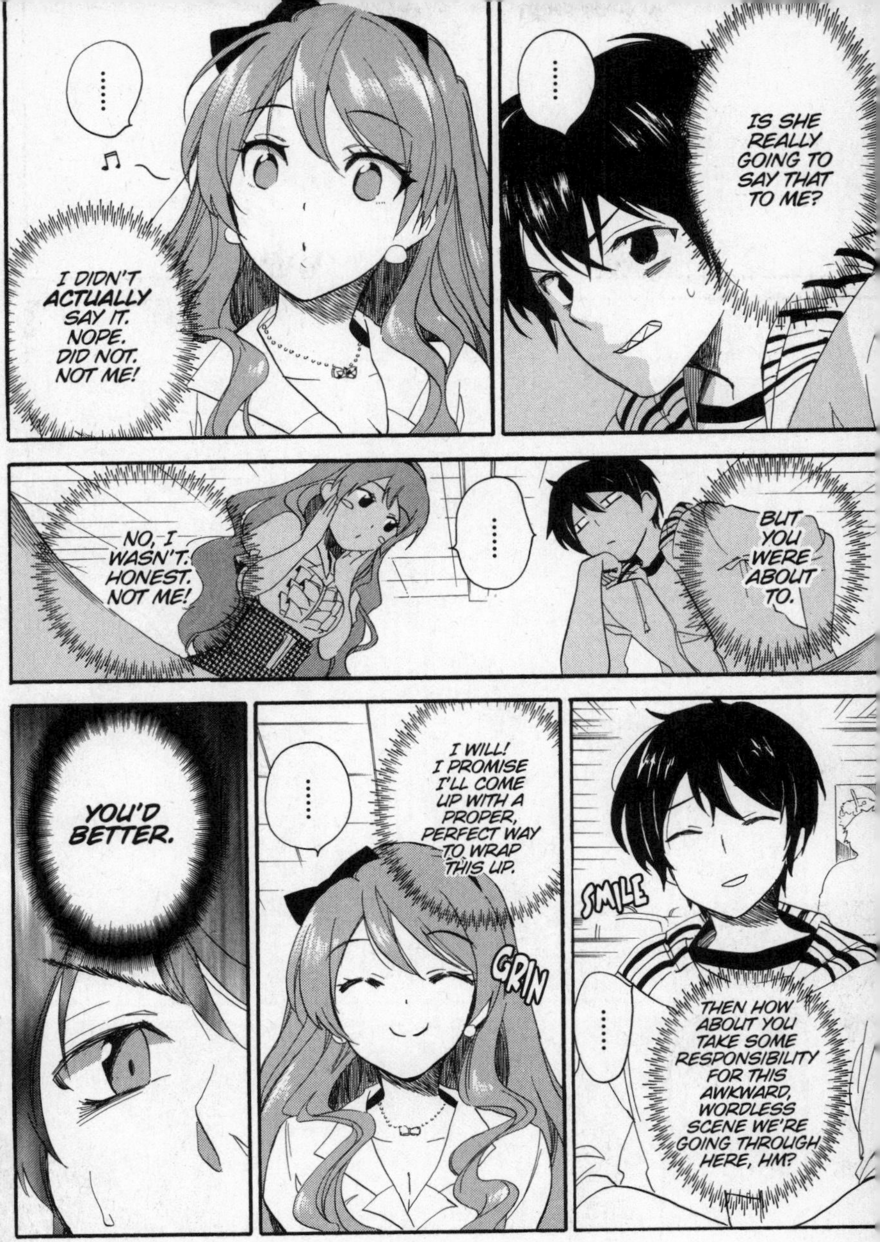
......
IS SHE REALLY GOING TO SAY THAT TO ME?
......
♪
I DIDN'T ACTUALLY SAY IT. NOPE. DID NOT. NOT ME!
BUT YOU WERE ABOUT TO.
......
NO, I WASN'T. HONEST. NOT ME!
SMILE
THEN HOW ABOUT YOU TAKE SOME RESPONSIBILITY FOR THIS AWKWARD, WORDLESS SCENE WE'RE GOING THROUGH HERE, HM?
......
I WILL! I PROMISE I'LL COME UP WITH A PROPER, PERFECT WAY TO WRAP THIS UP.
......
GRIN
YOU'D BETTER.

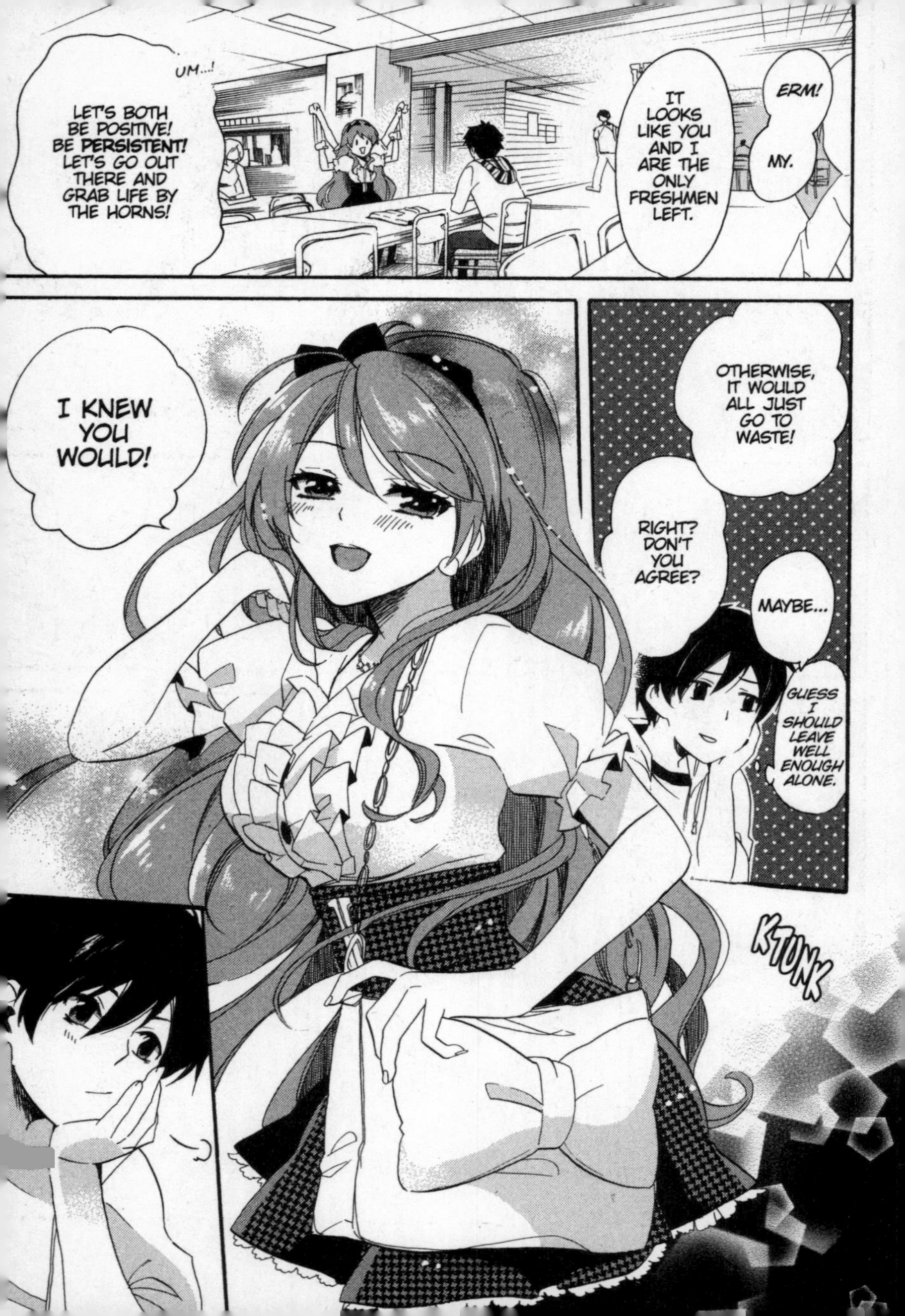
ERM!
MY.
IT LOOKS LIKE YOU AND I ARE THE ONLY FRESHMEN LEFT.
UM...!
LET'S BOTH BE POSITIVE! BE PERSISTENT! LET'S GO OUT THERE AND GRAB LIFE BY THE HORNS!
OTHERWISE, IT WOULD ALL JUST GO TO WASTE!
RIGHT? DON'T YOU AGREE?
MAYBE...
GUESS I SHOULD LEAVE WELL ENOUGH ALONE.
I KNEW YOU WOULD!
KTUNK

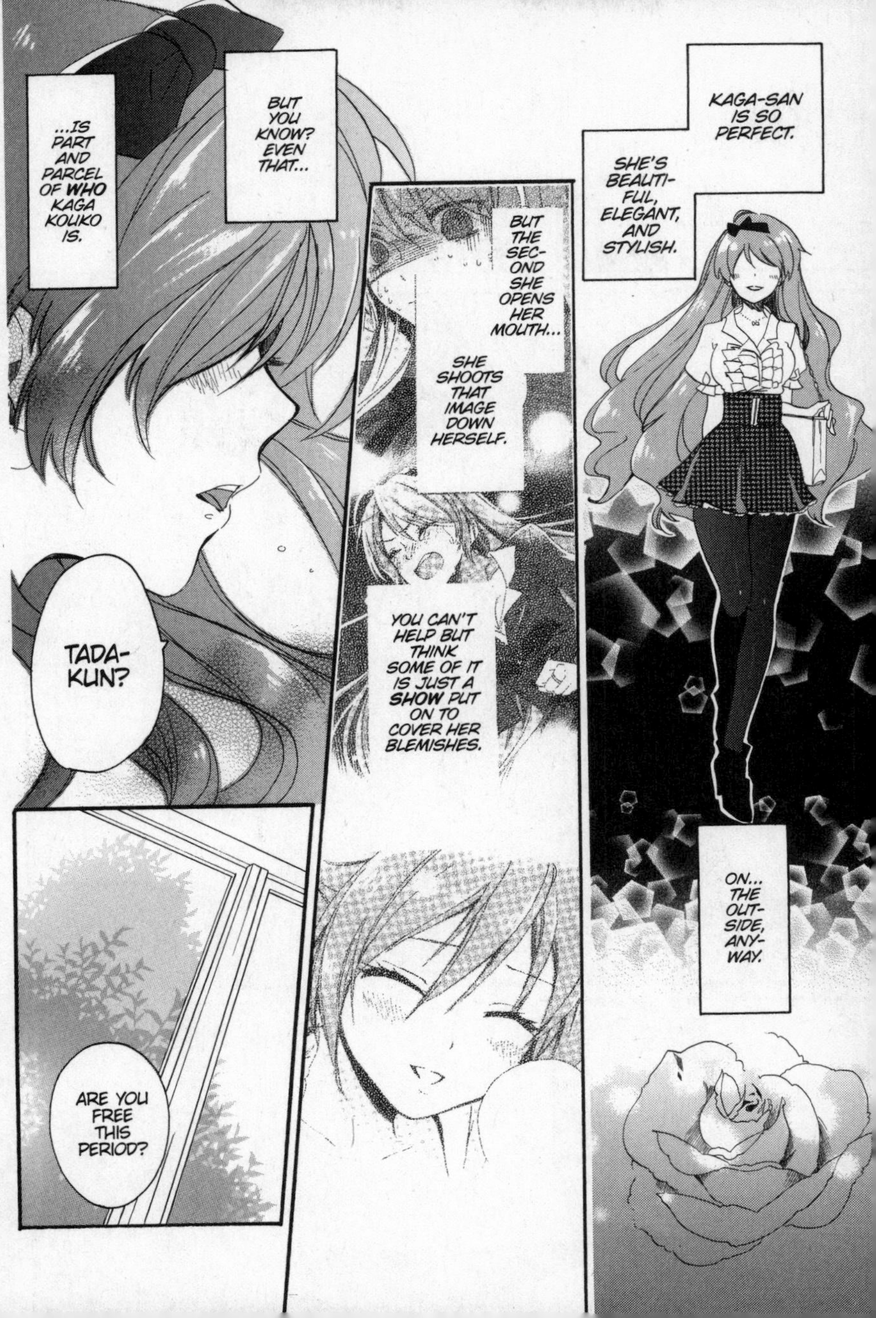
KAGA-SAN IS SO PERFECT.
SHE'S BEAUTI-FUL, ELEGANT, AND STYLISH.
ON... THE OUT-SIDE, ANY-WAY.
BUT THE SEC-OND SHE OPENS HER MOUTH...
SHE SHOOTS THAT IMAGE DOWN HERSELF.
YOU CAN'T HELP BUT THINK SOME OF IT IS JUST A SHOW PUT ON TO COVER HER BLEMISHES.
BUT YOU KNOW? EVEN THAT...
...IS PART AND PARCEL OF WHO KAGA KOUKO IS.
TADA-KUN?
ARE YOU FREE THIS PERIOD?

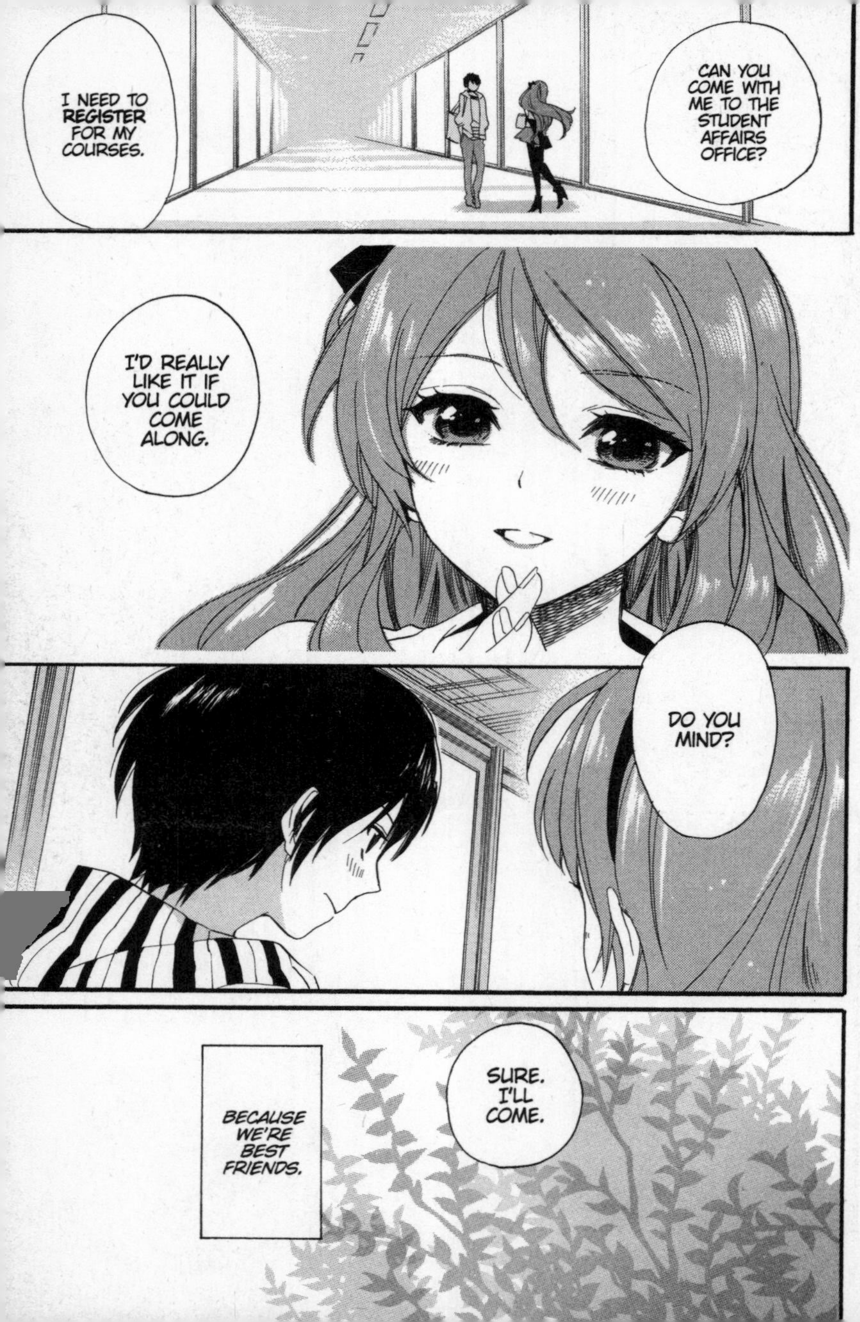
CAN YOU COME WITH ME TO THE STUDENT AFFAIRS OFFICE?
I NEED TO REGISTER FOR MY COURSES.
I'D REALLY LIKE IT IF YOU COULD COME ALONG.
DO YOU MIND?
SURE. I'LL COME.
BECAUSE WE'RE BEST FRIENDS.

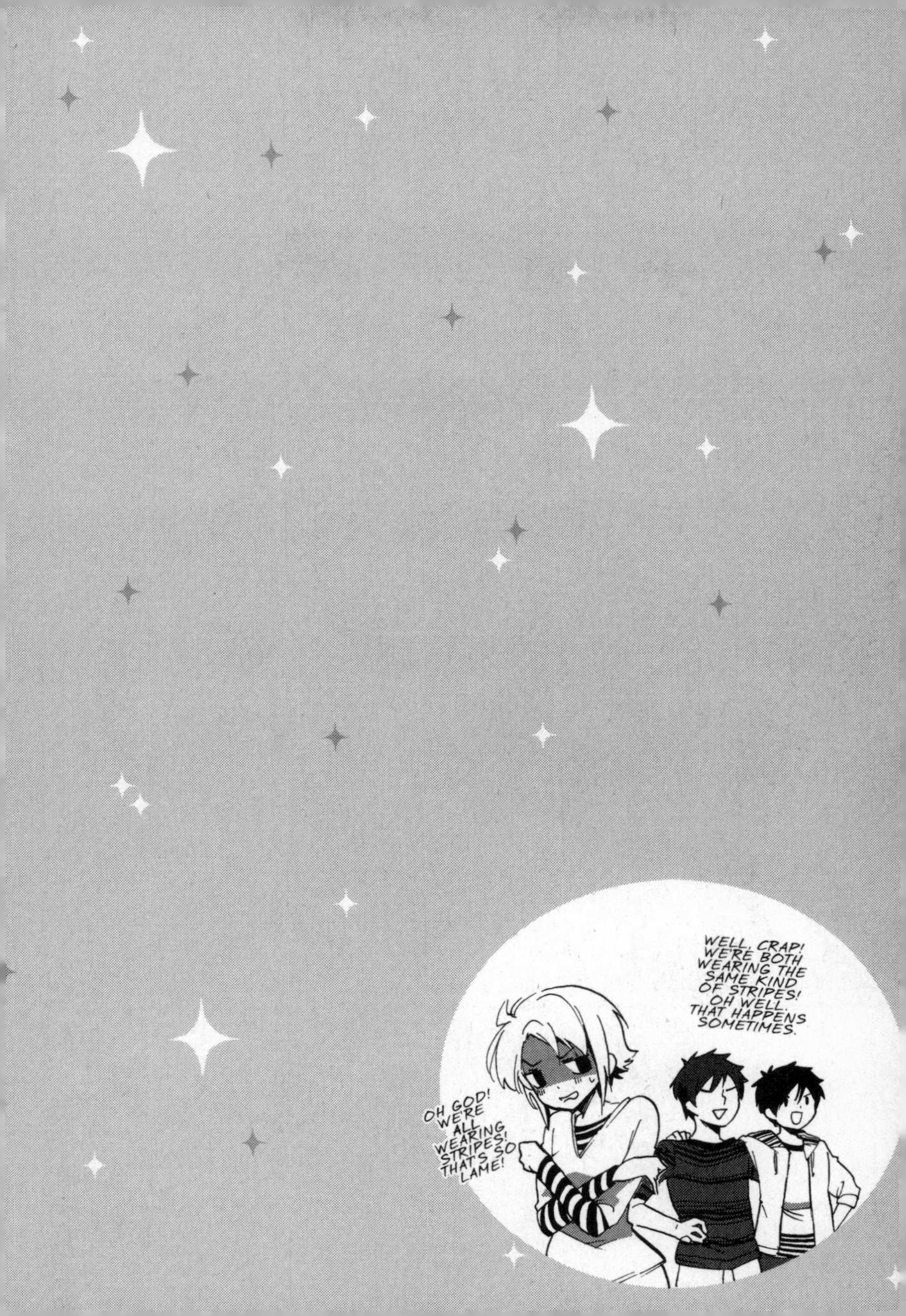
WELL, CRAP! WE'RE BOTH WEARING THE SAME KIND OF STRIPES! OH WELL. THAT HAPPENS SOMETIMES.
OH GOD! WE'RE ALL WEARING STRIPES! THAT'S SO LAME!

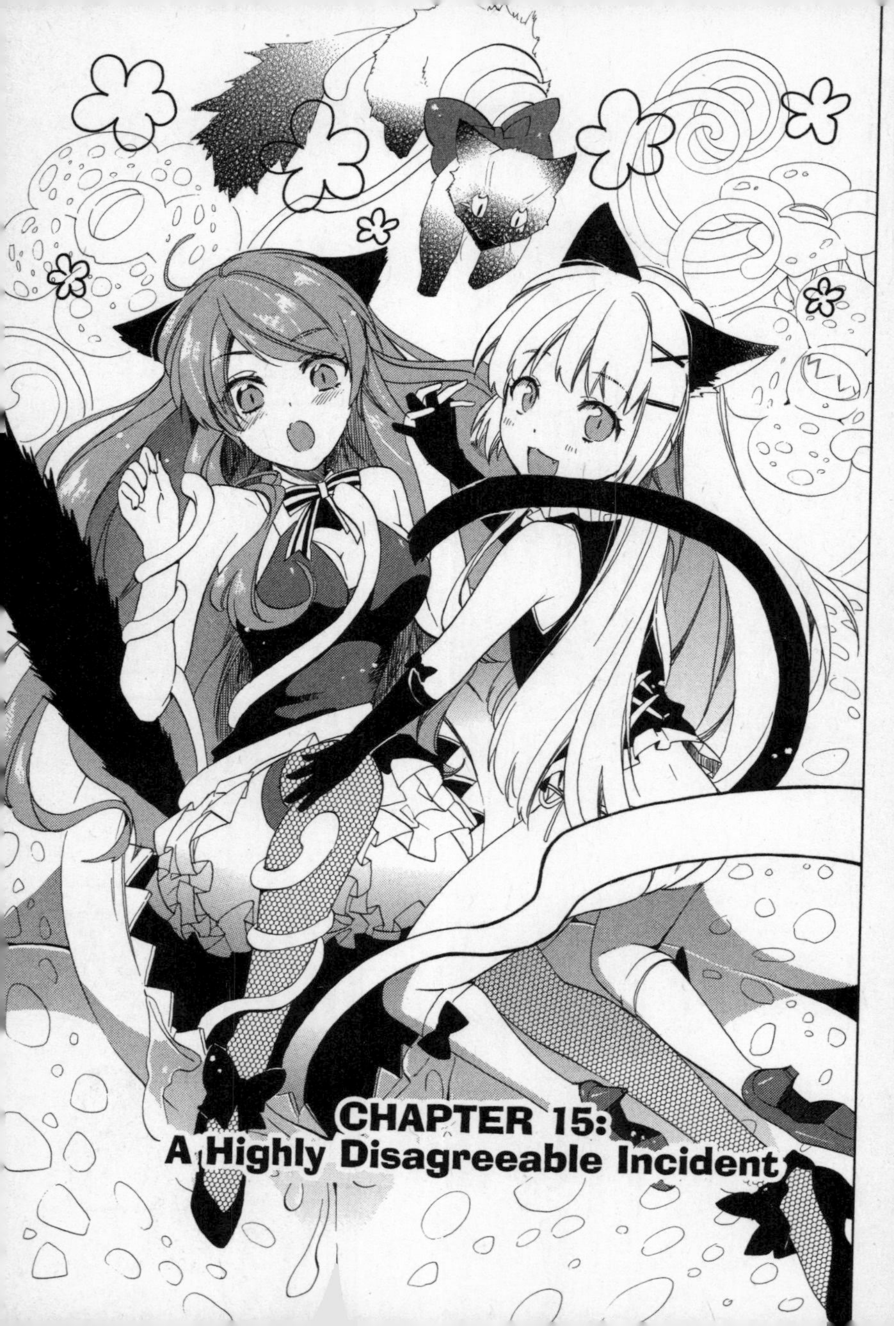
CHAPTER 15:
A Highly Disagreeable Incident

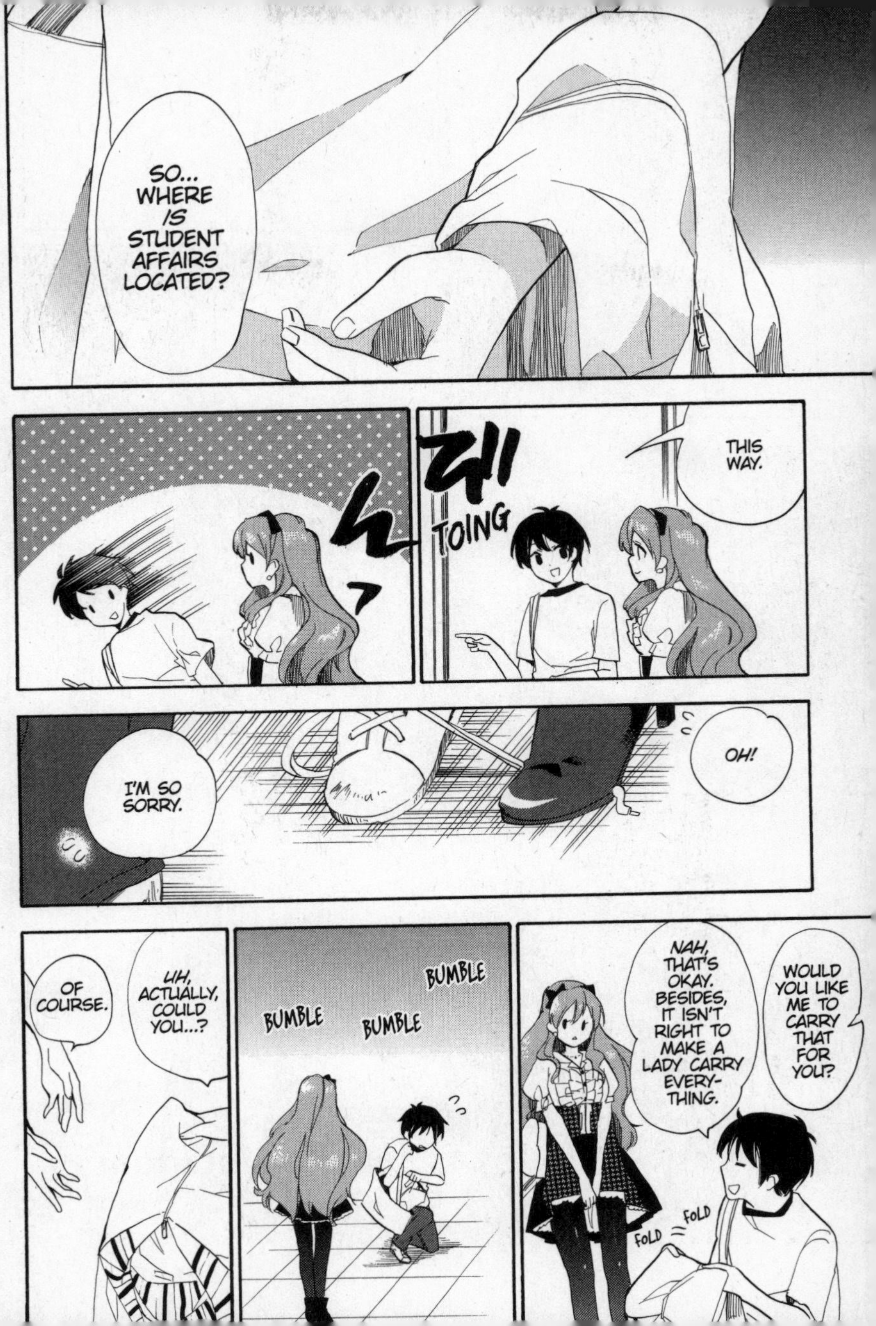
SO... WHERE IS STUDENT AFFAIRS LOCATED?
THIS WAY.
TOING
OH!
I'M SO SORRY.
WOULD YOU LIKE ME TO CARRY THAT FOR YOU?
NAH, THAT'S OKAY. BESIDES, IT ISN'T RIGHT TO MAKE A LADY CARRY EVERY-THING.
FOLD FOLD
BUMBLE
BUMBLE
BUMBLE
UH, ACTUALLY, COULD YOU...?
OF COURSE.

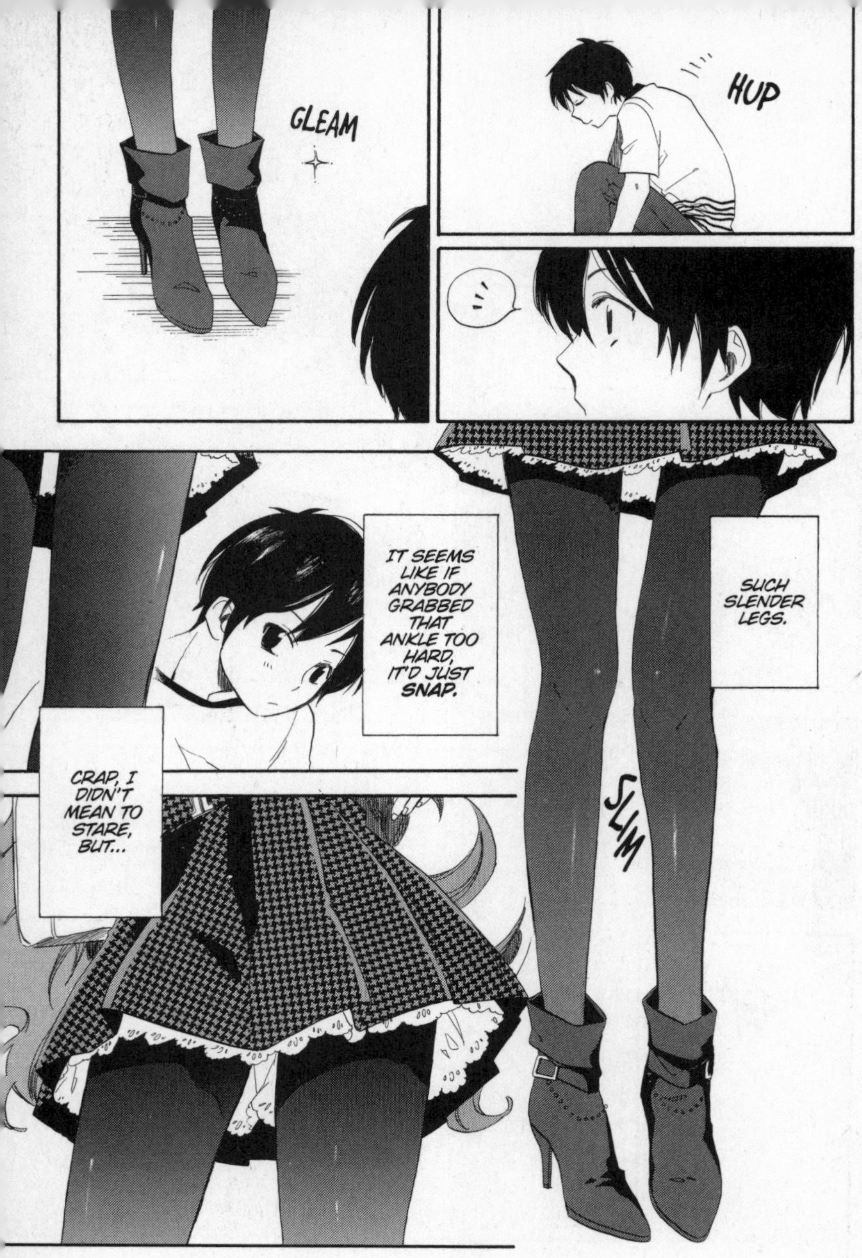
HUP
GLEAM
SUCH SLENDER LEGS.
SLIM
IT SEEMS LIKE IF ANYBODY GRABBED THAT ANKLE TOO HARD, IT'D JUST SNAP.
CRAP, I DIDN'T MEAN TO STARE, BUT...

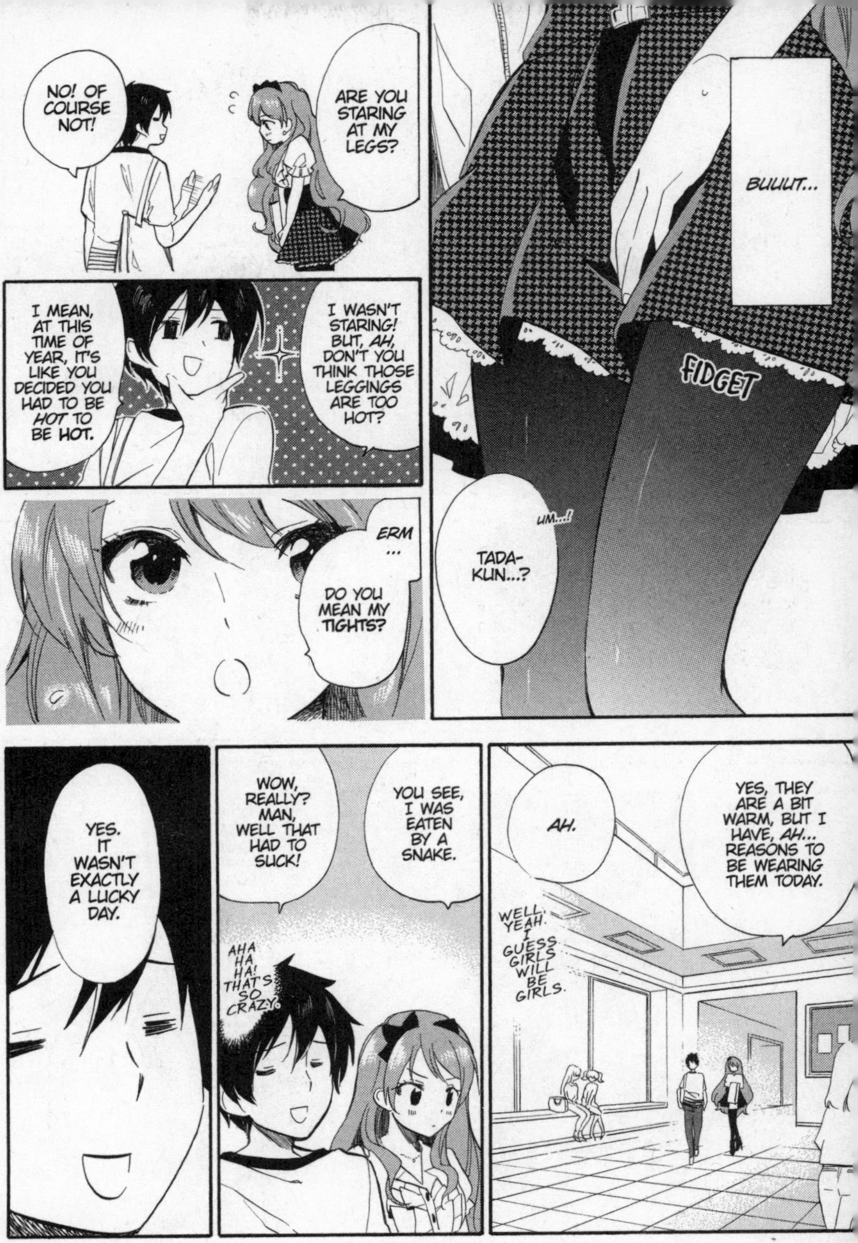
BUULLT...
FIDGET
UM...!
TADA-KUN...?
ARE YOU STARING AT MY LEGS?
NO! OF COURSE NOT!
I WASN'T STARING! BUT, AH, DON'T YOU THINK THOSE LEGGINGS ARE TOO HOT?
I MEAN, AT THIS TIME OF YEAR, IT'S LIKE YOU DECIDED YOU HAD TO BE HOT TO BE HOT.
ERM ...
DO YOU MEAN MY TIGHTS?
YES, THEY ARE A BIT WARM, BUT I HAVE, AH... REASONS TO BE WEARING THEM TODAY.
AH.
WELL, YEAH. I GUESS GIRLS WILL BE GIRLS.
YOU SEE, I WAS EATEN BY A SNAKE.
WOW, REALLY? MAN, WELL THAT HAD TO SUCK!
AHA HA HA! THAT'S SO CRAZY.
YES. IT WASN'T EXACTLY A LUCKY DAY.

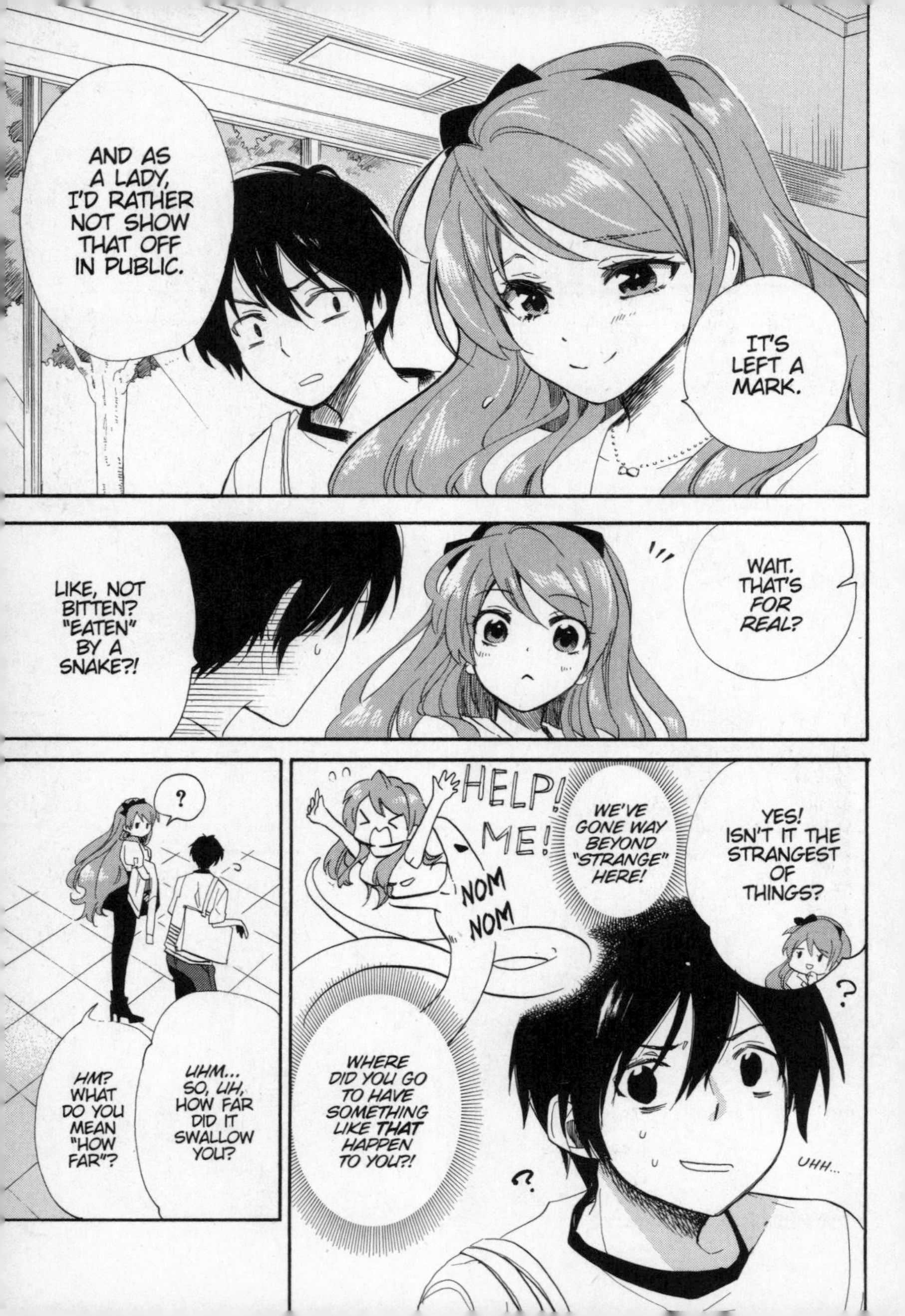
IT'S LEFT A MARK.
AND AS A LADY, I'D RATHER NOT SHOW THAT OFF IN PUBLIC.
WAIT. THAT'S FOR REAL?
LIKE, NOT BITTEN? "EATEN" BY A SNAKE?!
YES! ISN'T IT THE STRANGEST OF THINGS?
WE'VE GONE WAY BEYOND "STRANGE" HERE!
HELP! ME!
NOM NOM
WHERE DID YOU GO TO HAVE SOMETHING LIKE THAT HAPPEN TO YOU?!
?
UHH...
?
?
UHM... SO, UH, HOW FAR DID IT SWALLOW YOU?
HM? WHAT DO YOU MEAN "HOW FAR"?

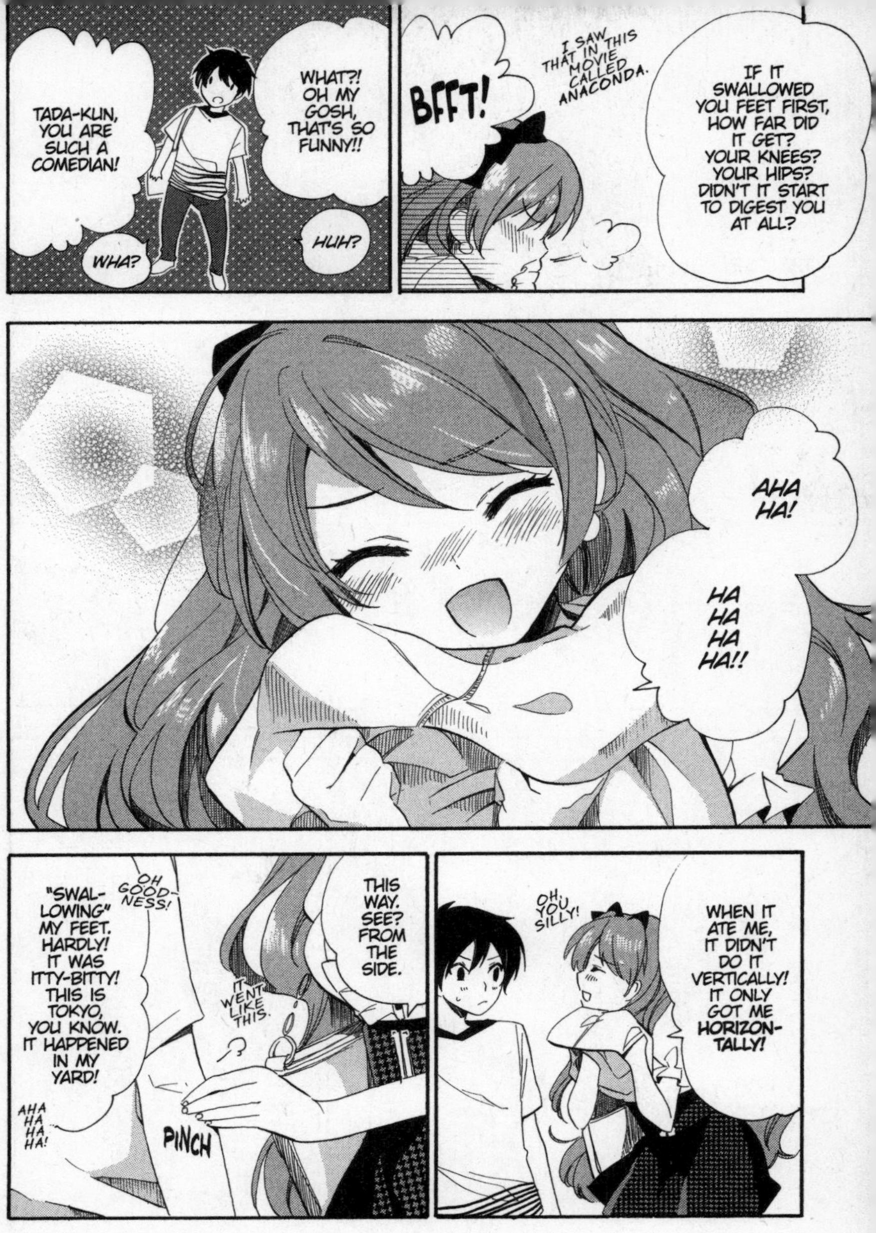
IF IT SWALLOWED YOU FEET FIRST, HOW FAR DID IT GET? YOUR KNEES? YOUR HIPS? DIDN'T IT START TO DIGEST YOU AT ALL?
I SAW THAT IN THIS MOVIE CALLED ANACONDA.
BFFT!
WHAT?! OH MY GOSH, THAT'S SO FUNNY!!
HUH?
TADA-KUN, YOU ARE SUCH A COMEDIAN!
WHA?
AHA HA!
HA HA HA HA!!
WHEN IT ATE ME, IT DIDN'T DO IT VERTICALLY! IT ONLY GOT ME HORIZONTALLY!
OH, YOU SILLY!
THIS WAY. SEE? FROM THE SIDE.
IT WENT LIKE THIS.
OH GOODNESS!
"SWALLOWING" MY FEET. HARDLY! IT WAS ITTY-BITTY! THIS IS TOKYO, YOU KNOW. IT HAPPENED IN MY YARD!
PINCH
AHA HA HA HA!

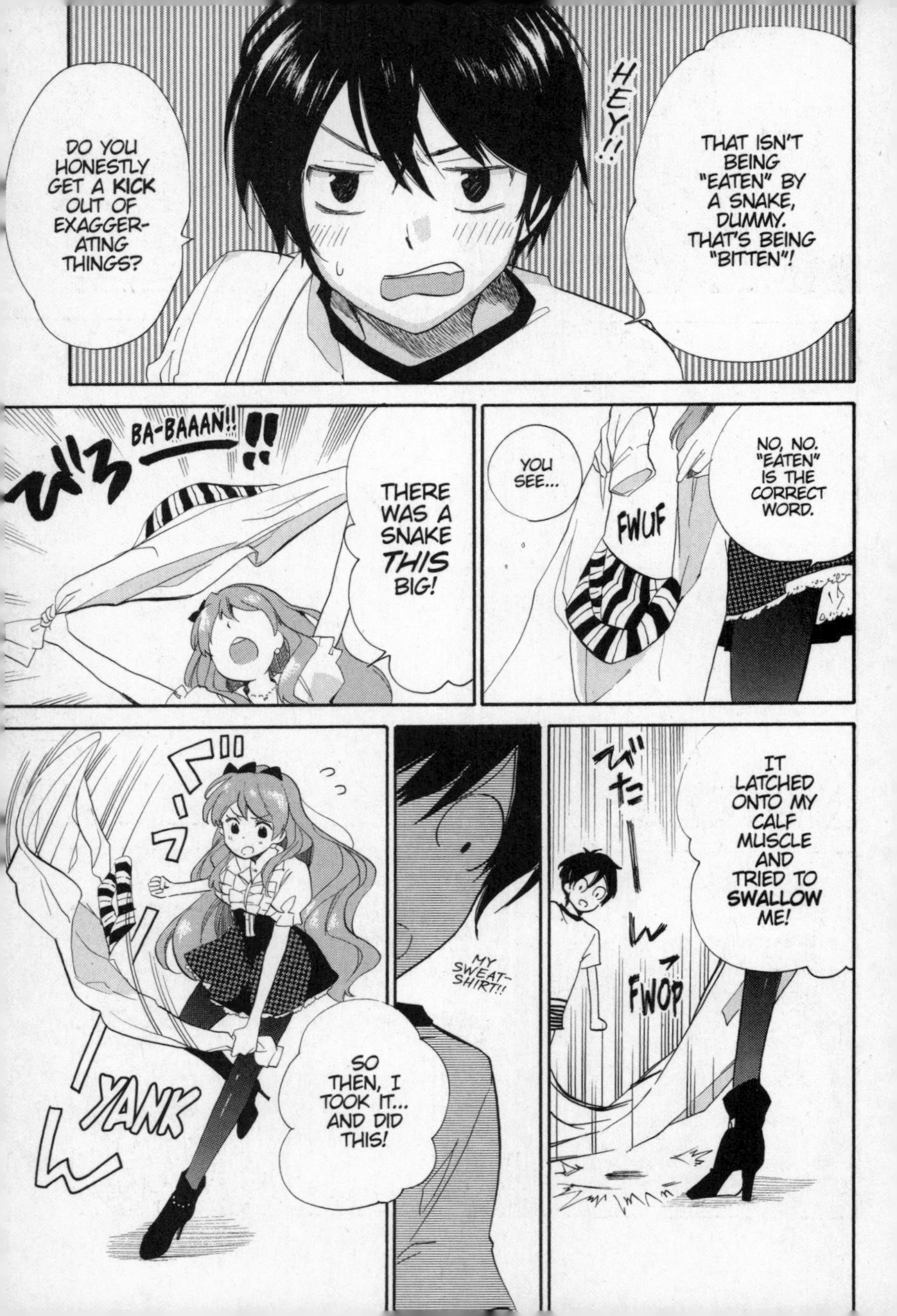
HEY!!
THAT ISN'T BEING "EATEN" BY A SNAKE, DUMMY. THAT'S BEING "BITTEN"!
DO YOU HONESTLY GET A KICK OUT OF EXAGGER-ATING THINGS?
NO, NO. "EATEN" IS THE CORRECT WORD.
YOU SEE...
FWUF
THERE WAS A SNAKE THIS BIG!
BA-BAAAN!!
びろーー!!
IT LATCHED ONTO MY CALF MUSCLE AND TRIED TO SWALLOW ME!
びたーん
FWOP
MY SWEAT-SHIRT!!
SO THEN, I TOOK IT... AND DID THIS!
YANK

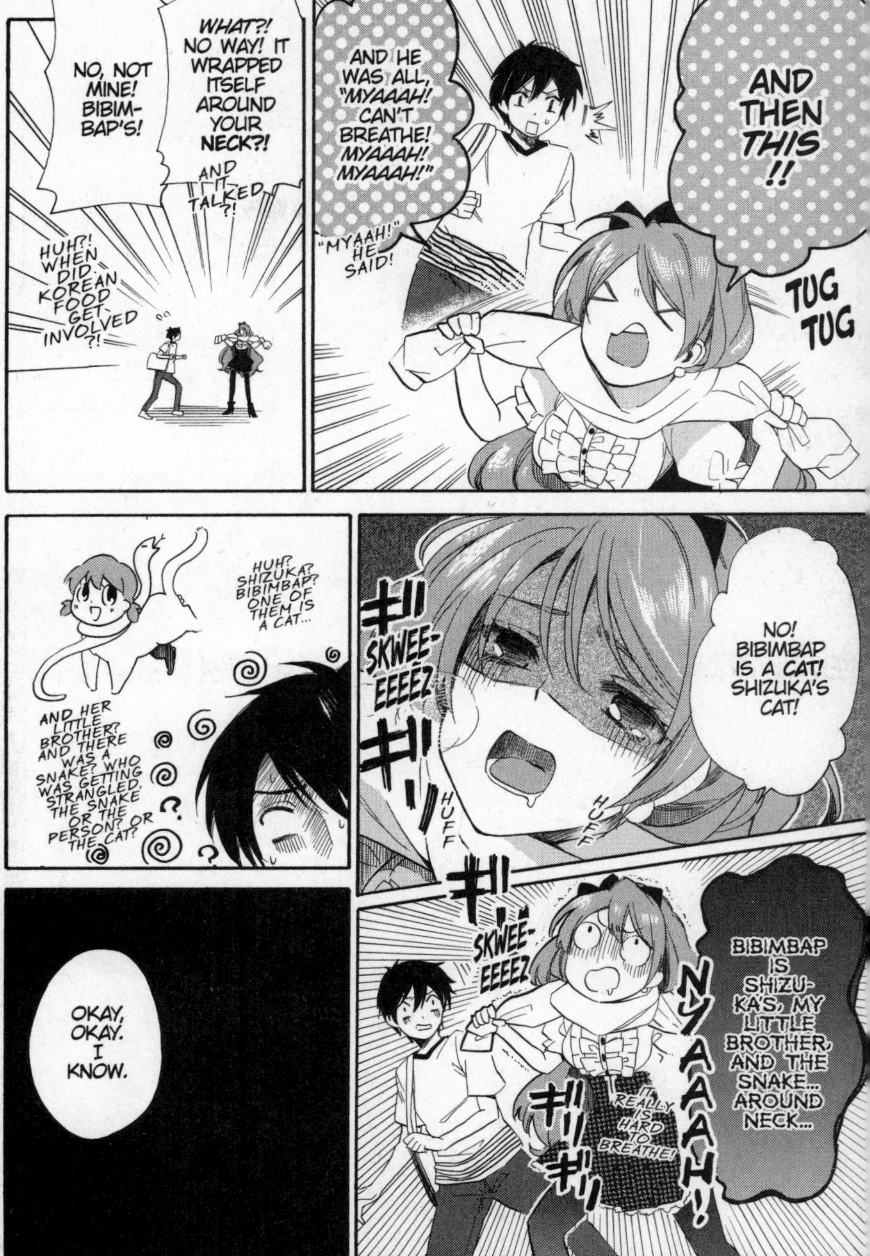
AND THEN THIS!!
AND HE WAS ALL, "MYAAAH! CAN'T BREATHE! MYAAAH! MYAAAH!"
TUG TUG
"MYAAH!" HE SAID!
WHAT?! NO WAY! IT WRAPPED ITSELF AROUND YOUR NECK?!
NO, NOT MINE! BIBIMBAP'S!
AND IT TALKED?!
HUH?! WHEN DID KOREAN FOOD GET INVOLVED?!
NO! BIBIMBAP IS A CAT! SHIZUKA'S CAT!
SKWEE-EEEEZ
HUFF HUFF
HUH? SHIZUKA? BIBIMBAP? ONE OF THEM IS A CAT...
AND HER LITTLE BROTHER? AND THERE WAS A SNAKE? WHO WAS GETTING STRANGLED, THE SNAKE OR THE PERSON? OR THE CAT?
BIBIMBAP IS SHIZUKA'S, MY LITTLE BROTHER, AND THE SNAKE... AROUND NECK...
NYAAAAH!
SKWEE-EEEEZ
IT REALLY IS HARD TO BREATHE!
OKAY, OKAY. I KNOW.

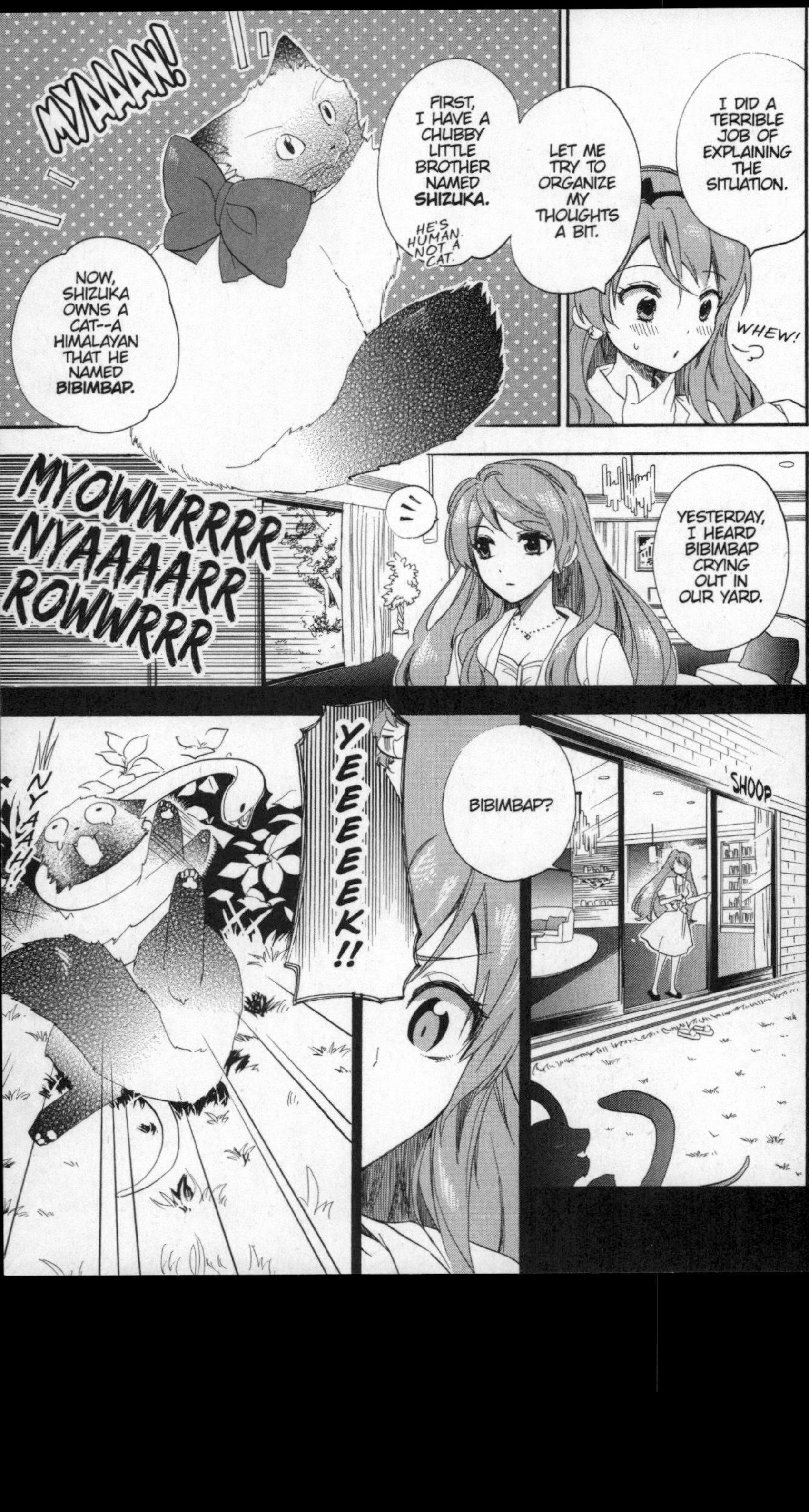
I DID A TERRIBLE JOB OF EXPLAINING THE SITUATION.
WHEW!
LET ME TRY TO ORGANIZE MY THOUGHTS A BIT.
FIRST, I HAVE A CHUBBY LITTLE BROTHER NAMED SHIZUKA.
HE'S HUMAN. NOT A CAT.
MYAAAN!
NOW, SHIZUKA OWNS A CAT--A HIMALAYAN THAT HE NAMED BIBIMBAP.
YESTERDAY, I HEARD BIBIMBAP CRYING OUT IN OUR YARD.
MYOWWRRRR NYAAAAARR ROWWRRR
SHOOP
BIBIMBAP?
YEEEEEK!!
NYAAAH!

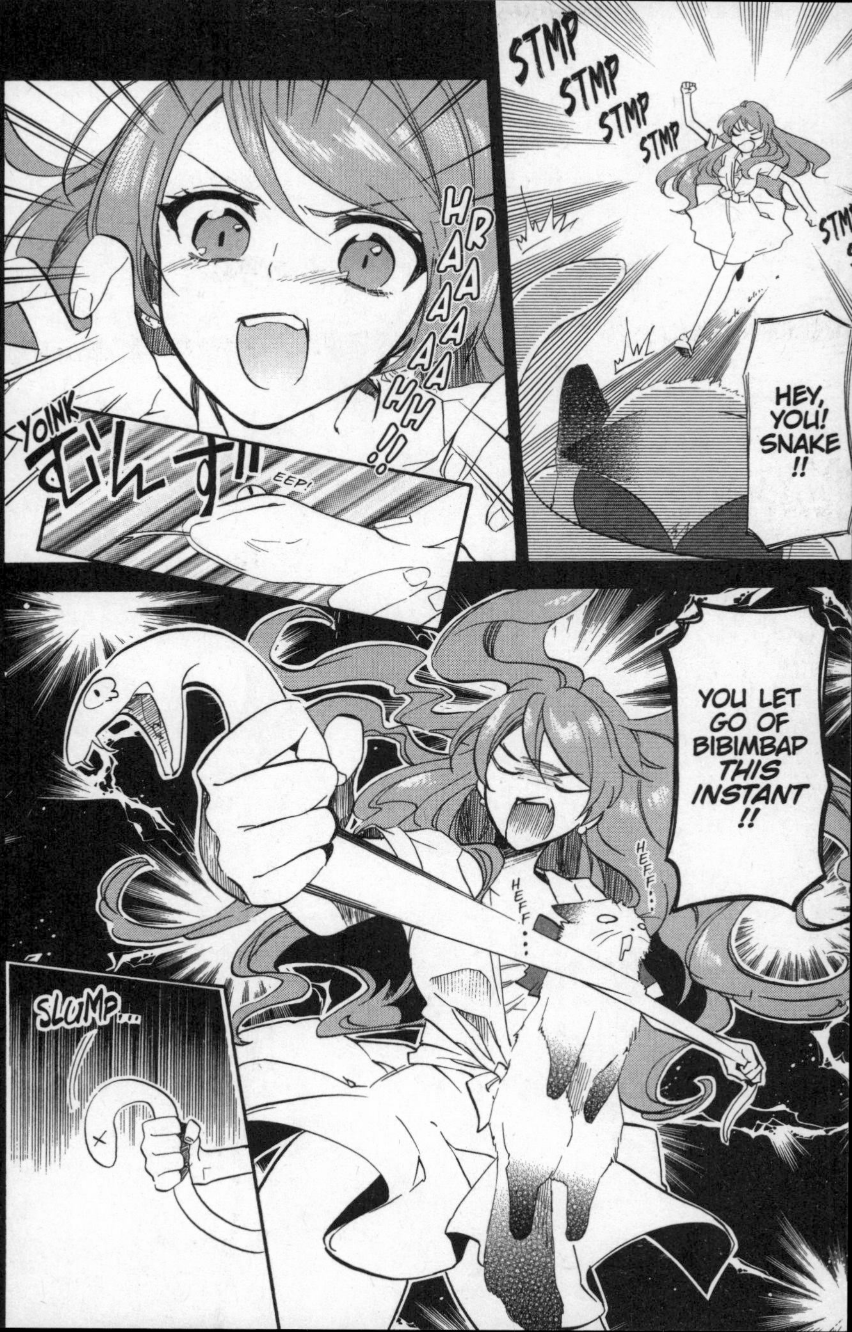
STMP
STMP
STMP
STMP
STMP
HEY, YOU! SNAKE !!
HRAAAAAAAHH !!
YOINK
むんず!!
EEP!
YOU LET GO OF BIBIMBAP *THIS INSTANT* !!
HEFF...
HEFF...
SLUMP...

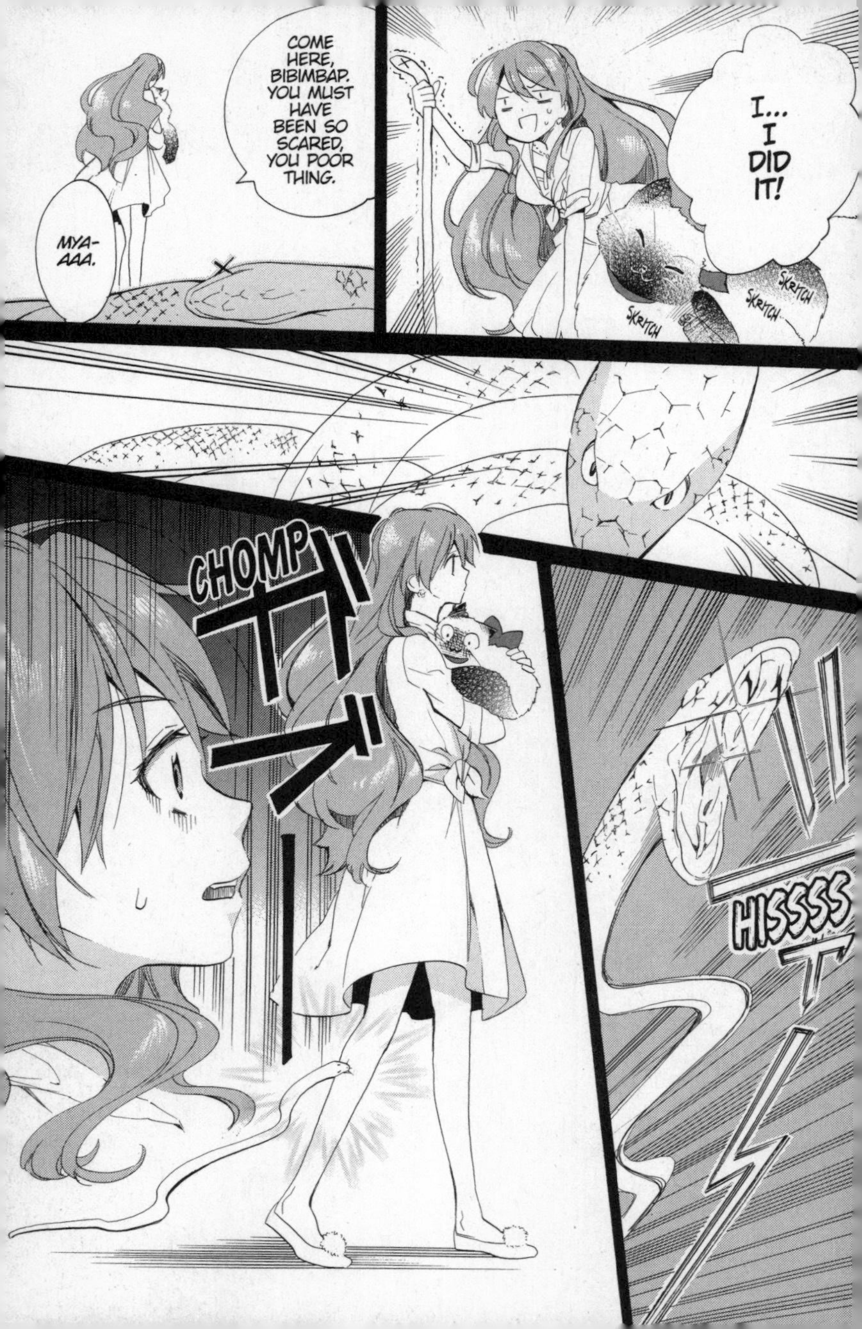
I... I DID IT!
SKRITCH
SKRITCH
SKRITCH
COME HERE, BIBIMBAP. YOU MUST HAVE BEEN SO SCARED, YOU POOR THING.
MYA-AAA.
HISSSS
CHOMP

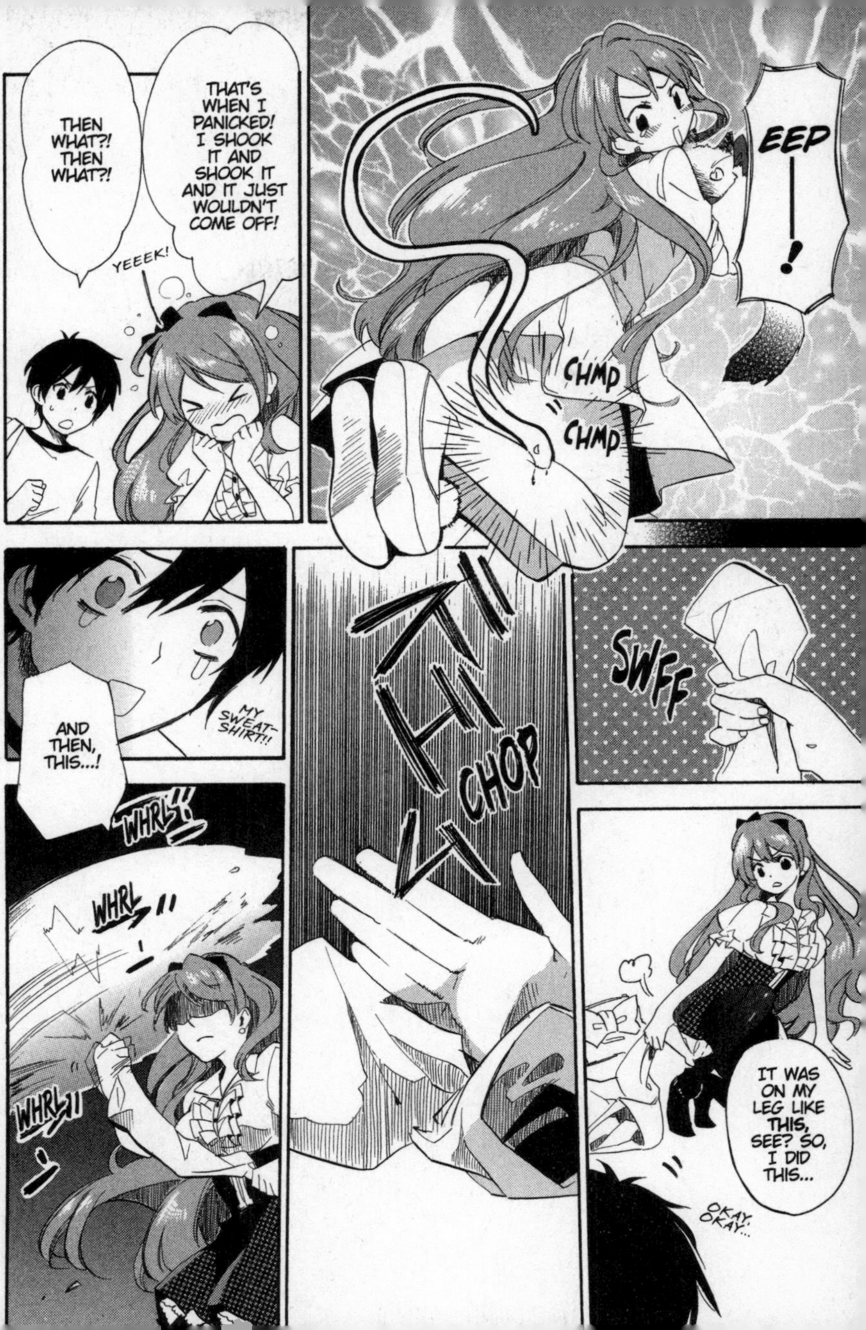
EEP—!
CHMP
CHMP
THAT'S WHEN I PANICKED! I SHOOK IT AND SHOOK IT AND IT JUST WOULDN'T COME OFF!
YEEEK!
THEN WHAT?! THEN WHAT?!
SWFF
IT WAS ON MY LEG LIKE THIS, SEE? SO, I DID THIS...
OKAY, OKAY...
CHOP
AND THEN, THIS...!
MY SWEAT-SHIRT!!
WHRL
WHRL
WHRL

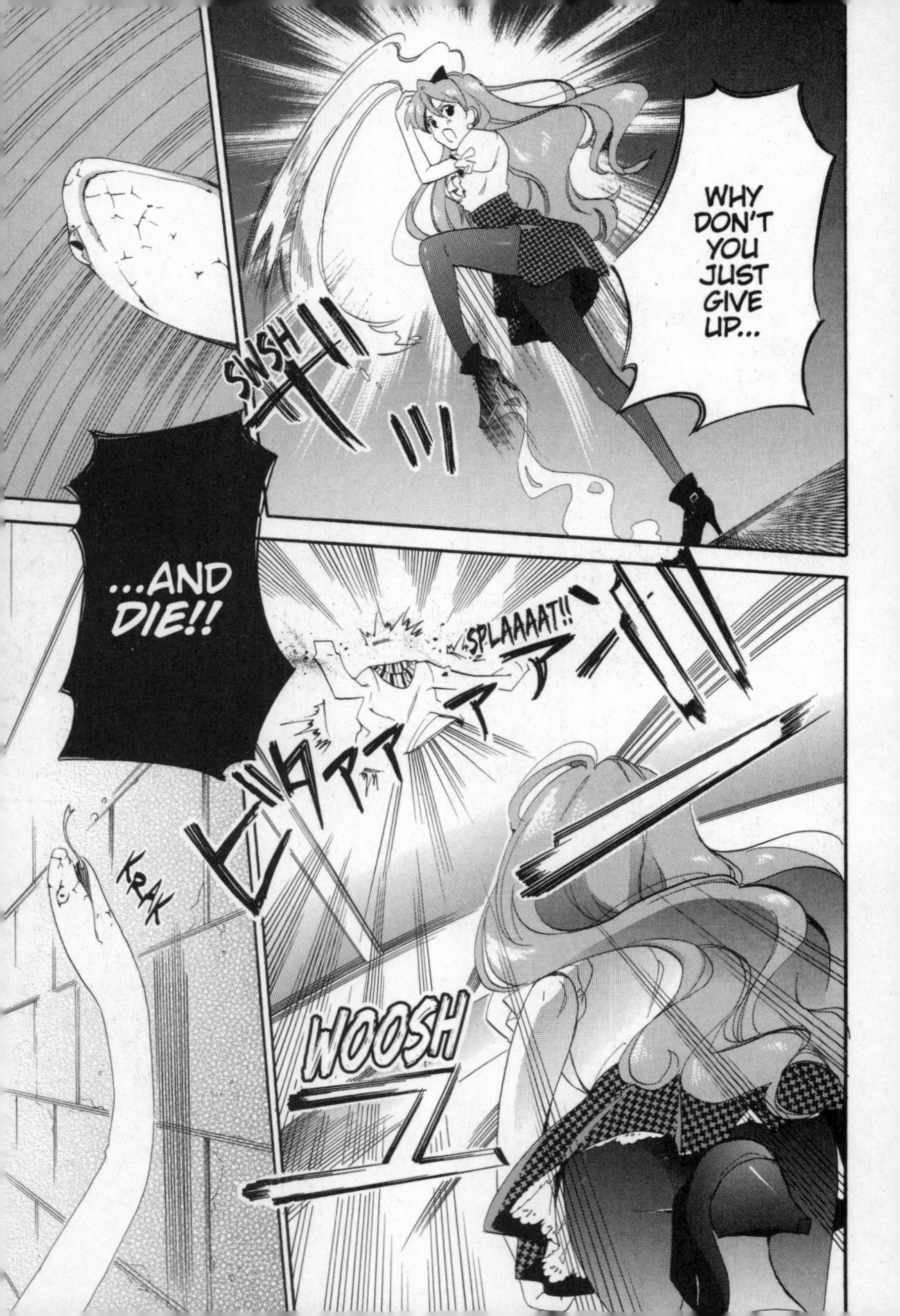
WHY DON'T YOU JUST GIVE UP...
SWSH
...AND DIE!!
SPLAAAAT!!
KRAK
WOOSH

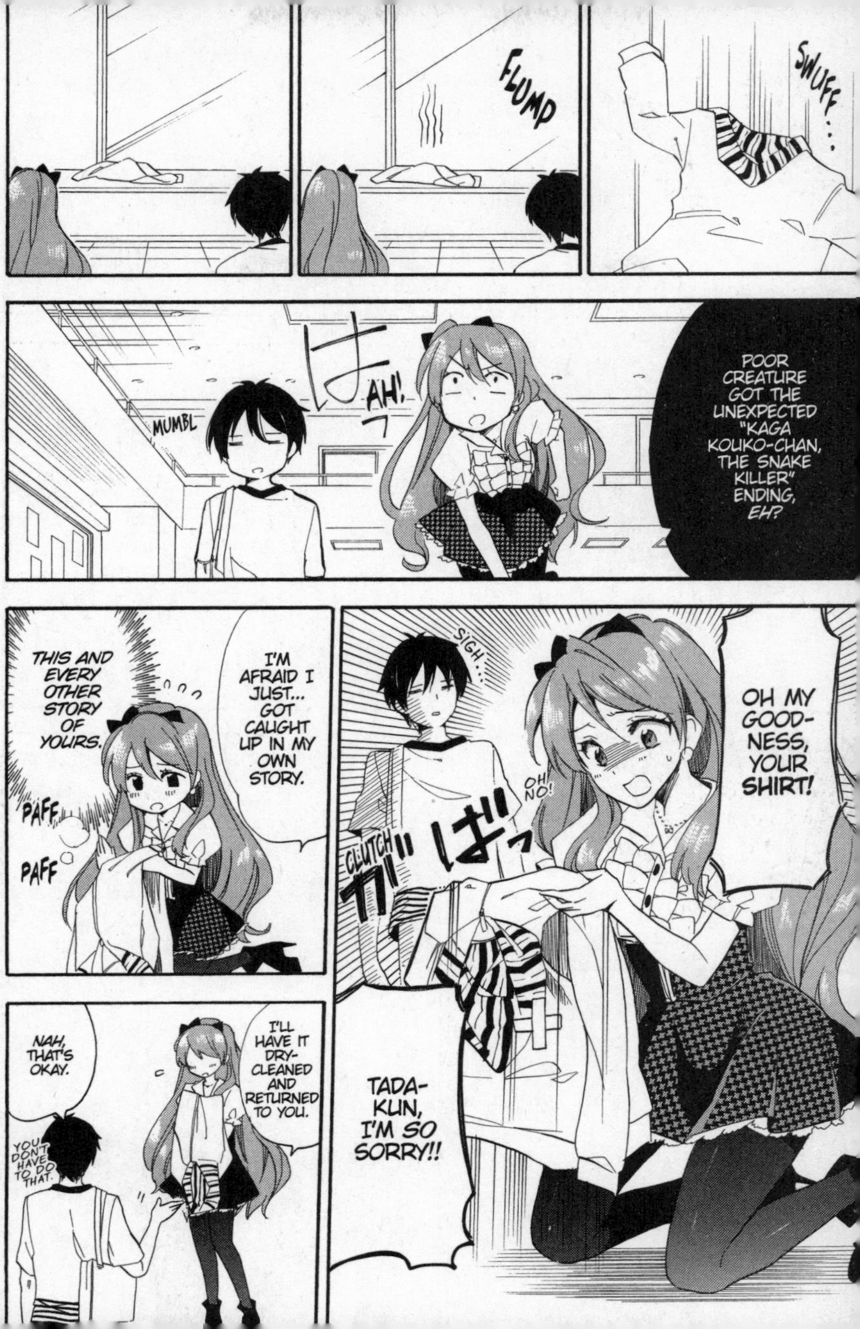
SWUFF...
FLUMP
POOR CREATURE GOT THE UNEXPECTED "KAGA KOUKO-CHAN, THE SNAKE KILLER" ENDING, EH?
は
AH!
MUMBL
OH MY GOODNESS, YOUR SHIRT!
SIGH...
OH NO!
ばっ
CLUTCH
ガ
TADA-KUN, I'M SO SORRY!!
I'M AFRAID I JUST... GOT CAUGHT UP IN MY OWN STORY.
THIS AND EVERY OTHER STORY OF YOURS.
PAFF
PAFF
I'LL HAVE IT DRY-CLEANED AND RETURNED TO YOU.
NAH, THAT'S OKAY.
YOU DON'T HAVE TO DO THAT.

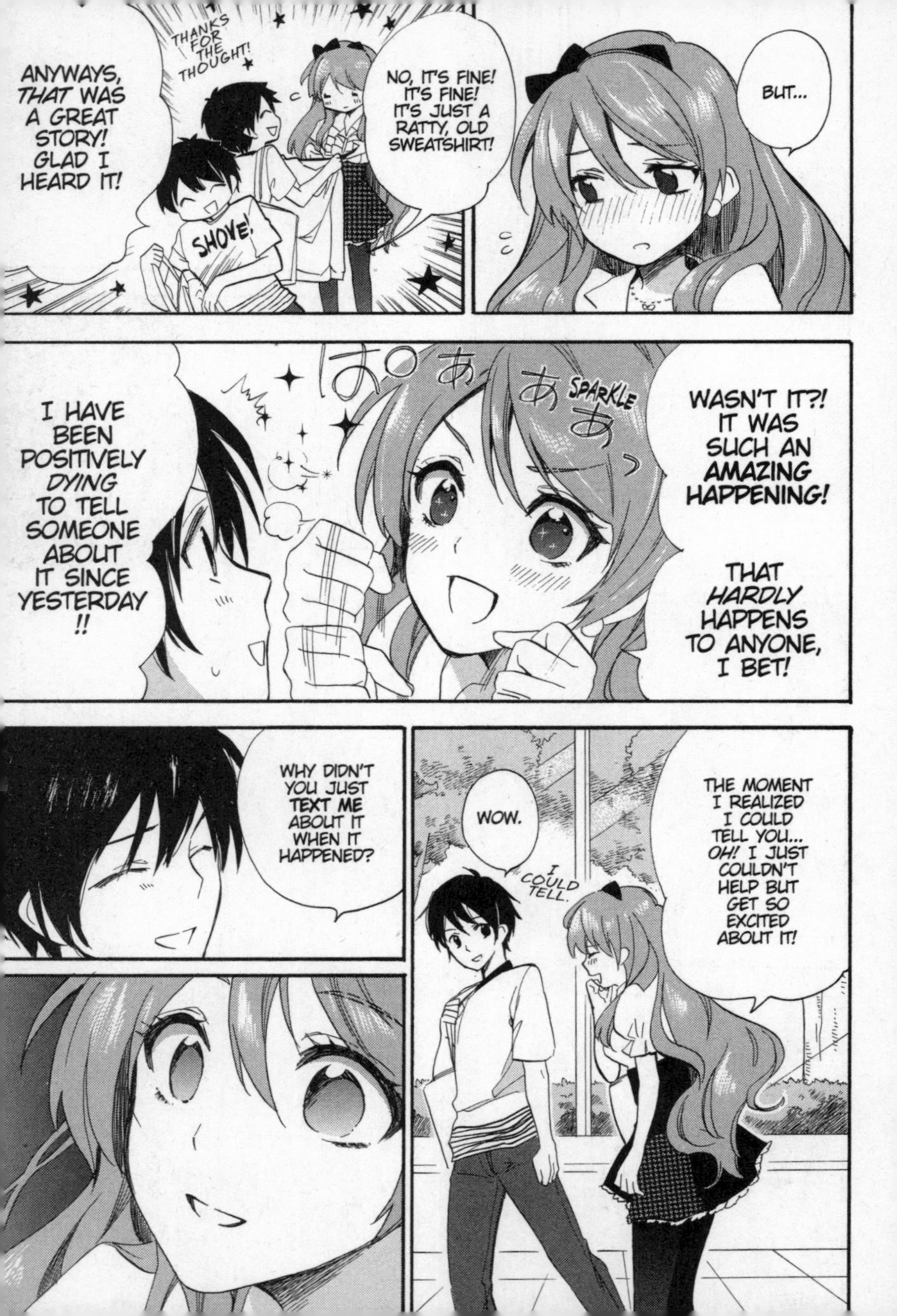
BUT...
NO, IT'S FINE! IT'S FINE! IT'S JUST A RATTY, OLD SWEATSHIRT!
THANKS FOR THE THOUGHT!
ANYWAYS, *THAT* WAS A GREAT STORY! GLAD I HEARD IT!
SHOVE!
WASN'T IT?! IT WAS SUCH AN **AMAZING HAPPENING!**
THAT *HARDLY* HAPPENS TO ANYONE, I BET!
SPARKLE
I HAVE BEEN POSITIVELY *DYING* TO TELL SOMEONE ABOUT IT SINCE YESTERDAY!!
THE MOMENT I REALIZED I COULD TELL YOU... *OH!* I JUST COULDN'T HELP BUT GET SO EXCITED ABOUT IT!
WOW.
I COULD TELL.
WHY DIDN'T YOU JUST **TEXT ME** ABOUT IT WHEN IT HAPPENED?

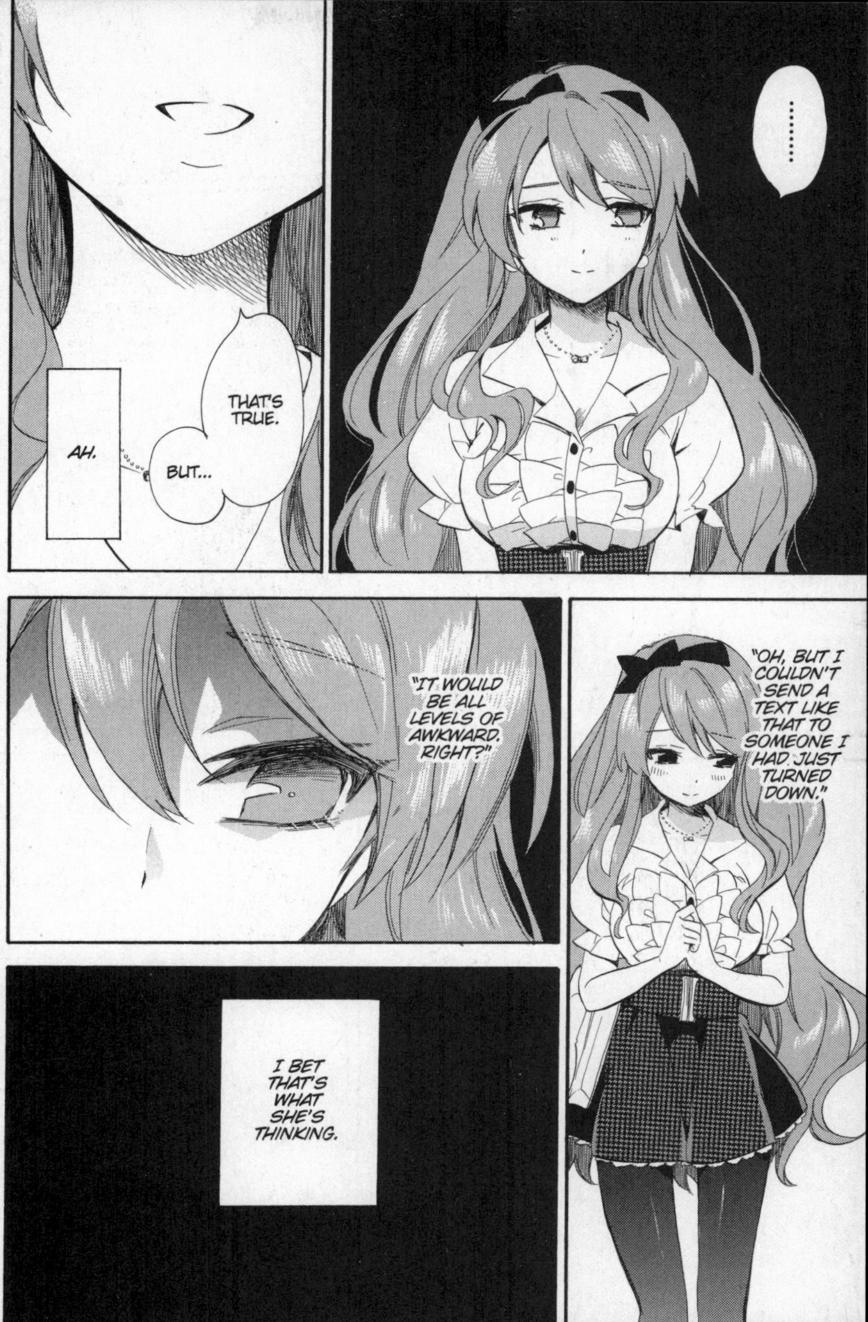
......
THAT'S TRUE.
BUT...
AH.
"OH, BUT I COULDN'T SEND A TEXT LIKE THAT TO SOMEONE I HAD JUST TURNED DOWN."
"IT WOULD BE ALL LEVELS OF AWKWARD. RIGHT?"
I BET THAT'S WHAT SHE'S THINKING.

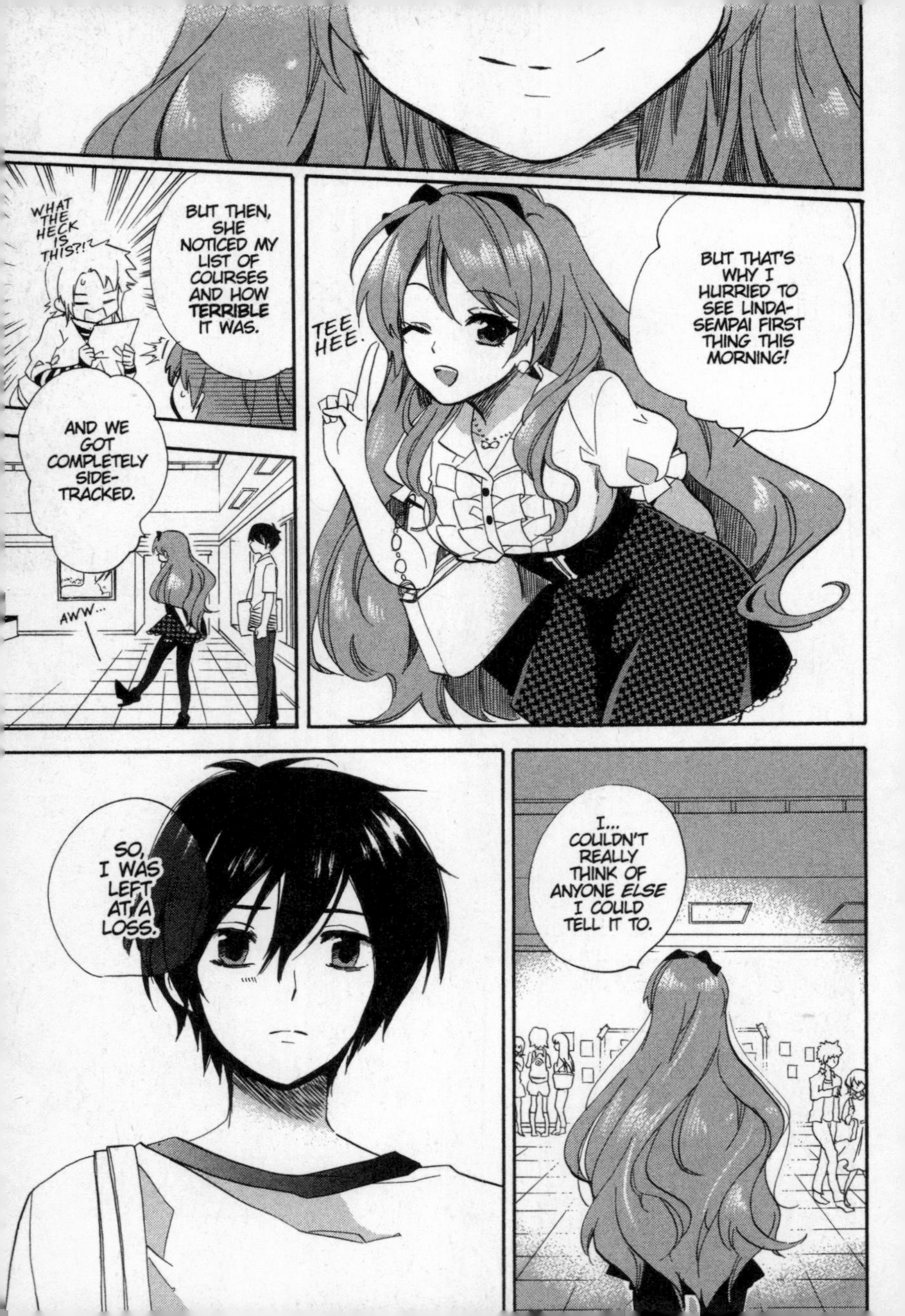
BUT THAT'S WHY I HURRIED TO SEE LINDA-SEMPAI FIRST THING THIS MORNING!
TEE HEE.
BUT THEN, SHE NOTICED MY LIST OF COURSES AND HOW TERRIBLE IT WAS.
WHAT THE HECK IS THIS?!?
AND WE GOT COMPLETELY SIDE-TRACKED.
AWW...
I... COULDN'T REALLY THINK OF ANYONE *ELSE* I COULD TELL IT TO.
SO, I WAS LEFT AT A LOSS.

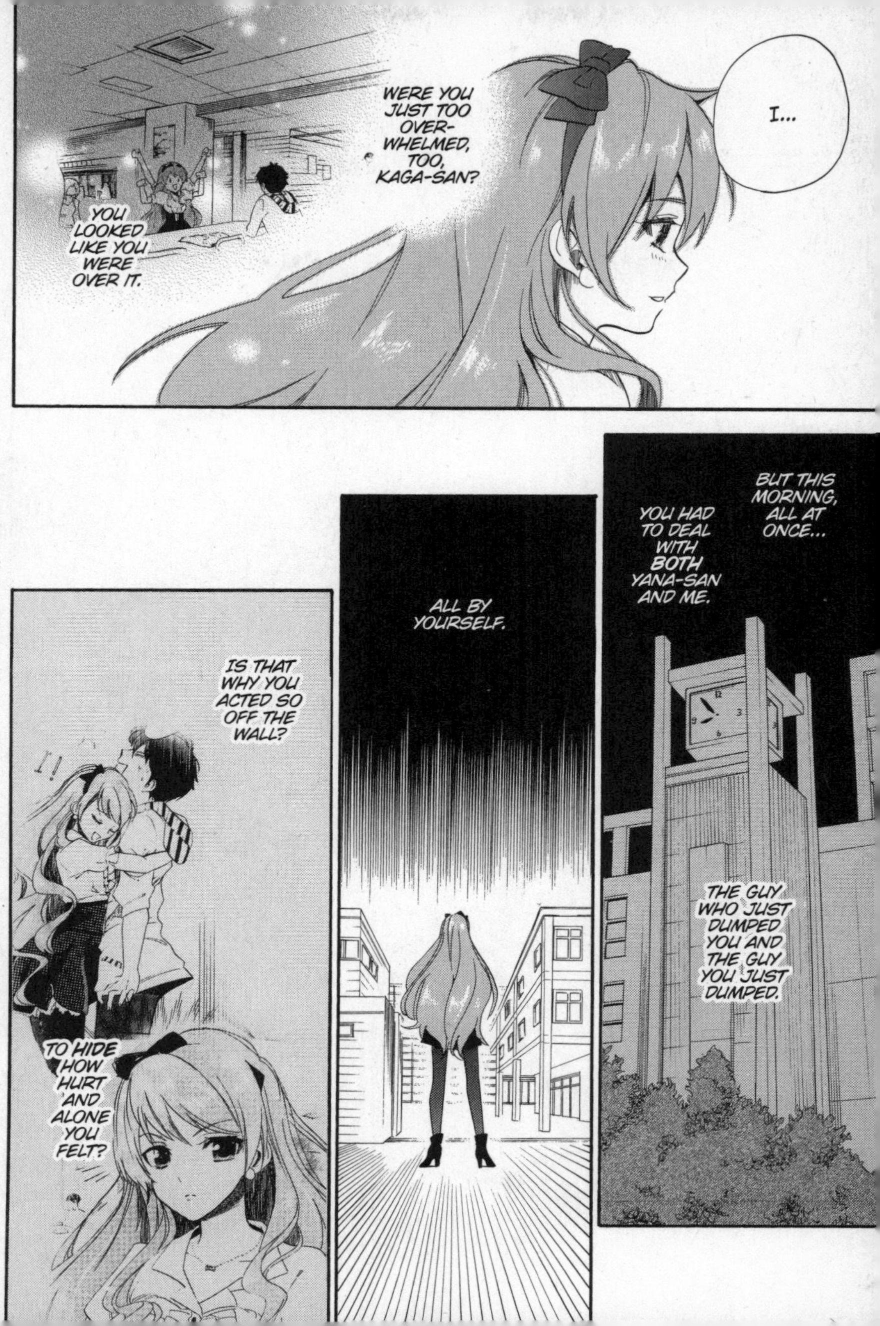
I...
WERE YOU JUST TOO OVER-WHELMED, TOO, KAGA-SAN?
YOU LOOKED LIKE YOU WERE OVER IT.
BUT THIS MORNING, ALL AT ONCE...
YOU HAD TO DEAL WITH BOTH YANA-SAN AND ME.
THE GUY WHO JUST DUMPED YOU AND THE GUY YOU JUST DUMPED.
ALL BY YOURSELF.
IS THAT WHY YOU ACTED SO OFF THE WALL?
!!
TO HIDE HOW HURT AND ALONE YOU FELT?

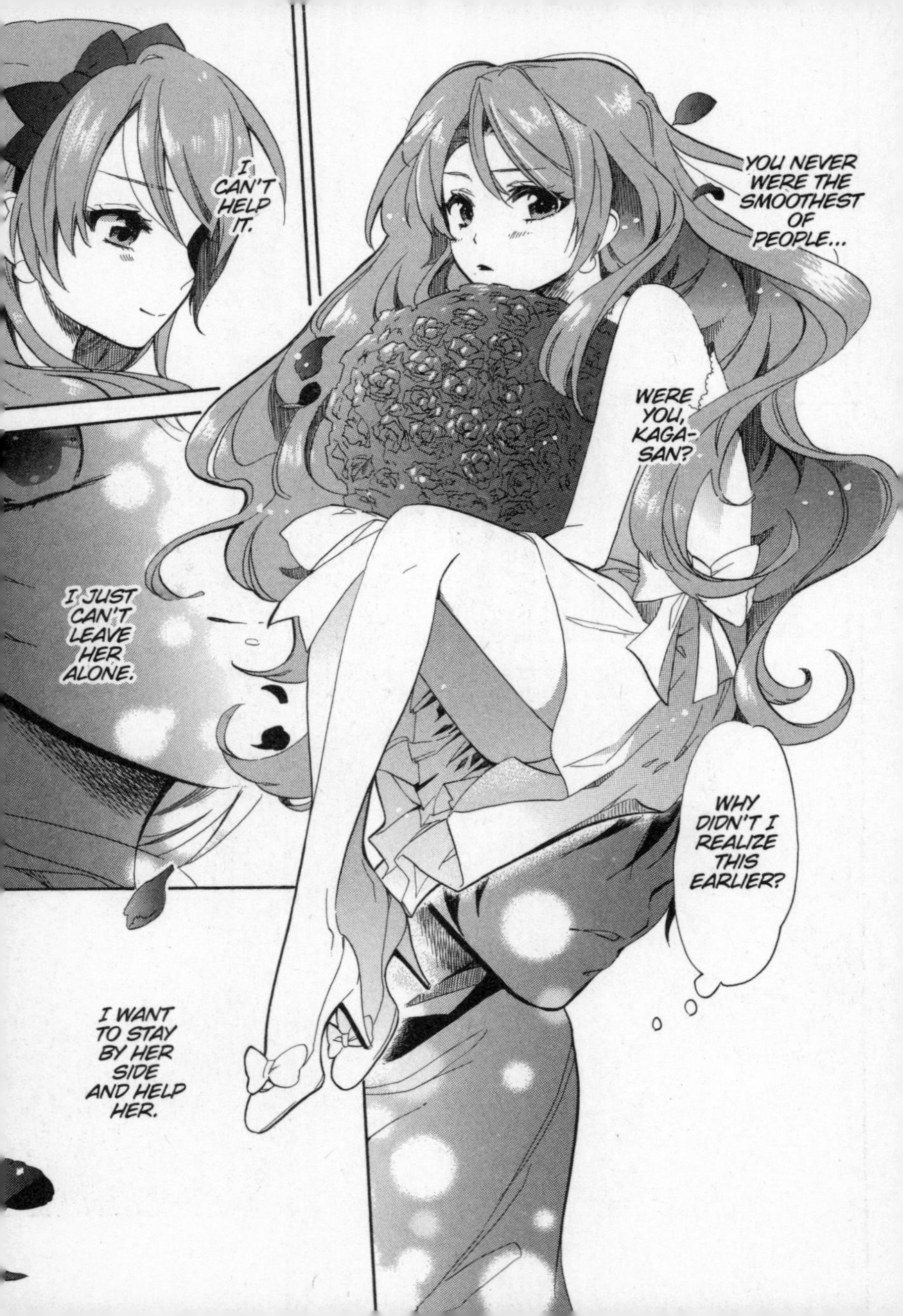
YOU NEVER WERE THE SMOOTHEST OF PEOPLE...
WERE YOU, KAGA-SAN?
WHY DIDN'T I REALIZE THIS EARLIER?
I CAN'T HELP IT.
I JUST CAN'T LEAVE HER ALONE.
I WANT TO STAY BY HER SIDE AND HELP HER.

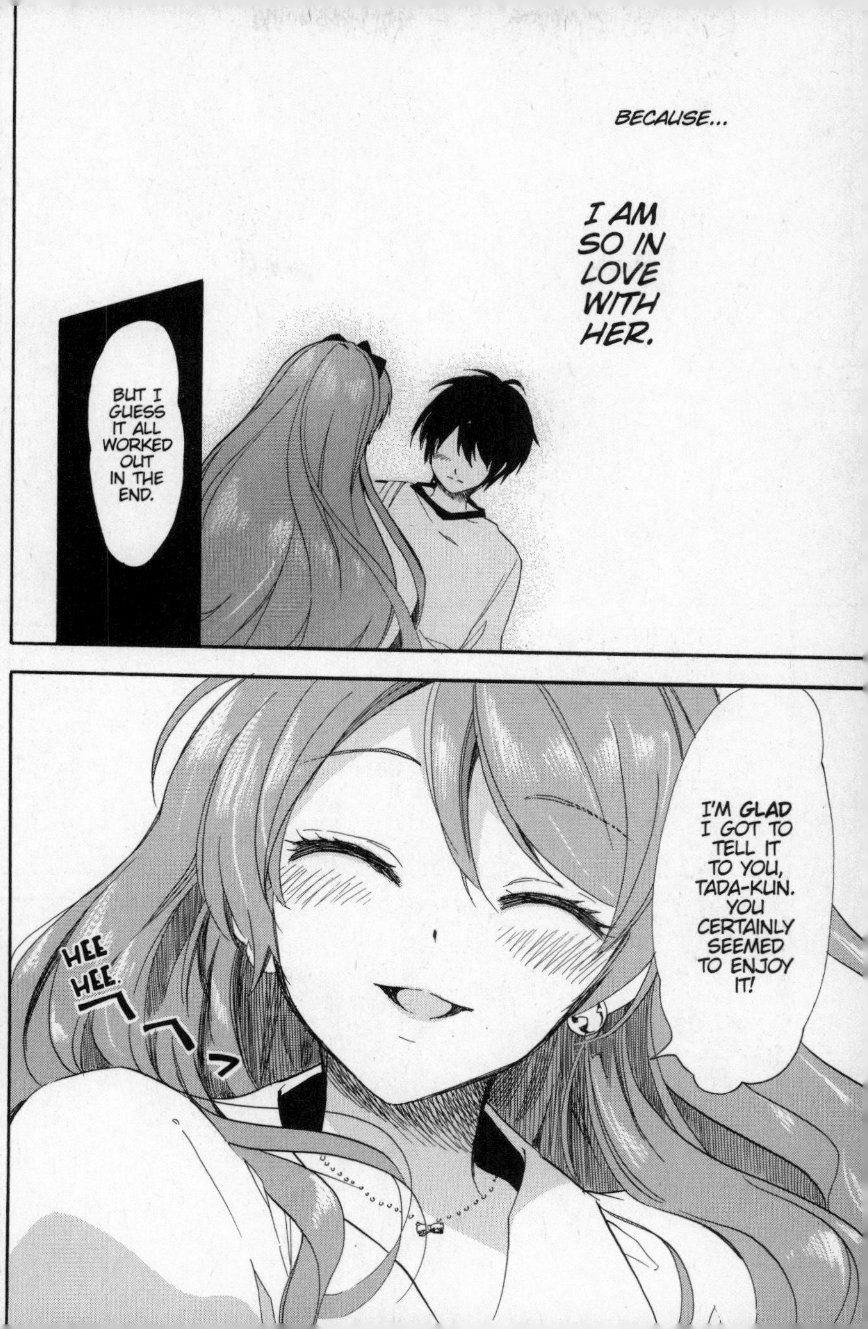
BECAUSE...
I AM SO IN LOVE WITH HER.
BUT I GUESS IT ALL WORKED OUT IN THE END.
I'M GLAD I GOT TO TELL IT TO YOU, TADA-KUN. YOU CERTAINLY SEEMED TO ENJOY IT!
HEE HEE.

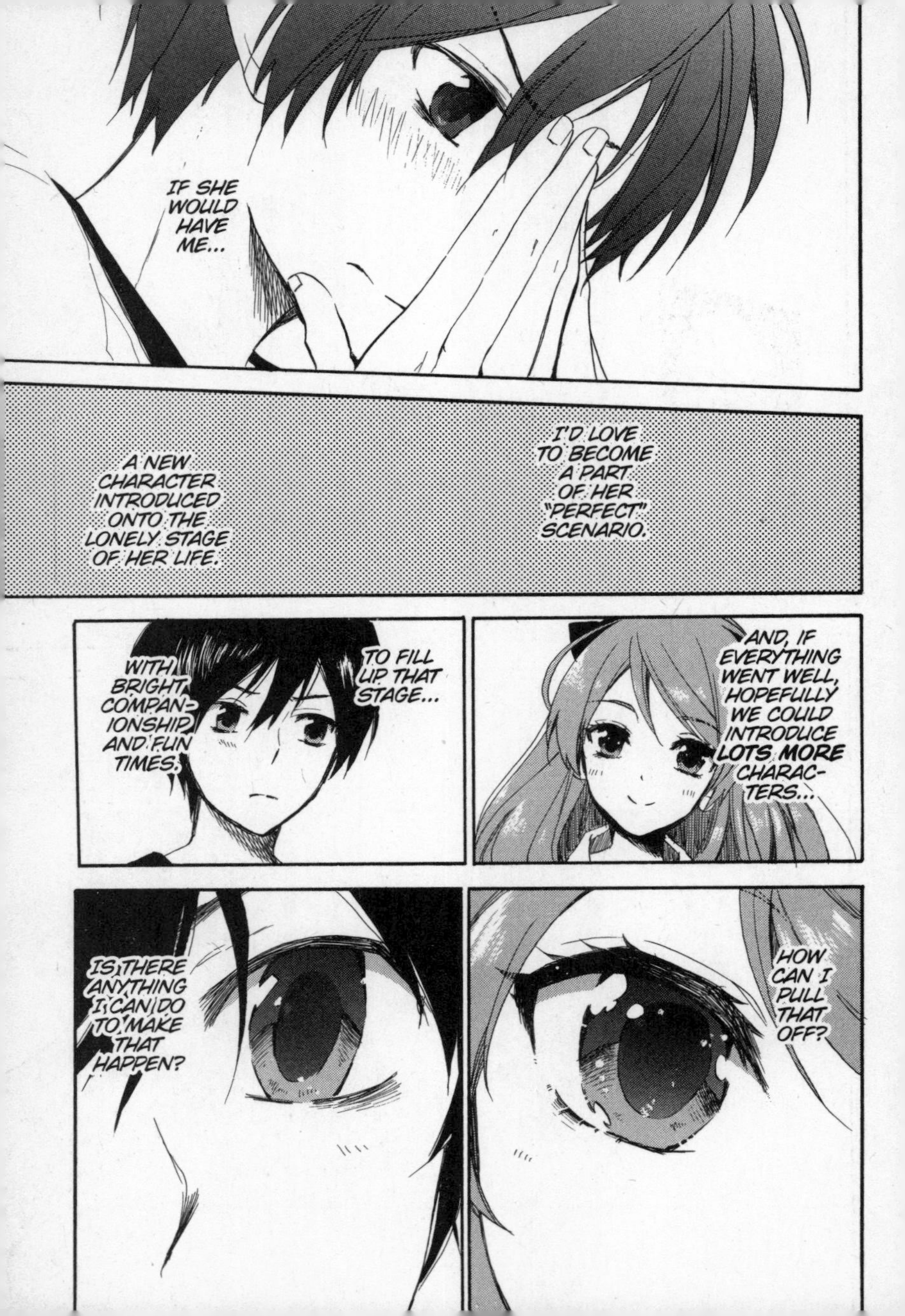
IF SHE WOULD HAVE ME...
I'D LOVE TO BECOME A PART OF HER "PERFECT" SCENARIO.
A NEW CHARACTER INTRODUCED ONTO THE LONELY STAGE OF HER LIFE.
AND, IF EVERYTHING WENT WELL, HOPEFULLY WE COULD INTRODUCE **LOTS MORE** CHARACTERS...
TO FILL UP THAT STAGE...
WITH BRIGHT COMPANIONSHIP AND FUN TIMES.
HOW CAN I PULL THAT OFF?
IS THERE ANYTHING I CAN DO TO MAKE THAT HAPPEN?

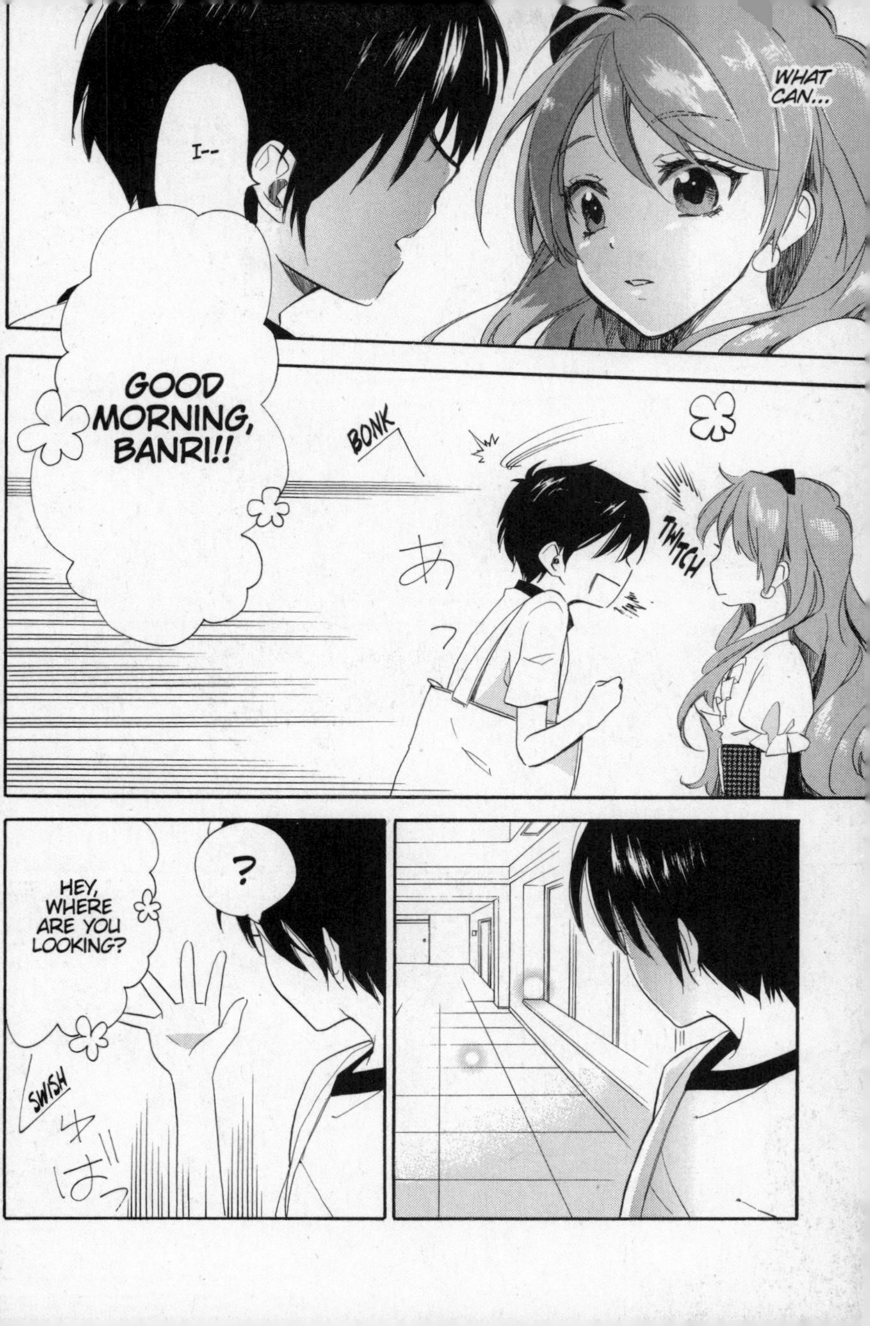

WHAT CAN...
I--
GOOD MORNING, BANRI!!
BONK
TWITCH
あっ
?
HEY, WHERE ARE YOU LOOKING?
SWISH
ばっ

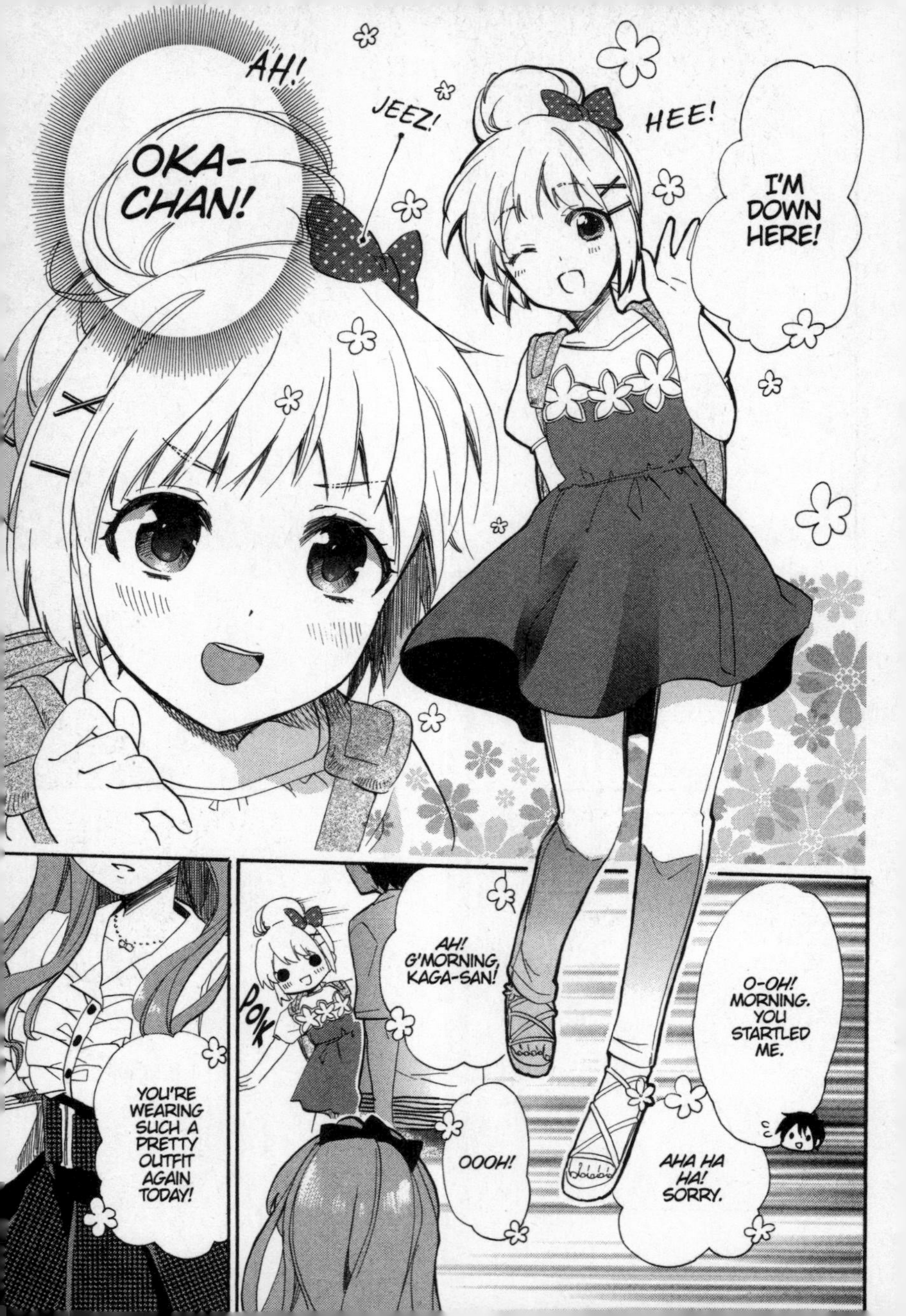
HEE!
I'M DOWN HERE!
AH!
OKA-CHAN!
JEEZ!
O-OH! MORNING. YOU STARTLED ME.
AHA HA HA! SORRY.
AH! G'MORNING, KAGA-SAN!
POK
OOOH!
YOU'RE WEARING SUCH A PRETTY OUTFIT AGAIN TODAY!

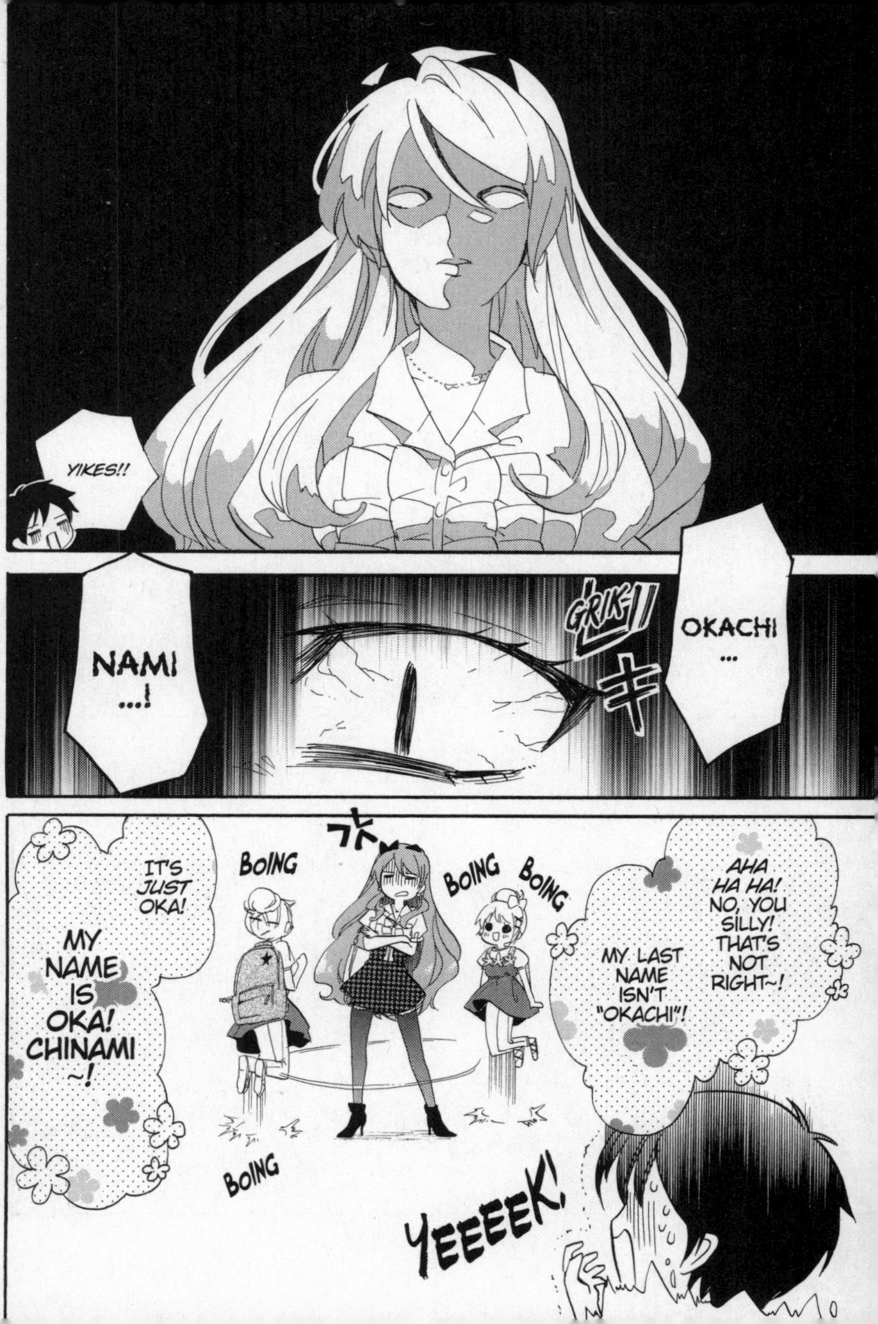
YIKES!!
OKACHI ...
GRIK
NAMI ...!
AHA HA HA! NO, YOU SILLY! THAT'S NOT RIGHT~!
MY LAST NAME ISN'T "OKACHI"!
BOING
BOING
BOING
IT'S JUST OKA!
MY NAME IS OKA! CHINAMI ~!
BOING
YEEEEK!

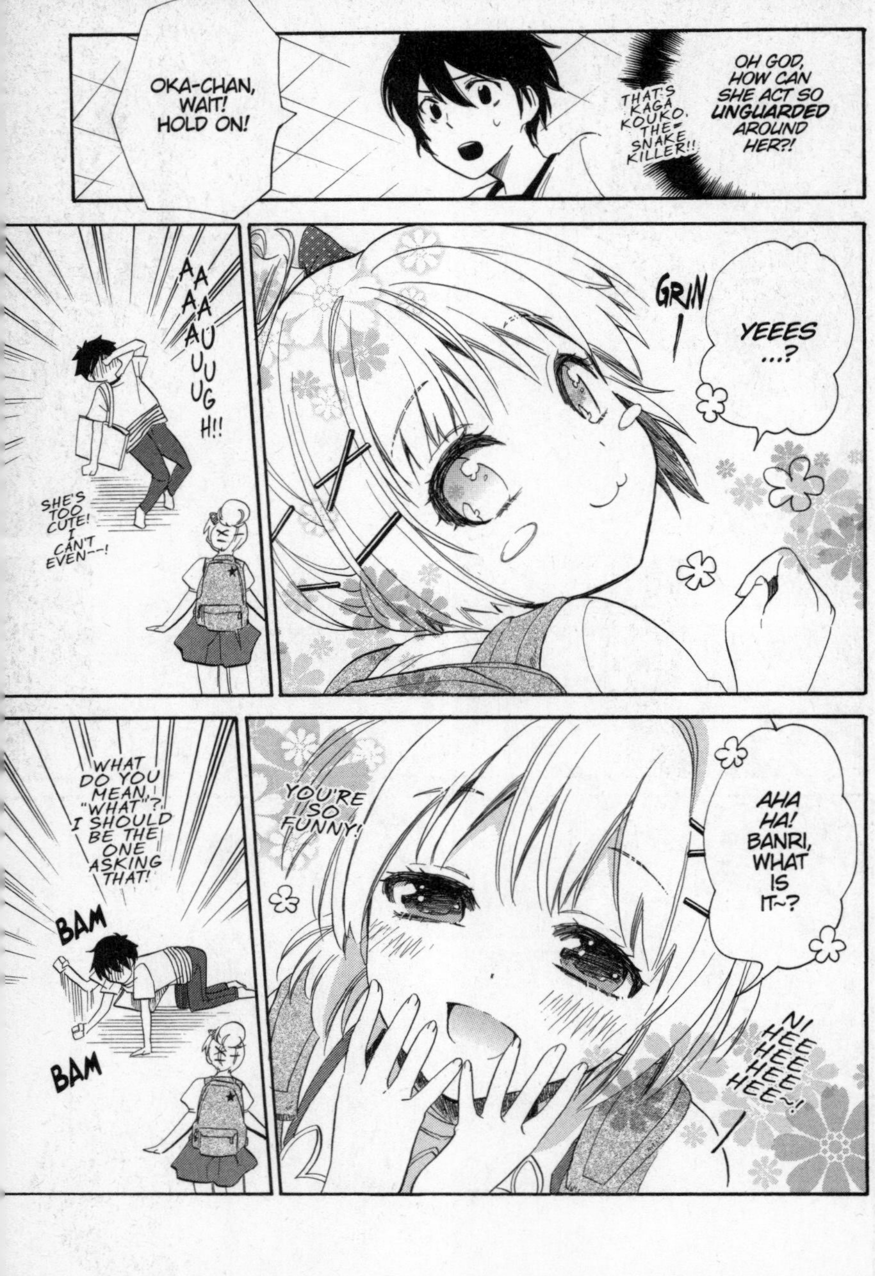
OH GOD, HOW CAN SHE ACT SO UNGUARDED AROUND HER?!
THAT'S KAGA KOUKO, THE SNAKE KILLER!!
OKA-CHAN, WAIT! HOLD ON!
GRIN
YEEES ...?
AAAAAUUUGH!!
SHE'S TOO CUTE! I CAN'T EVEN--!
AHA HA! BANRI, WHAT IS IT~?
YOU'RE SO FUNNY!
NI HEE HEE HEE HEE~!
WHAT DO YOU MEAN, "WHAT"? I SHOULD BE THE ONE ASKING THAT!
BAM
BAM

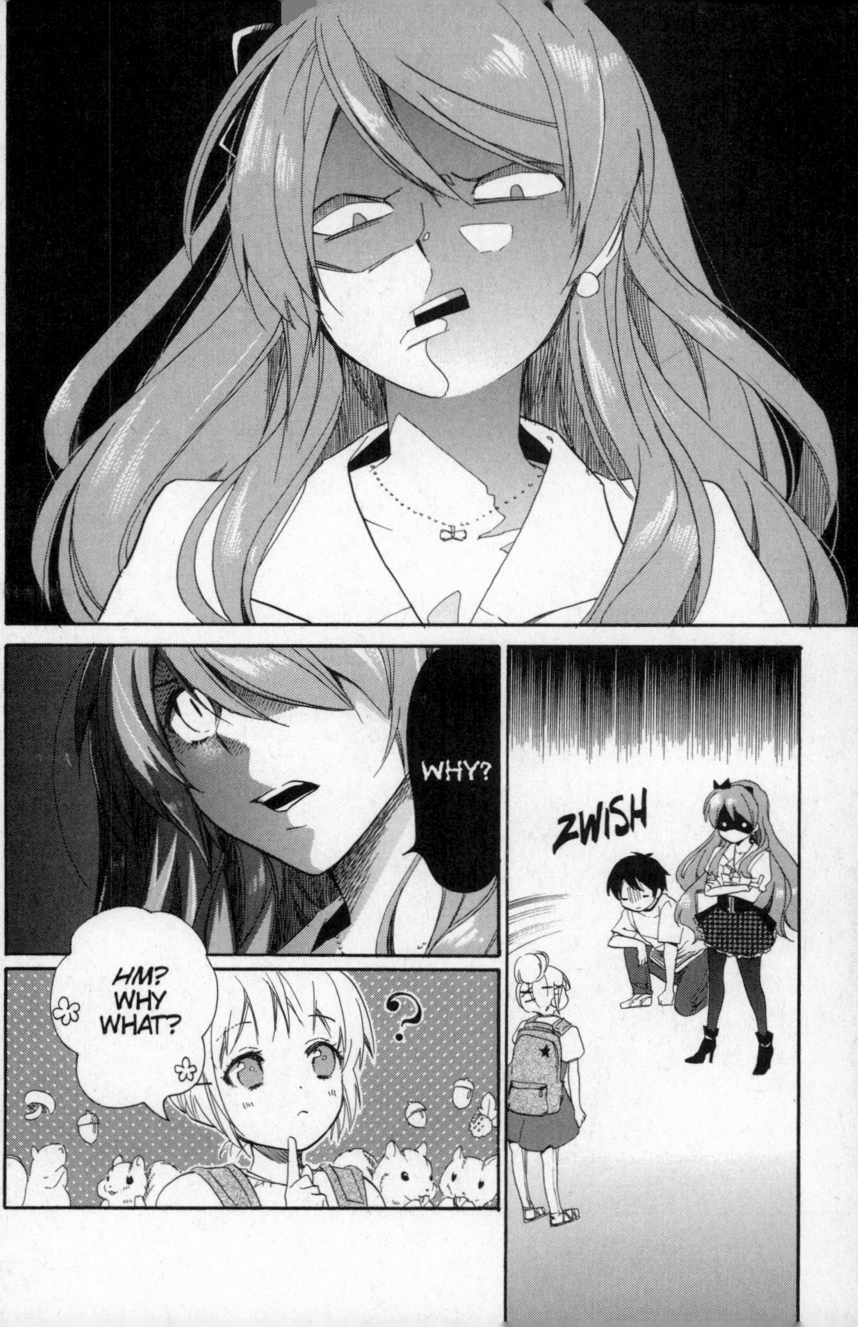
ZWISH
WHY?
HM? WHY WHAT?

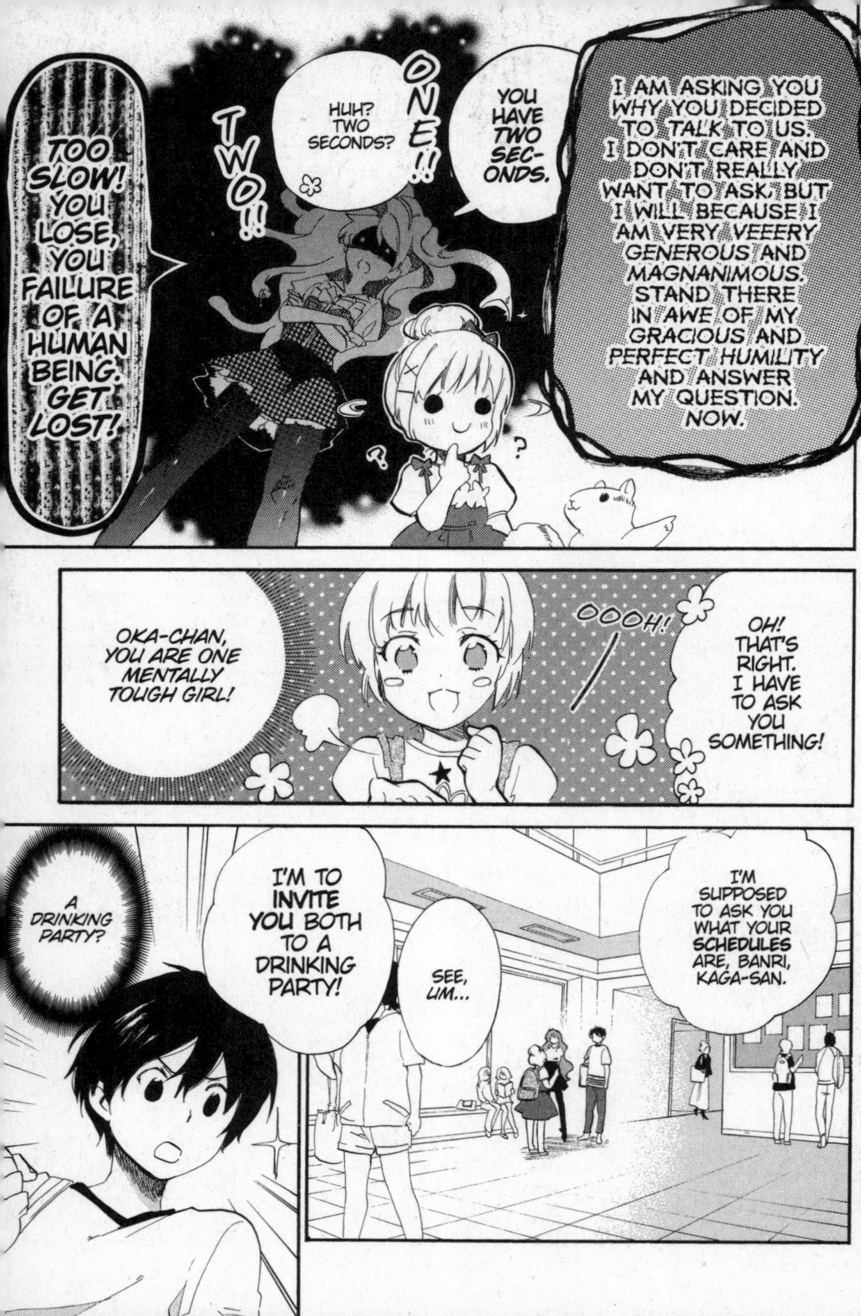
I AM ASKING YOU WHY YOU DECIDED TO TALK TO US. I DON'T CARE AND DON'T REALLY WANT TO ASK, BUT I WILL BECAUSE I AM VERY VEEERY GENEROUS AND MAGNANIMOUS. STAND THERE IN AWE OF MY GRACIOUS AND PERFECT HUMILITY AND ANSWER MY QUESTION. NOW.
YOU HAVE TWO SEC-ONDS.
ONE!!
HUH? TWO SECONDS?
TWO!!
TOO SLOW! YOU LOSE, YOU FAILURE OF A HUMAN BEING. GET LOST!
OH! THAT'S RIGHT. I HAVE TO ASK YOU SOMETHING!
OOOH!
OKA-CHAN, YOU ARE ONE MENTALLY TOUGH GIRL!
I'M SUPPOSED TO ASK YOU WHAT YOUR SCHEDULES ARE, BANRI, KAGA-SAN.
SEE, UM...
I'M TO INVITE YOU BOTH TO A DRINKING PARTY!
A DRINKING PARTY?

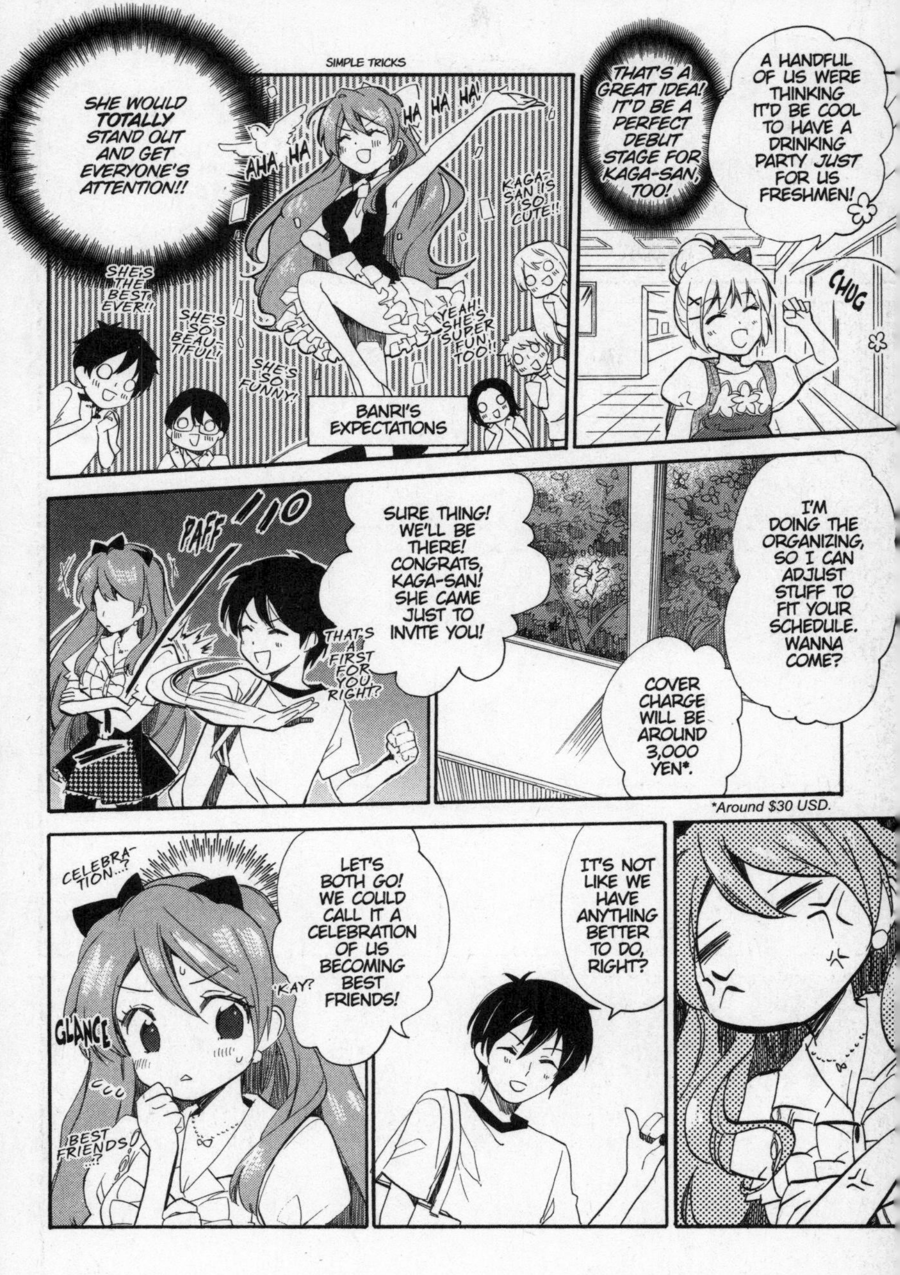
A HANDFUL OF US WERE THINKING IT'D BE COOL TO HAVE A DRINKING PARTY JUST FOR US FRESHMEN!
THAT'S A GREAT IDEA! IT'D BE A PERFECT DEBUT STAGE FOR KAGA-SAN, TOO!
CHUG
SHE WOULD TOTALLY STAND OUT AND GET EVERYONE'S ATTENTION!!
HA HA HA!
AHA HA
KAGA-SAN IS SO CUTE!!
YEAH! SHE'S SUPER FUN TOO!!
SHE'S THE BEST EVER!!
SHE'S SO BEAUTIFUL!
SHE'S SO FUNNY!
BANRI'S EXPECTATIONS
I'M DOING THE ORGANIZING, SO I CAN ADJUST STUFF TO FIT YOUR SCHEDULE. WANNA COME?
COVER CHARGE WILL BE AROUND 3,000 YEN*.
SURE THING! WE'LL BE THERE! CONGRATS, KAGA-SAN! SHE CAME JUST TO INVITE YOU!
PAFF
THAT'S A FIRST FOR YOU, RIGHT?
IT'S NOT LIKE WE HAVE ANYTHING BETTER TO DO, RIGHT?
LET'S BOTH GO! WE COULD CALL IT A CELEBRATION OF US BECOMING BEST FRIENDS!
'KAY?
CELEBRATION...?
GLANCE
BEST FRIENDS...?

*Around $30 USD.

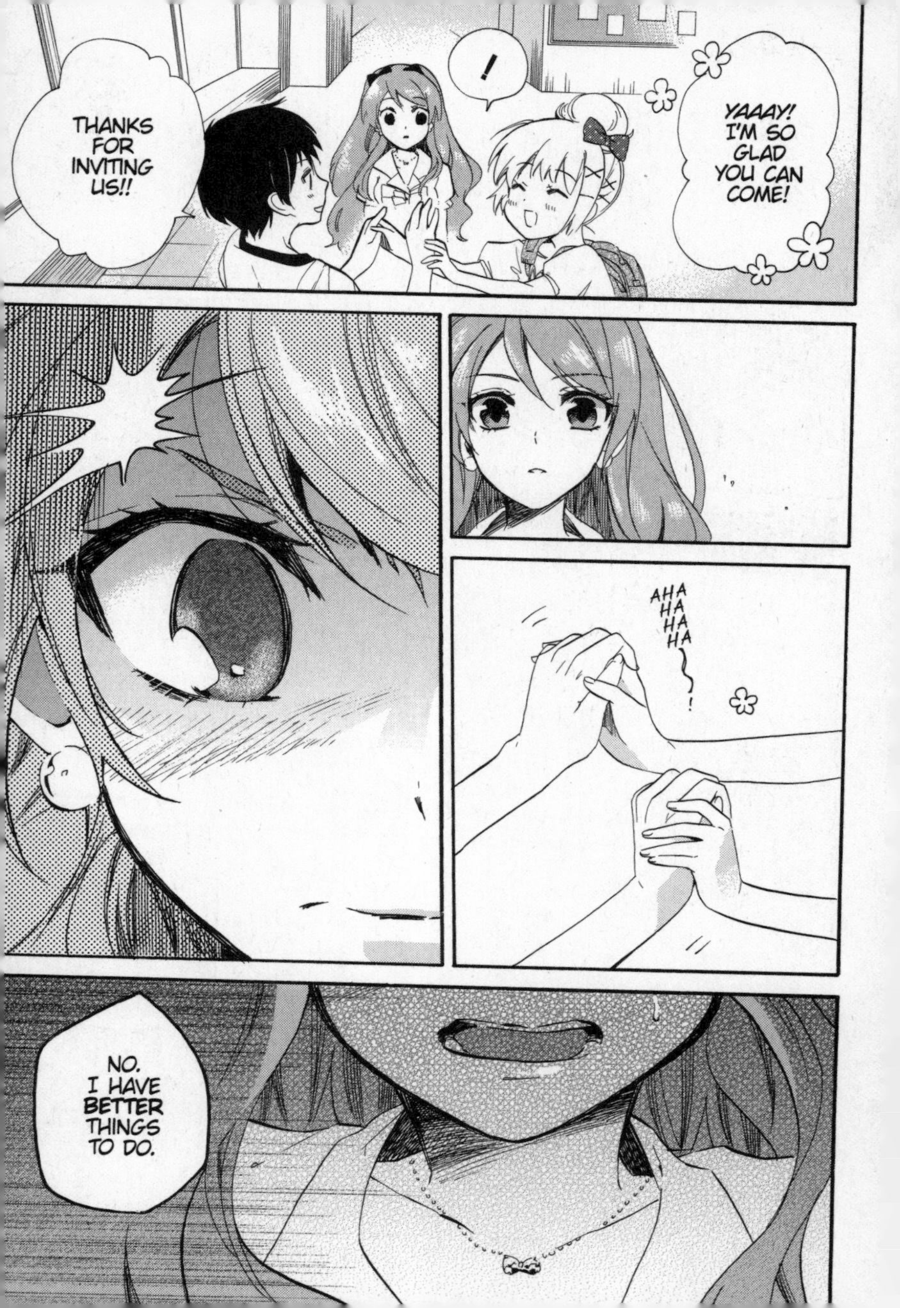
YAAAY! I'M SO GLAD YOU CAN COME!
!
THANKS FOR INVITING US!!
AHAHAHAHA~!
NO. I HAVE BETTER THINGS TO DO.

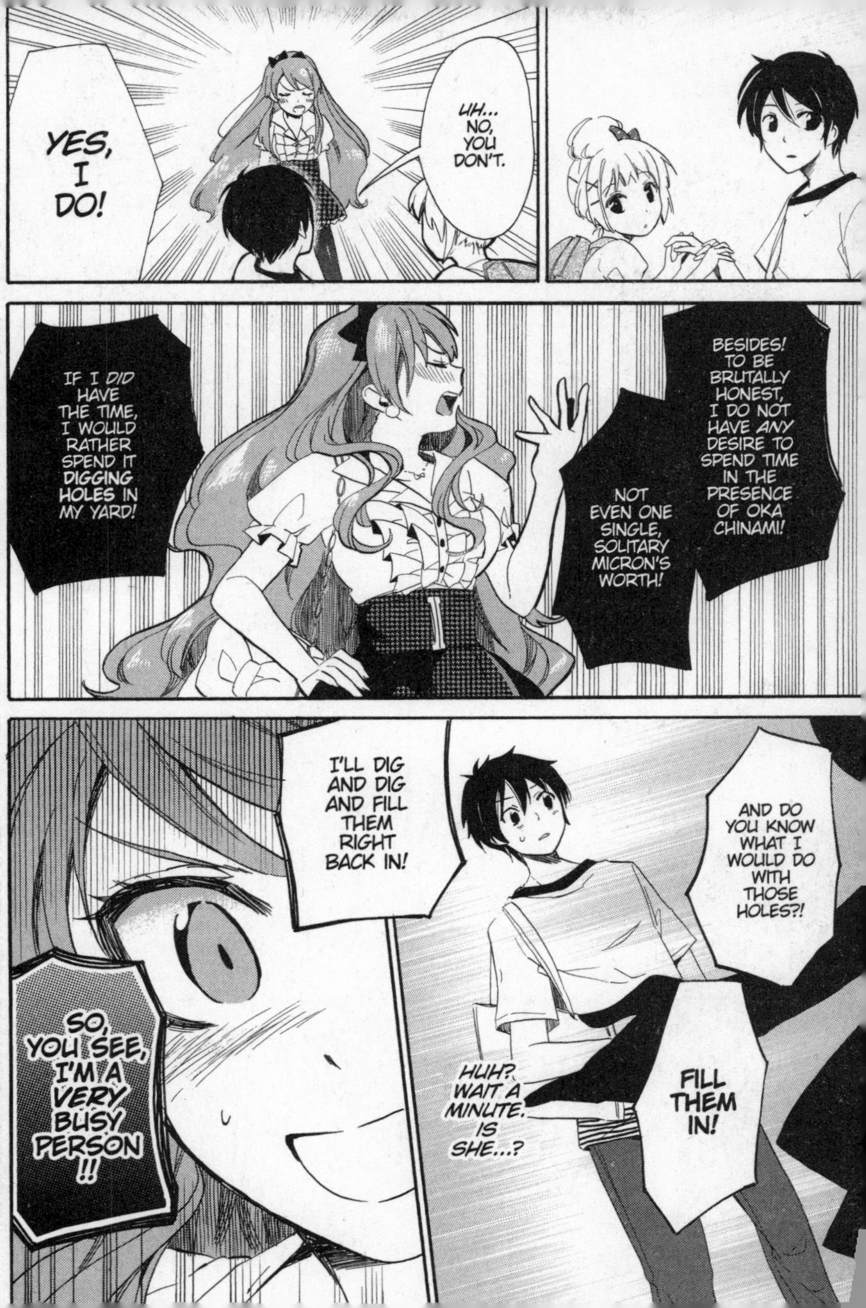
UH... NO, YOU DON'T.
YES, I DO!
BESIDES! TO BE BRUTALLY HONEST, I DO NOT HAVE ANY DESIRE TO SPEND TIME IN THE PRESENCE OF OKA CHINAMI!
NOT EVEN ONE SINGLE, SOLITARY MICRON'S WORTH!
IF I DID HAVE THE TIME, I WOULD RATHER SPEND IT DIGGING HOLES IN MY YARD!
AND DO YOU KNOW WHAT I WOULD DO WITH THOSE HOLES?!
I'LL DIG AND DIG AND FILL THEM RIGHT BACK IN!
FILL THEM IN!
HUH? WAIT A MINUTE. IS SHE...?
SO, YOU SEE, I'M A VERY BUSY PERSON!!

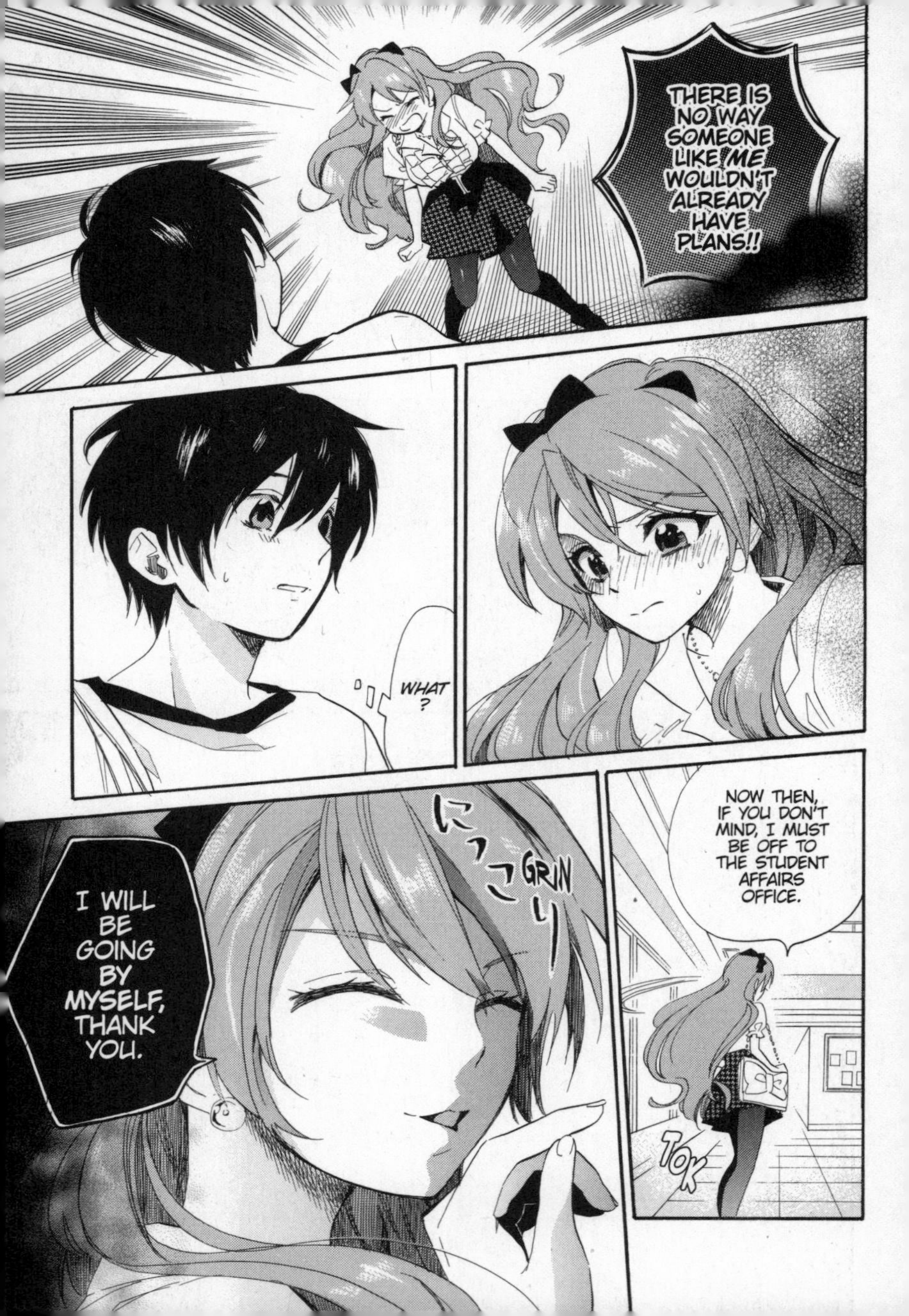
THERE IS NO WAY SOMEONE LIKE *ME* WOULDN'T ALREADY HAVE PLANS!!
WHAT?
NOW THEN, IF YOU DON'T MIND, I MUST BE OFF TO THE STUDENT AFFAIRS OFFICE.
TOK
にっこり
GRIN
I WILL BE GOING BY MYSELF, THANK YOU.

ZOOM

WAIT! LET ME GO WITH--

HARUMPH!

OH DEAR.

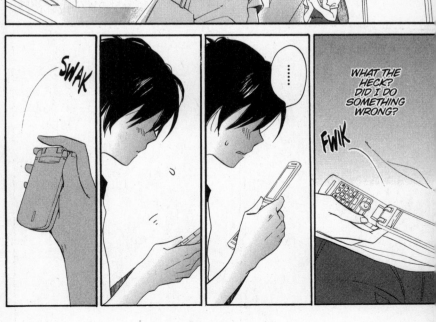

SWAK

WHAT THE HECK? DID I DO SOMETHING WRONG?

FWIK

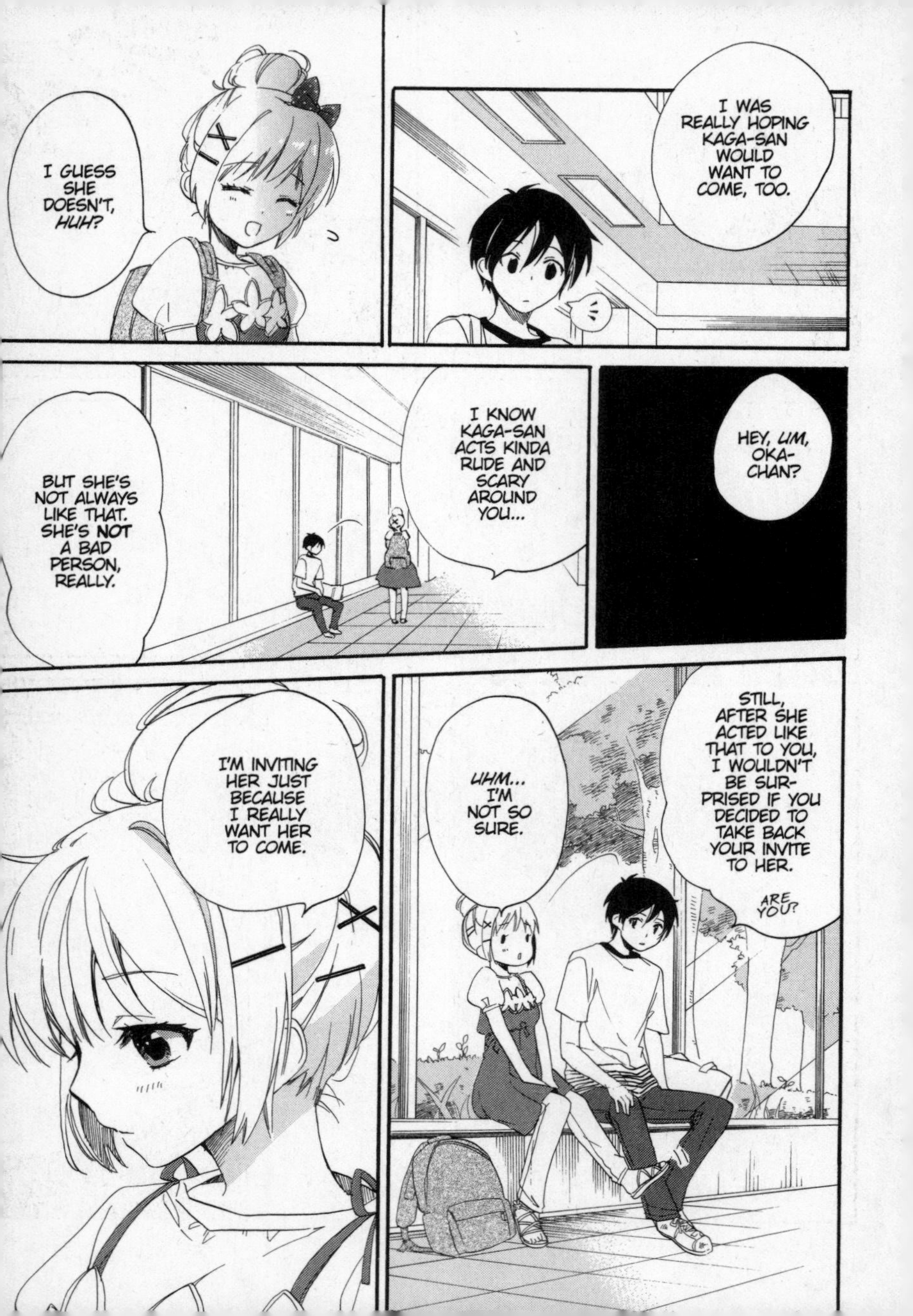
I WAS REALLY HOPING KAGA-SAN WOULD WANT TO COME, TOO.
I GUESS SHE DOESN'T, *HUH?*
HEY, *UM,* OKA-CHAN?
I KNOW KAGA-SAN ACTS KINDA RUDE AND SCARY AROUND YOU...
BUT SHE'S NOT ALWAYS LIKE THAT. SHE'S **NOT** A BAD PERSON, REALLY.
STILL, AFTER SHE ACTED LIKE THAT TO YOU, I WOULDN'T BE SUR-PRISED IF YOU DECIDED TO TAKE BACK YOUR INVITE TO HER.
ARE YOU?
UHM... I'M NOT SO SURE.
I'M INVITING HER JUST BECAUSE I REALLY WANT HER TO COME.

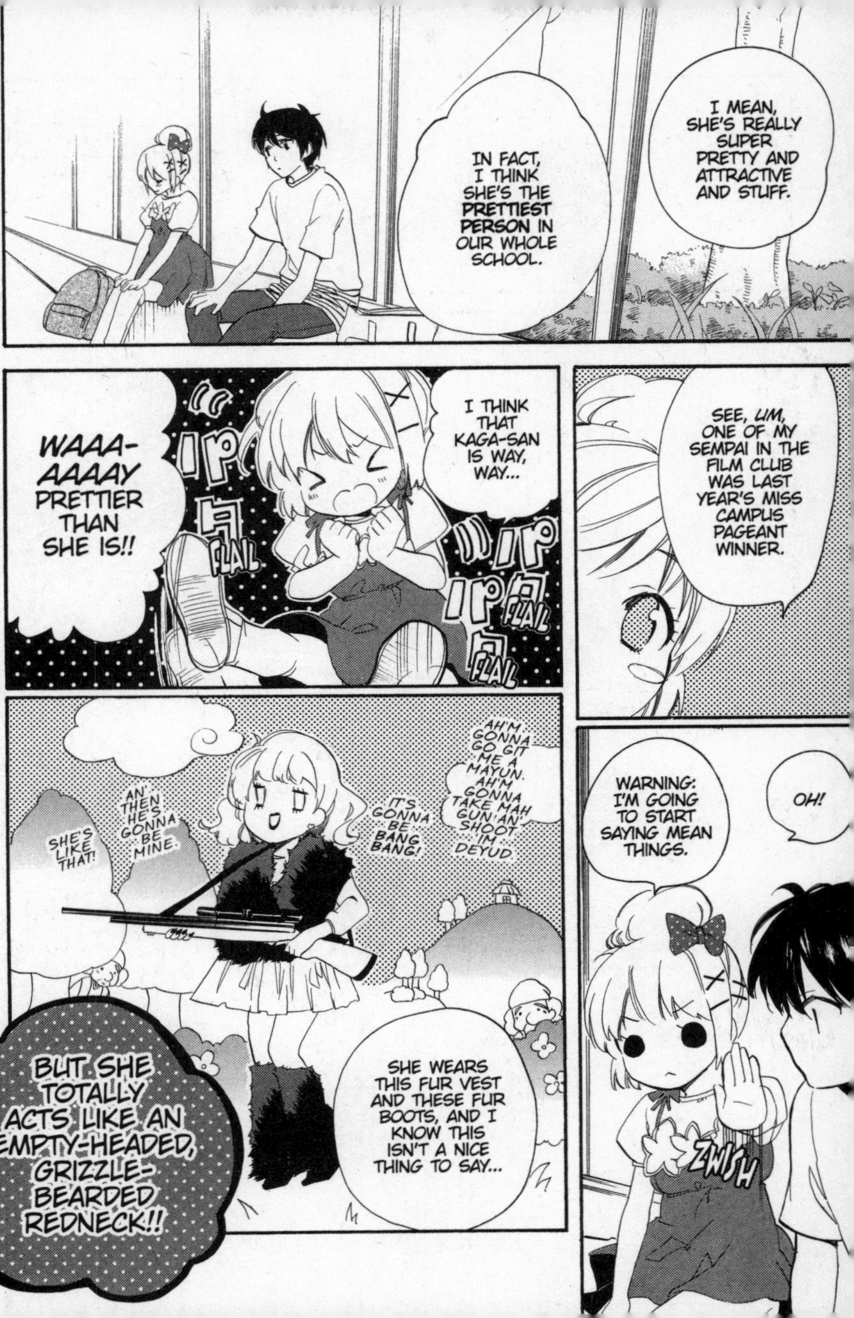
I MEAN, SHE'S REALLY SUPER PRETTY AND ATTRACTIVE AND STUFF.
IN FACT, I THINK SHE'S THE PRETTIEST PERSON IN OUR WHOLE SCHOOL.
SEE, UM, ONE OF MY SEMPAI IN THE FILM CLUB WAS LAST YEAR'S MISS CAMPUS PAGEANT WINNER.
I THINK THAT KAGA-SAN IS WAY, WAY...
WAAAAAAAY PRETTIER THAN SHE IS!!
FLAIL
FLAIL
FLAIL
OH!
WARNING: I'M GOING TO START SAYING MEAN THINGS.
ZWISH
AH'M GONNA GO GIT ME A MAYUN. AH'M GONNA TAKE MAH GUN AN' SHOOT 'IM DEYUD
IT'S GONNA BE BANG BANG!
AN' THEN HE'S GONNA BE MINE.
SHE'S LIKE THAT!
SHE WEARS THIS FUR VEST AND THESE FUR BOOTS, AND I KNOW THIS ISN'T A NICE THING TO SAY...
BUT SHE TOTALLY ACTS LIKE AN EMPTY-HEADED, GRIZZLE-BEARDED REDNECK!!

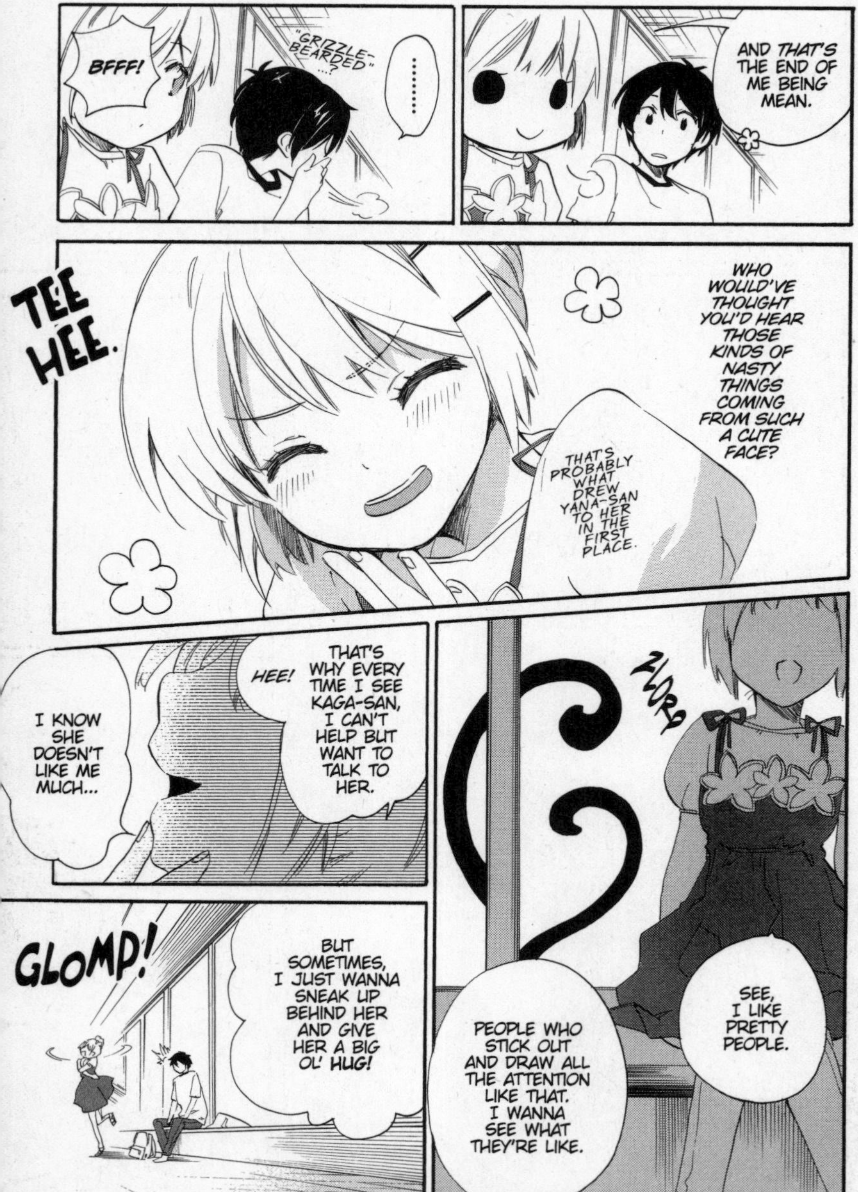
AND THAT'S THE END OF ME BEING MEAN.
BFFF!
"GRIZZLE-BEARDED"...?
....
WHO WOULD'VE THOUGHT YOU'D HEAR THOSE KINDS OF NASTY THINGS COMING FROM SUCH A CUTE FACE?
THAT'S PROBABLY WHAT DREW YANA-SAN TO HER IN THE FIRST PLACE.
TEE HEE.
ZLORP
SEE, I LIKE PRETTY PEOPLE.
PEOPLE WHO STICK OUT AND DRAW ALL THE ATTENTION LIKE THAT. I WANNA SEE WHAT THEY'RE LIKE.
HEE!
THAT'S WHY EVERY TIME I SEE KAGA-SAN, I CAN'T HELP BUT WANT TO TALK TO HER.
I KNOW SHE DOESN'T LIKE ME MUCH...
BUT SOMETIMES, I JUST WANNA SNEAK UP BEHIND HER AND GIVE HER A BIG OL' HUG!
GLOMP!

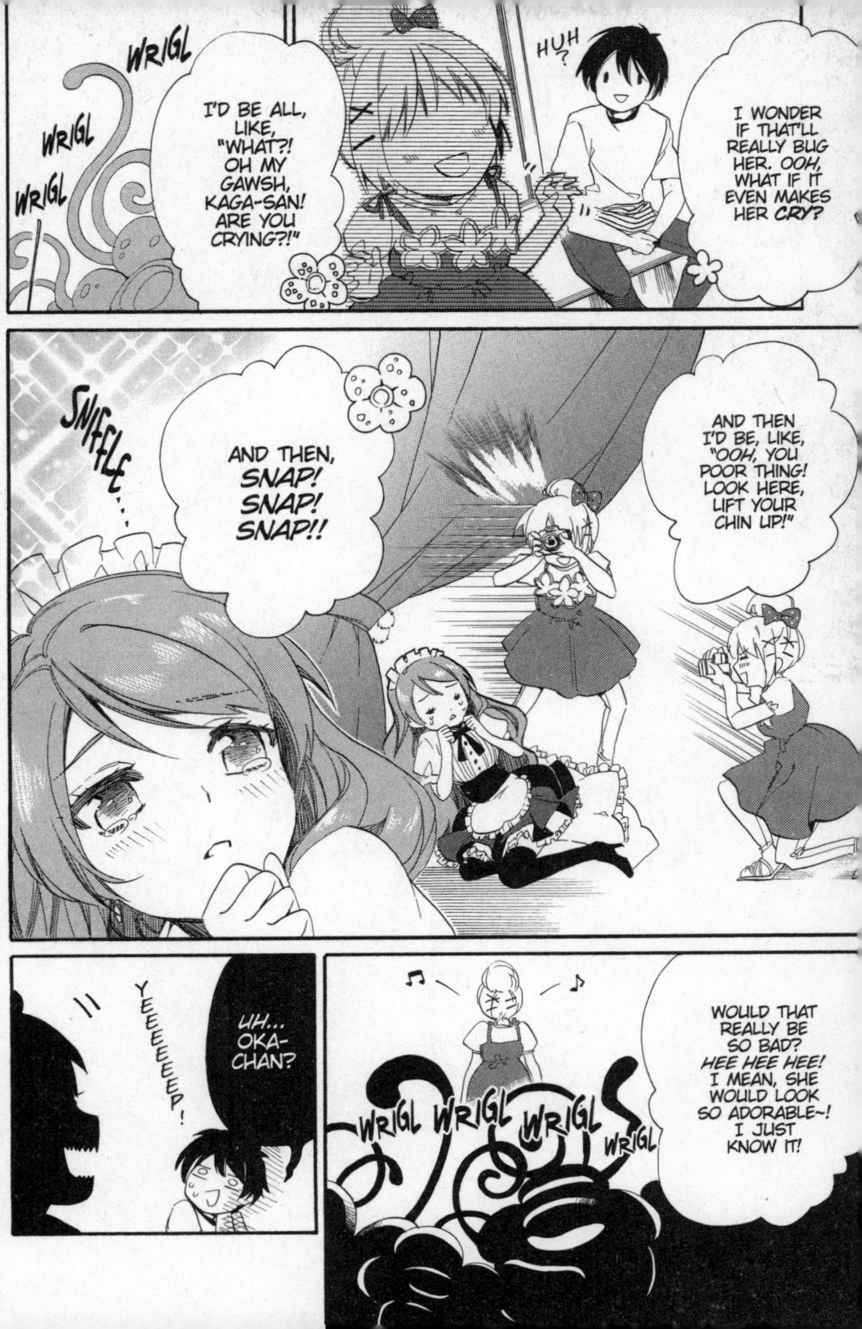
I WONDER IF THAT'LL REALLY BUG HER. *OOH*, WHAT IF IT EVEN MAKES HER ***CRY?***
HUH?
I'D BE ALL, LIKE, "WHAT?! OH MY GAWSH, KAGA-SAN! ARE YOU CRYING?!"
WRIGL
WRIGL
WRIGL
AND THEN I'D BE, LIKE, "*OOH*, YOU POOR THING! LOOK HERE, LIFT YOUR CHIN UP!"
AND THEN, ***SNAP! SNAP! SNAP!!***
SNIFFLE...
WOULD THAT REALLY BE SO BAD? *HEE HEE HEE!* I MEAN, SHE WOULD LOOK SO ADORABLE~! I JUST KNOW IT!
WRIGL WRIGL WRIGL WRIGL
UH... OKA-CHAN?
YEEEEEEP!

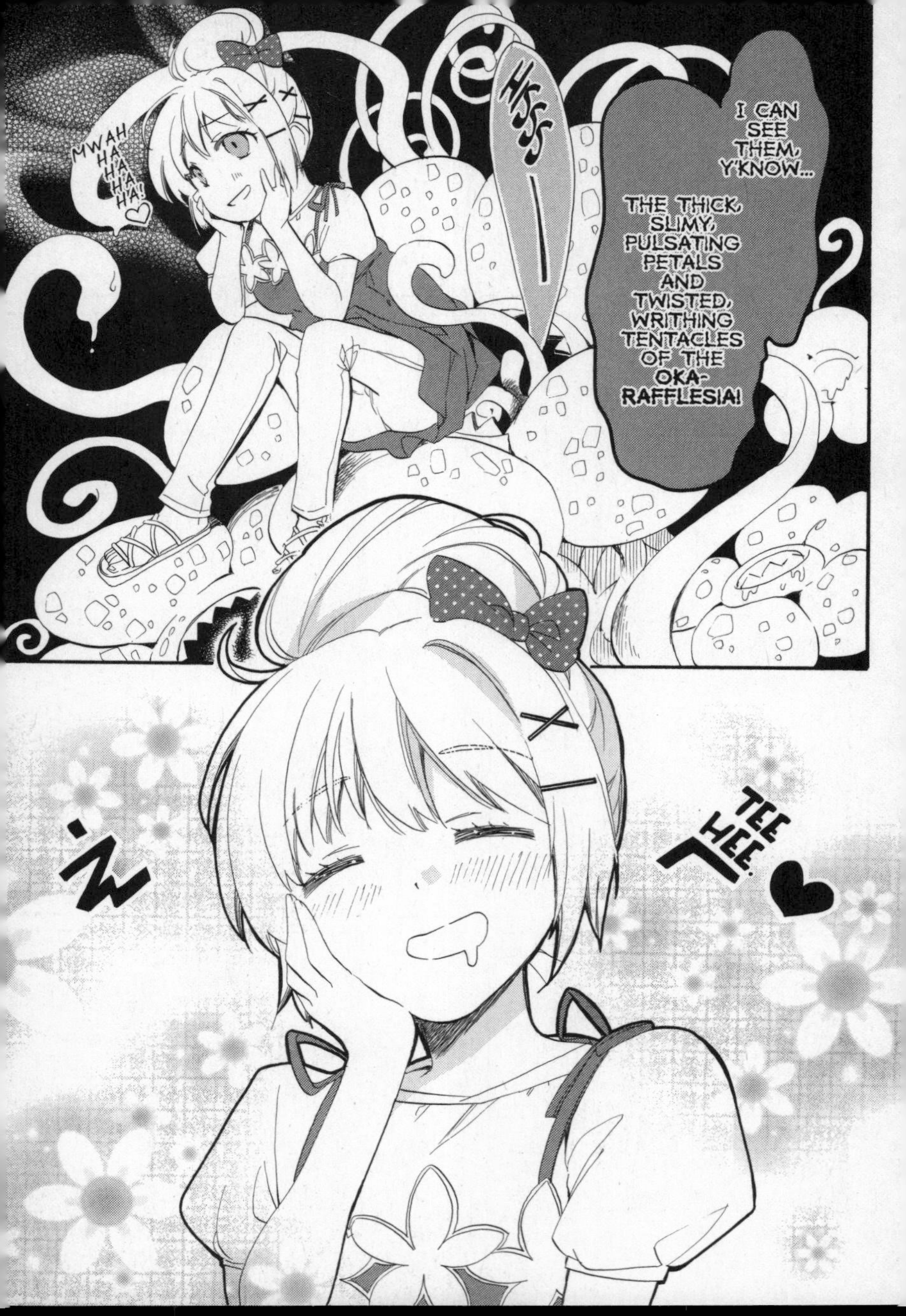
I CAN SEE THEM, Y'KNOW...
THE THICK, SLIMY, PULSATING PETALS AND TWISTED, WRITHING TENTACLES OF THE OKA-RAFFLESIA!
HSSS—
MWAH HA HA HA HA!
TEE HEE
N

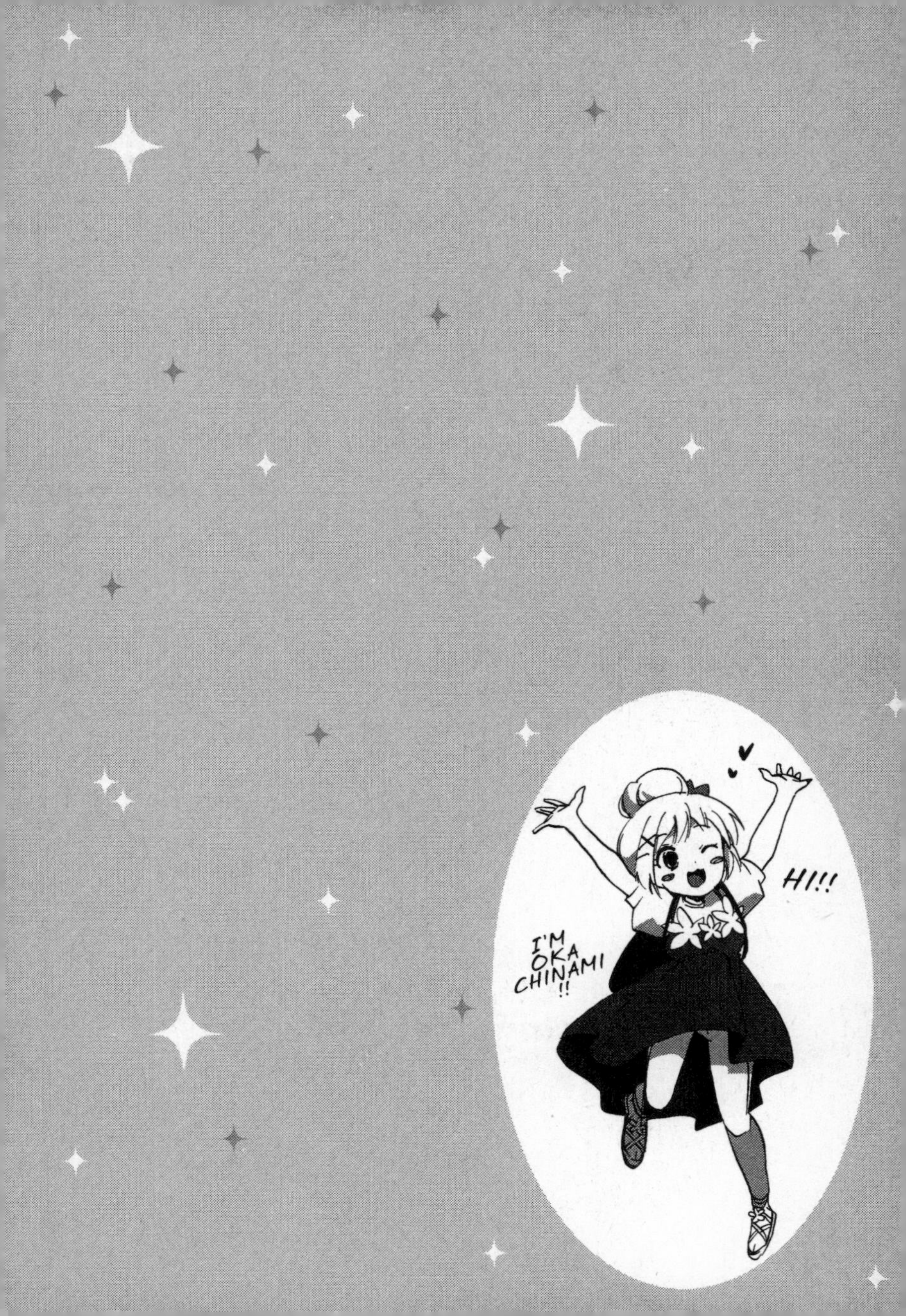
HI!!
I'M OKA CHINAMI !!

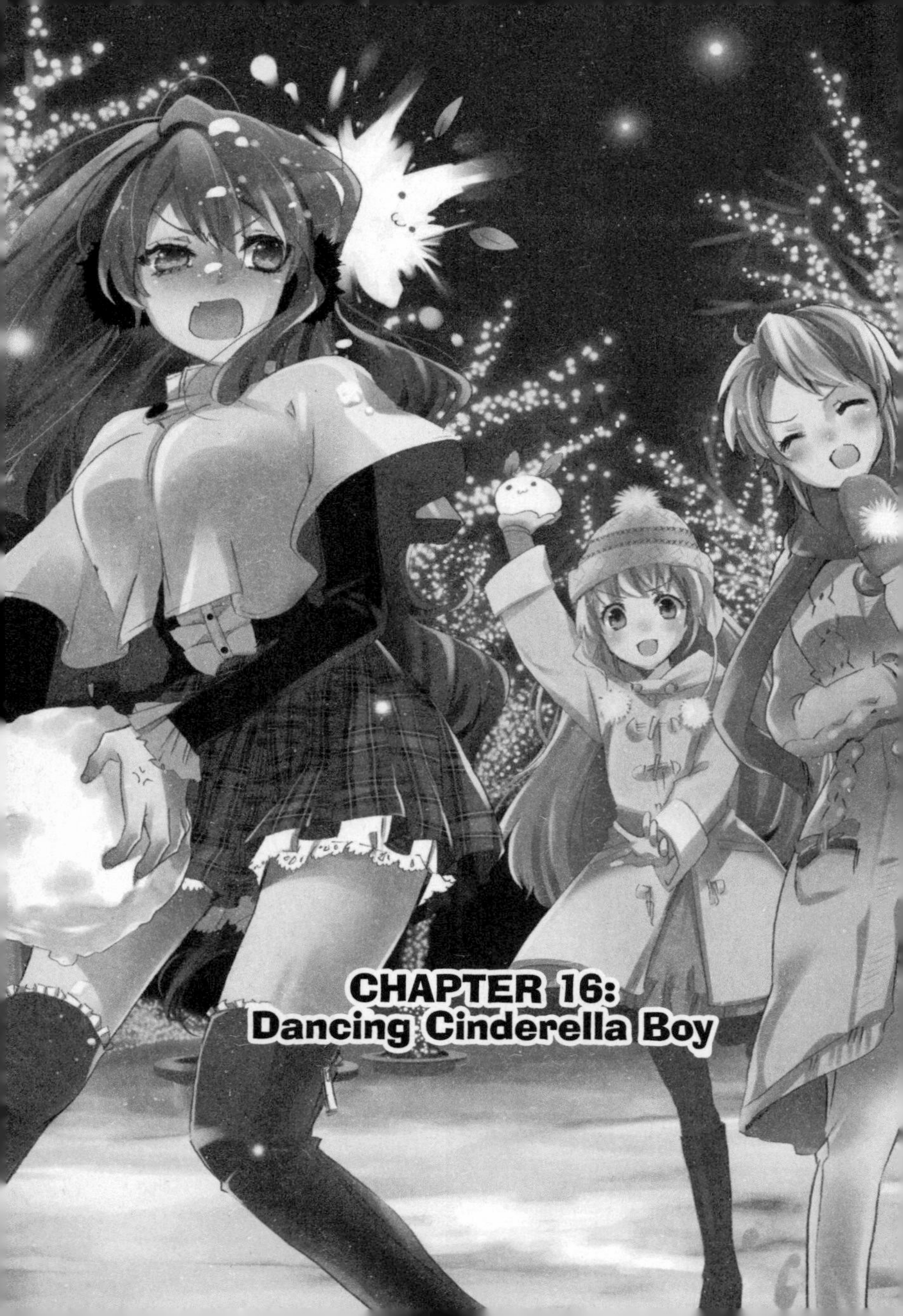
CHAPTER 16:
Dancing Cinderella Boy

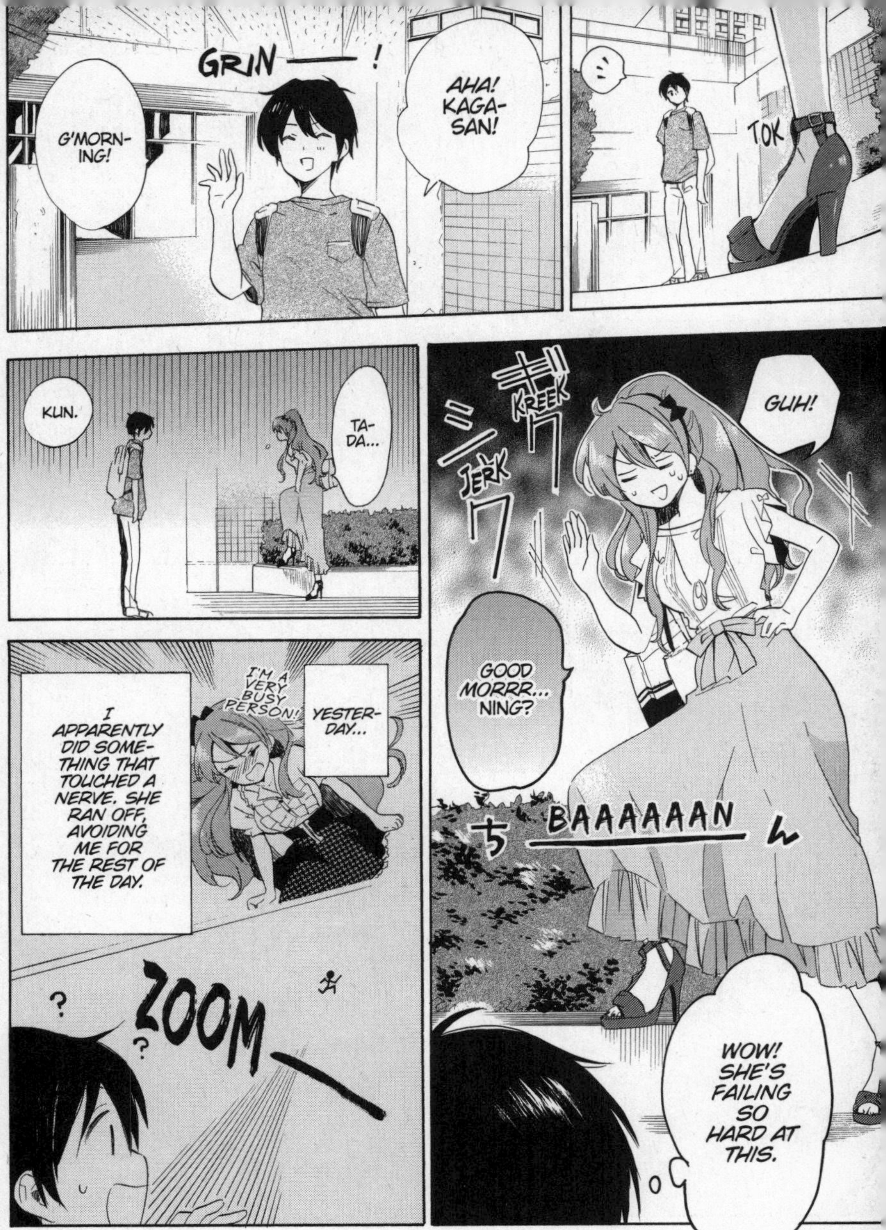

TOK
AHA! KAGA-SAN!
GRIN—!
G'MORNING!
KREEK
JERK
GUH!
GOOD MORRR... NING?
BAAAAAAN
WOW! SHE'S FAILING SO HARD AT THIS.
TA-DA...
KUN.
YESTERDAY...
I'M A VERY BUSY PERSON!
I APPARENTLY DID SOMETHING THAT TOUCHED A NERVE. SHE RAN OFF, AVOIDING ME FOR THE REST OF THE DAY.
ZOOM

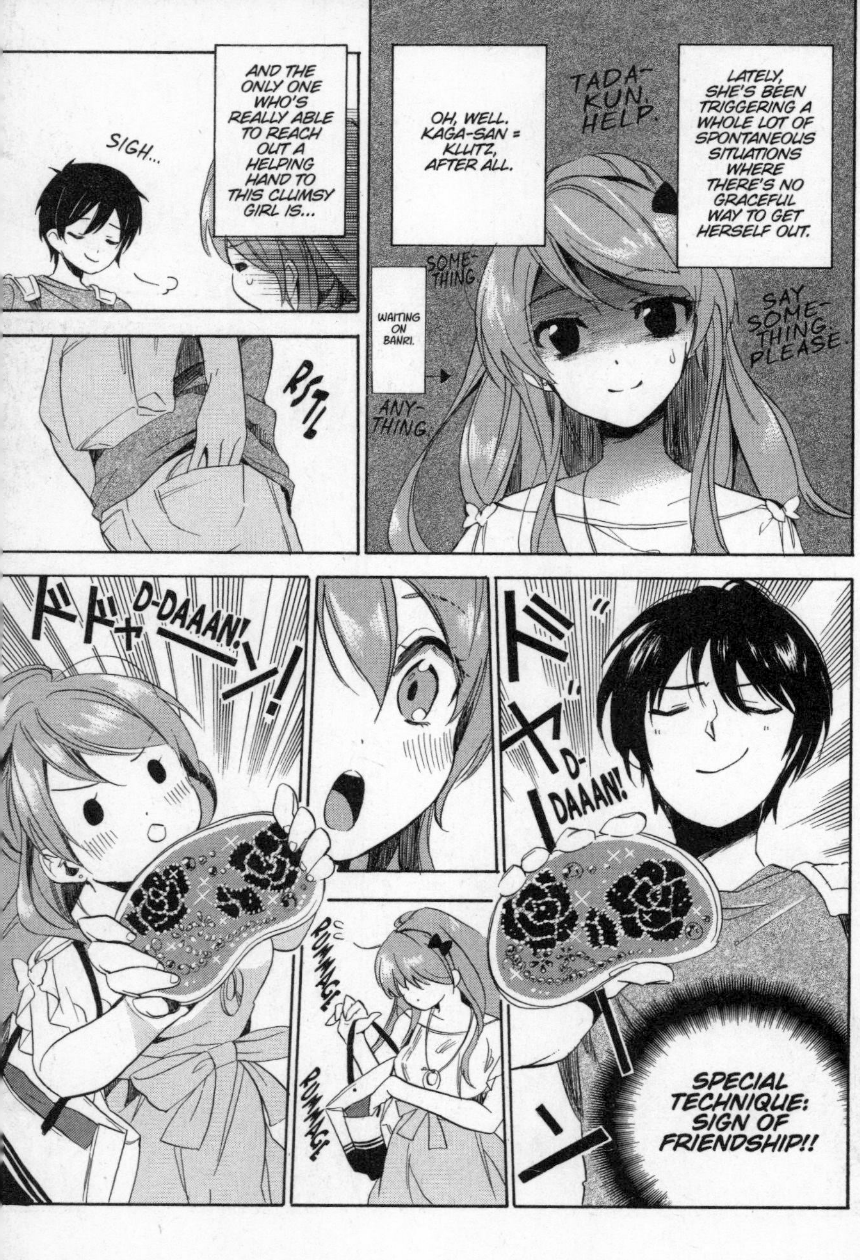
LATELY, SHE'S BEEN TRIGGERING A WHOLE LOT OF SPONTANEOUS SITUATIONS WHERE THERE'S NO GRACEFUL WAY TO GET HERSELF OUT.
TADA-KUN, HELP.
OH, WELL. KAGA-SAN = KLUTZ, AFTER ALL.
SAY SOMETHING, PLEASE.
SOMETHING.
WAITING ON BANRI.
ANYTHING.
AND THE ONLY ONE WHO'S REALLY ABLE TO REACH OUT A HELPING HAND TO THIS CLUMSY GIRL IS...
SIGH...
RSTL
D-DAAAN!
SPECIAL TECHNIQUE: SIGN OF FRIENDSHIP!!
RUMMAGE RUMMAGE
D-DAAAN!

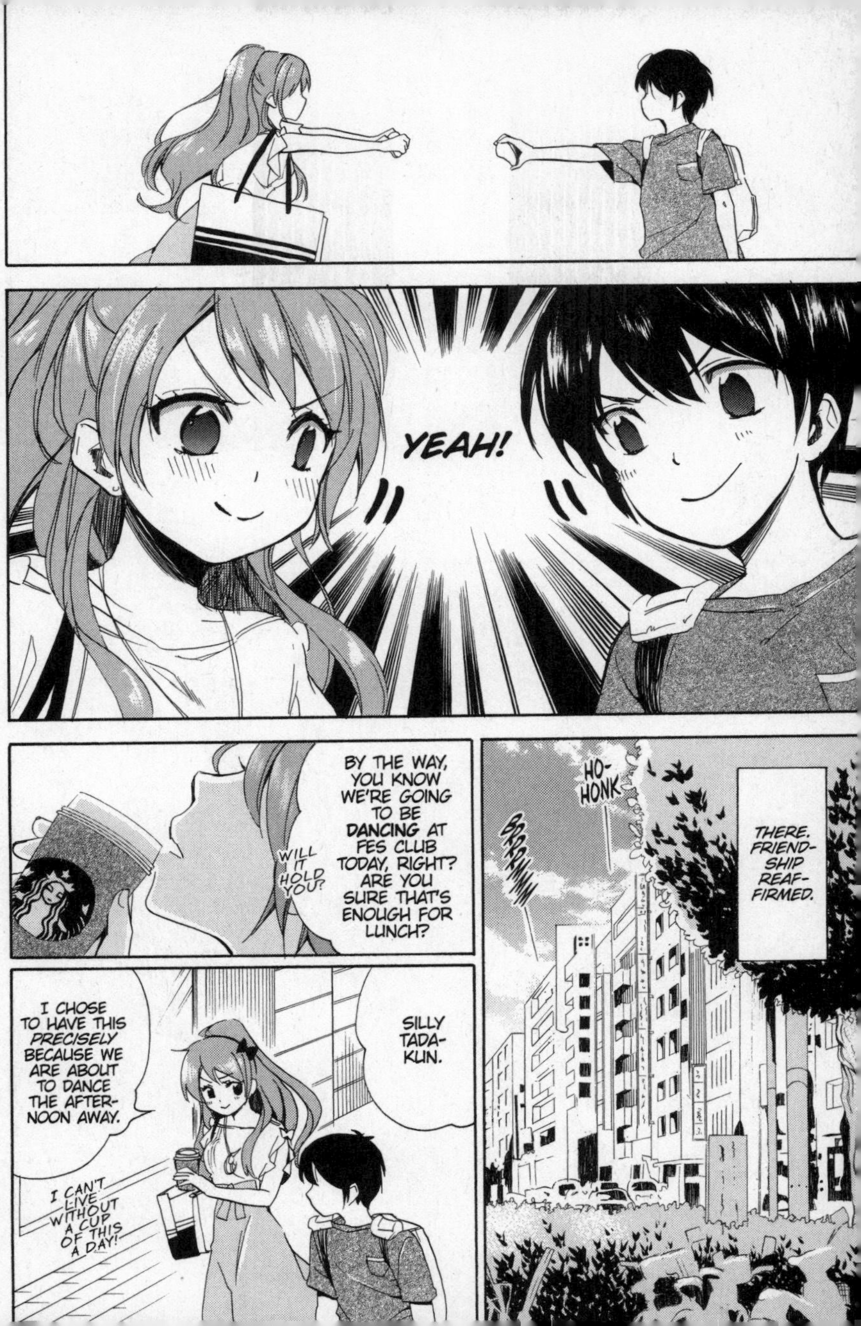

YEAH!
HO-HONK
BRRRMMMM
THERE. FRIEND-SHIP REAF-FIRMED.
BY THE WAY, YOU KNOW WE'RE GOING TO BE **DANCING** AT FES CLUB TODAY, RIGHT? ARE YOU SURE THAT'S ENOUGH FOR LUNCH?
WILL IT HOLD YOU?
SILLY TADA-KUN.
I CHOSE TO HAVE THIS *PRECISELY* BECAUSE WE ARE ABOUT TO DANCE THE AFTER-NOON AWAY.
I CAN'T LIVE WITHOUT A CUP OF THIS A DAY!

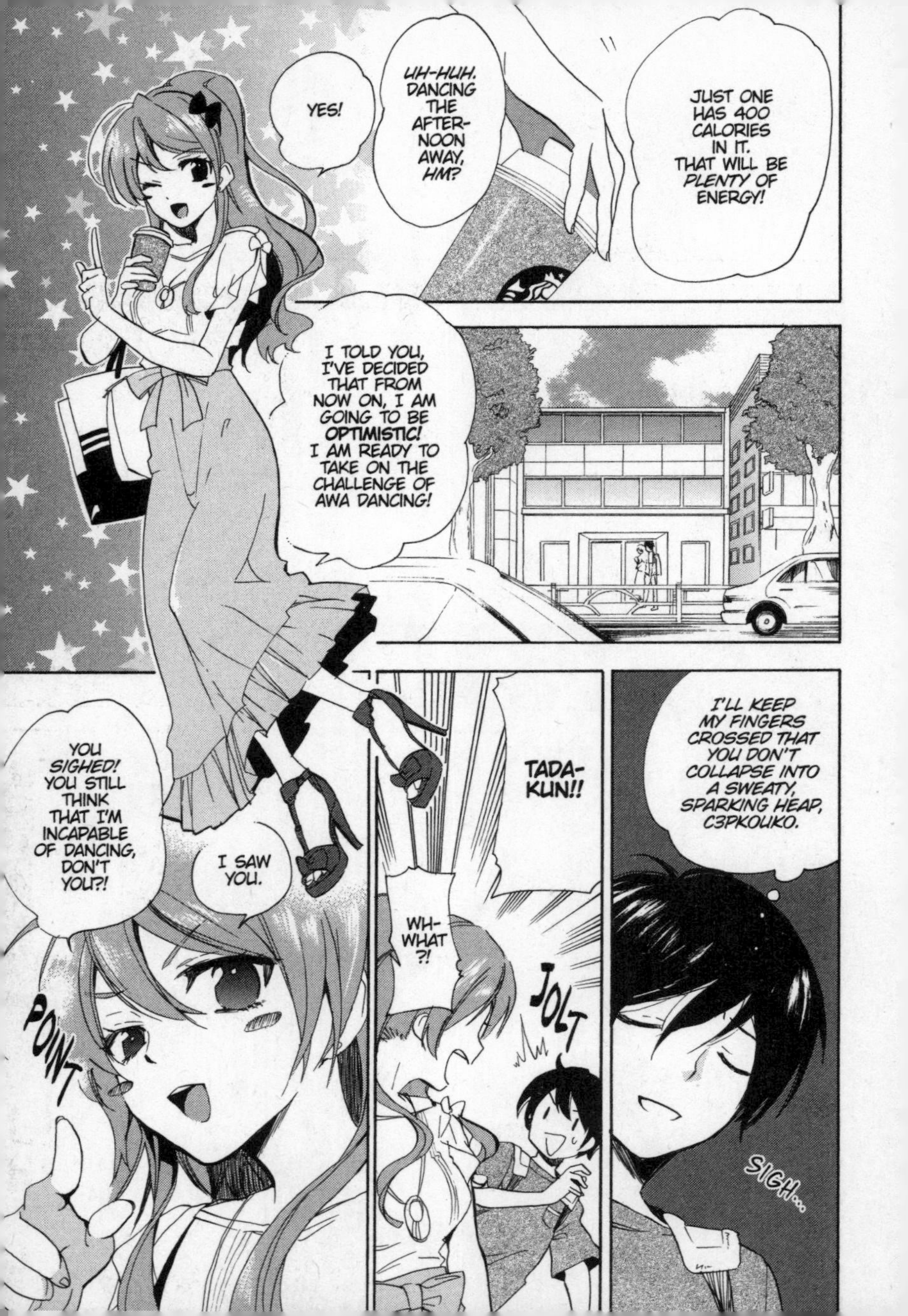
JUST ONE HAS 400 CALORIES IN IT. THAT WILL BE PLENTY OF ENERGY!
UH-HUH. DANCING THE AFTER-NOON AWAY, HM?
YES!
I TOLD YOU, I'VE DECIDED THAT FROM NOW ON, I AM GOING TO BE OPTIMISTIC! I AM READY TO TAKE ON THE CHALLENGE OF AWA DANCING!
I'LL KEEP MY FINGERS CROSSED THAT YOU DON'T COLLAPSE INTO A SWEATY, SPARKING HEAP, C3PKOUKO.
SIGH...
TADA-KUN!!
WH-WHAT?!
JOLT
YOU SIGHED! YOU STILL THINK THAT I'M INCAPABLE OF DANCING, DON'T YOU?!
I SAW YOU.
POINT

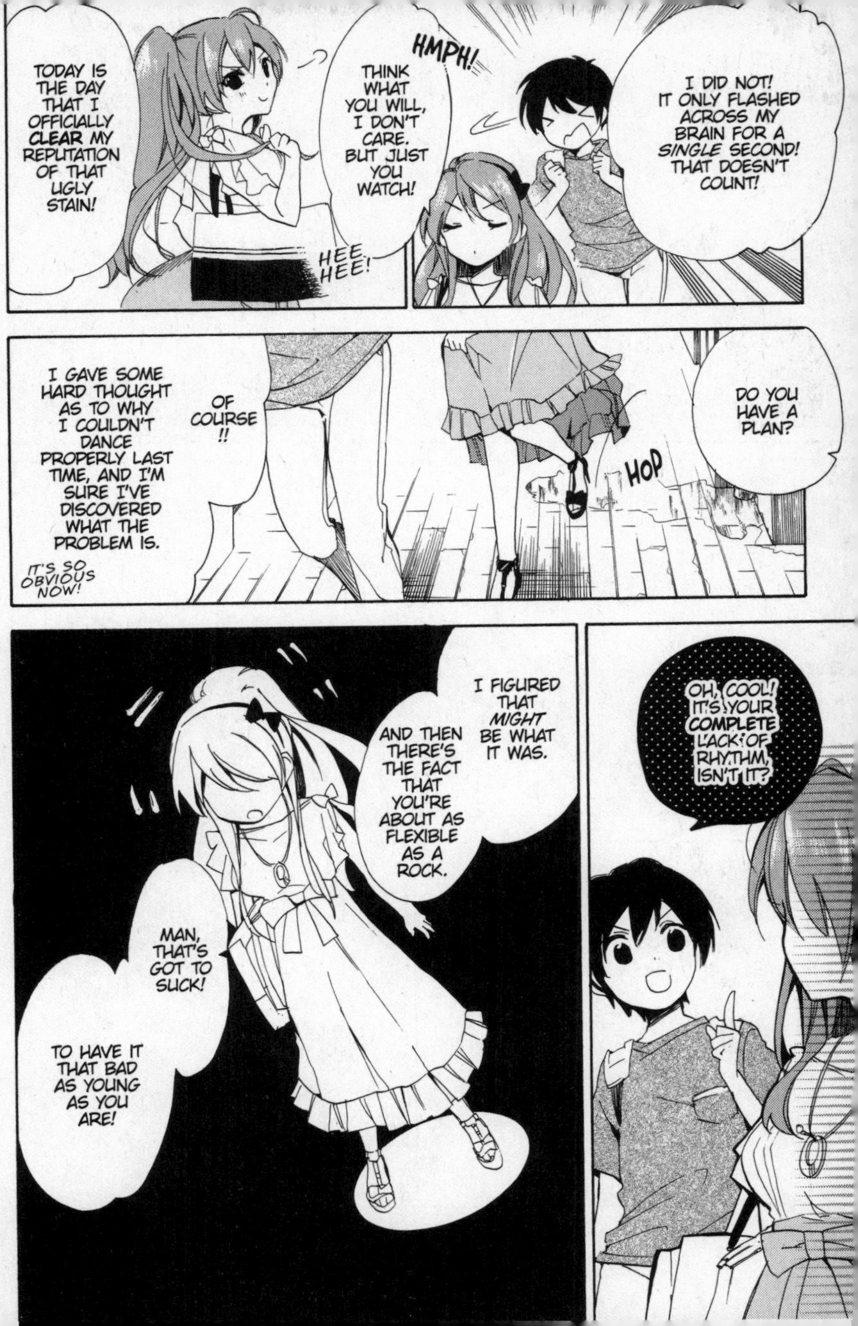
I DID NOT! IT ONLY FLASHED ACROSS MY BRAIN FOR A *SINGLE* SECOND! THAT DOESN'T COUNT!
HMPH!
THINK WHAT YOU WILL, I DON'T CARE. BUT JUST YOU WATCH!
HEE HEE!
TODAY IS THE DAY THAT I OFFICIALLY **CLEAR** MY REPUTATION OF THAT UGLY STAIN!
DO YOU HAVE A PLAN?
HOP
OF COURSE!!
I GAVE SOME HARD THOUGHT AS TO WHY I COULDN'T DANCE PROPERLY LAST TIME, AND I'M SURE I'VE DISCOVERED WHAT THE PROBLEM IS.
IT'S SO OBVIOUS NOW!
OH, COOL! IT'S YOUR COMPLETE LACK OF RHYTHM, ISN'T IT?
I FIGURED THAT *MIGHT* BE WHAT IT WAS.
AND THEN THERE'S THE FACT THAT YOU'RE ABOUT AS FLEXIBLE AS A ROCK.
MAN, THAT'S GOT TO SUCK!
TO HAVE IT THAT BAD AS YOUNG AS YOU ARE!

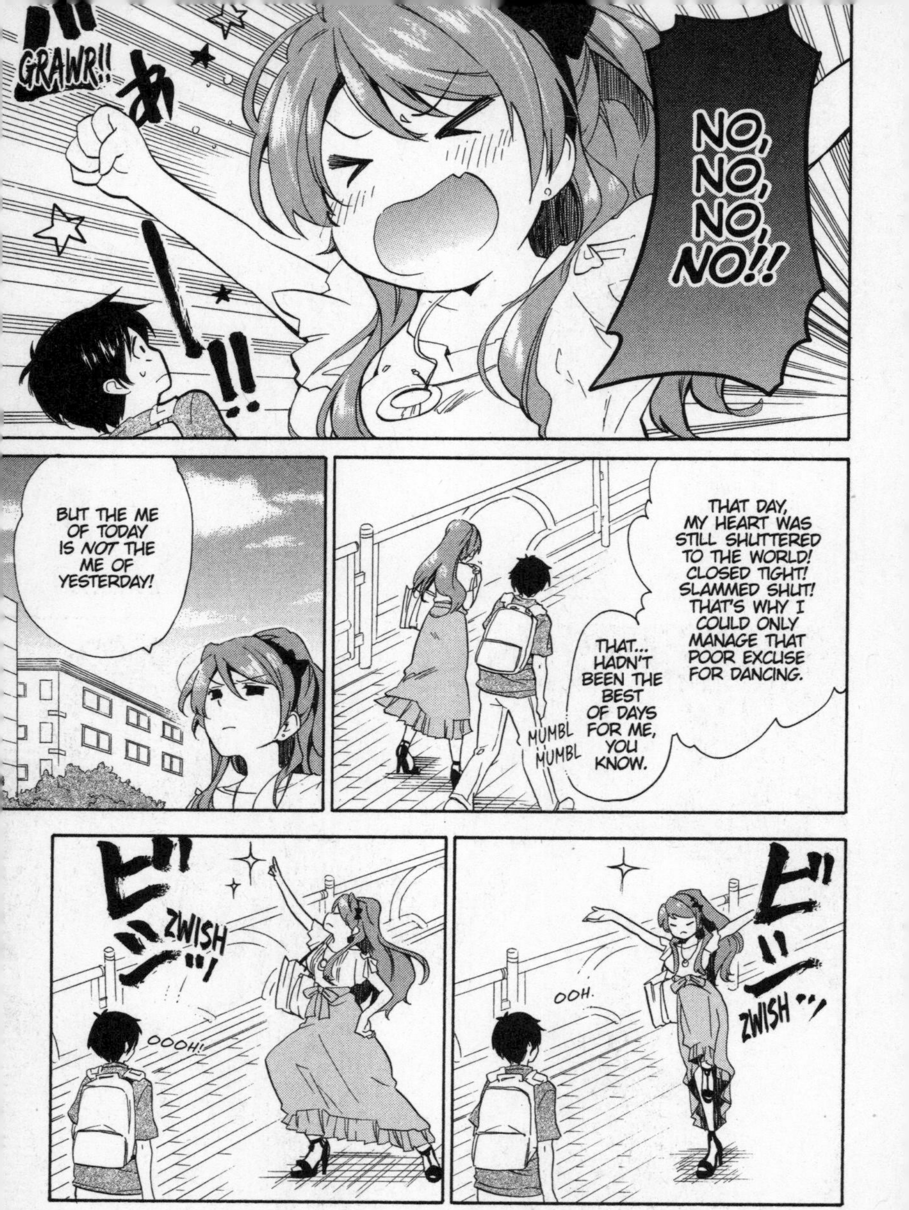
NO, NO, NO, NO!!
GRAWR!!
THAT DAY, MY HEART WAS STILL SHUTTERED TO THE WORLD! CLOSED TIGHT! SLAMMED SHUT! THAT'S WHY I COULD ONLY MANAGE THAT POOR EXCUSE FOR DANCING.
THAT... HADN'T BEEN THE BEST OF DAYS FOR ME, YOU KNOW.
MUMBL MUMBL
BUT THE ME OF TODAY IS *NOT* THE ME OF YESTERDAY!
OOH.
ZWISH
ZWISH
OOOH!

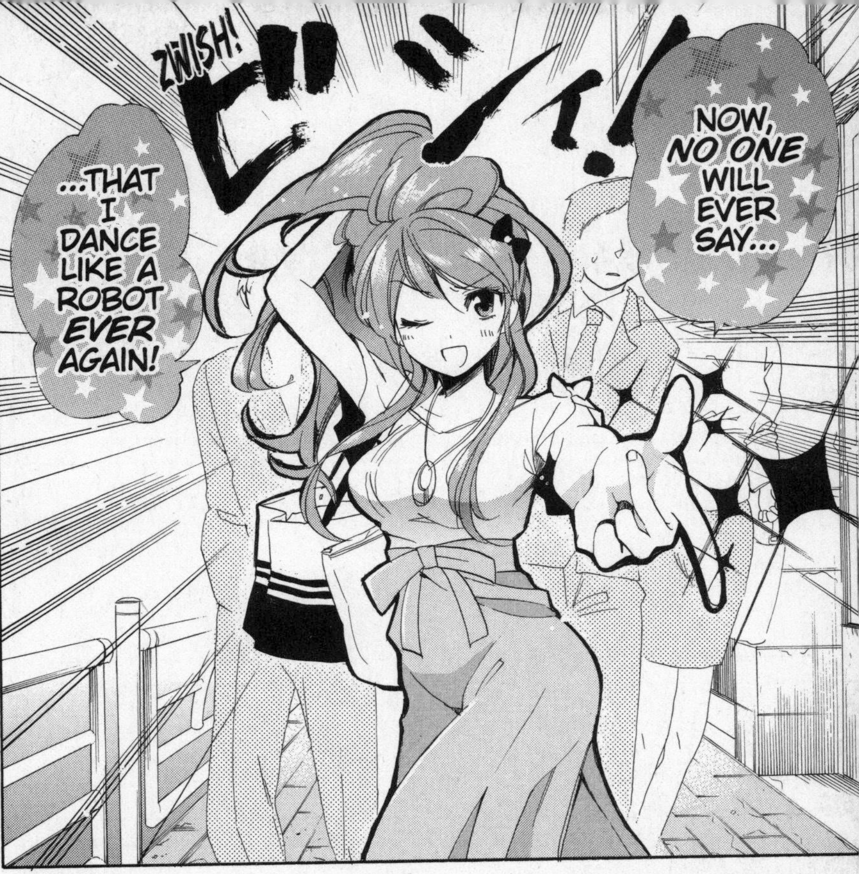
ZWISH!
NOW, NO ONE WILL EVER SAY...
...THAT I DANCE LIKE A ROBOT EVER AGAIN!
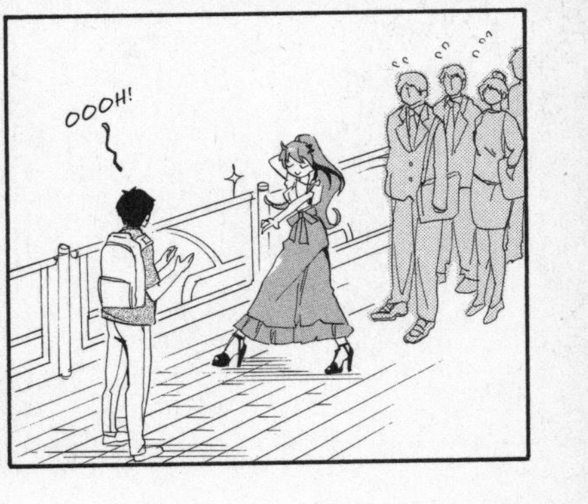
OOOH!
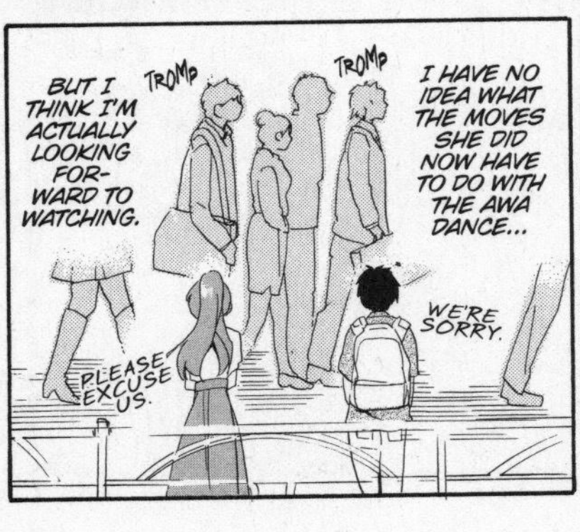
TROMP
I HAVE NO IDEA WHAT THE MOVES SHE DID NOW HAVE TO DO WITH THE AWA DANCE...
TROMP
BUT I THINK I'M ACTUALLY LOOKING FOR-WARD TO WATCHING.
WE'RE SORRY.
PLEASE EXCUSE US.

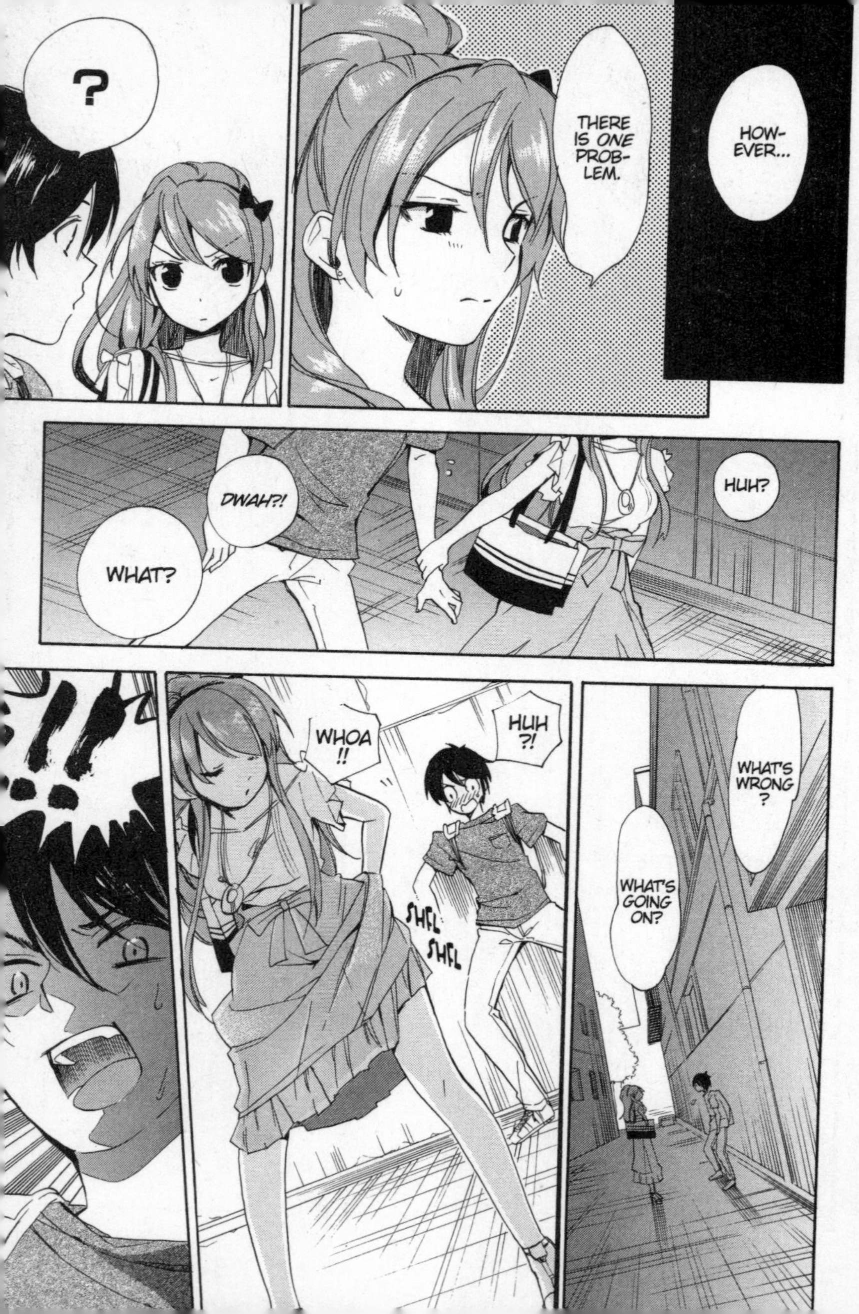
HOW-EVER...
THERE IS ONE PROB-LEM.
?
HUH?
DWAH?!
WHAT?
WHAT'S WRONG?
WHAT'S GOING ON?
HUH?!
WHOA!!
SHFL SHFL
!!

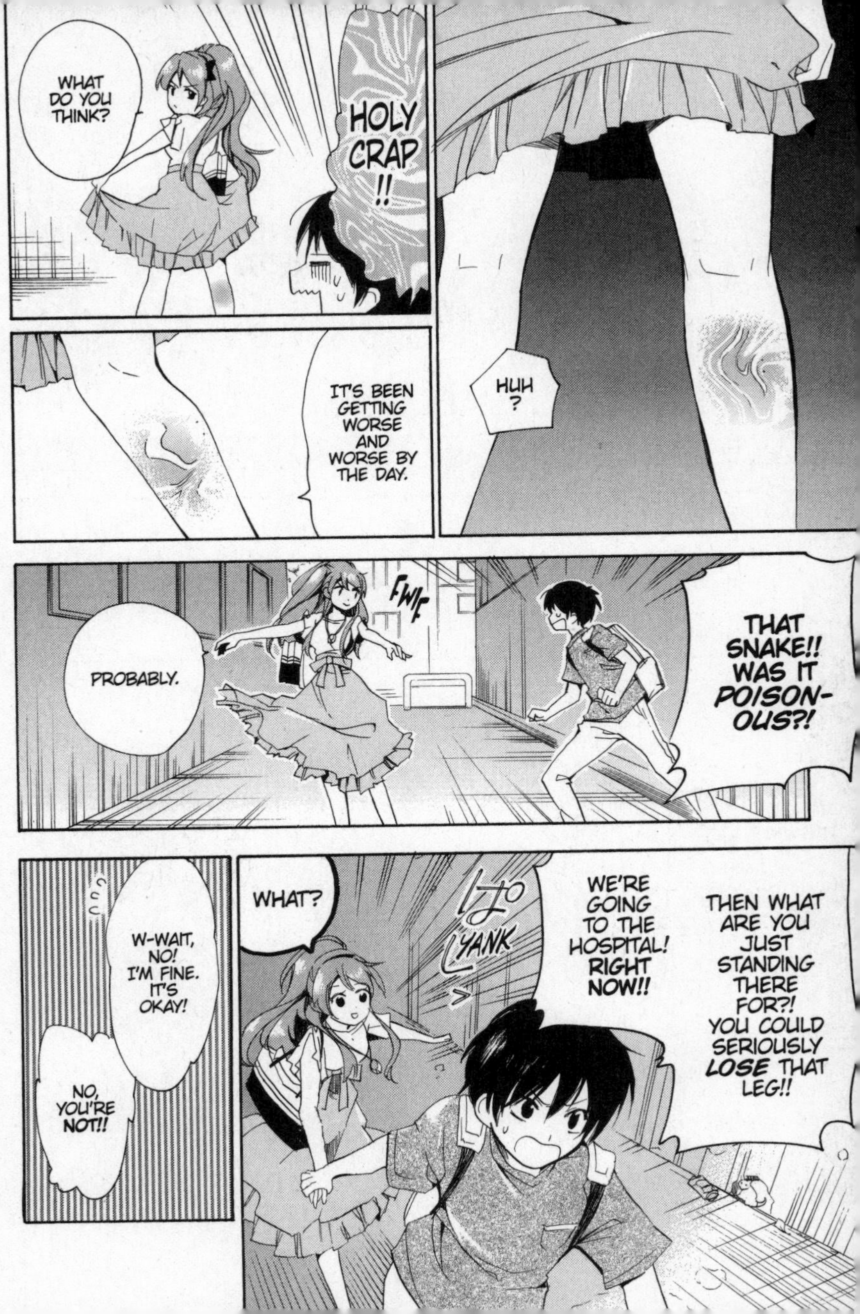
HUH ?
HOLY CRAP !!
WHAT DO YOU THINK?
IT'S BEEN GETTING WORSE AND WORSE BY THE DAY.
THAT SNAKE!! WAS IT POISON-OUS?!
FWIP
PROBABLY.
THEN WHAT ARE YOU JUST STANDING THERE FOR?! YOU COULD SERIOUSLY LOSE THAT LEG!!
WE'RE GOING TO THE HOSPITAL! RIGHT NOW!!
YANK
WHAT?
W-WAIT, NO! I'M FINE. IT'S OKAY!
NO, YOU'RE NOT!!

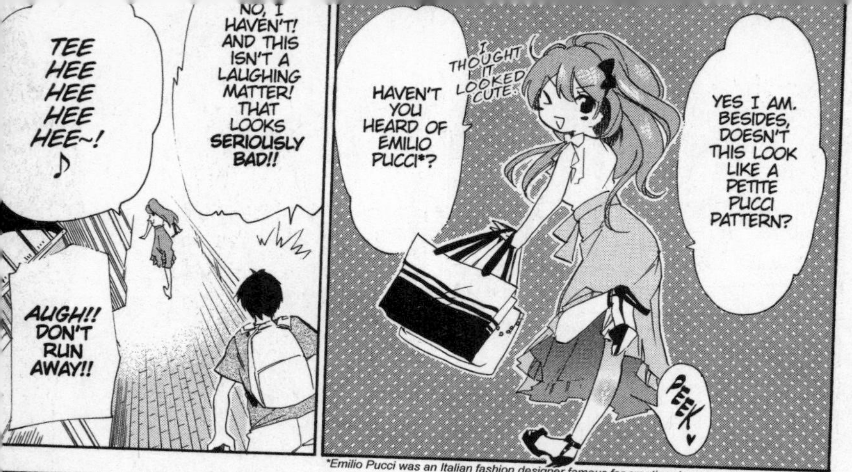
YES I AM. BESIDES, DOESN'T THIS LOOK LIKE A PETITE PUCCI PATTERN?
I THOUGHT IT LOOKED CUTE.
HAVEN'T YOU HEARD OF EMILIO PUCCI*?
PEEK ♥
NO, I HAVEN'T! AND THIS ISN'T A LAUGHING MATTER! THAT LOOKS SERIOUSLY BAD!!
TEE HEE HEE HEE HEE~! ♪
AUGH!! DON'T RUN AWAY!!

*Emilio Pucci was an Italian fashion designer famous for creating dresses with geometric prints.

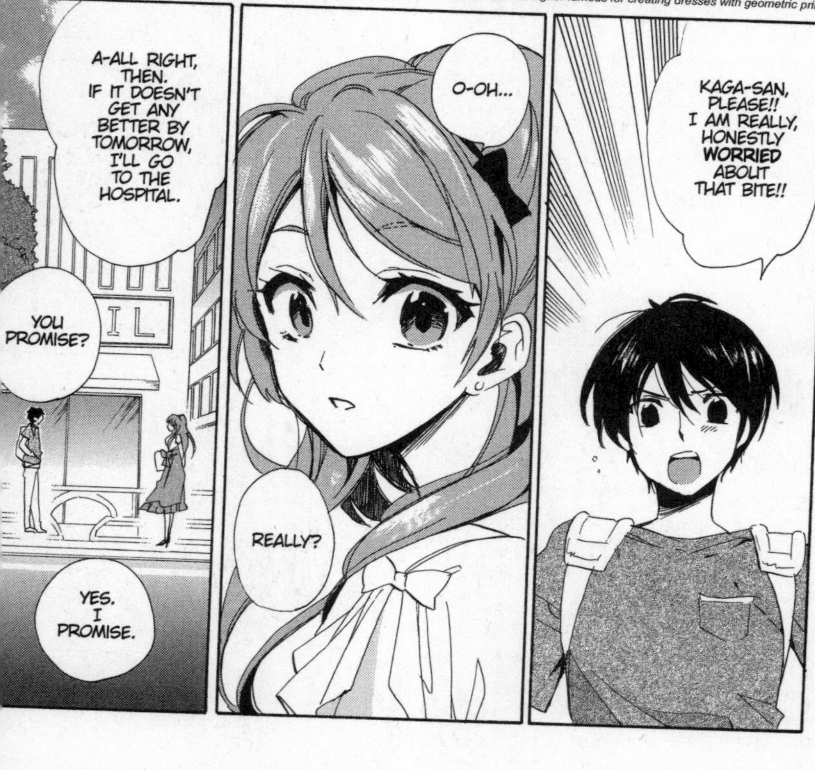
KAGA-SAN, PLEASE!! I AM REALLY, HONESTLY WORRIED ABOUT THAT BITE!!
O-OH...
REALLY?
A-ALL RIGHT, THEN. IF IT DOESN'T GET ANY BETTER BY TOMORROW, I'LL GO TO THE HOSPITAL.
YOU PROMISE?
YES. I PROMISE.

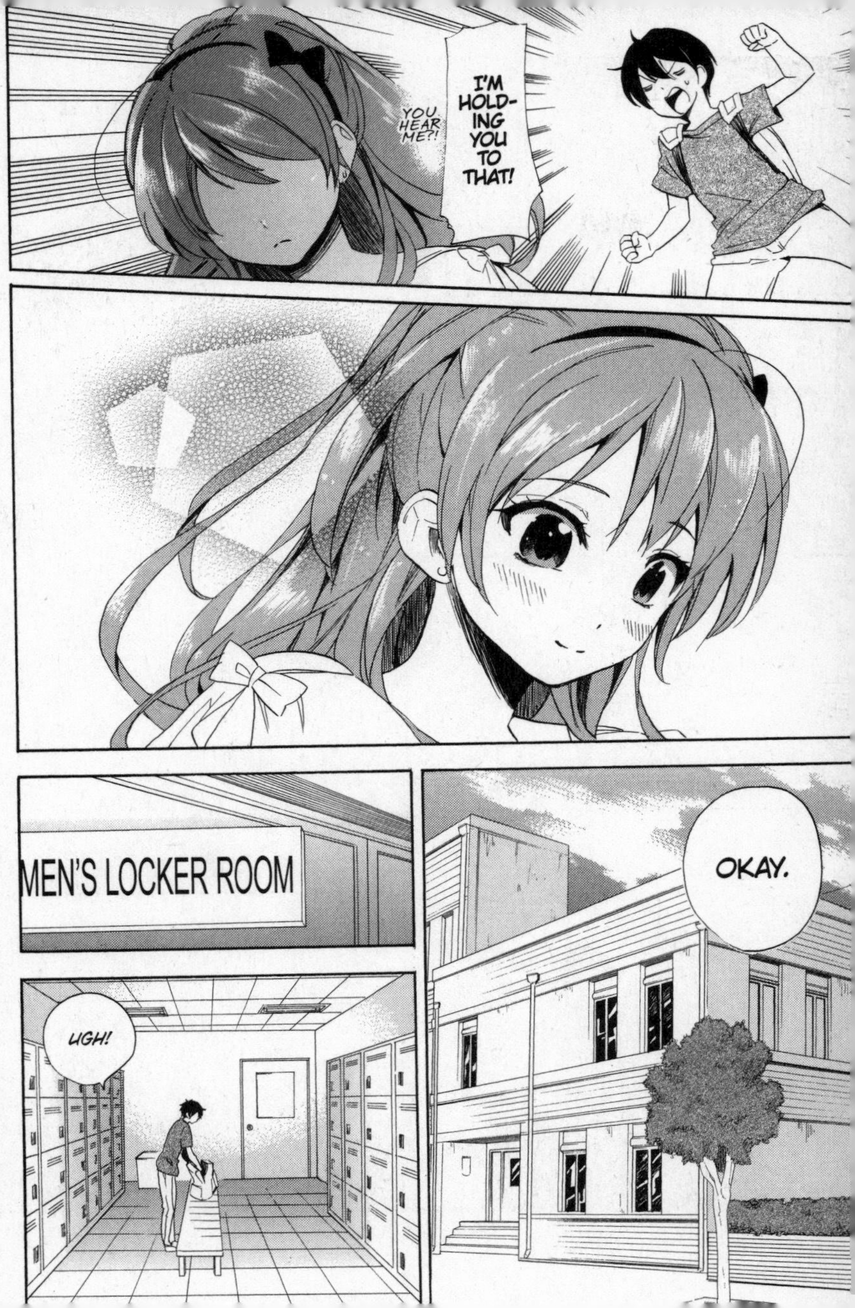
I'M HOLDING YOU TO THAT!
YOU HEAR ME?!
OKAY.
MEN'S LOCKER ROOM
UGH!

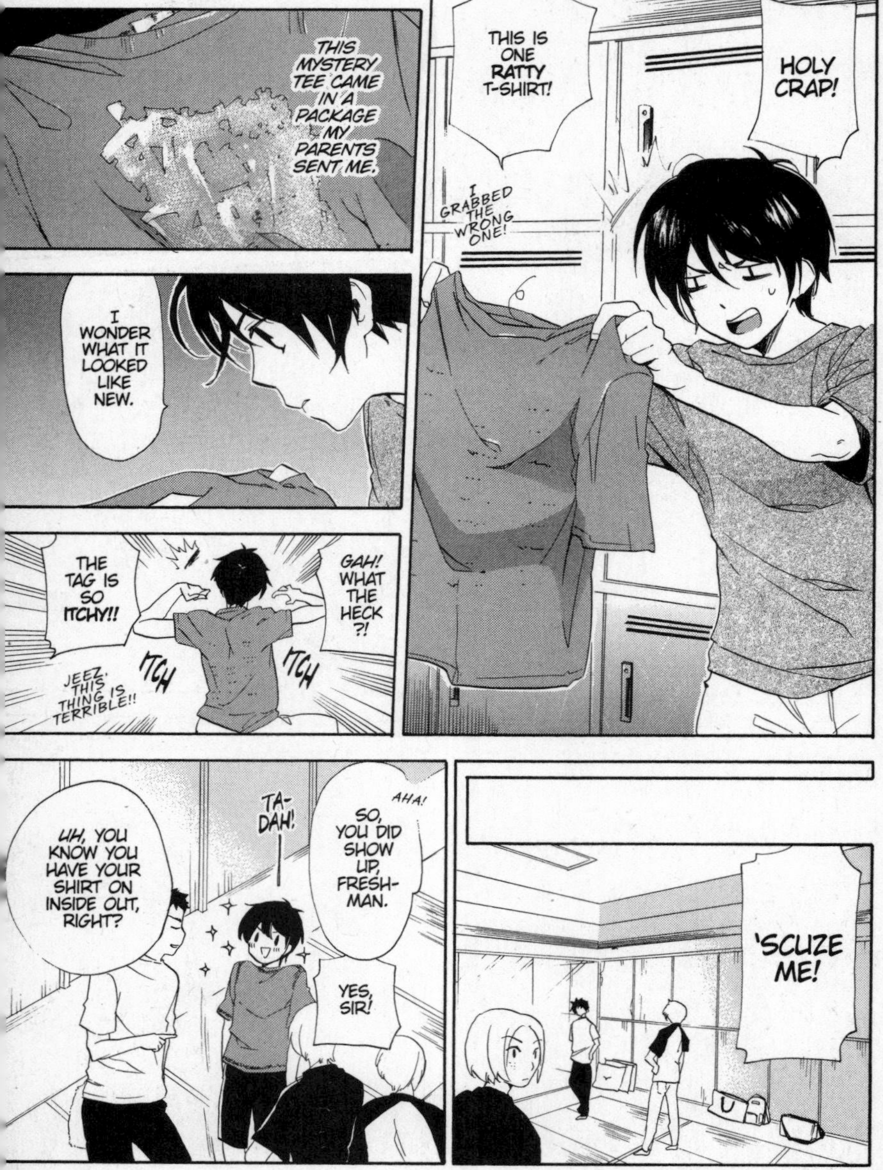
HOLY CRAP!
THIS IS ONE RATTY T-SHIRT!
I GRABBED THE WRONG ONE!
THIS MYSTERY TEE CAME IN A PACKAGE MY PARENTS SENT ME.
I WONDER WHAT IT LOOKED LIKE NEW.
GAH! WHAT THE HECK?!
THE TAG IS SO ITCHY!!
ITCH
ITCH
JEEZ. THIS THING IS TERRIBLE!!
'SCUZE ME!
AHA!
SO, YOU DID SHOW UP, FRESHMAN.
TA-DAH!
YES, SIR!
UH, YOU KNOW YOU HAVE YOUR SHIRT ON INSIDE OUT, RIGHT?

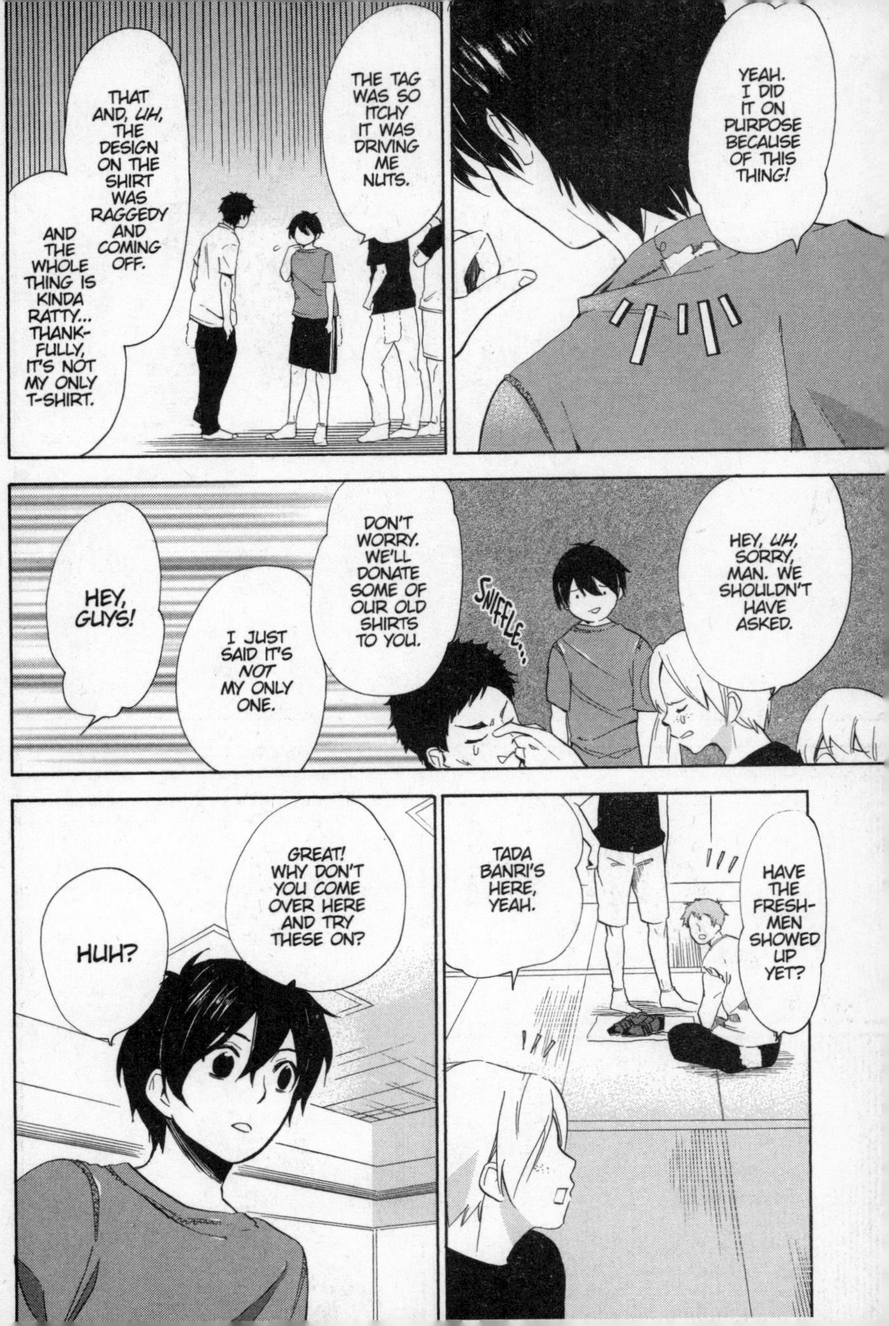
YEAH. I DID IT ON PURPOSE BECAUSE OF THIS THING!
THE TAG WAS SO ITCHY IT WAS DRIVING ME NUTS.
THAT AND, *UH*, THE DESIGN ON THE SHIRT WAS RAGGEDY AND COMING OFF. AND THE WHOLE THING IS KINDA RATTY... THANKFULLY, IT'S NOT MY ONLY T-SHIRT.
HEY, *UH*, SORRY, MAN. WE SHOULDN'T HAVE ASKED.
SNIFFLE...
DON'T WORRY. WE'LL DONATE SOME OF OUR OLD SHIRTS TO YOU.
I JUST SAID IT'S *NOT* MY ONLY ONE.
HEY, GUYS!
HAVE THE FRESHMEN SHOWED UP YET?
TADA BANRI'S HERE, YEAH.
GREAT! WHY DON'T YOU COME OVER HERE AND TRY THESE ON?
HUH?

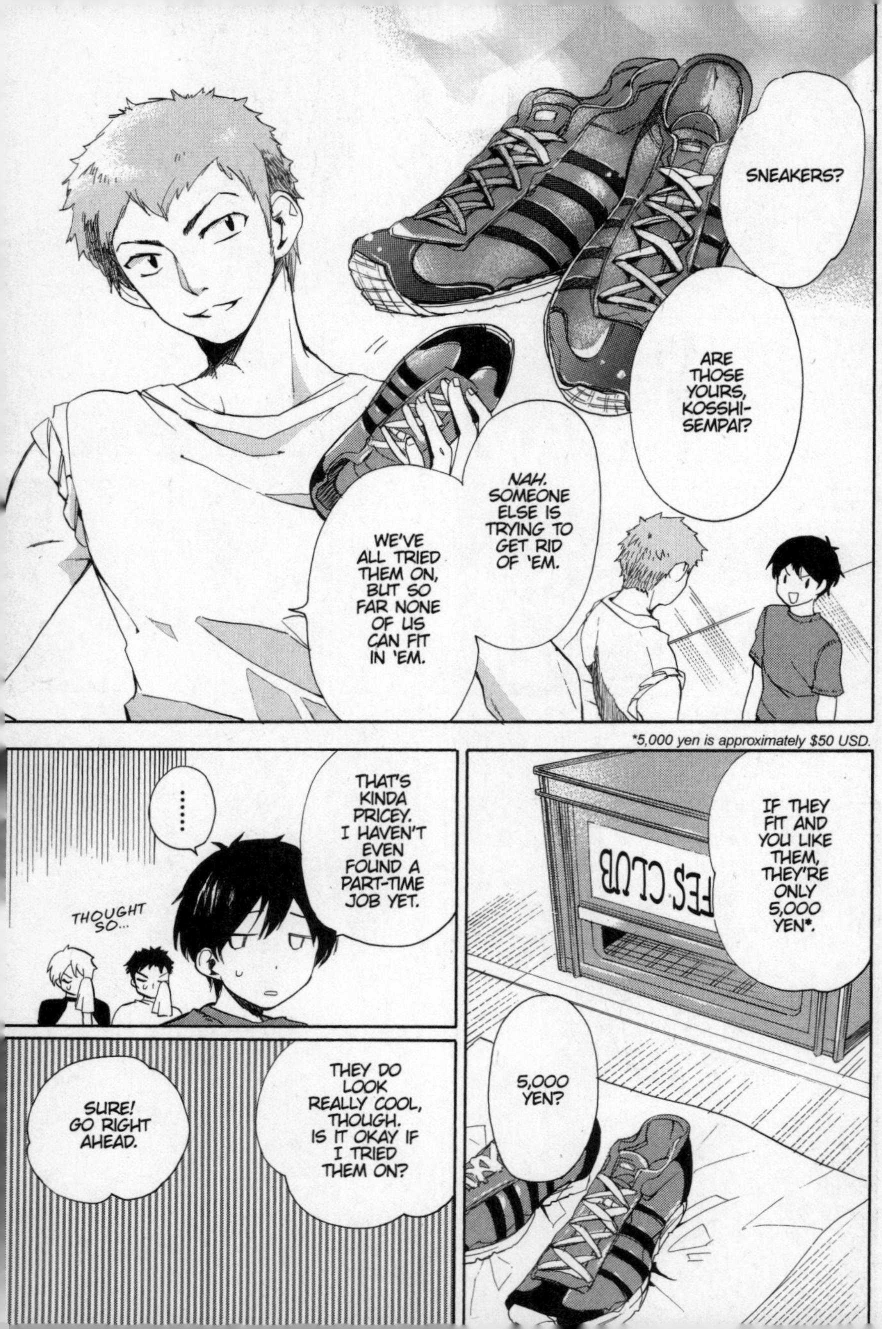
SNEAKERS?
ARE THOSE YOURS, KOSSHI-SEMPAI?
NAH. SOMEONE ELSE IS TRYING TO GET RID OF 'EM.
WE'VE ALL TRIED THEM ON, BUT SO FAR NONE OF US CAN FIT IN 'EM.
IF THEY FIT AND YOU LIKE THEM, THEY'RE ONLY 5,000 YEN*.
FES CLUB
5,000 YEN?
THAT'S KINDA PRICEY. I HAVEN'T EVEN FOUND A PART-TIME JOB YET.
......
THOUGHT SO...
THEY DO LOOK REALLY COOL, THOUGH. IS IT OKAY IF I TRIED THEM ON?
SURE! GO RIGHT AHEAD.

*5,000 yen is approximately $50 USD.

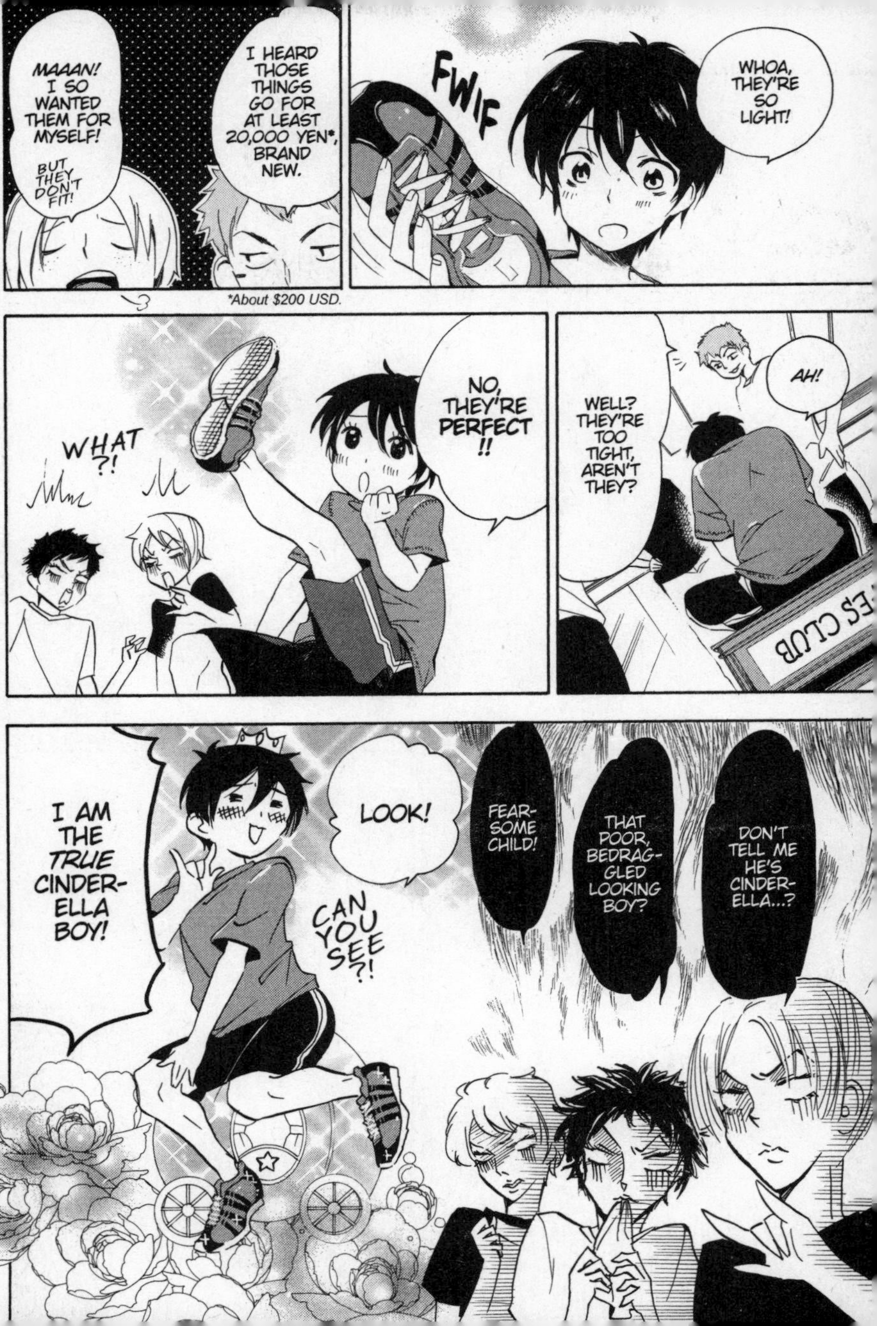
FWIF
WHOA, THEY'RE SO LIGHT!
I HEARD THOSE THINGS GO FOR AT LEAST 20,000 YEN*, BRAND NEW.
MAAAN! I SO WANTED THEM FOR MYSELF!
BUT THEY DON'T FIT!
AH!
WELL? THEY'RE TOO TIGHT, AREN'T THEY?
NO, THEY'RE PERFECT!!
WHAT?!
DON'T TELL ME HE'S CINDER-ELLA...?
THAT POOR, BEDRAG-GLED LOOKING BOY?
FEAR-SOME CHILD!
LOOK!
I AM THE TRUE CINDER-ELLA BOY!
CAN YOU SEE?!
*About $200 USD.

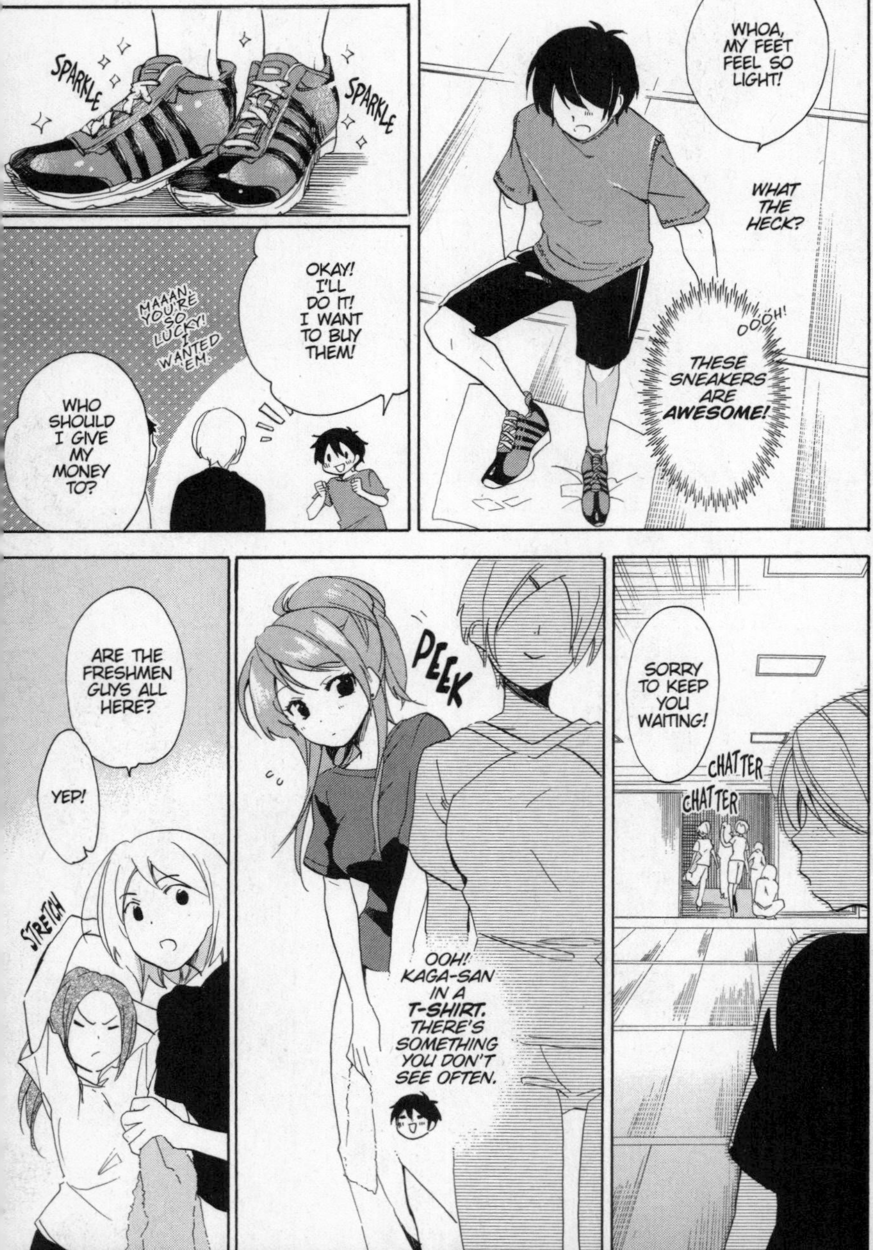
WHOA, MY FEET FEEL SO LIGHT!
WHAT THE HECK?
OOOOH!
THESE SNEAKERS ARE **AWESOME!**
SPARKLE
SPARKLE
OKAY! I'LL DO IT! I WANT TO BUY THEM!
MAAAN. YOU'RE SO LUCKY! I WANTED 'EM.
WHO SHOULD I GIVE MY MONEY TO?
SORRY TO KEEP YOU WAITING!
CHATTER
CHATTER
PEEK
OOH! KAGA-SAN IN A **T-SHIRT.** THERE'S SOMETHING YOU DON'T SEE OFTEN.
ARE THE FRESHMEN GUYS ALL HERE?
YEP!
STRETCH

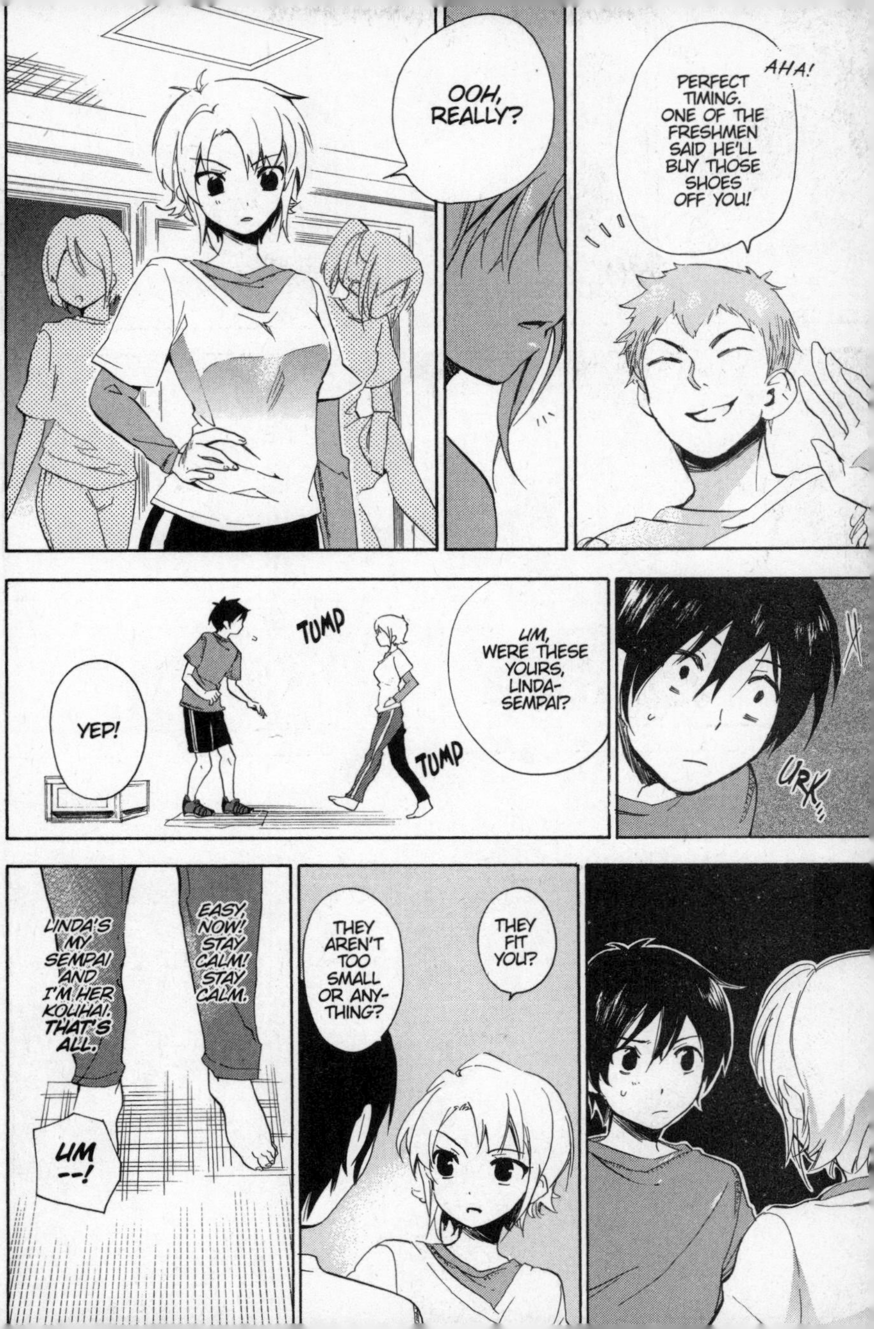
AHA!
PERFECT TIMING. ONE OF THE FRESHMEN SAID HE'LL BUY THOSE SHOES OFF YOU!
OOH, REALLY?
URK...
UM, WERE THESE YOURS, LINDA-SEMPAI?
TUMP
TUMP
YEP!
THEY FIT YOU?
THEY AREN'T TOO SMALL OR ANYTHING?
EASY, NOW! STAY CALM! STAY CALM.
LINDA'S MY SEMPAI AND I'M HER KOUHAI. THAT'S ALL.
UM--!

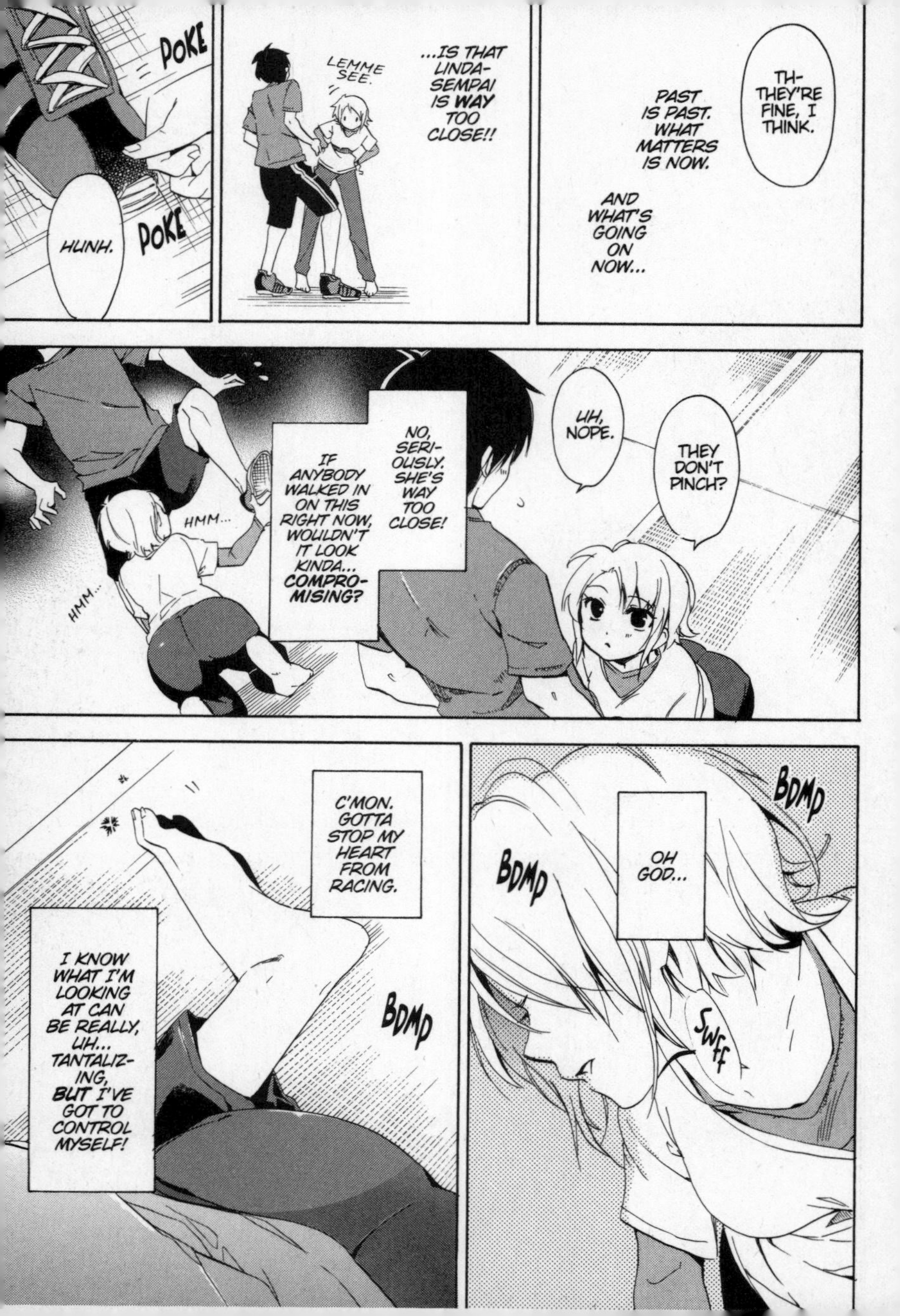
TH-THEY'RE FINE, I THINK.
PAST IS PAST. WHAT MATTERS IS NOW.
AND WHAT'S GOING ON NOW...
...IS THAT LINDA-SEMPAI IS WAY TOO CLOSE!!
LEMME SEE.
POKE
HUNH.
POKE
THEY DON'T PINCH?
UH, NOPE.
NO, SERIOUSLY. SHE'S WAY TOO CLOSE!
IF ANYBODY WALKED IN ON THIS RIGHT NOW, WOULDN'T IT LOOK KINDA... COMPROMISING?
HMM...
HMM...
BDMP
OH GOD...
BDMP
SWFF
C'MON. GOTTA STOP MY HEART FROM RACING.
BDMP
I KNOW WHAT I'M LOOKING AT CAN BE REALLY, UH... TANTALIZING, BUT I'VE GOT TO CONTROL MYSELF!

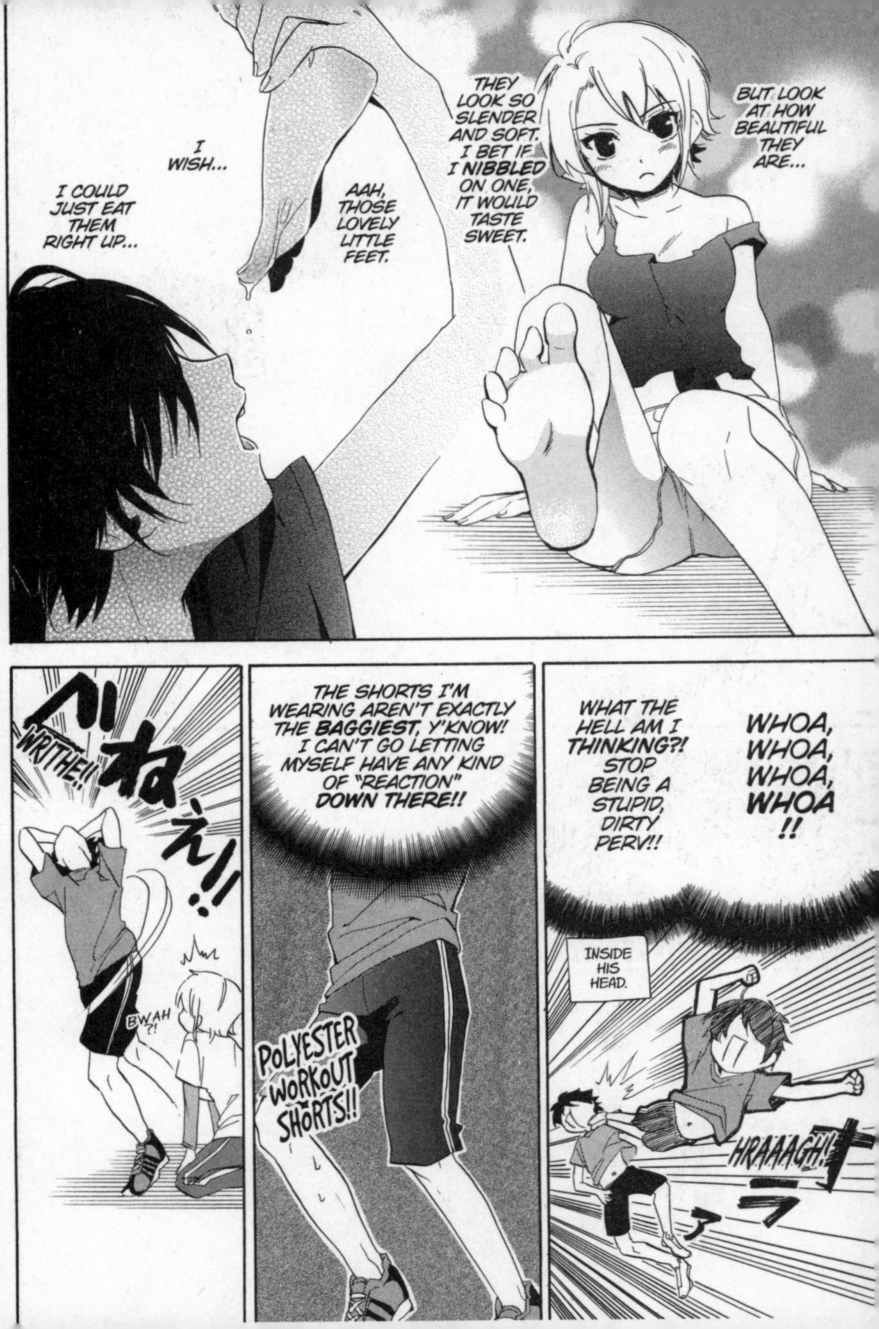
BUT LOOK AT HOW BEAUTIFUL THEY ARE...
THEY LOOK SO SLENDER AND SOFT. I BET IF I NIBBLED ON ONE, IT WOULD TASTE SWEET.
AAH, THOSE LOVELY LITTLE FEET.
I WISH...
I COULD JUST EAT THEM RIGHT UP...
WHOA, WHOA, WHOA, WHOA!!
WHAT THE HELL AM I THINKING?! STOP BEING A STUPID, DIRTY PERV!!
INSIDE HIS HEAD.
HRAAAGH!
THE SHORTS I'M WEARING AREN'T EXACTLY THE BAGGIEST, Y'KNOW! I CAN'T GO LETTING MYSELF HAVE ANY KIND OF "REACTION" DOWN THERE!!
POLYESTER WORKOUT SHORTS!!
くねえ!!
WRITHE!!
BWAH?!

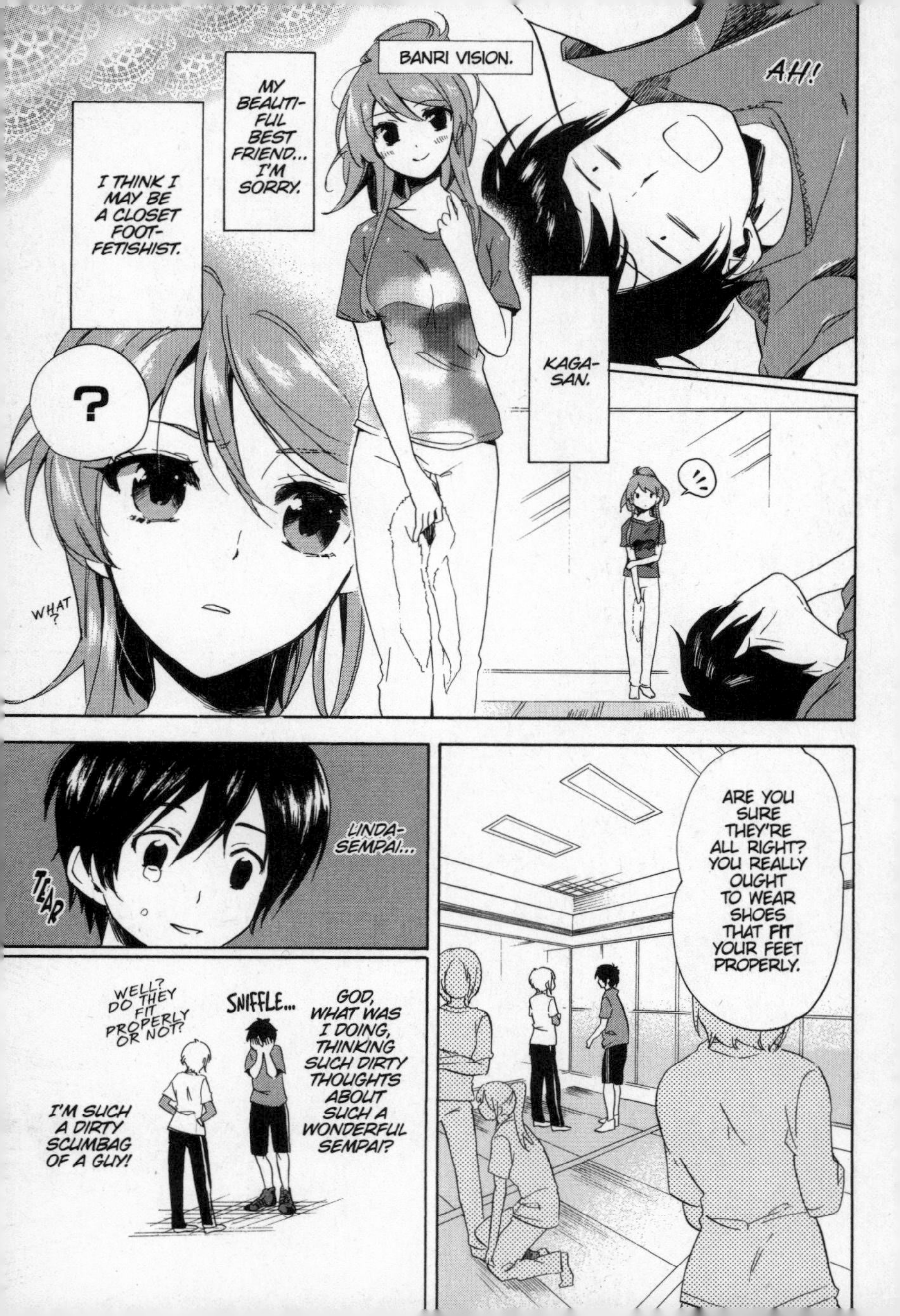
AH!
KAGA-SAN.
BANRI VISION.
MY BEAUTIFUL BEST FRIEND... I'M SORRY.
I THINK I MAY BE A CLOSET FOOT-FETISHIST.
?
WHAT?
ARE YOU SURE THEY'RE ALL RIGHT? YOU REALLY OUGHT TO WEAR SHOES THAT FIT YOUR FEET PROPERLY.
LINDA-SEMPAI...
TEAR
GOD, WHAT WAS I DOING, THINKING SUCH DIRTY THOUGHTS ABOUT SUCH A WONDERFUL SEMPAI?
SNIFFLE...
WELL? DO THEY FIT PROPERLY OR NOT?
I'M SUCH A DIRTY SCUMBAG OF A GUY!

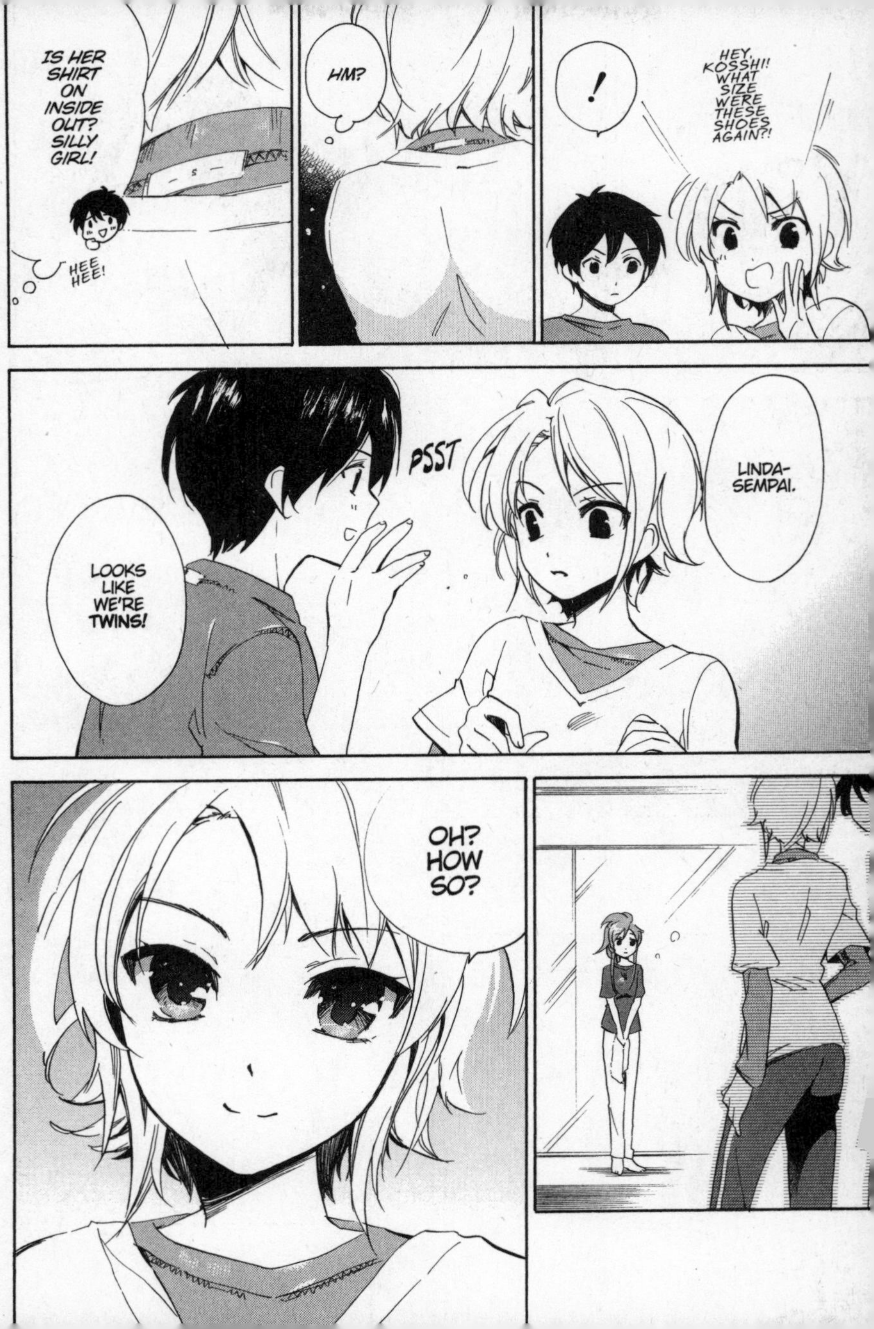
HEY, KOSSHI! WHAT SIZE WERE THESE SHOES AGAIN?!
!
HM?
IS HER SHIRT ON INSIDE OUT? SILLY GIRL!
HEE HEE!
LINDA-SEMPAI.
PSST
LOOKS LIKE WE'RE TWINS!
OH? HOW SO?

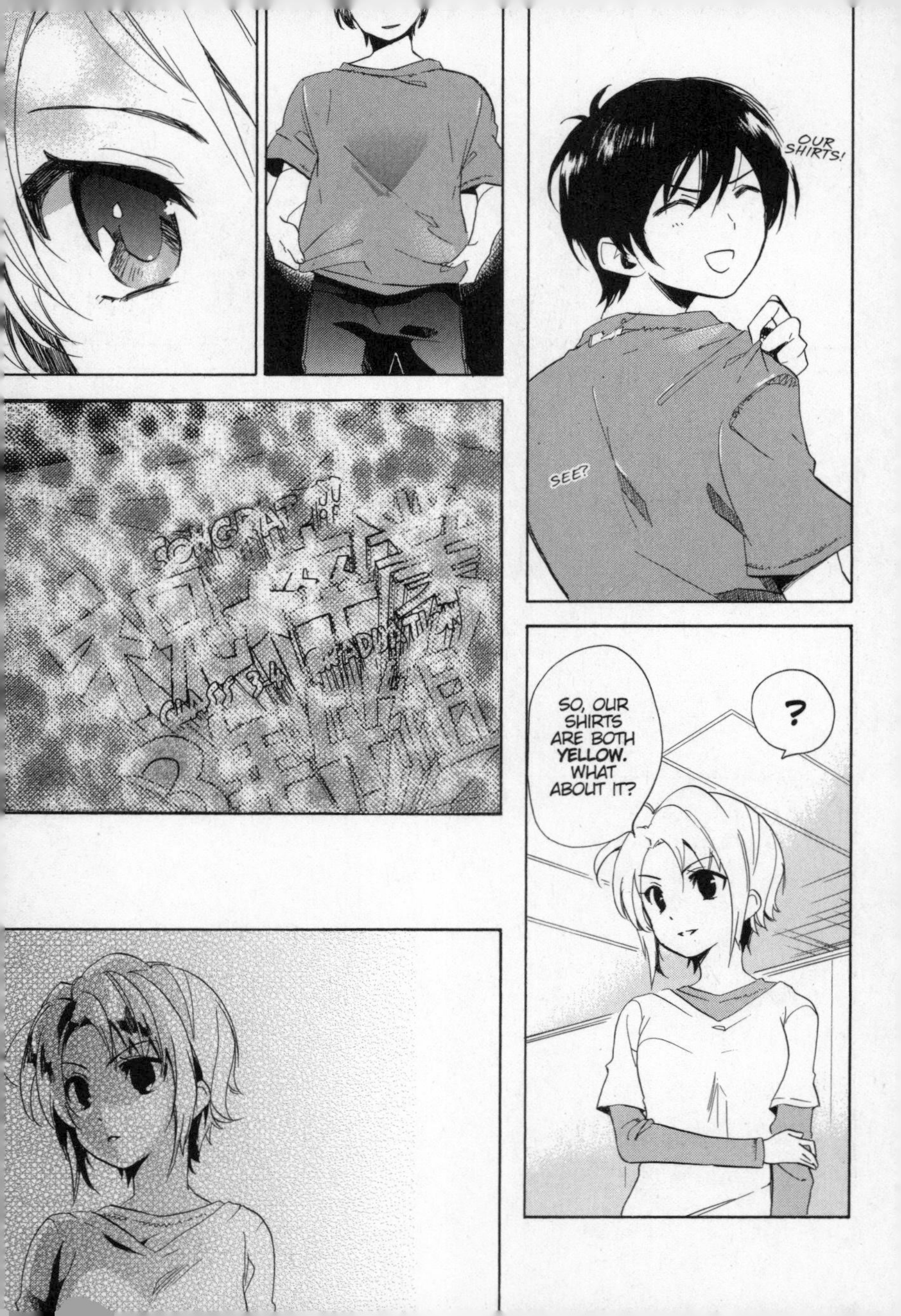
OUR SHIRTS!
SEE?
SO, OUR SHIRTS ARE BOTH YELLOW. WHAT ABOUT IT?
?

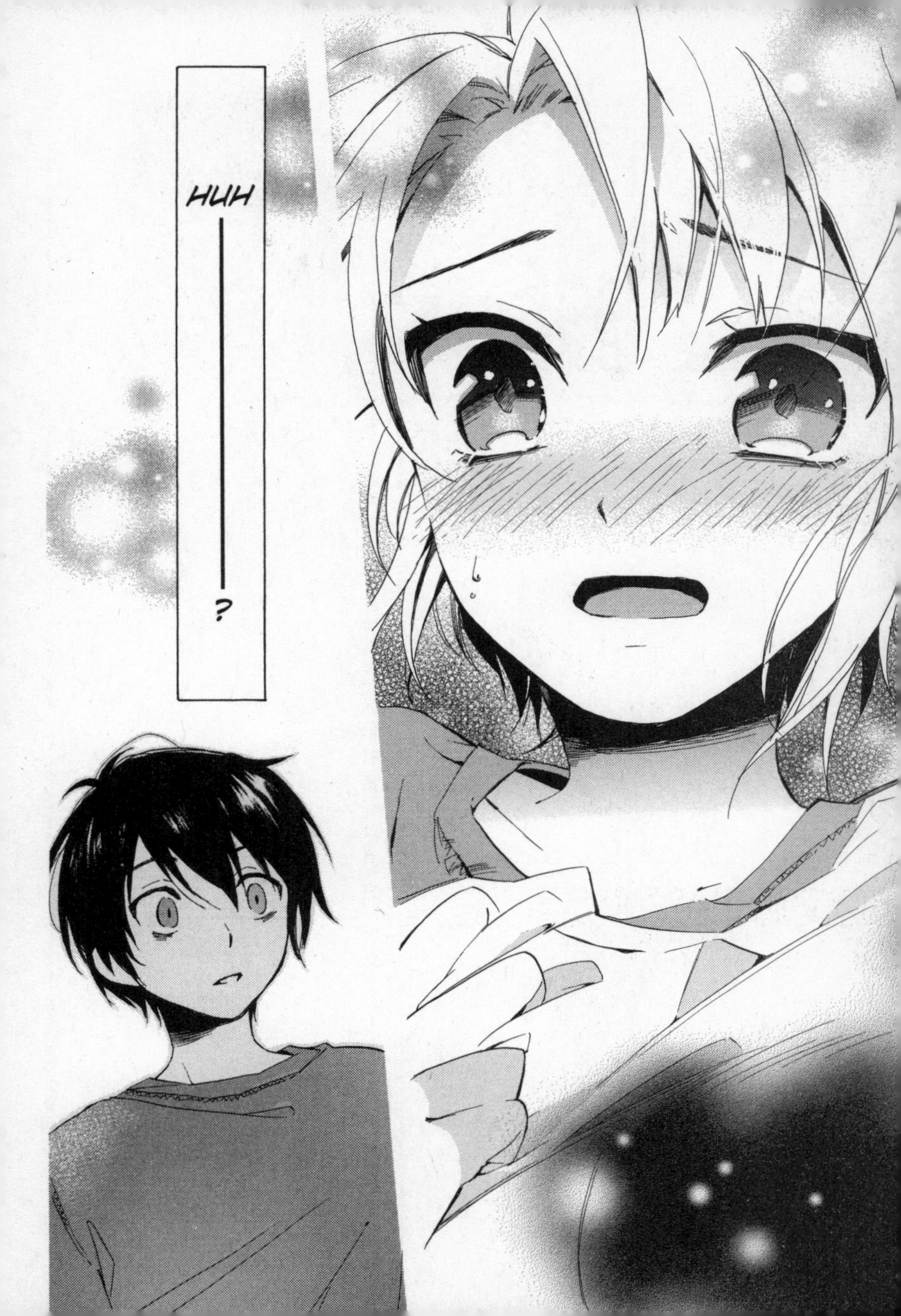
HUH——?

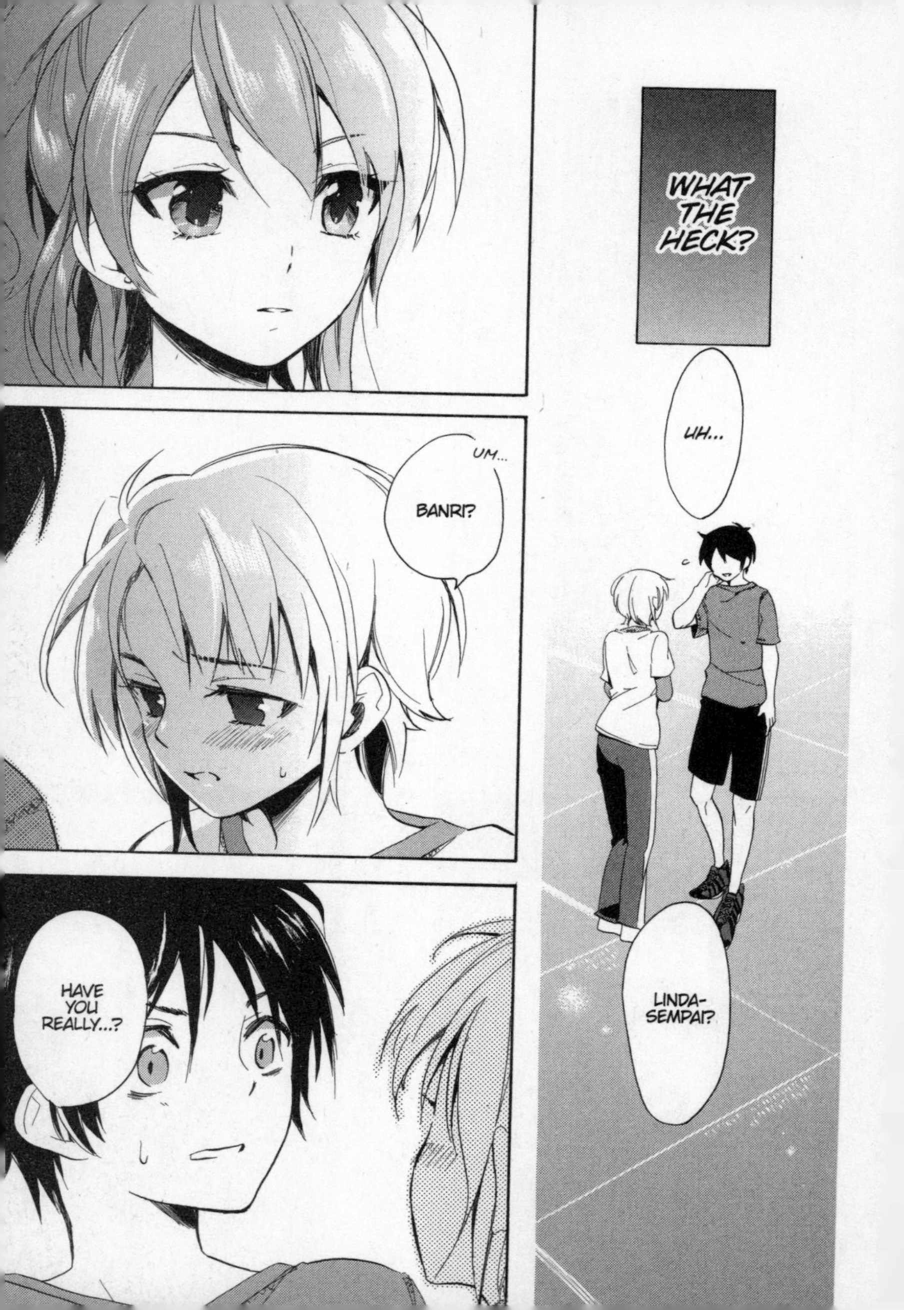
WHAT THE HECK?
UH...
LINDA-SEMPAI?
UM... BANRI?
HAVE YOU REALLY...?

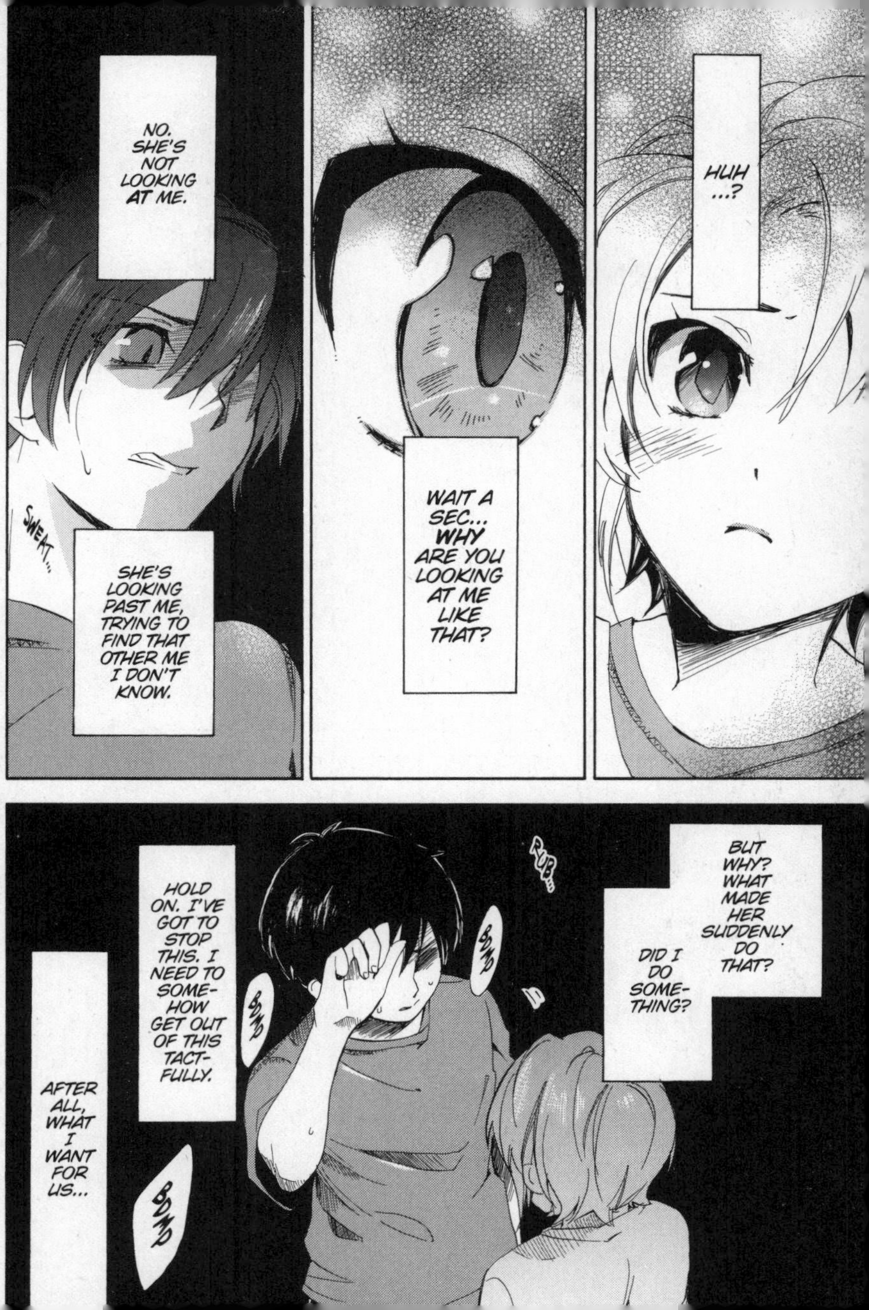
HUH ...?
WAIT A SEC... WHY ARE YOU LOOKING AT ME LIKE THAT?
NO. SHE'S NOT LOOKING AT ME.
SWEAT...
SHE'S LOOKING PAST ME, TRYING TO FIND THAT OTHER ME I DON'T KNOW.
BUT WHY? WHAT MADE HER SUDDENLY DO THAT?
DID I DO SOME-THING?
RUB...
BDMP
BDMP
HOLD ON. I'VE GOT TO STOP THIS. I NEED TO SOME-HOW GET OUT OF THIS TACT-FULLY.
BDMP
AFTER ALL, WHAT I WANT FOR US...

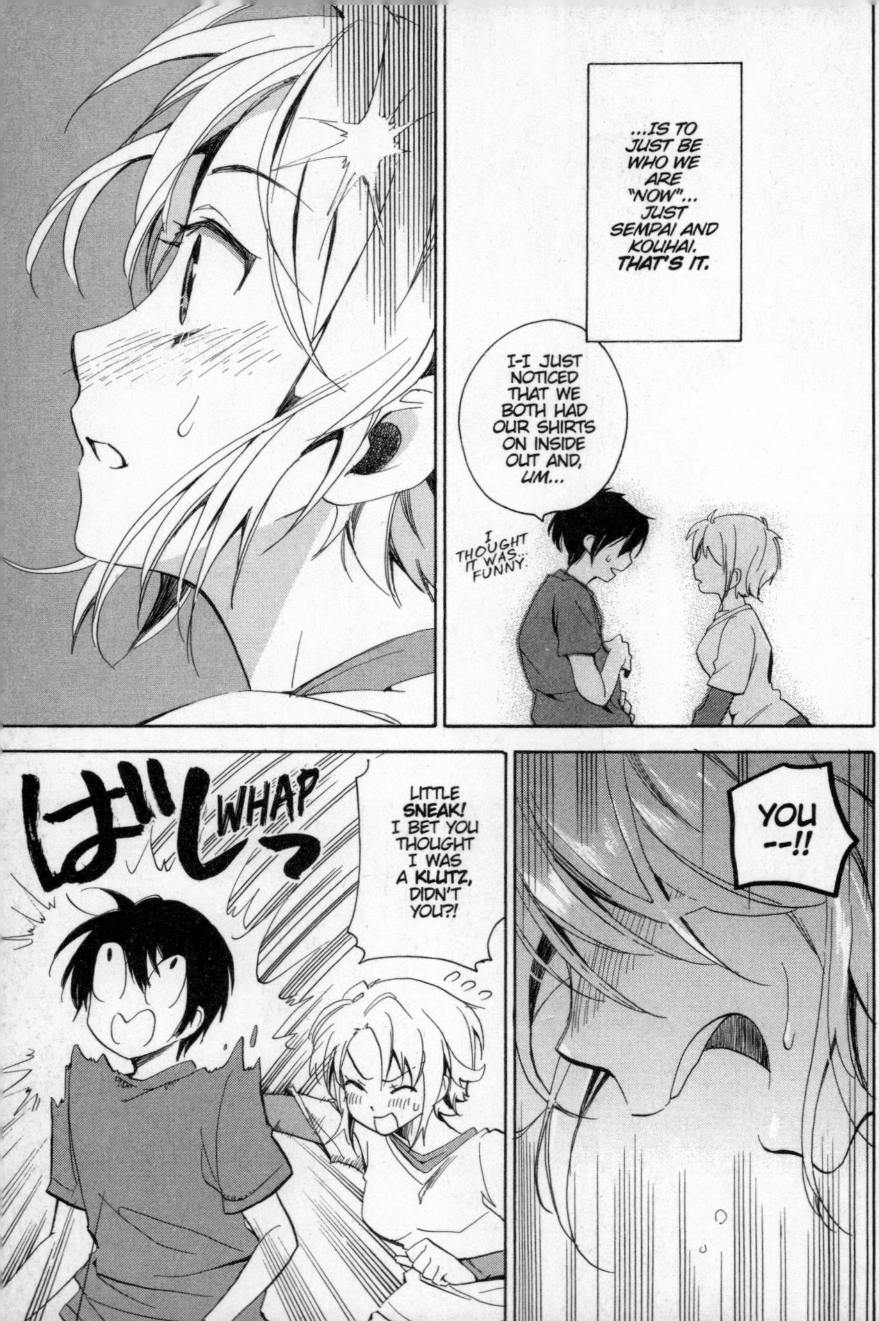
...IS TO JUST BE WHO WE ARE "NOW"... JUST SEMPAI AND KOUHAI. THAT'S IT.
I-I JUST NOTICED THAT WE BOTH HAD OUR SHIRTS ON INSIDE OUT AND, UM...
I THOUGHT IT WAS... FUNNY.
YOU --!!
ばしっ
WHAP
LITTLE SNEAK! I BET YOU THOUGHT I WAS A KLUTZ, DIDN'T YOU?!

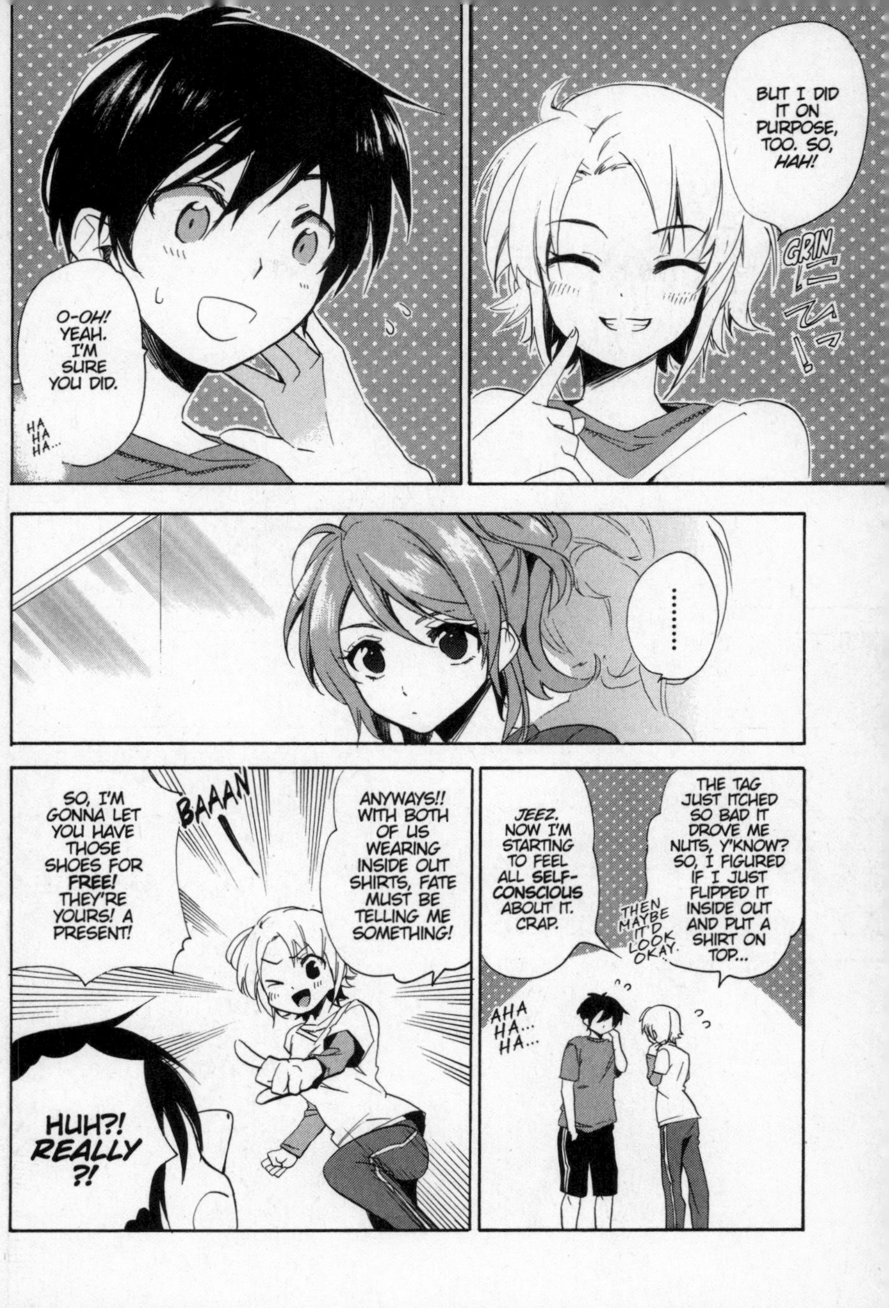
BUT I DID IT ON PURPOSE, TOO. SO, *HAH!*
GRIN
O-OH! YEAH. I'M SURE YOU DID.
HA HA HA...
......
THE TAG JUST ITCHED SO BAD IT DROVE ME NUTS, Y'KNOW? SO, I FIGURED IF I JUST FLIPPED IT INSIDE OUT AND PUT A SHIRT ON TOP...
THEN MAYBE IT'D LOOK OKAY.
JEEZ. NOW I'M STARTING TO FEEL ALL SELF-CONSCIOUS ABOUT IT. CRAP.
AHA HA... HA...
ANYWAYS!! WITH BOTH OF US WEARING INSIDE OUT SHIRTS, FATE MUST BE TELLING ME SOMETHING!
BAAAN
SO, I'M GONNA LET YOU HAVE THOSE SHOES FOR FREE! THEY'RE YOURS! A PRESENT!
HUH?! REALLY?!

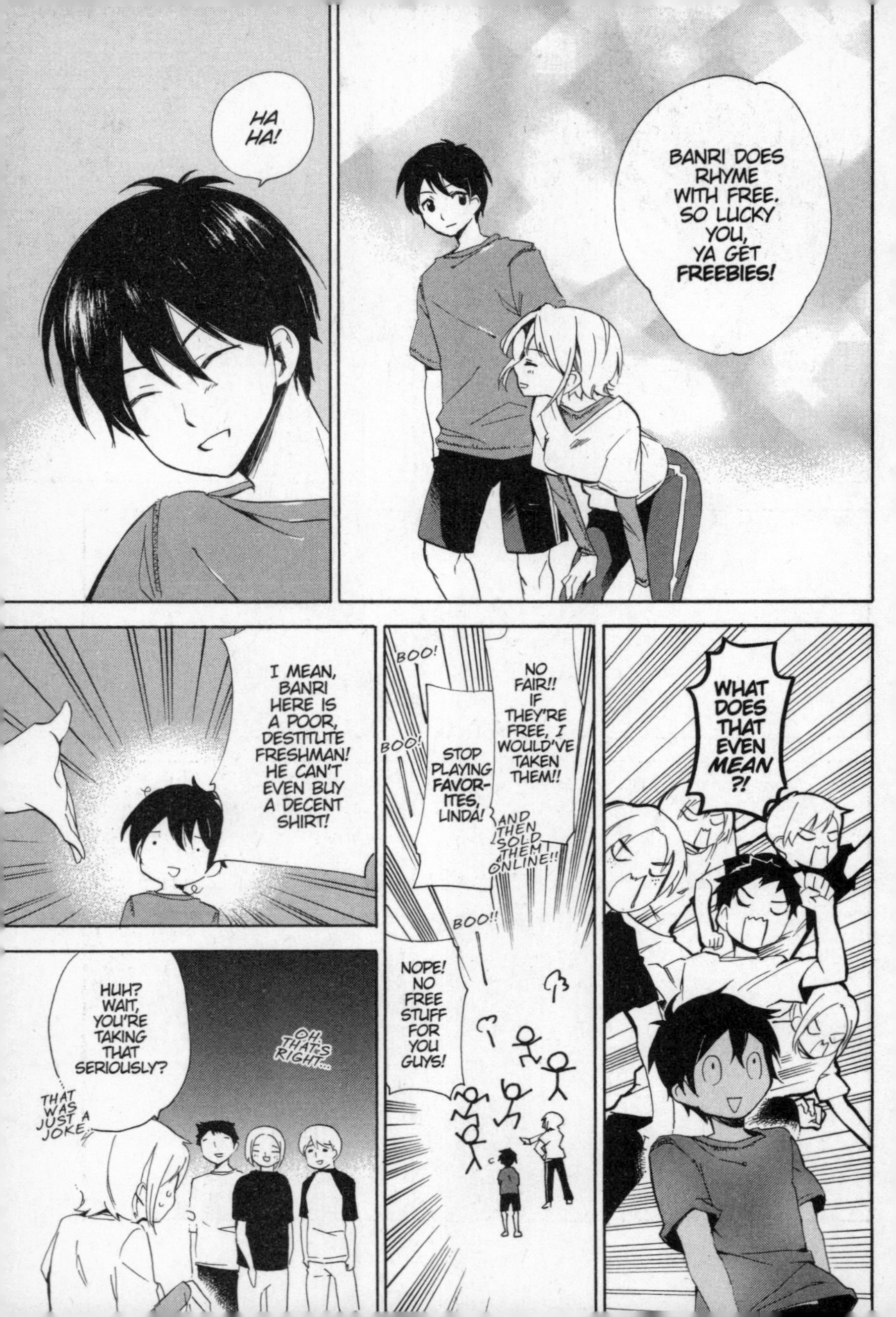
BANRI DOES RHYME WITH FREE. SO LUCKY YOU, YA GET FREEBIES!
HA HA!
WHAT DOES THAT EVEN MEAN?!
NO FAIR!! IF THEY'RE FREE, I WOULD'VE TAKEN THEM!!
BOO!
STOP PLAYING FAVOR-ITES, LINDA!
BOO!
AND THEN SOLD THEM ONLINE!!
BOO!!
NOPE! NO FREE STUFF FOR YOU GUYS!
I MEAN, BANRI HERE IS A POOR, DESTITUTE FRESHMAN! HE CAN'T EVEN BUY A DECENT SHIRT!
HUH? WAIT, YOU'RE TAKING THAT SERIOUSLY?
OH, THAT'S RIGHT...
THAT WAS JUST A JOKE...

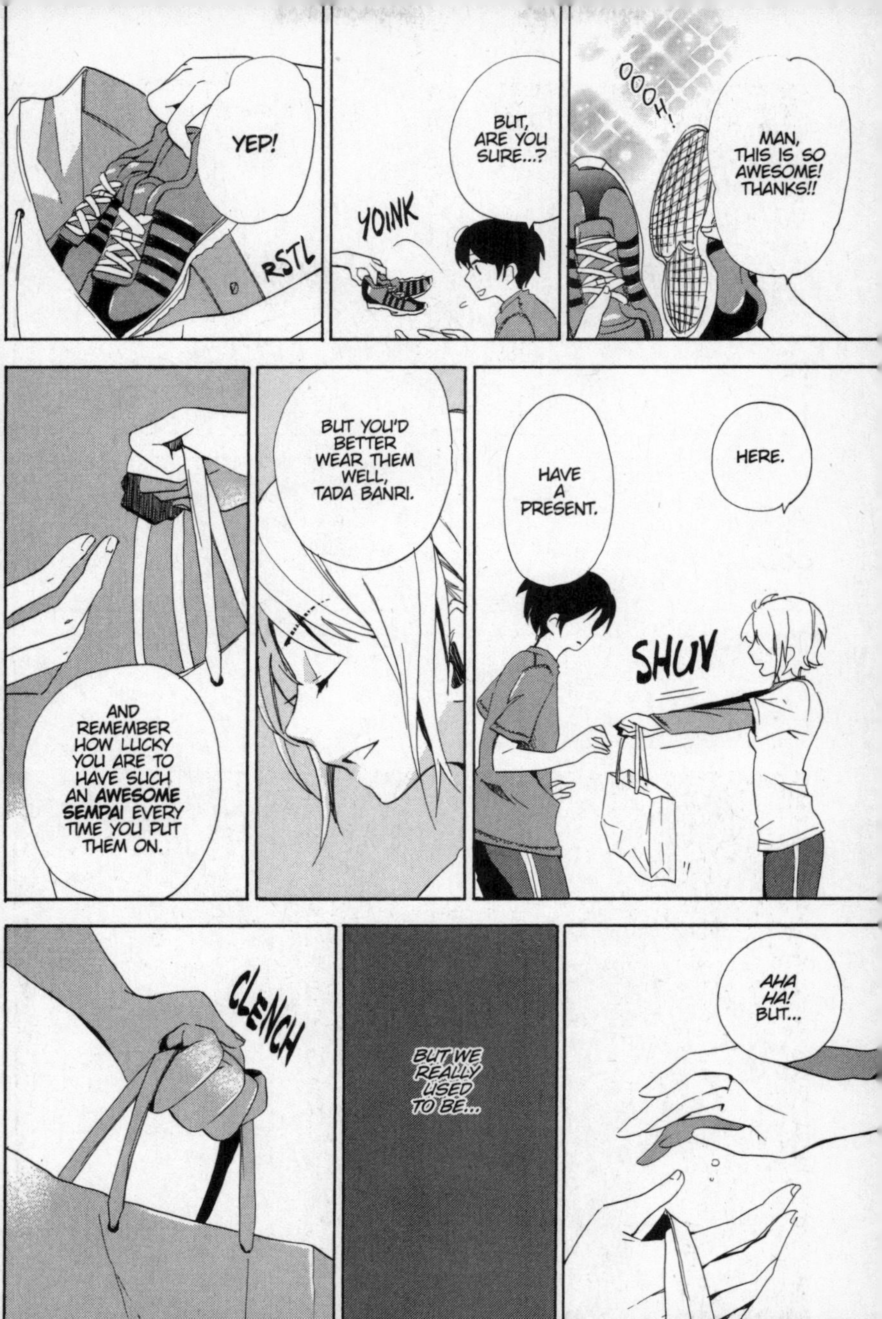
OOOH!
MAN, THIS IS SO AWESOME! THANKS!!
BUT, ARE YOU SURE...?
YOINK
YEP!
RSTL
HERE.
HAVE A PRESENT.
SHUV
BUT YOU'D BETTER WEAR THEM WELL, TADA BANRI.
AND REMEMBER HOW LUCKY YOU ARE TO HAVE SUCH AN **AWESOME SEMPAI** EVERY TIME YOU PUT THEM ON.
AHA HA! BUT...
BUT WE REALLY USED TO BE...
CLENCH

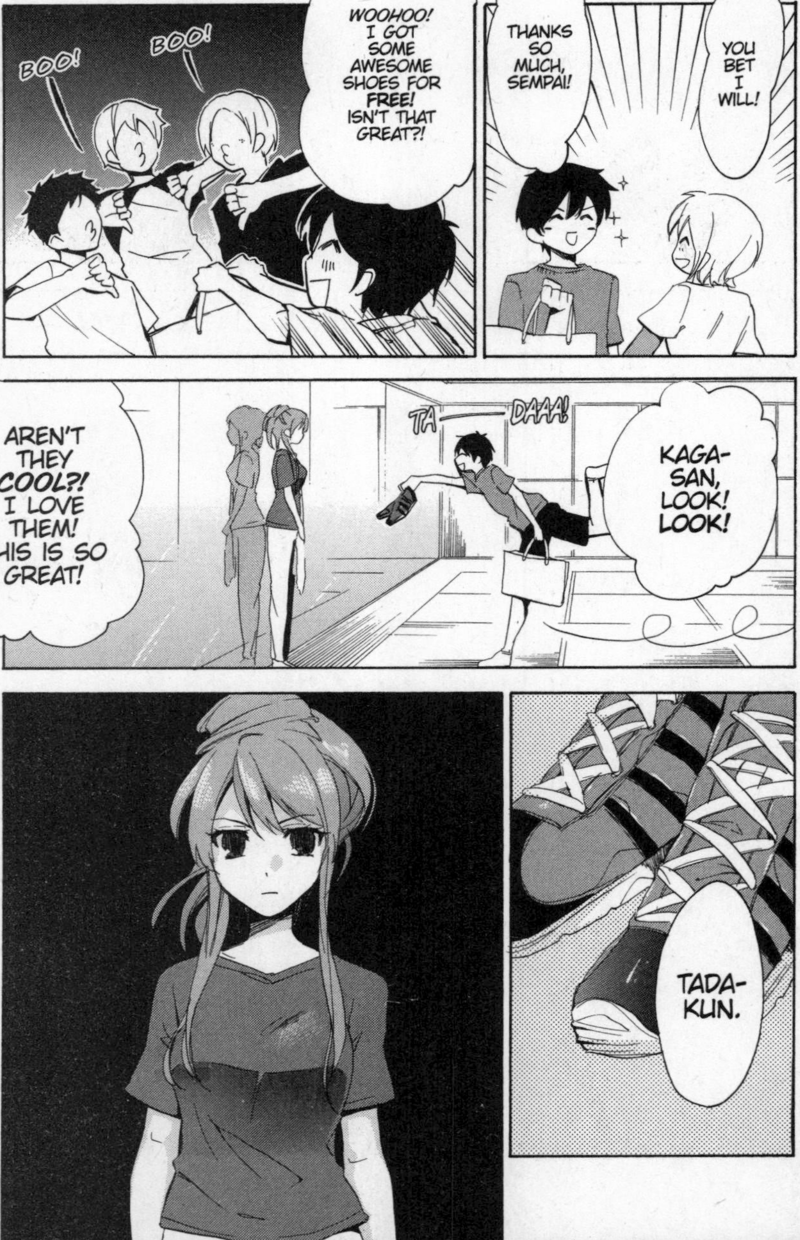
YOU BET I WILL!
THANKS SO MUCH, SEMPAI!
WOOHOO! I GOT SOME AWESOME SHOES FOR FREE! ISN'T THAT GREAT?!
BOO!
BOO!
KAGA-SAN, LOOK! LOOK!
TA—DAAA!
AREN'T THEY COOL?! I LOVE THEM! THIS IS SO GREAT!
TADA-KUN.

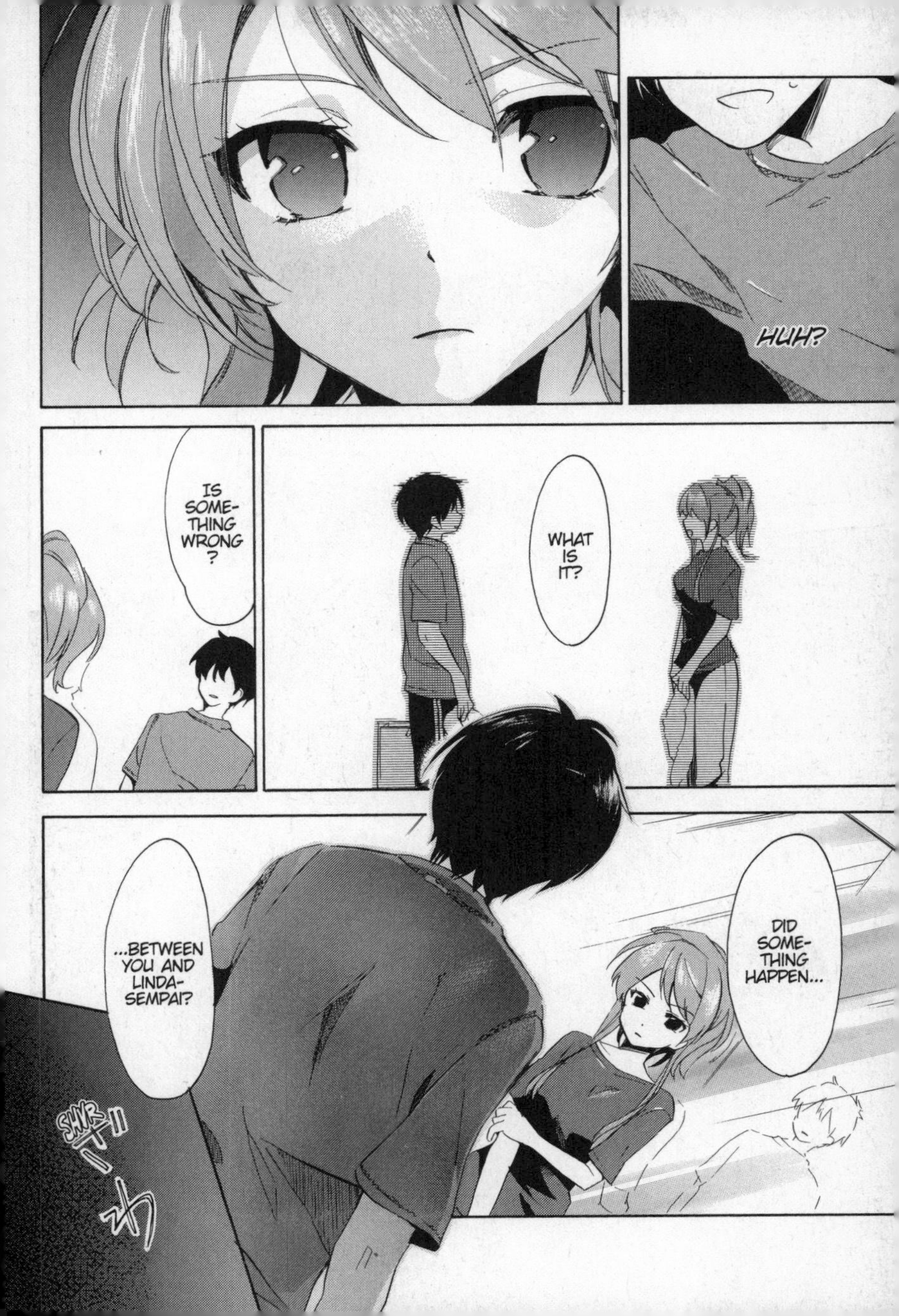
HUH?
WHAT IS IT?
IS SOMETHING WRONG?
DID SOMETHING HAPPEN...
...BETWEEN YOU AND LINDA-SEMPAI?
SHYR

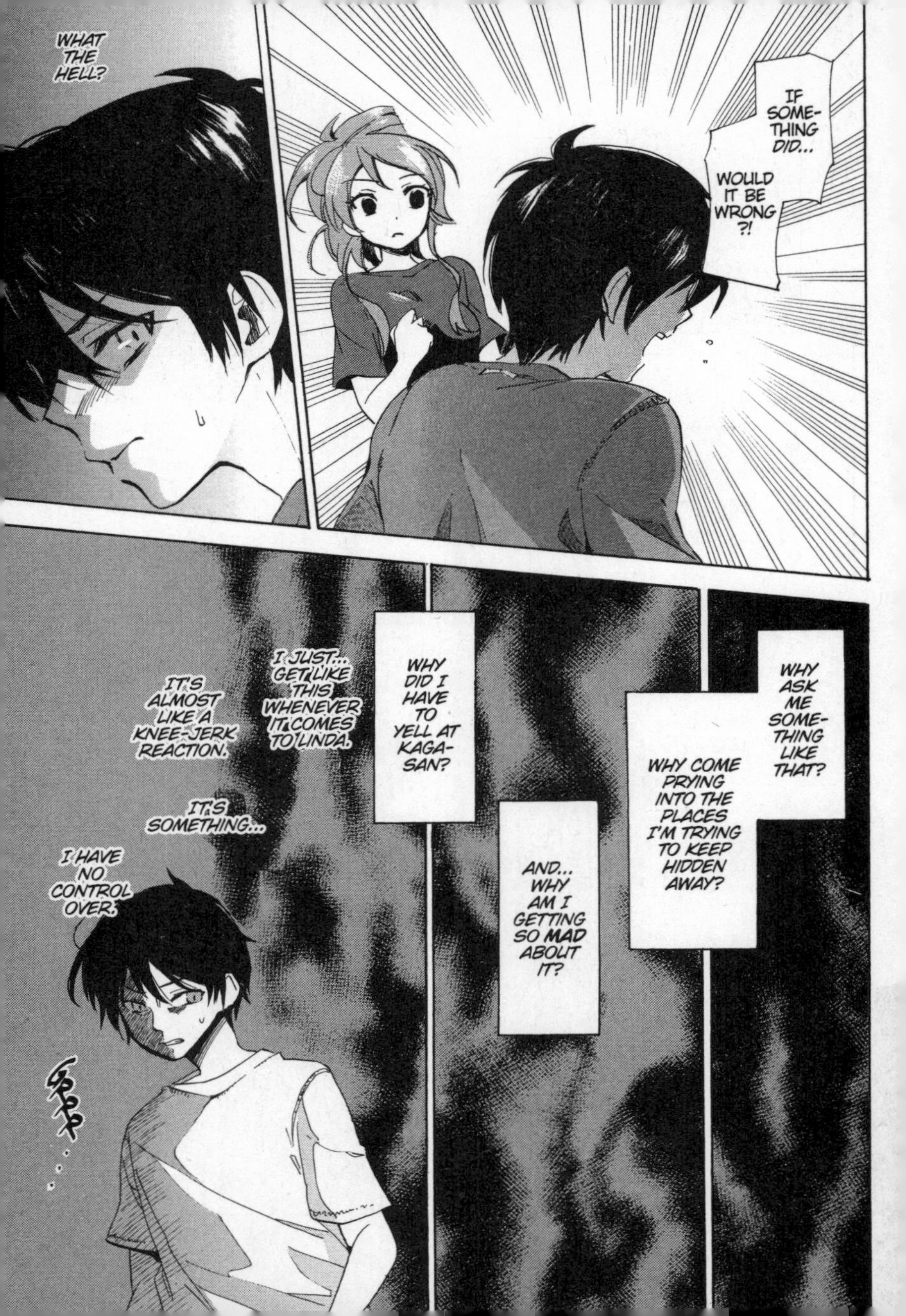
IF SOMETHING DID...
WOULD IT BE WRONG?!
WHAT THE HELL?
WHY ASK ME SOMETHING LIKE THAT?
WHY COME PRYING INTO THE PLACES I'M TRYING TO KEEP HIDDEN AWAY?
AND... WHY AM I GETTING SO MAD ABOUT IT?
WHY DID I HAVE TO YELL AT KAGA-SAN?
I JUST... GET LIKE THIS WHENEVER IT COMES TO LINDA.
IT'S ALMOST LIKE A KNEE-JERK REACTION.
IT'S SOMETHING...
I HAVE NO CONTROL OVER.
GRRR...

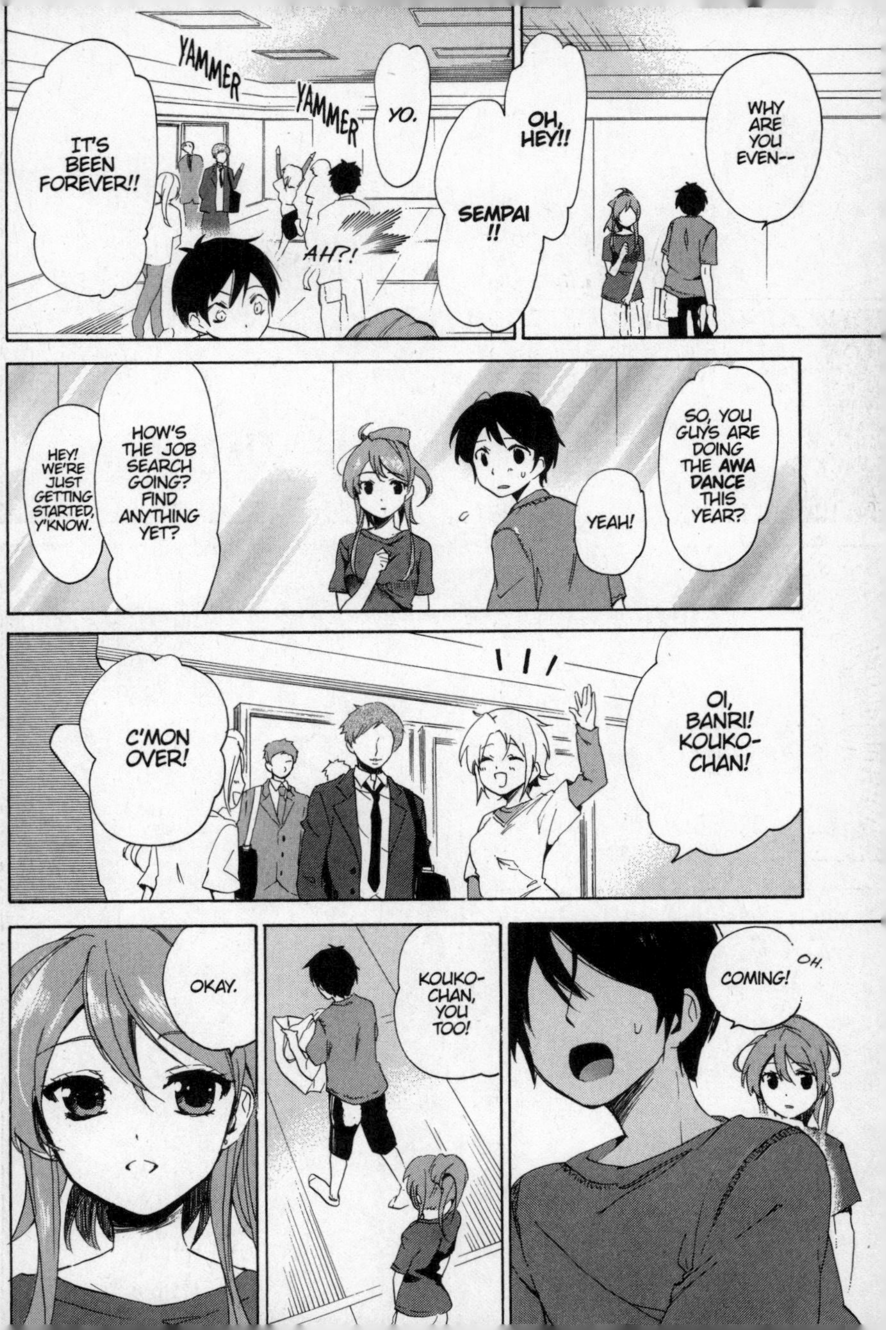
WHY ARE YOU EVEN--
OH, HEY!!
SEMPAI!!
YO.
YAMMER
YAMMER
AH?!
IT'S BEEN FOREVER!!
SO, YOU GUYS ARE DOING THE AWA DANCE THIS YEAR?
YEAH!
HOW'S THE JOB SEARCH GOING? FIND ANYTHING YET?
HEY! WE'RE JUST GETTING STARTED, Y'KNOW.
OI, BANRI! KOUKO-CHAN!
C'MON OVER!
OH.
COMING!
KOUKO-CHAN, YOU TOO!
OKAY.

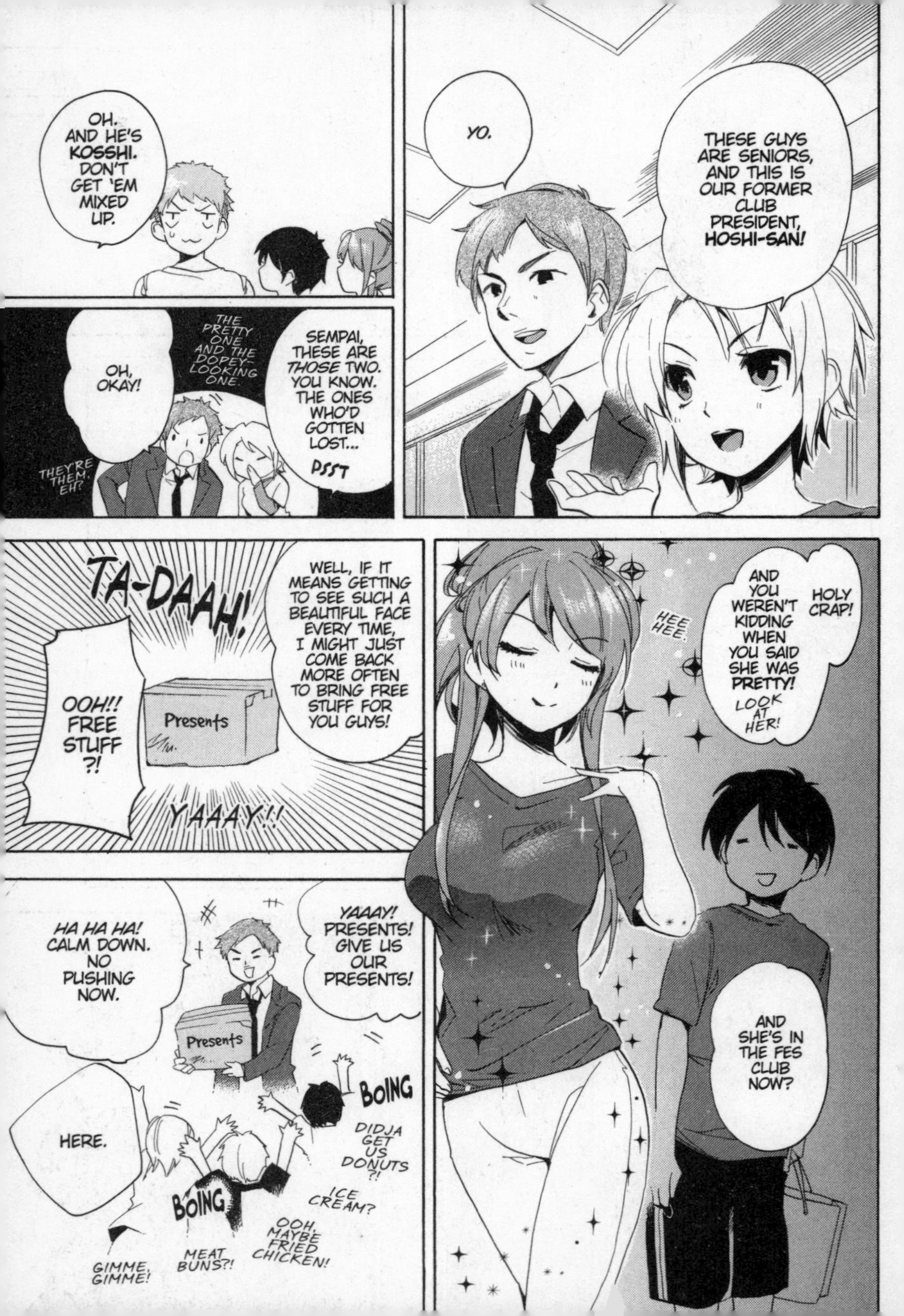
THESE GUYS ARE SENIORS, AND THIS IS OUR FORMER CLUB PRESIDENT, HOSHI-SAN!
YO.
OH. AND HE'S KOSSHI. DON'T GET 'EM MIXED UP.
SEMPAI, THESE ARE THOSE TWO. YOU KNOW. THE ONES WHO'D GOTTEN LOST...
PSST
THE PRETTY ONE AND THE DOPEY-LOOKING ONE.
OH, OKAY!
THEY'RE THEM, EH?
HOLY CRAP!
AND YOU WEREN'T KIDDING WHEN YOU SAID SHE WAS PRETTY!
LOOK AT HER!
HEE HEE.
AND SHE'S IN THE FES CLUB NOW?
WELL, IF IT MEANS GETTING TO SEE SUCH A BEAUTIFUL FACE EVERY TIME, I MIGHT JUST COME BACK MORE OFTEN TO BRING FREE STUFF FOR YOU GUYS!
TA-DAAH!
Presents
OOH!! FREE STUFF?!
YAAAY!!
YAAAY! PRESENTS! GIVE US OUR PRESENTS!
HA HA HA! CALM DOWN. NO PUSHING NOW.
Presents
BOING
DIDJA GET US DONUTS?!
HERE.
ICE CREAM?
OOH, MAYBE FRIED CHICKEN!
BOING
MEAT BUNS?!
GIMME, GIMME!

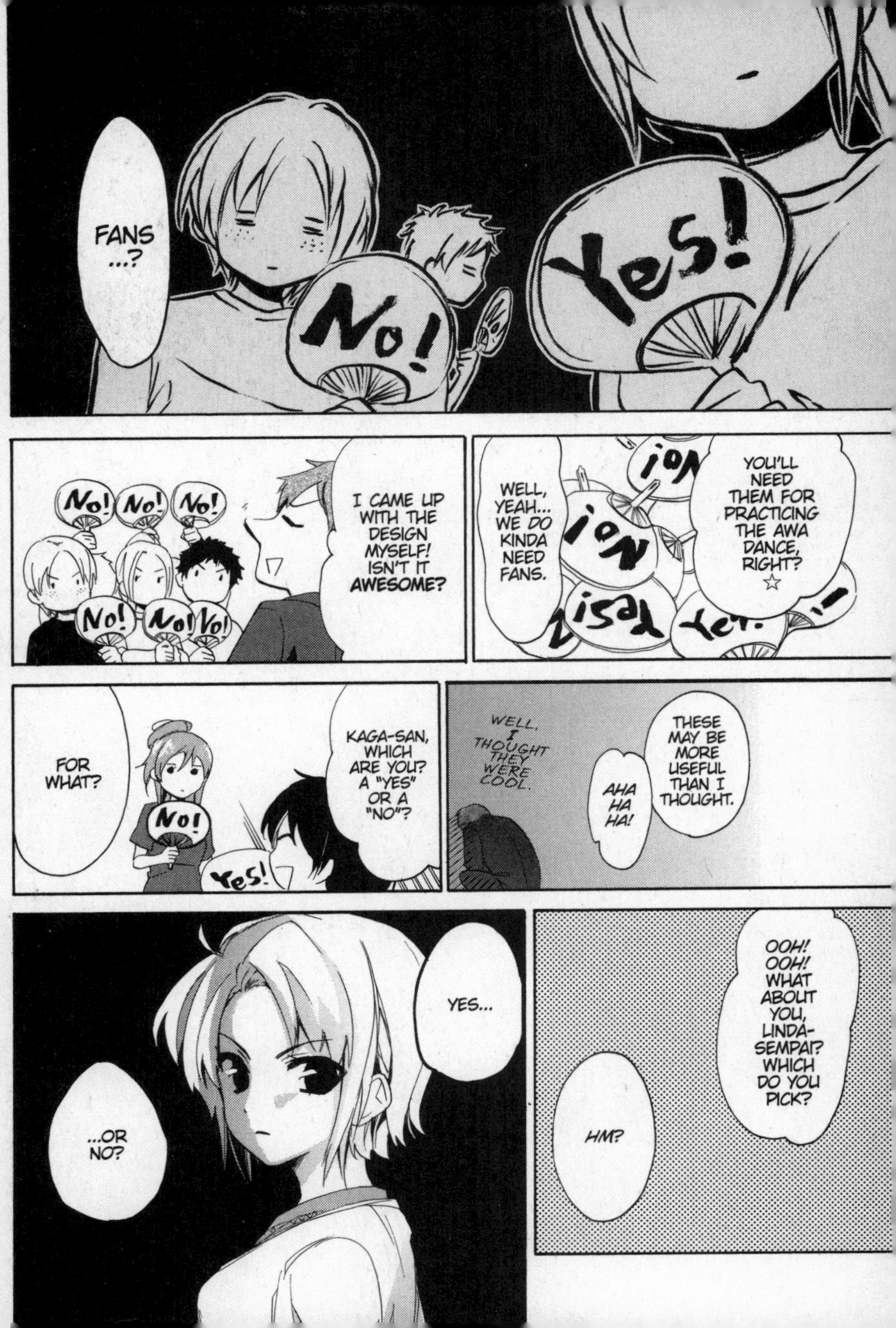
Yes!
No!
FANS ...?
YOU'LL NEED THEM FOR PRACTICING THE AWA DANCE, RIGHT? ☆
WELL, YEAH... WE DO KINDA NEED FANS.
I CAME UP WITH THE DESIGN MYSELF! ISN'T IT AWESOME?
THESE MAY BE MORE USEFUL THAN I THOUGHT.
AHA HA HA!
WELL, I THOUGHT THEY WERE COOL.
KAGA-SAN, WHICH ARE YOU? A "YES" OR A "NO"?
Yes!
No!
FOR WHAT?
OOH! OOH! WHAT ABOUT YOU, LINDA-SEMPAI? WHICH DO YOU PICK?
HM?
YES...
...OR NO?

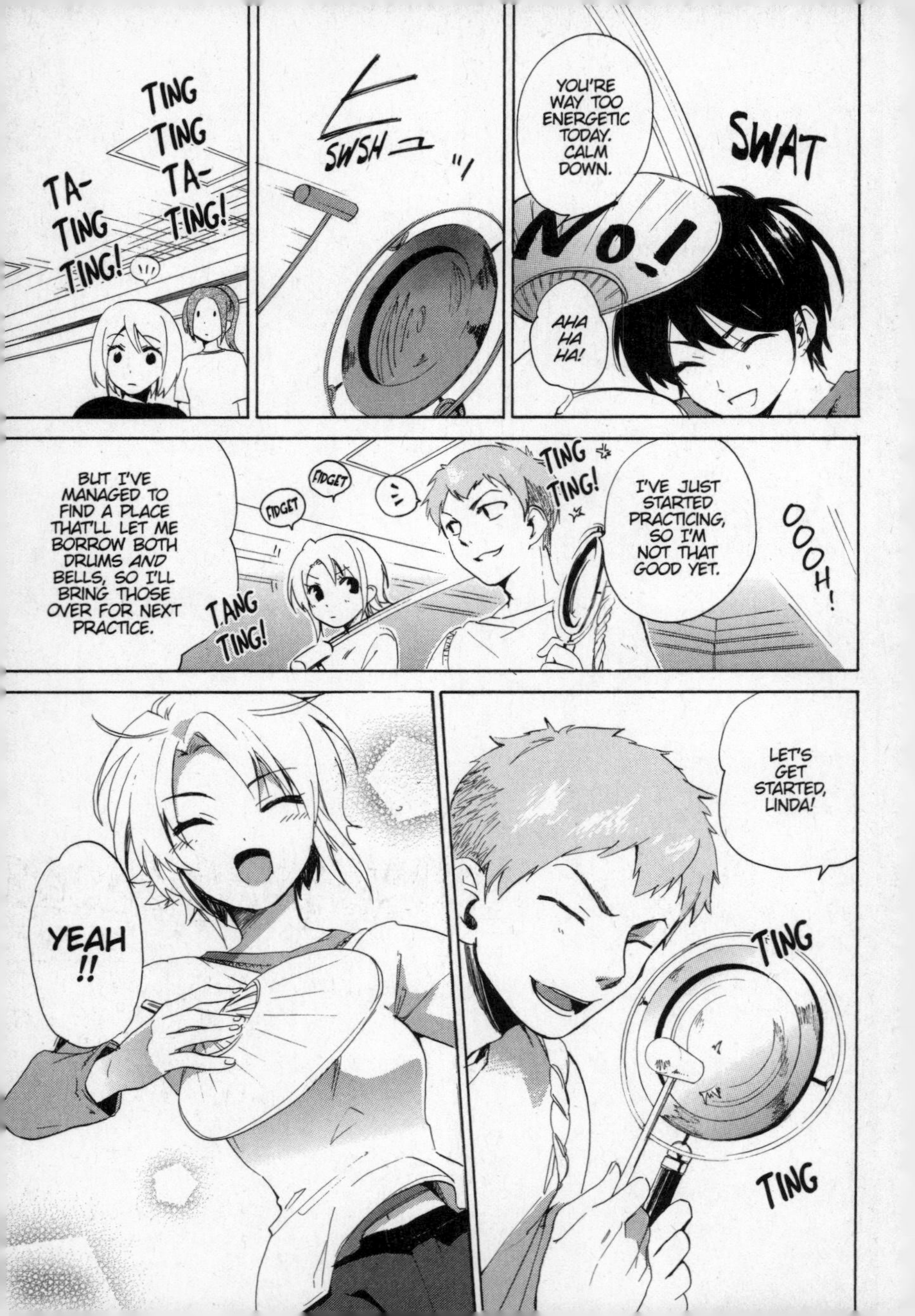
YOU'RE WAY TOO ENERGETIC TODAY. CALM DOWN.
SWAT
NO!
AHA HA HA!
SWSH
TING TING TA-TING!
TA-TING TING!
OOOOH!
I'VE JUST STARTED PRACTICING, SO I'M NOT THAT GOOD YET.
TING TING!
FIDGET
FIDGET
BUT I'VE MANAGED TO FIND A PLACE THAT'LL LET ME BORROW BOTH DRUMS AND BELLS, SO I'LL BRING THOSE OVER FOR NEXT PRACTICE.
TANG TING!
LET'S GET STARTED, LINDA!
TING
TING
YEAH!!

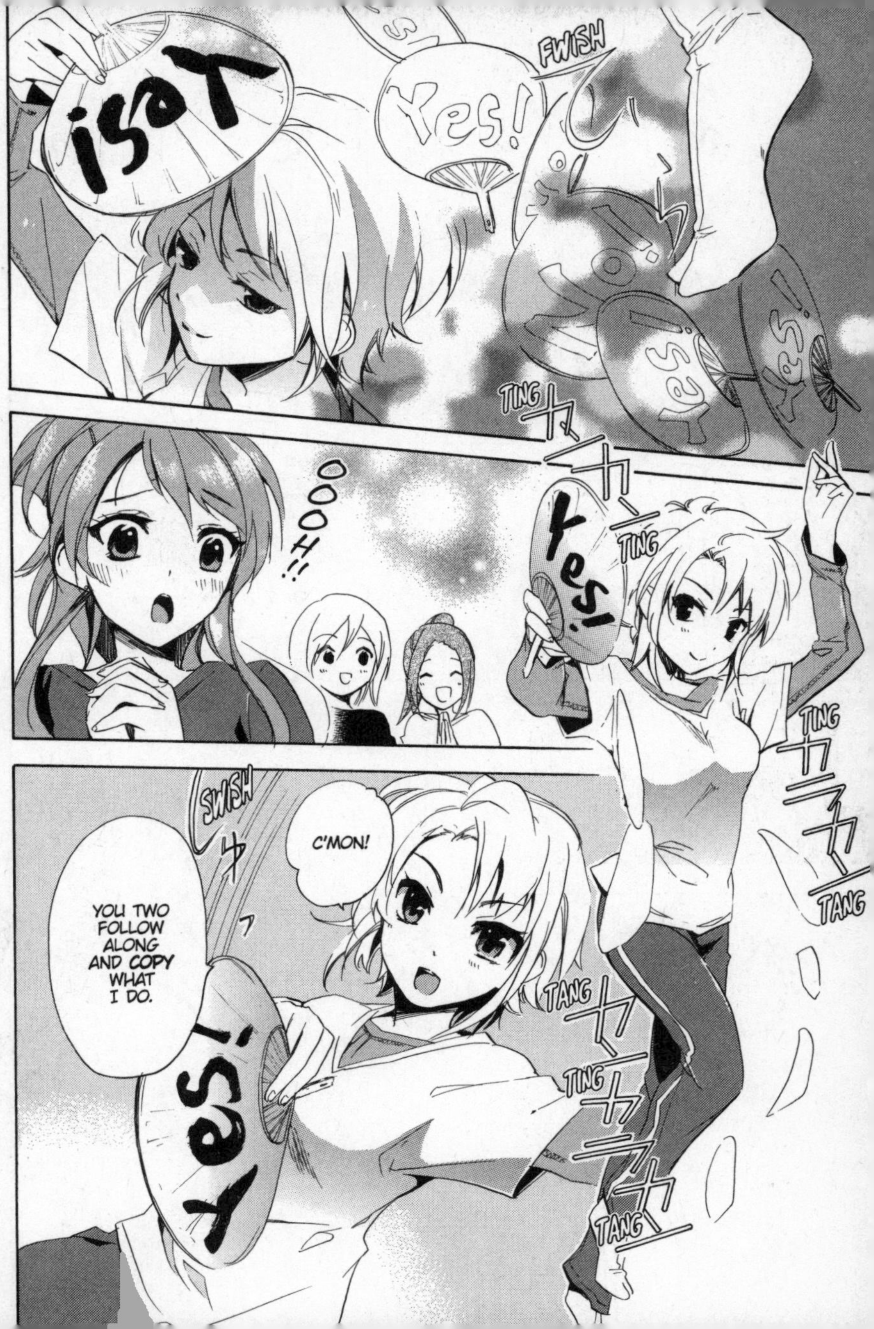
FWISH
Yes!
TING
TING
Yes!
OOOOH!!
TING
TANG
SWISH
C'MON!
YOU TWO FOLLOW ALONG AND COPY WHAT I DO.
TANG
TING
TANG
Yes!

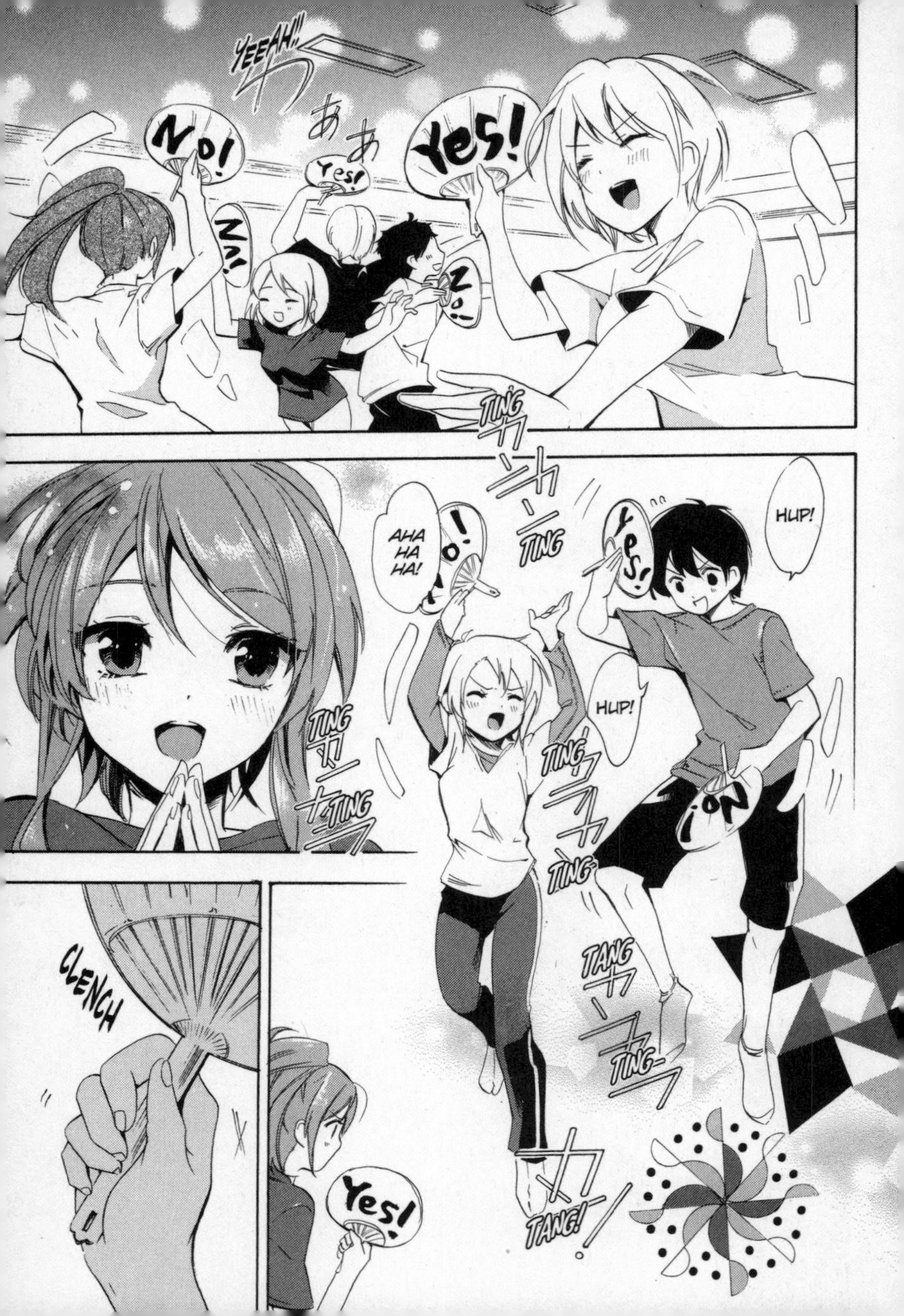
YEEAH!!
あ
あ
Yes!
Yes!
No!
No!
No!
HUP!
Yes!
AHA HA HA!
No!
TING
TING
HUP!
TING
TING
No!
TING
TANG
TING
TANG!
TING
TING
CLENCH
Yes!

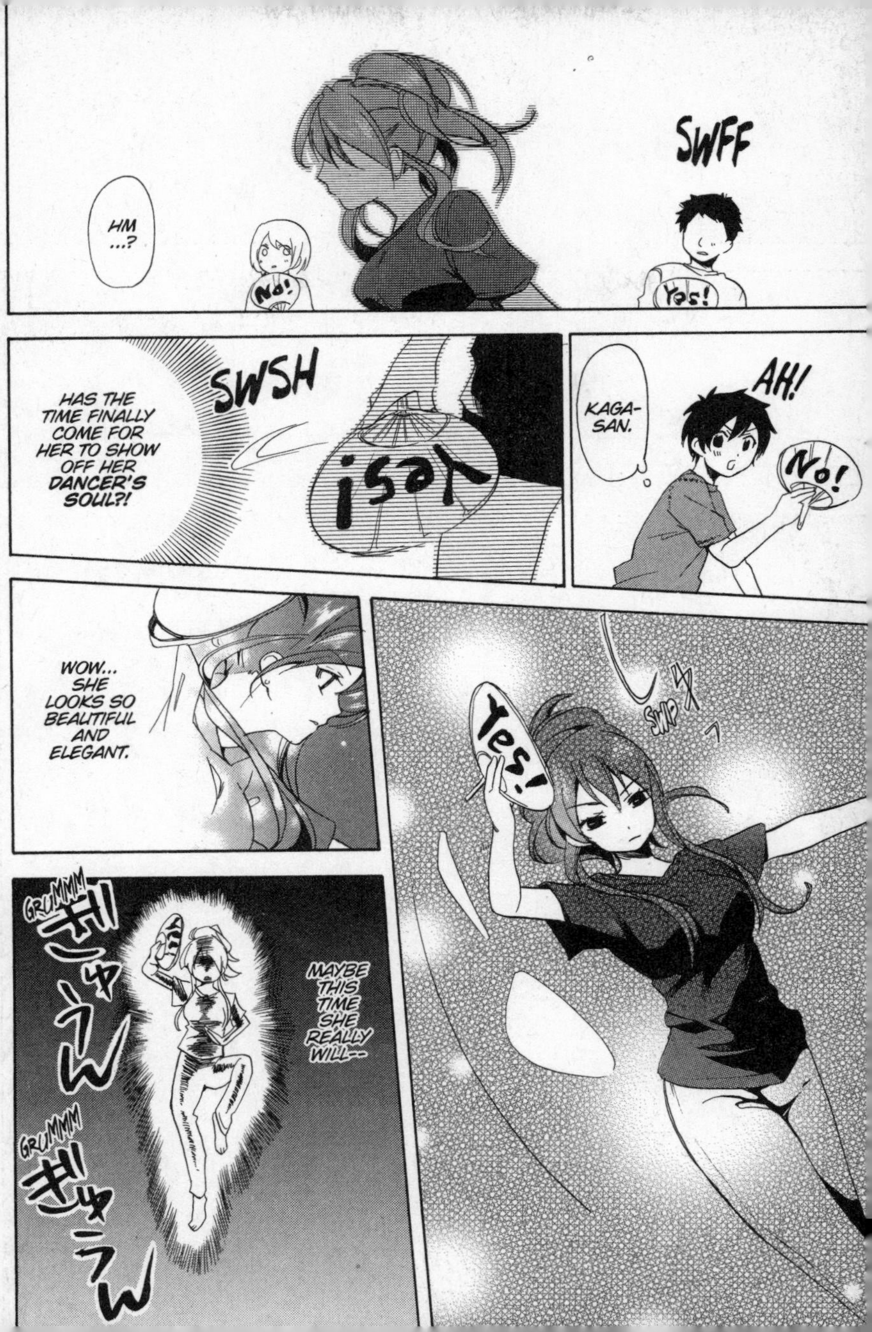
SWFF
Yes!
HM ...?
No!
AH!
KAGA-SAN.
No!
SWSH
Yes!
HAS THE TIME FINALLY COME FOR HER TO SHOW OFF HER DANCER'S SOUL?!
SWIP
Yes!
WOW... SHE LOOKS SO BEAUTIFUL AND ELEGANT.
MAYBE THIS TIME SHE REALLY WILL--
GRUMMM
GRUMMM

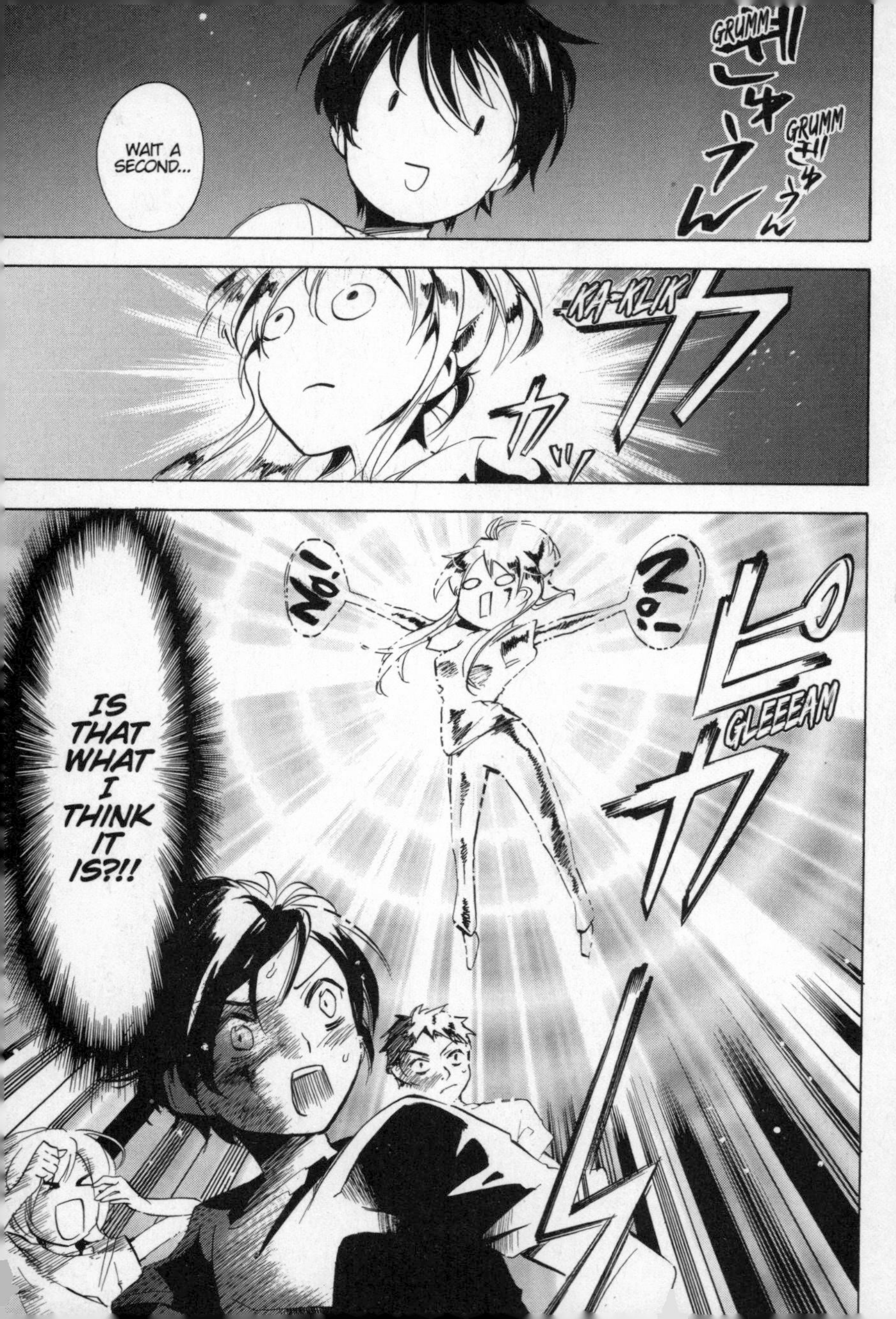
GRUMM
GRUMM
WAIT A SECOND...
KA-KLIK
No!
No!
GLEEEAM
IS THAT WHAT I THINK IT IS?!!

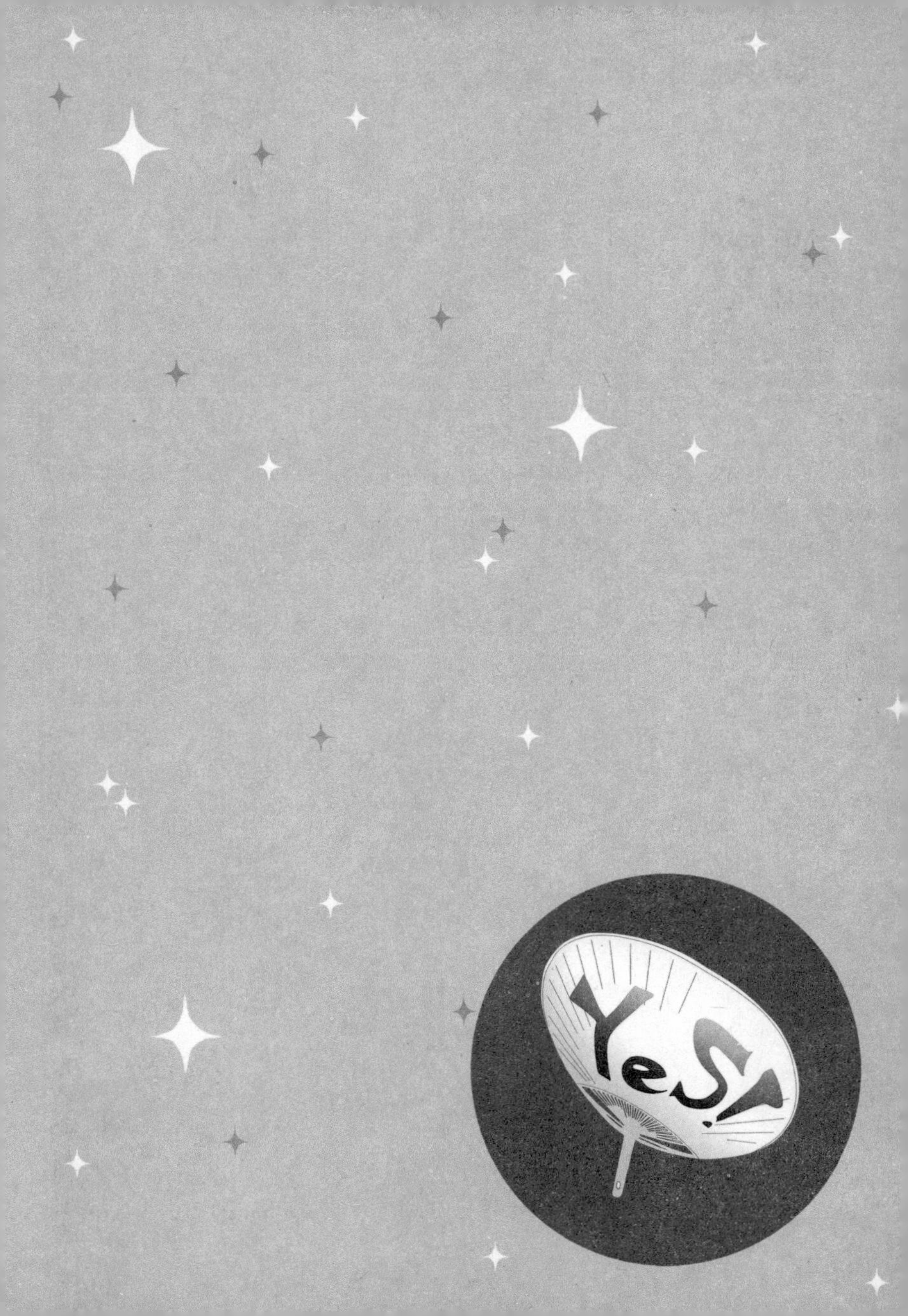
Yes!

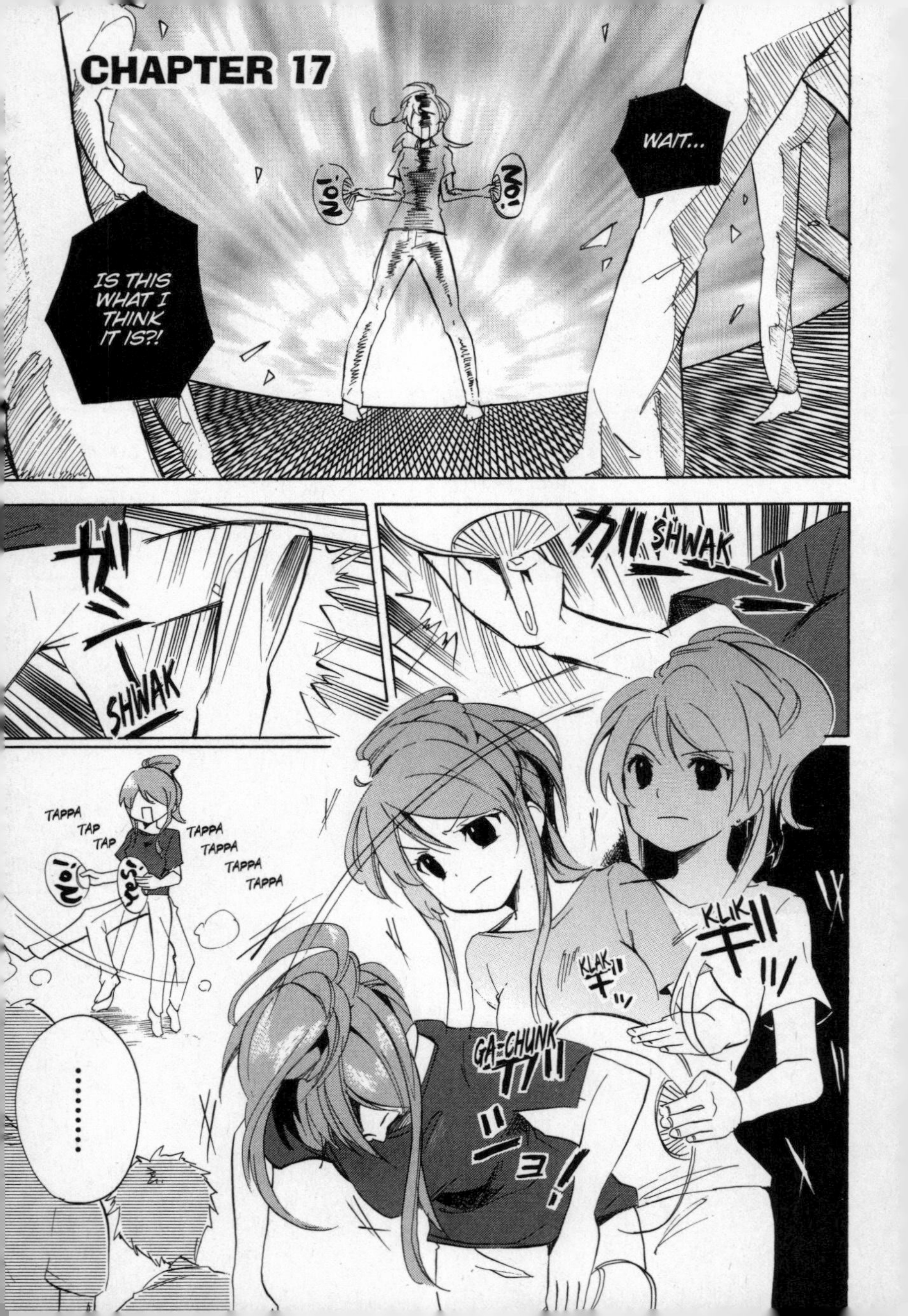
CHAPTER 17
WAIT...
IS THIS WHAT I THINK IT IS?!
NO!
NO!
SHWAK
SHWAK
KLIK
KLAK
GA-CHUNK
TAPPA TAP TAP
TAPPA TAPPA TAPPA TAPPA
NO!
YES!
......

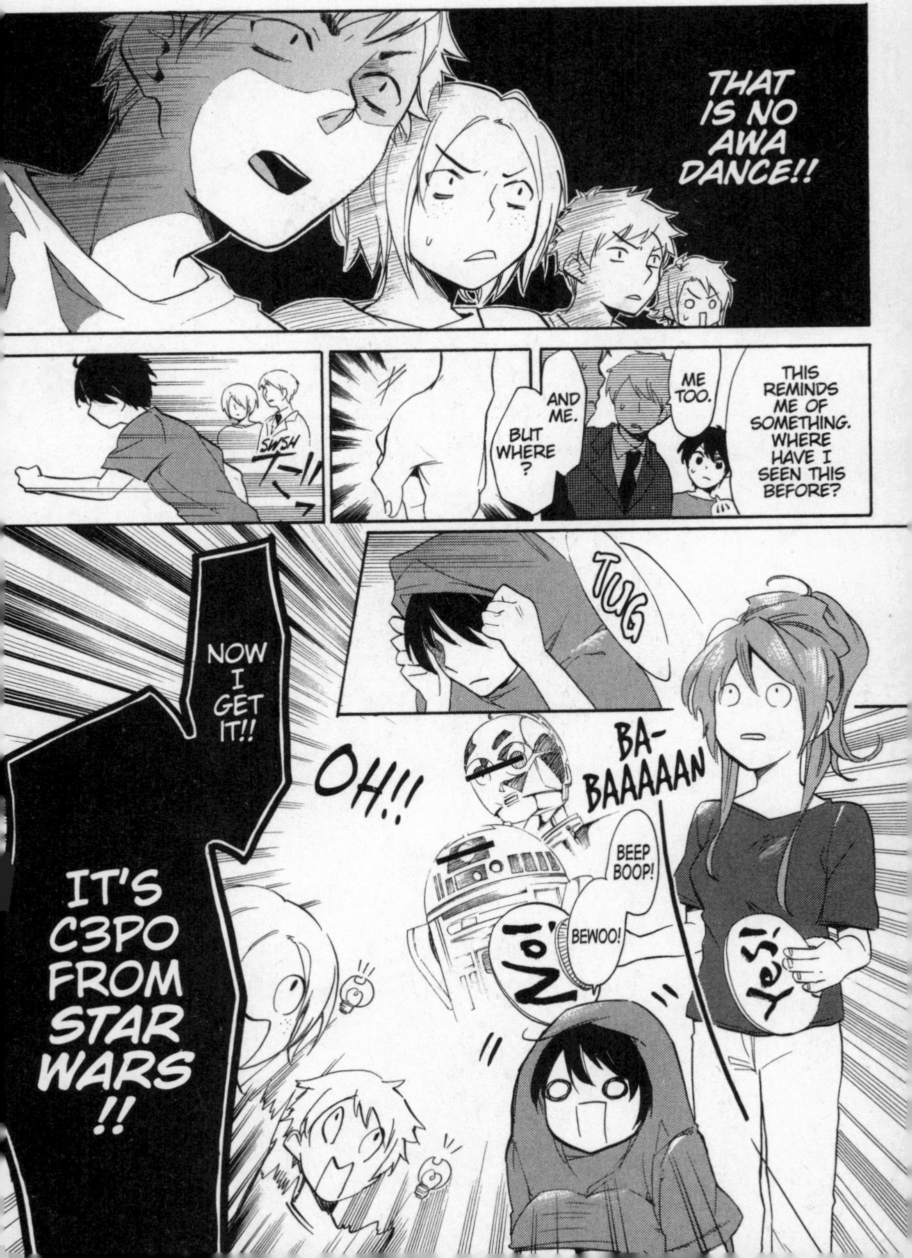
THAT IS NO AWA DANCE!!
THIS REMINDS ME OF SOMETHING. WHERE HAVE I SEEN THIS BEFORE?
ME TOO.
AND ME. BUT WHERE?
SWSH
TUG
BA-BAAAAAN
OH!!
BEEP BOOP!
BEWOO!
Yes!
No!
NOW I GET IT!!
IT'S C3PO FROM STAR WARS!!

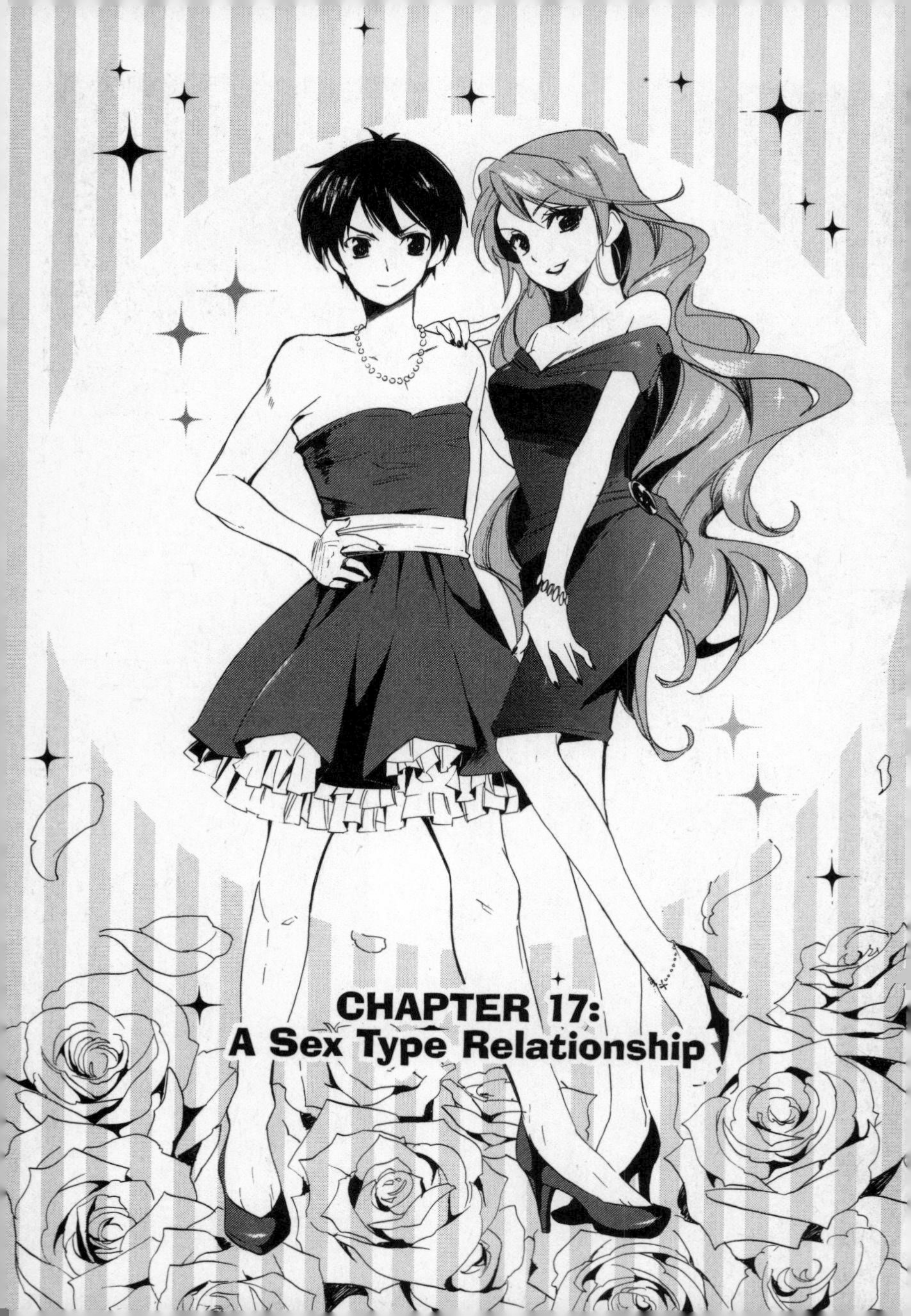

CHAPTER 17: A Sex Type Relationship

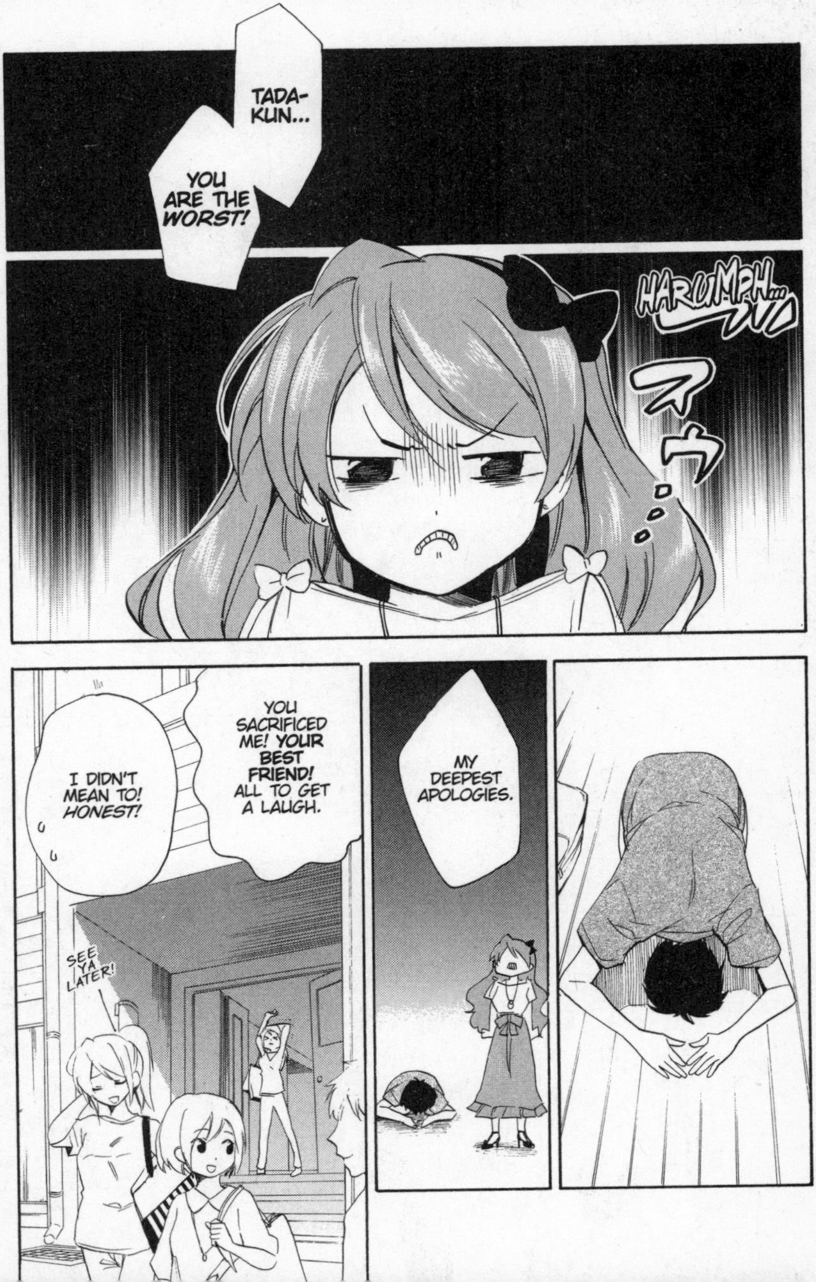
TADA-KUN...
YOU ARE THE WORST!
HARUMPH...
スゥ
MY DEEPEST APOLOGIES.
YOU SACRIFICED ME! YOUR BEST FRIEND! ALL TO GET A LAUGH.
I DIDN'T MEAN TO! HONEST!
SEE YA LATER!

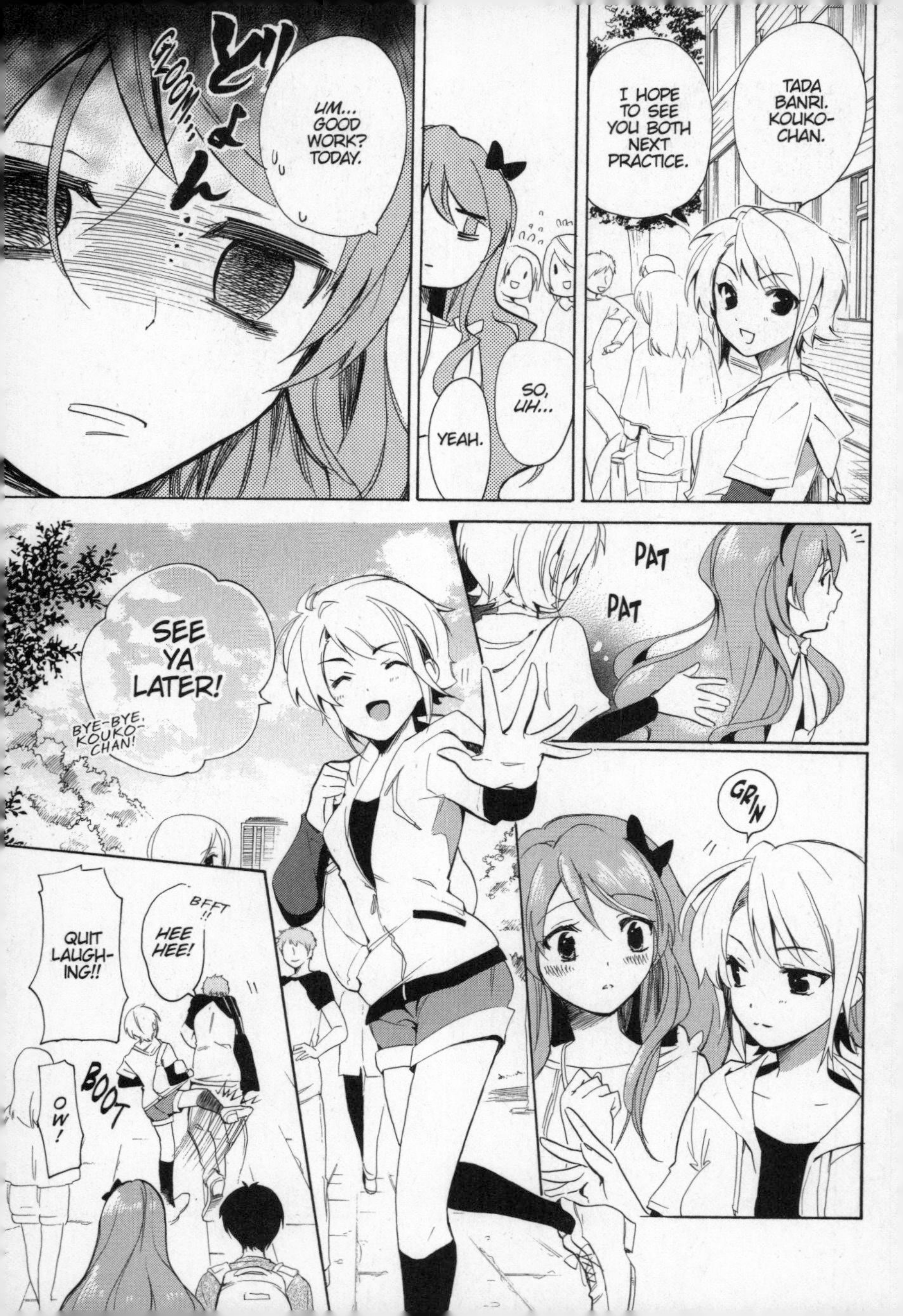
TADA BANRI. KOUKO-CHAN.
I HOPE TO SEE YOU BOTH NEXT PRACTICE.
SO, UH...
YEAH.
UM... GOOD WORK? TODAY.
GLOOM...
PAT
PAT
GRIN
SEE YA LATER!
BYE-BYE, KOUKO-CHAN!
BFFT!!
HEE HEE!
QUIT LAUGHING!!
BOOT
OW!

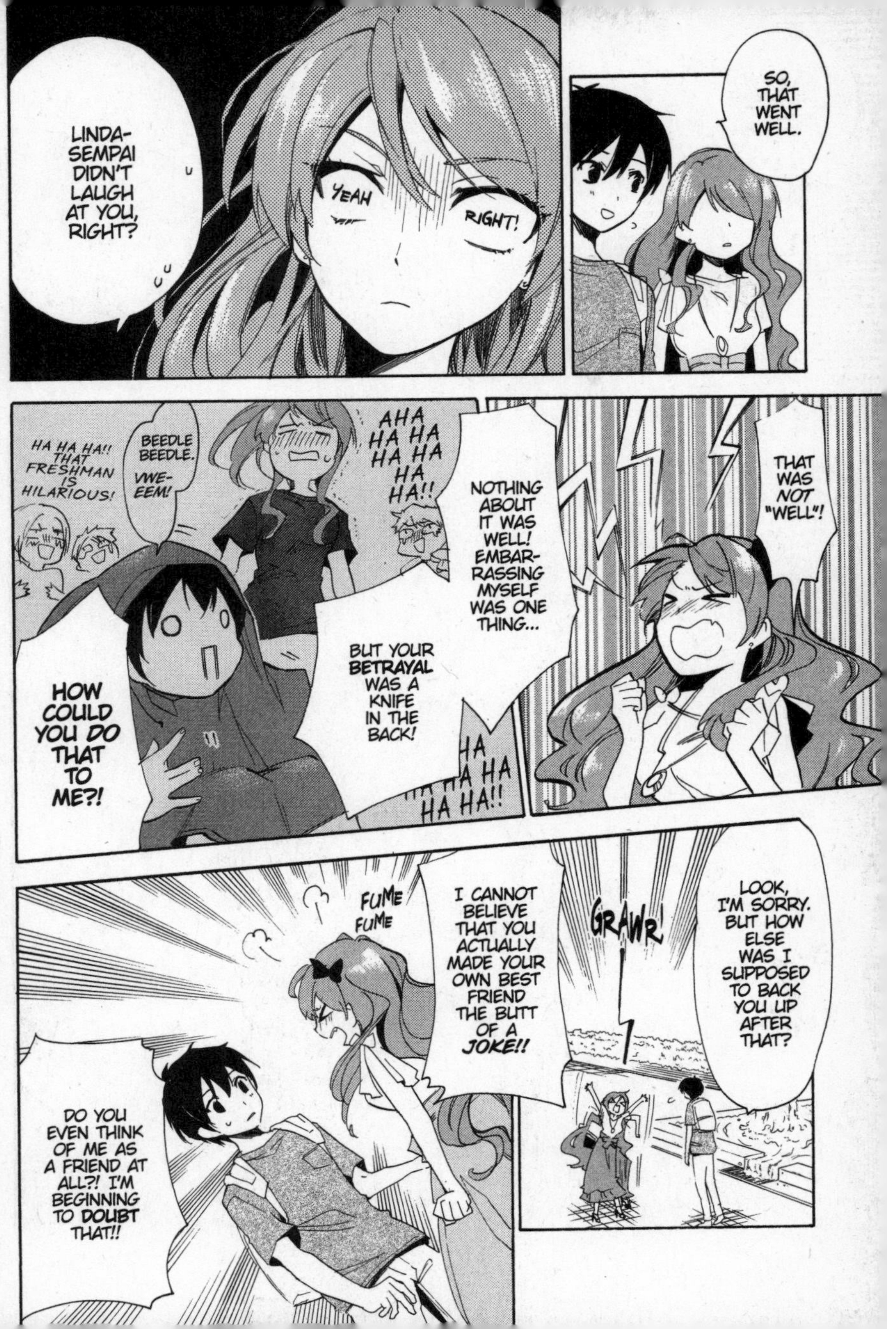
SO, THAT WENT WELL.
LINDA-SEMPAI DIDN'T LAUGH AT YOU, RIGHT?
YEAH RIGHT!
THAT WAS NOT "WELL"!
NOTHING ABOUT IT WAS WELL! EMBARRASSING MYSELF WAS ONE THING...
AHA HA HA HA HA HA HA!!
BEEDLE BEEDLE. VWE-EEM!
HA HA HA!! THAT FRESHMAN IS HILARIOUS!
BUT YOUR BETRAYAL WAS A KNIFE IN THE BACK!
HA HA HA HA HA!!
HOW COULD YOU DO THAT TO ME?!
LOOK, I'M SORRY. BUT HOW ELSE WAS I SUPPOSED TO BACK YOU UP AFTER THAT?
GRAWR!
I CANNOT BELIEVE THAT YOU ACTUALLY MADE YOUR OWN BEST FRIEND THE BUTT OF A JOKE!!
FUME FUME
DO YOU EVEN THINK OF ME AS A FRIEND AT ALL?! I'M BEGINNING TO DOUBT THAT!!

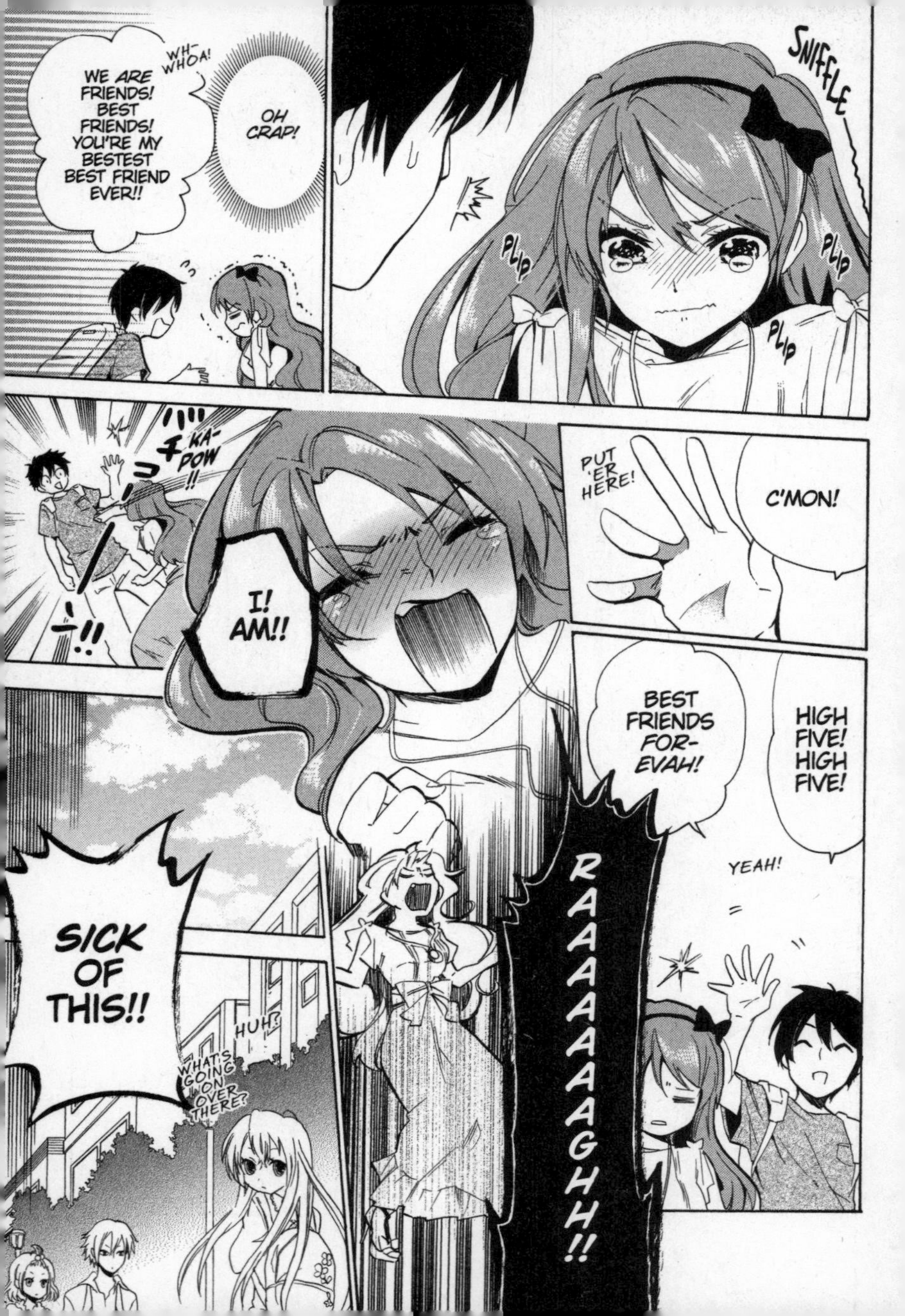
SNIFFLE
PLIP
PLIP
PLIP
WE ARE FRIENDS! BEST FRIENDS! YOU'RE MY BESTEST BEST FRIEND EVER!!
WH-WHOA!
OH CRAP!
C'MON!
PUT 'ER HERE!
HIGH FIVE! HIGH FIVE!
BEST FRIENDS FOR-EVAH!
YEAH!
I! AM!!
RAAAAAAAAGHH!!
KA-POW!!
SICK OF THIS!!
HUH?
WHAT'S GOING ON OVER THERE?

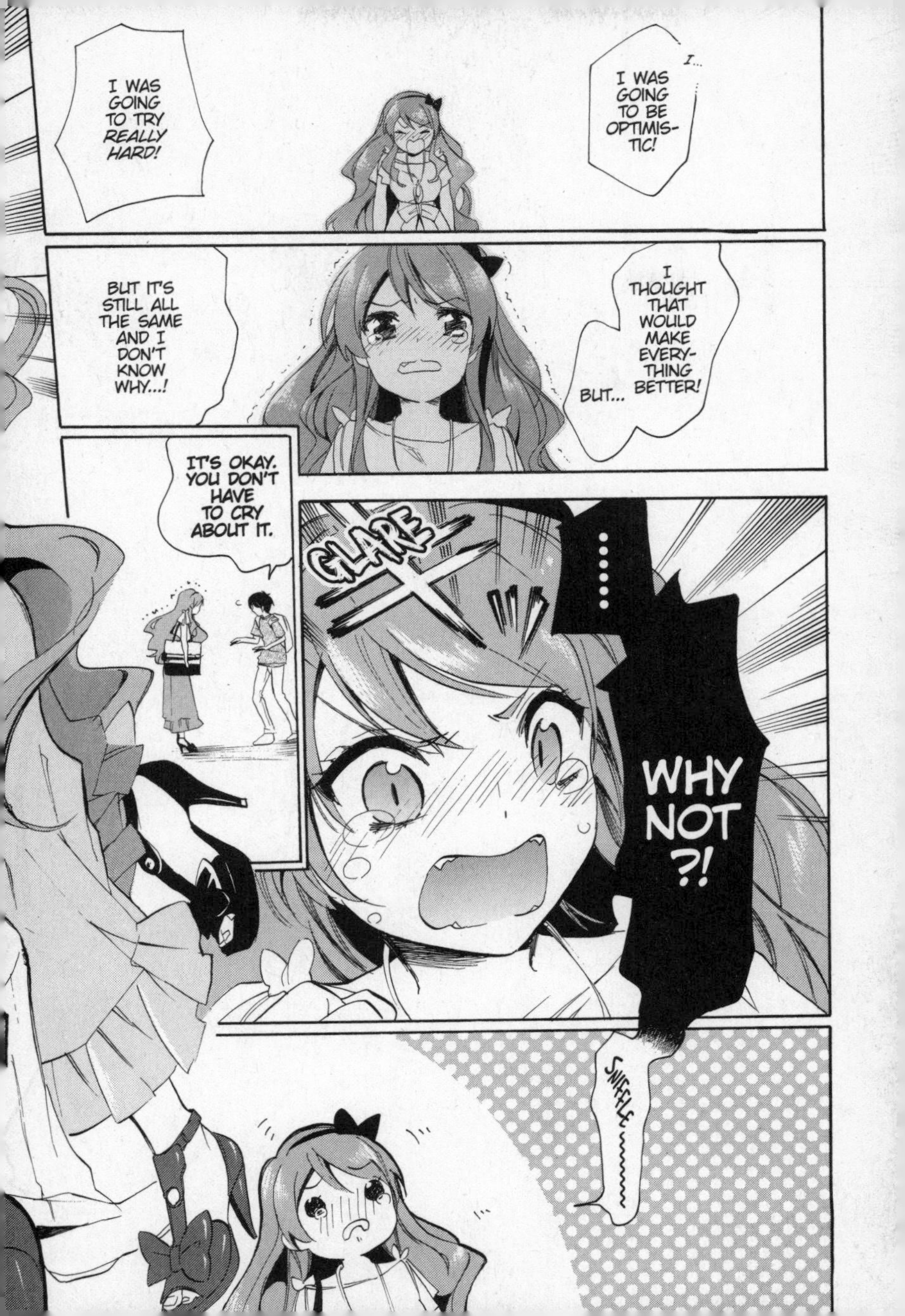

I...
I WAS GOING TO BE OPTIMISTIC!
I WAS GOING TO TRY REALLY HARD!
I THOUGHT THAT WOULD MAKE EVERYTHING BETTER!
BUT...
BUT IT'S STILL ALL THE SAME AND I DON'T KNOW WHY...!
IT'S OKAY. YOU DON'T HAVE TO CRY ABOUT IT.
GLARE
......
WHY NOT ?!
SNIFFLE

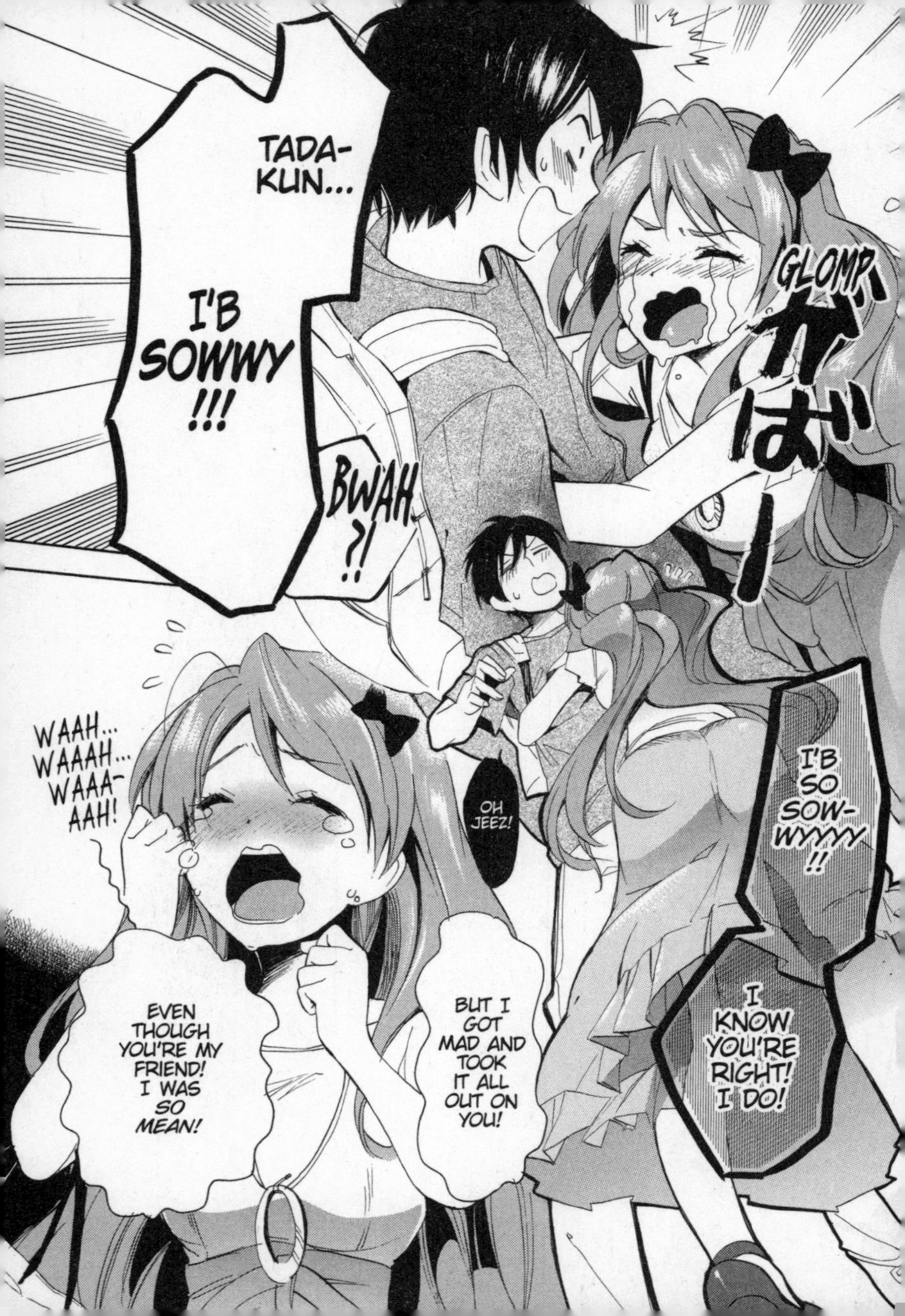
GLOMP
がばー
TADA-KUN...
I'B SOWWY!!!
BWAH?!
I'B SO SOW-WYYYY!!
I KNOW YOU'RE RIGHT! I DO!
OH JEEZ!
BUT I GOT MAD AND TOOK IT ALL OUT ON YOU!
EVEN THOUGH YOU'RE MY FRIEND! I WAS SO MEAN!
WAAH... WAAAH... WAAA-AAH!

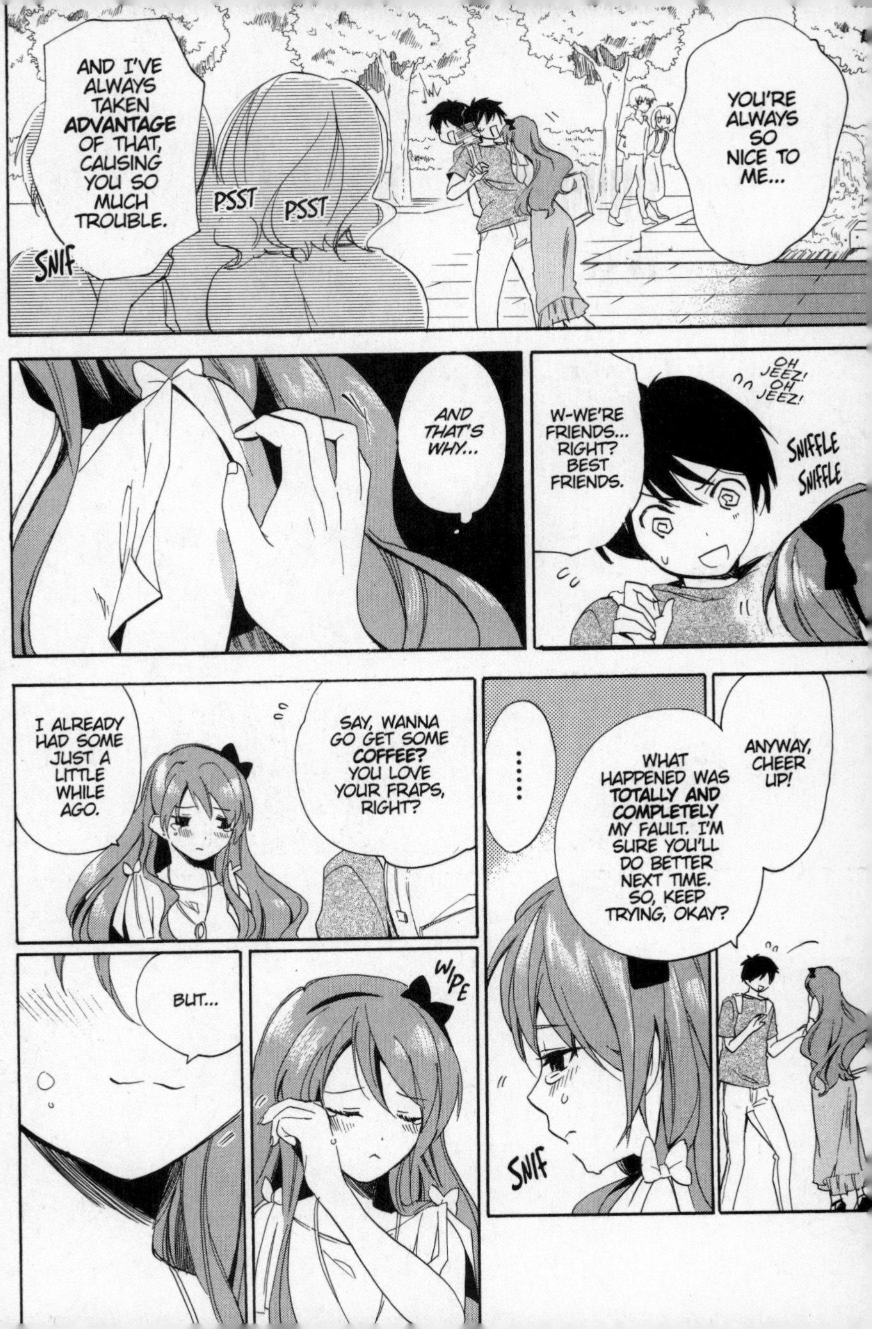
YOU'RE ALWAYS SO NICE TO ME...
PSST
PSST
AND I'VE ALWAYS TAKEN ADVANTAGE OF THAT, CAUSING YOU SO MUCH TROUBLE.
SNIF
OH JEEZ! OH JEEZ!
W-WE'RE FRIENDS... RIGHT? BEST FRIENDS.
SNIFFLE SNIFFLE
AND THAT'S WHY...
ANYWAY, CHEER UP!
WHAT HAPPENED WAS TOTALLY AND COMPLETELY MY FAULT. I'M SURE YOU'LL DO BETTER NEXT TIME. SO, KEEP TRYING, OKAY?
......
SNIF
SAY, WANNA GO GET SOME COFFEE? YOU LOVE YOUR FRAPS, RIGHT?
I ALREADY HAD SOME JUST A LITTLE WHILE AGO.
WIPE
BUT...

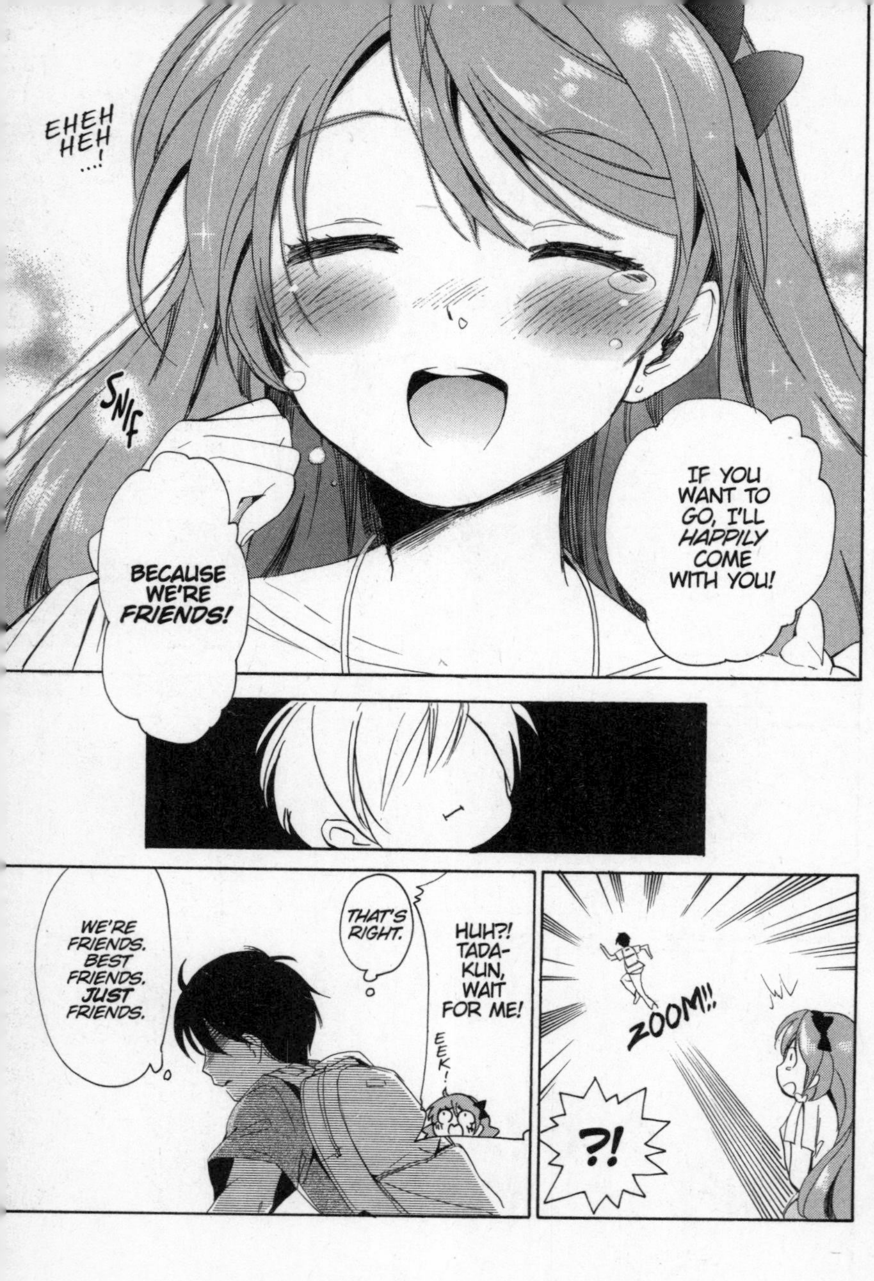
EHEH HEH ....!
IF YOU WANT TO GO, I'LL HAPPILY COME WITH YOU!
SNIF
BECAUSE WE'RE FRIENDS!
ZOOM!!
?!
HUH?! TADA-KUN, WAIT FOR ME!
THAT'S RIGHT.
EEK!
WE'RE FRIENDS. BEST FRIENDS. JUST FRIENDS.

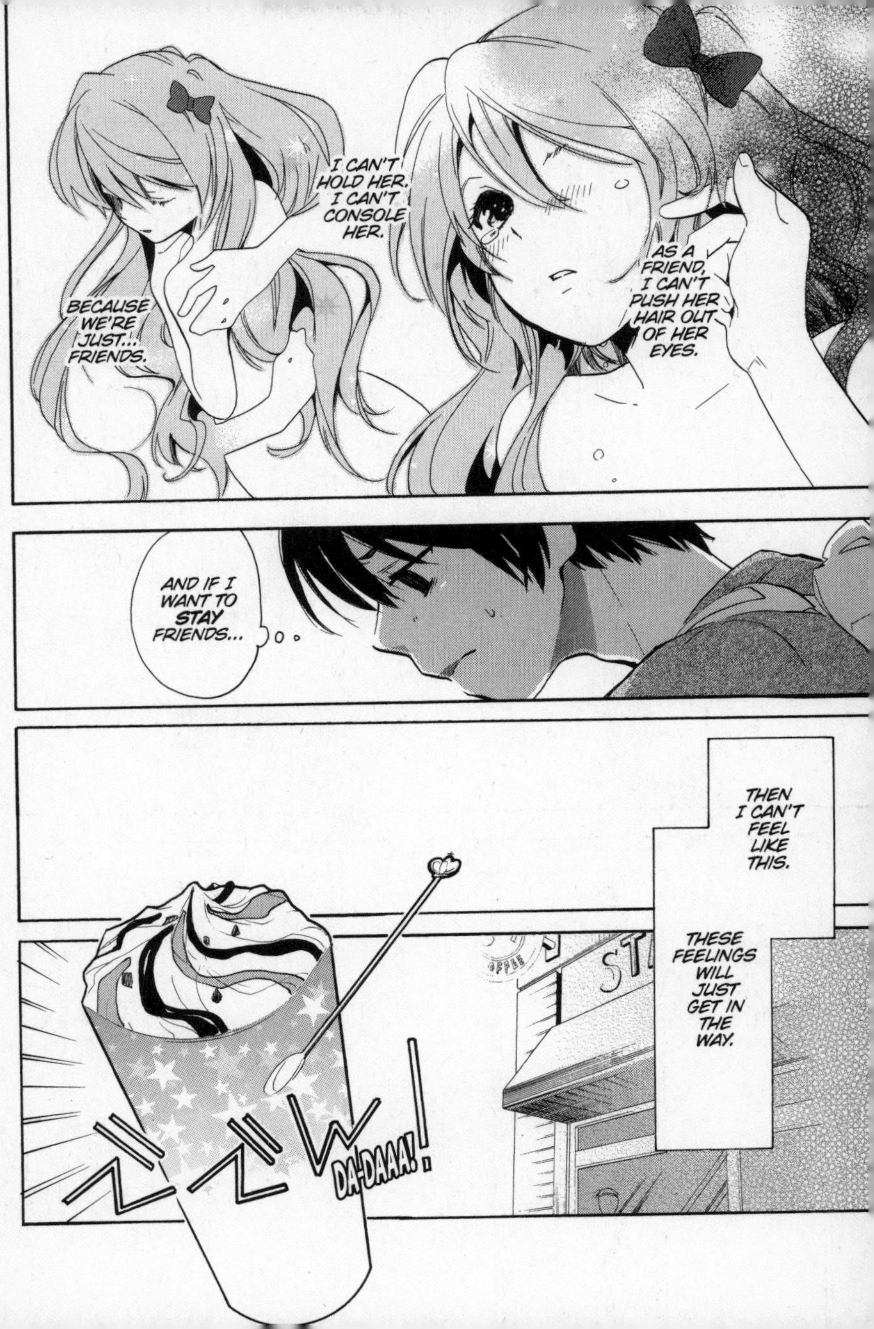
AS A FRIEND, I CAN'T PUSH HER HAIR OUT OF HER EYES.
I CAN'T HOLD HER. I CAN'T CONSOLE HER.
BECAUSE WE'RE JUST... FRIENDS.
AND IF I WANT TO STAY FRIENDS...
THEN I CAN'T FEEL LIKE THIS.
THESE FEELINGS WILL JUST GET IN THE WAY.
DA-DAAA!

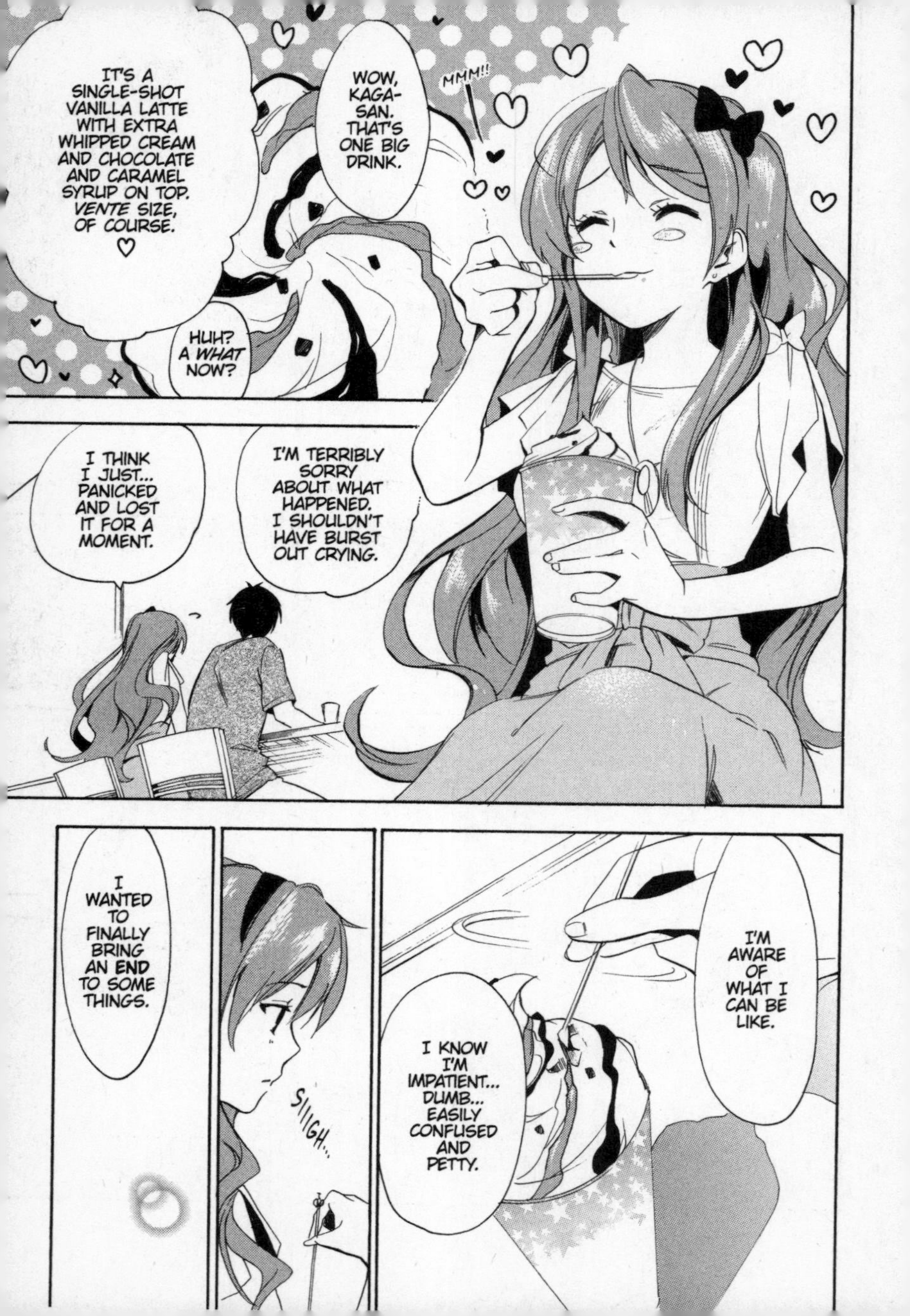
MMM!!
WOW, KAGA-SAN. THAT'S ONE BIG DRINK.
IT'S A SINGLE-SHOT VANILLA LATTE WITH EXTRA WHIPPED CREAM AND CHOCOLATE AND CARAMEL SYRUP ON TOP. VENTE SIZE, OF COURSE. ♡
HUH? A WHAT NOW?
I'M TERRIBLY SORRY ABOUT WHAT HAPPENED. I SHOULDN'T HAVE BURST OUT CRYING.
I THINK I JUST... PANICKED AND LOST IT FOR A MOMENT.
I'M AWARE OF WHAT I CAN BE LIKE.
I KNOW I'M IMPATIENT... DUMB... EASILY CONFUSED AND PETTY.
SIIIGH...
I WANTED TO FINALLY BRING AN END TO SOME THINGS.

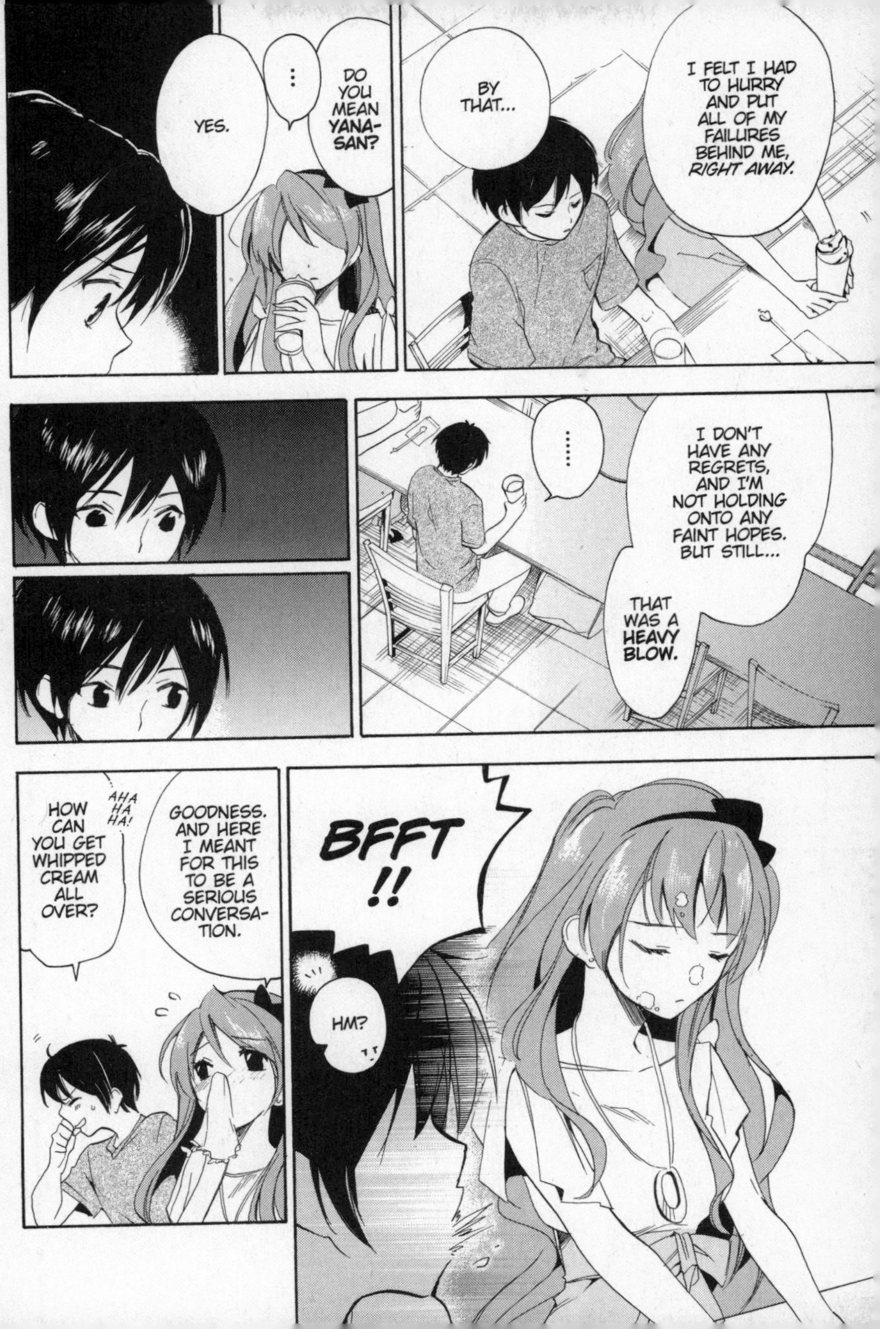
I FELT I HAD TO HURRY AND PUT ALL OF MY FAILURES BEHIND ME, *RIGHT AWAY.*
BY THAT...
DO YOU MEAN YANA-SAN?
...
YES.
I DON'T HAVE ANY REGRETS, AND I'M NOT HOLDING ONTO ANY FAINT HOPES. BUT STILL...
THAT WAS A **HEAVY BLOW.**
......
BFFT!!
HM?
GOODNESS. AND HERE I MEANT FOR THIS TO BE A SERIOUS CONVERSATION.
AHA HA HA!
HOW CAN YOU GET WHIPPED CREAM ALL OVER?

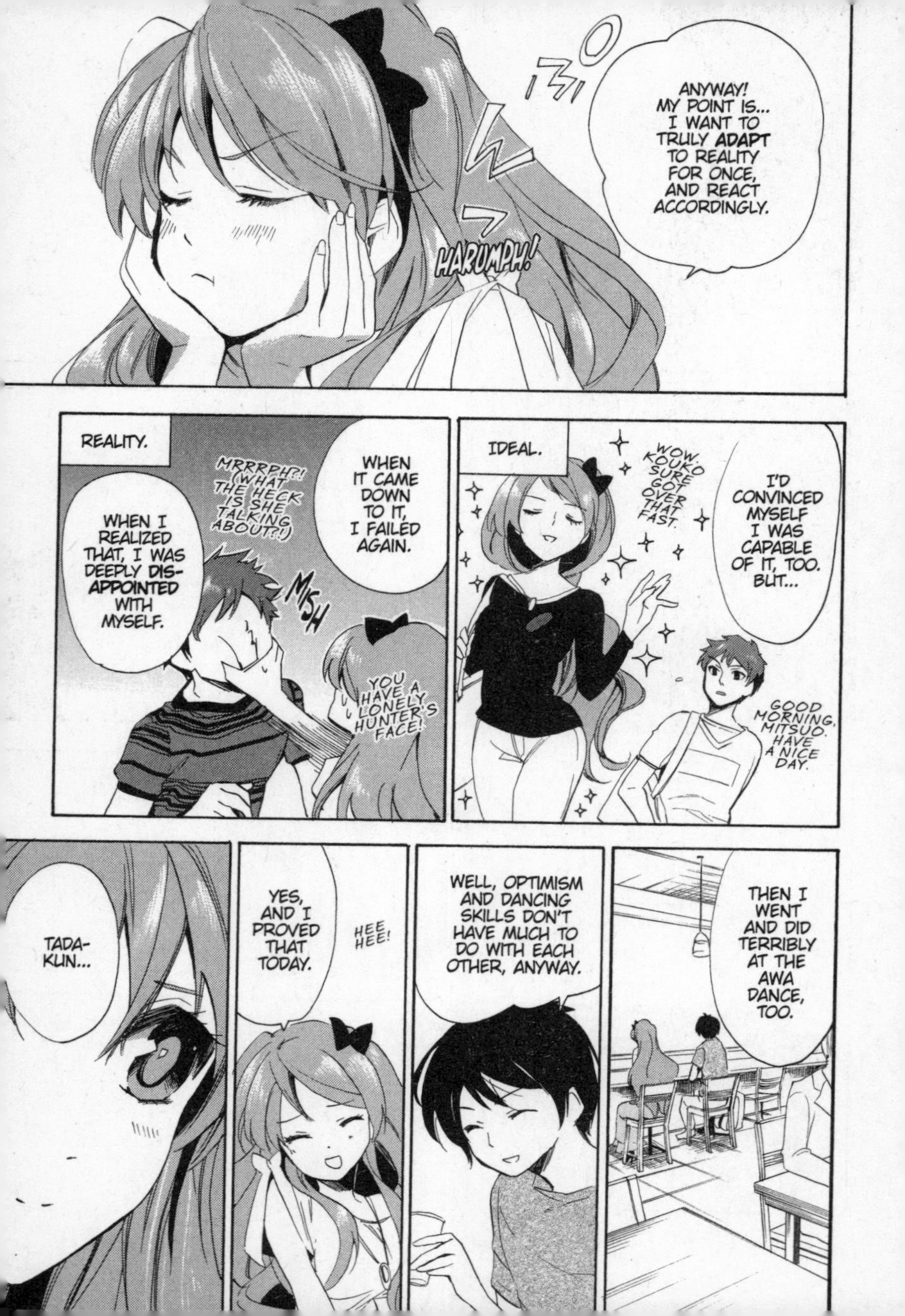
ANYWAY! MY POINT IS... I WANT TO TRULY **ADAPT** TO REALITY FOR ONCE, AND REACT ACCORDINGLY.
HARUMPH!
I'D CONVINCED MYSELF I WAS CAPABLE OF IT, TOO. BUT...
WOW. KOUKO SURE GOT OVER THAT FAST.
IDEAL.
GOOD MORNING, MITSUO. HAVE A NICE DAY.
WHEN IT CAME DOWN TO IT, I FAILED AGAIN.
MRRRPH?! (WHAT THE HECK IS SHE TALKING ABOUT?!)
REALITY.
WHEN I REALIZED THAT, I WAS DEEPLY **DIS-APPOINTED** WITH MYSELF.
MISH
YOU HAVE A LONELY HUNTER'S FACE!
THEN I WENT AND DID TERRIBLY AT THE AWA DANCE, TOO.
WELL, OPTIMISM AND DANCING SKILLS DON'T HAVE MUCH TO DO WITH EACH OTHER, ANYWAY.
YES, AND I PROVED THAT TODAY.
HEE HEE!
TADA-KUN...

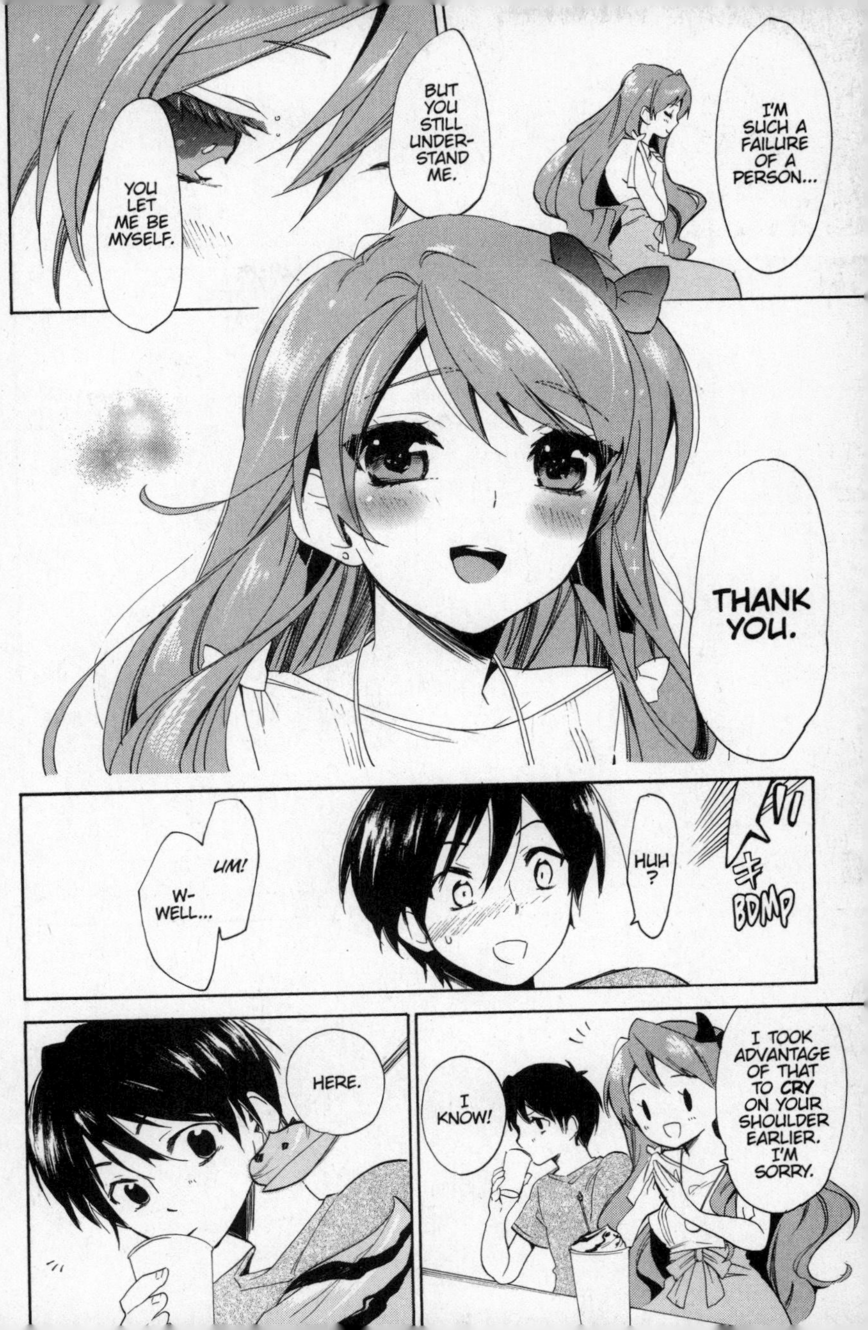
I'M SUCH A FAILURE OF A PERSON...
BUT YOU STILL UNDER-STAND ME.
YOU LET ME BE MYSELF.
THANK YOU.
BDMP
HUH?
UM!
W-WELL...
I TOOK ADVANTAGE OF THAT TO CRY ON YOUR SHOULDER EARLIER. I'M SORRY.
I KNOW!
HERE.

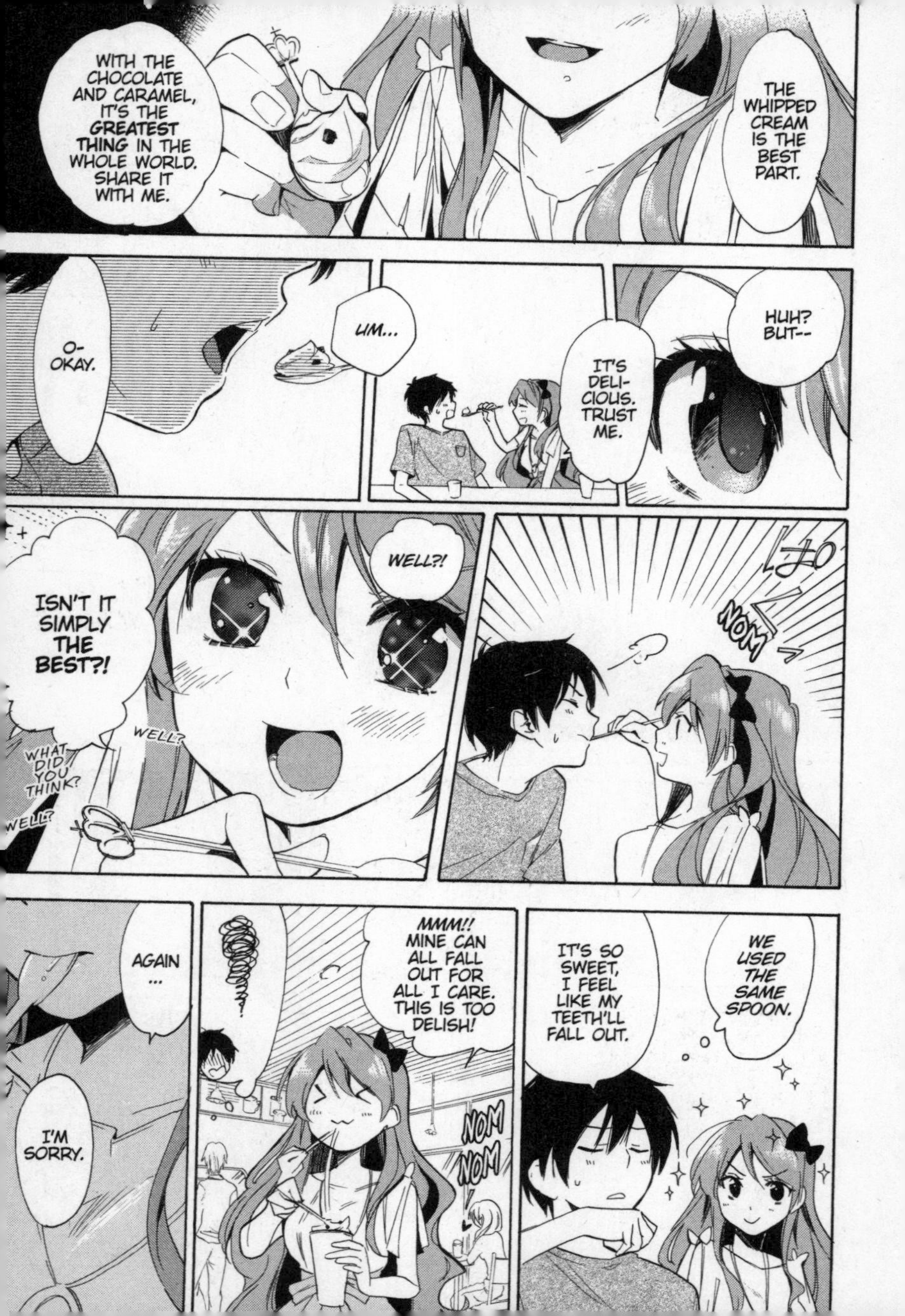
THE WHIPPED CREAM IS THE BEST PART.
WITH THE CHOCOLATE AND CARAMEL, IT'S THE GREATEST THING IN THE WHOLE WORLD. SHARE IT WITH ME.
HUH? BUT--
IT'S DELICIOUS. TRUST ME.
UM...
O-OKAY.
NOM
WELL?!
ISN'T IT SIMPLY THE BEST?!
WELL?
WHAT DID YOU THINK?
WELL?
WE USED THE SAME SPOON.
IT'S SO SWEET, I FEEL LIKE MY TEETH'LL FALL OUT.
MMM!! MINE CAN ALL FALL OUT FOR ALL I CARE. THIS IS TOO DELISH!
NOM NOM
AGAIN ...
I'M SORRY.

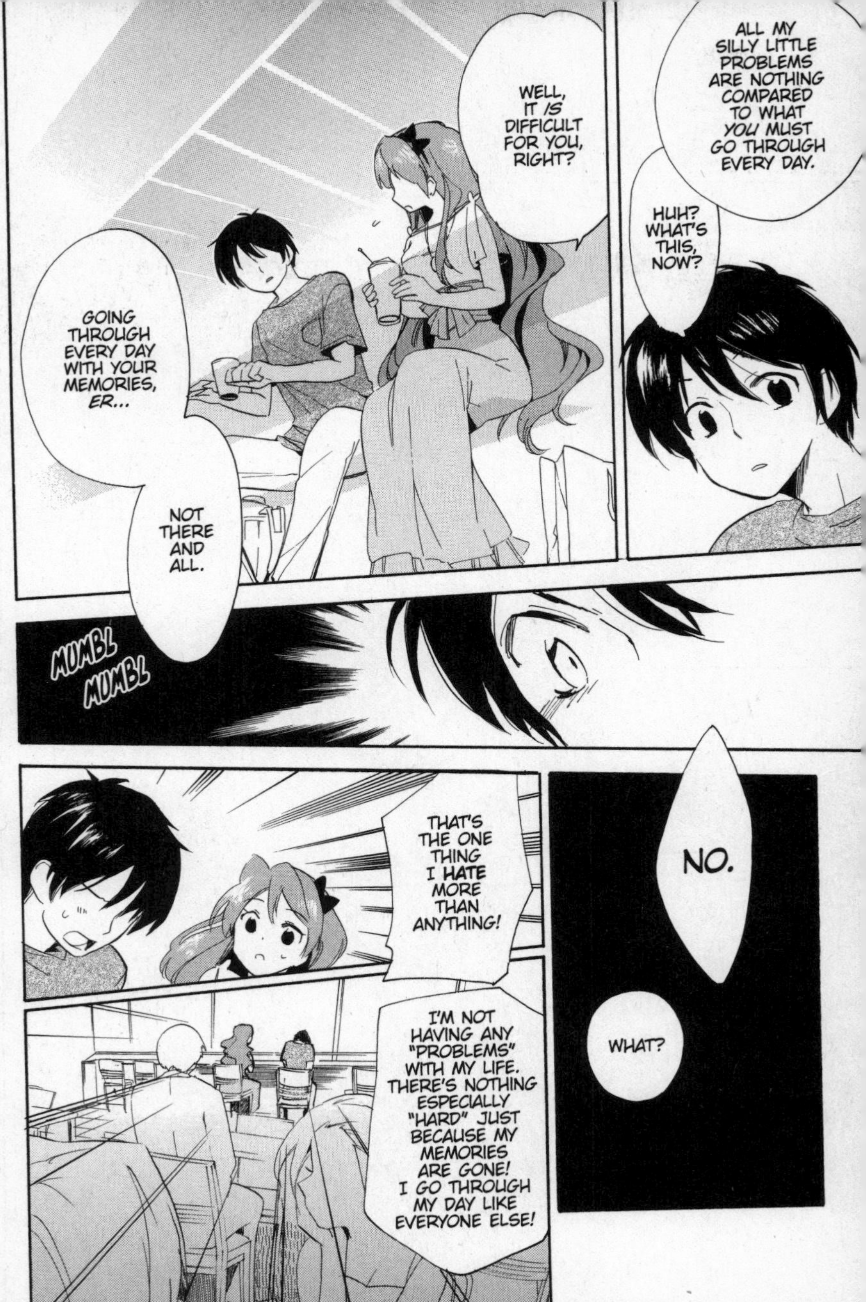
ALL MY SILLY LITTLE PROBLEMS ARE NOTHING COMPARED TO WHAT *YOU* MUST GO THROUGH EVERY DAY.
HUH? WHAT'S THIS, NOW?
WELL, IT *IS* DIFFICULT FOR YOU, RIGHT?
GOING THROUGH EVERY DAY WITH YOUR MEMORIES, *ER...*
NOT THERE AND ALL.
MUMBL MUMBL
NO.
WHAT?
THAT'S THE ONE THING I HATE MORE THAN ANYTHING!
I'M NOT HAVING ANY "PROBLEMS" WITH MY LIFE. THERE'S NOTHING ESPECIALLY "HARD" JUST BECAUSE MY MEMORIES ARE GONE! I GO THROUGH MY DAY LIKE EVERYONE ELSE!

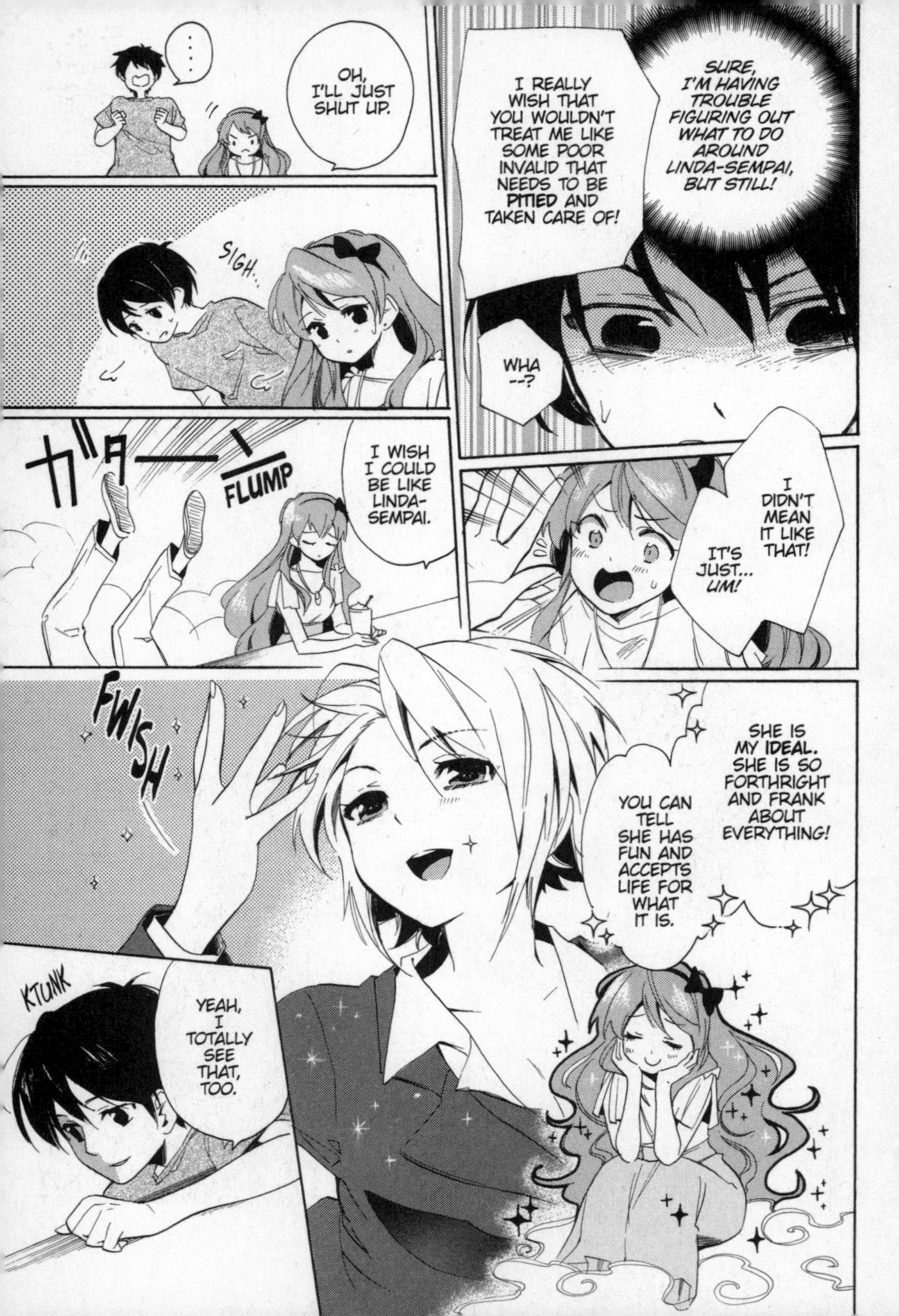
SURE, I'M HAVING TROUBLE FIGURING OUT WHAT TO DO AROUND LINDA-SEMPAI, BUT STILL!
I REALLY WISH THAT YOU WOULDN'T TREAT ME LIKE SOME POOR INVALID THAT NEEDS TO BE **PITIED** AND TAKEN CARE OF!
WHA --?
OH, I'LL JUST SHUT UP.
· · · ·
SIGH...
I DIDN'T MEAN IT LIKE THAT!
IT'S JUST... UM!
I WISH I COULD BE LIKE LINDA-SEMPAI.
FLUMP
ガターーン
SHE IS MY **IDEAL.** SHE IS SO FORTHRIGHT AND FRANK ABOUT EVERYTHING!
YOU CAN TELL SHE HAS FUN AND ACCEPTS LIFE FOR WHAT IT IS.
FWISH
KTUNK
YEAH, I TOTALLY SEE THAT, TOO.

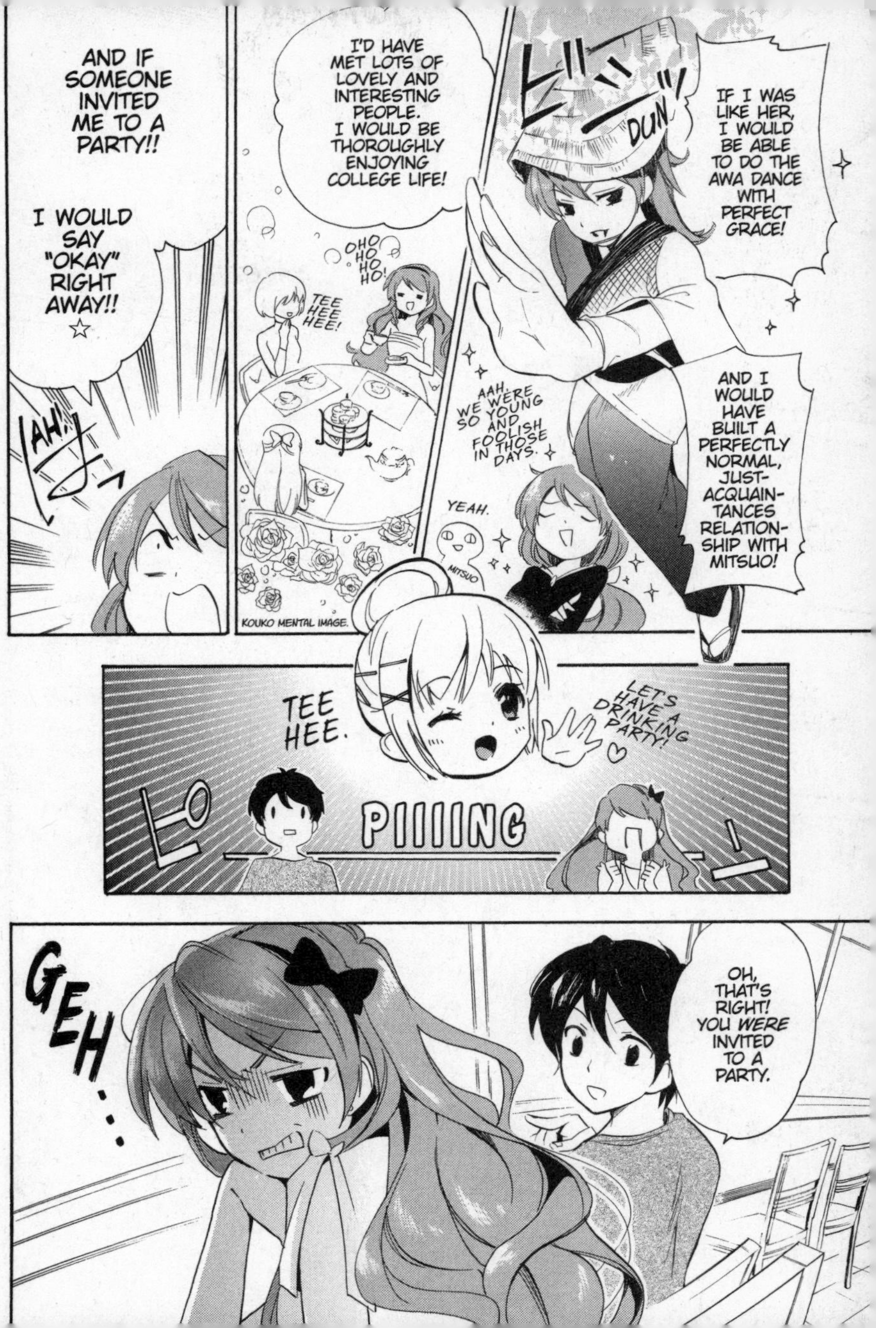

IF I WAS LIKE HER, I WOULD BE ABLE TO DO THE AWA DANCE WITH PERFECT GRACE!
DUN
AND I WOULD HAVE BUILT A PERFECTLY NORMAL, JUST-ACQUAINTANCES RELATIONSHIP WITH MITSUO!
AAH. WE WERE SO YOUNG AND FOOLISH IN THOSE DAYS.
YEAH.
MITSUO
I'D HAVE MET LOTS OF LOVELY AND INTERESTING PEOPLE. I WOULD BE THOROUGHLY ENJOYING COLLEGE LIFE!
OHO HO HO HO!
TEE HEE HEE!
KOUKO MENTAL IMAGE.
AND IF SOMEONE INVITED ME TO A PARTY!!
I WOULD SAY "OKAY" RIGHT AWAY!! ☆
AH!
LET'S HAVE A DRINKING PARTY! ♡
TEE HEE.
PIIIING
OH, THAT'S RIGHT! YOU WERE INVITED TO A PARTY.
GEH...

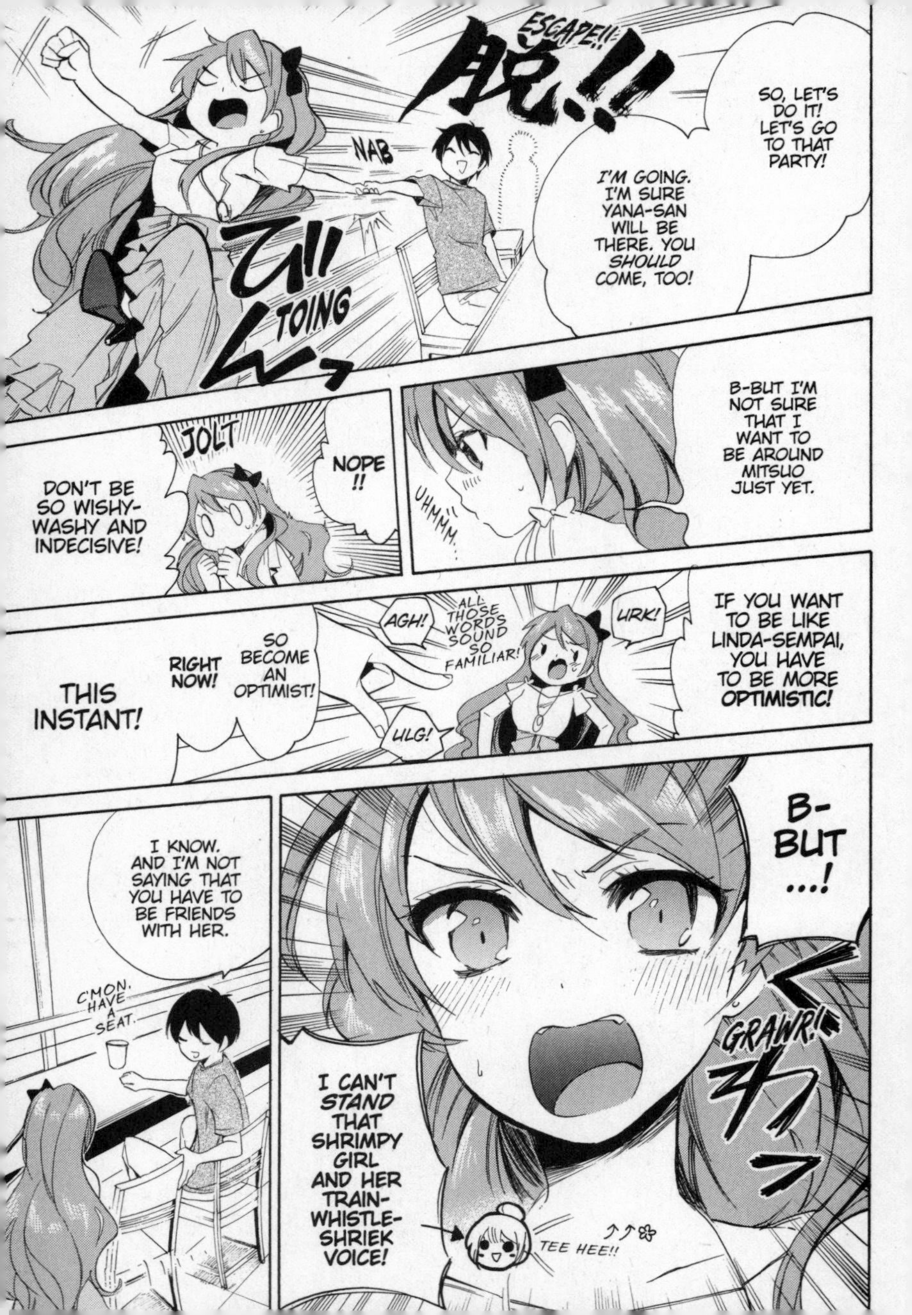
SO, LET'S DO IT! LET'S GO TO THAT PARTY!
I'M GOING. I'M SURE YANA-SAN WILL BE THERE. YOU SHOULD COME, TOO!
ESCAPE!!
NAB
TOING
B-BUT I'M NOT SURE THAT I WANT TO BE AROUND MITSUO JUST YET.
UHMMM...
NOPE!!
JOLT
DON'T BE SO WISHY-WASHY AND INDECISIVE!
IF YOU WANT TO BE LIKE LINDA-SEMPAI, YOU HAVE TO BE MORE OPTIMISTIC!
URK!
ALL THOSE WORDS SOUND SO FAMILIAR!
AGH!
ULG!
SO BECOME AN OPTIMIST!
RIGHT NOW!
THIS INSTANT!
B-BUT...!
GRAWR!
I CAN'T STAND THAT SHRIMPY GIRL AND HER TRAIN-WHISTLE-SHRIEK VOICE!
TEE HEE!!
I KNOW. AND I'M NOT SAYING THAT YOU HAVE TO BE FRIENDS WITH HER.
C'MON. HAVE A SEAT.

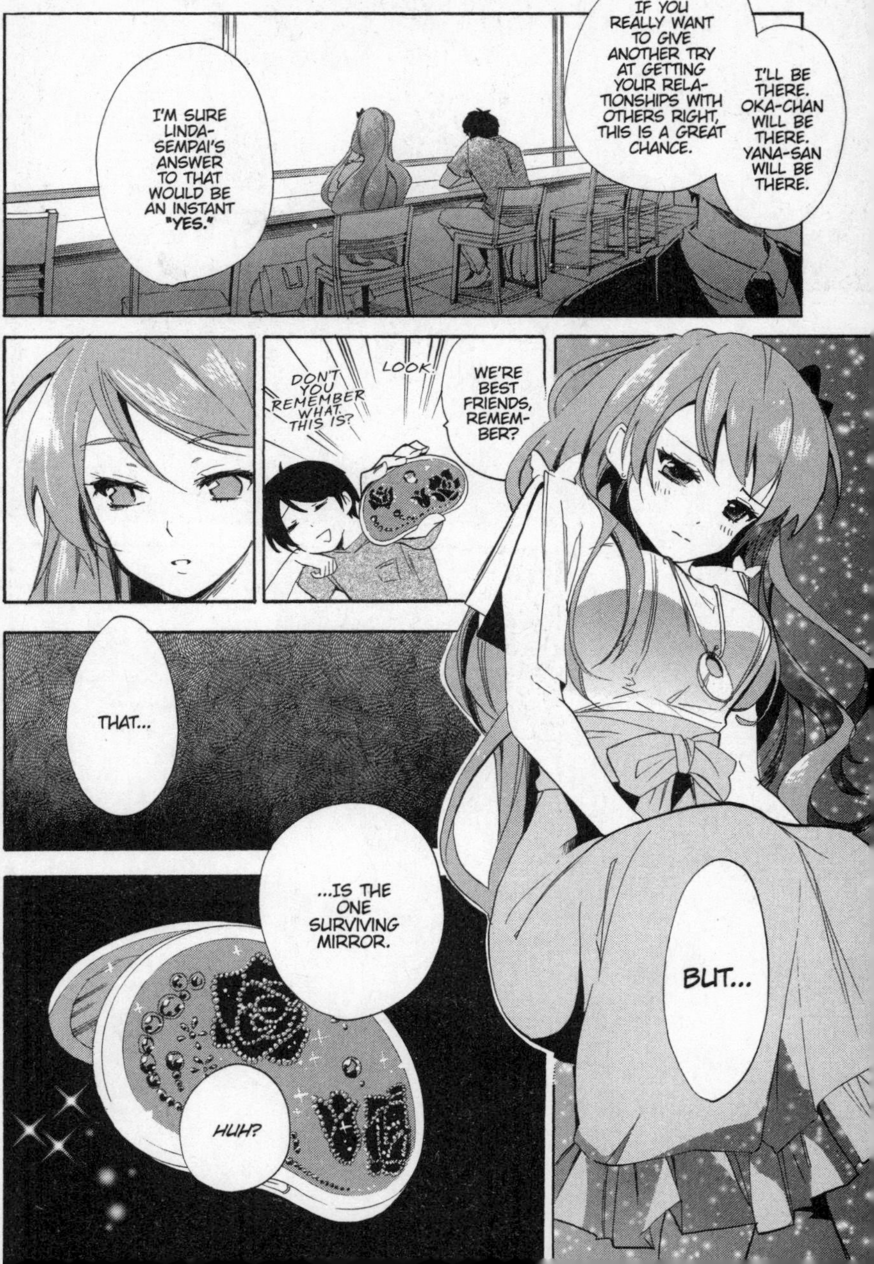
I'LL BE THERE. OKA-CHAN WILL BE THERE. YANA-SAN WILL BE THERE.
IF YOU REALLY WANT TO GIVE ANOTHER TRY AT GETTING YOUR RELATIONSHIPS WITH OTHERS RIGHT, THIS IS A GREAT CHANCE.
I'M SURE LINDA-SEMPAI'S ANSWER TO THAT WOULD BE AN INSTANT "YES."
WE'RE BEST FRIENDS, REMEMBER?
LOOK!
DON'T YOU REMEMBER WHAT THIS IS?
THAT...
...IS THE ONE SURVIVING MIRROR.
BUT...
HUH?

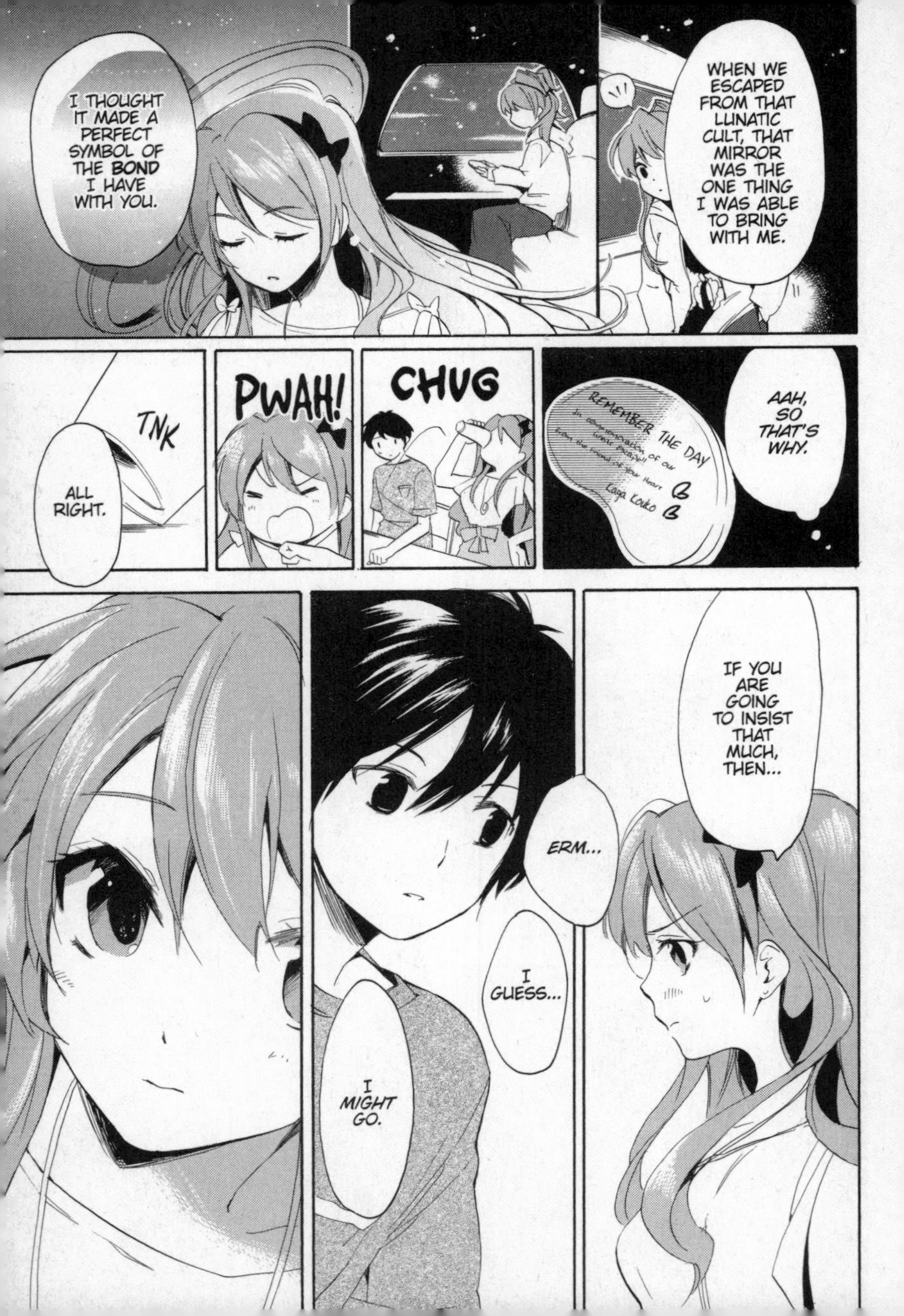
WHEN WE ESCAPED FROM THAT LUNATIC CULT, THAT MIRROR WAS THE ONE THING I WAS ABLE TO BRING WITH ME.
I THOUGHT IT MADE A PERFECT SYMBOL OF THE BOND I HAVE WITH YOU.
AAH, SO THAT'S WHY.
REMEMBER THE DAY
In commemoration of our lunatic escape!!
From the friend of your Heart
Kaga Kouko
CHUG
PWAH!
TNK
ALL RIGHT.
IF YOU ARE GOING TO INSIST THAT MUCH, THEN...
ERM...
I GUESS...
I MIGHT GO.

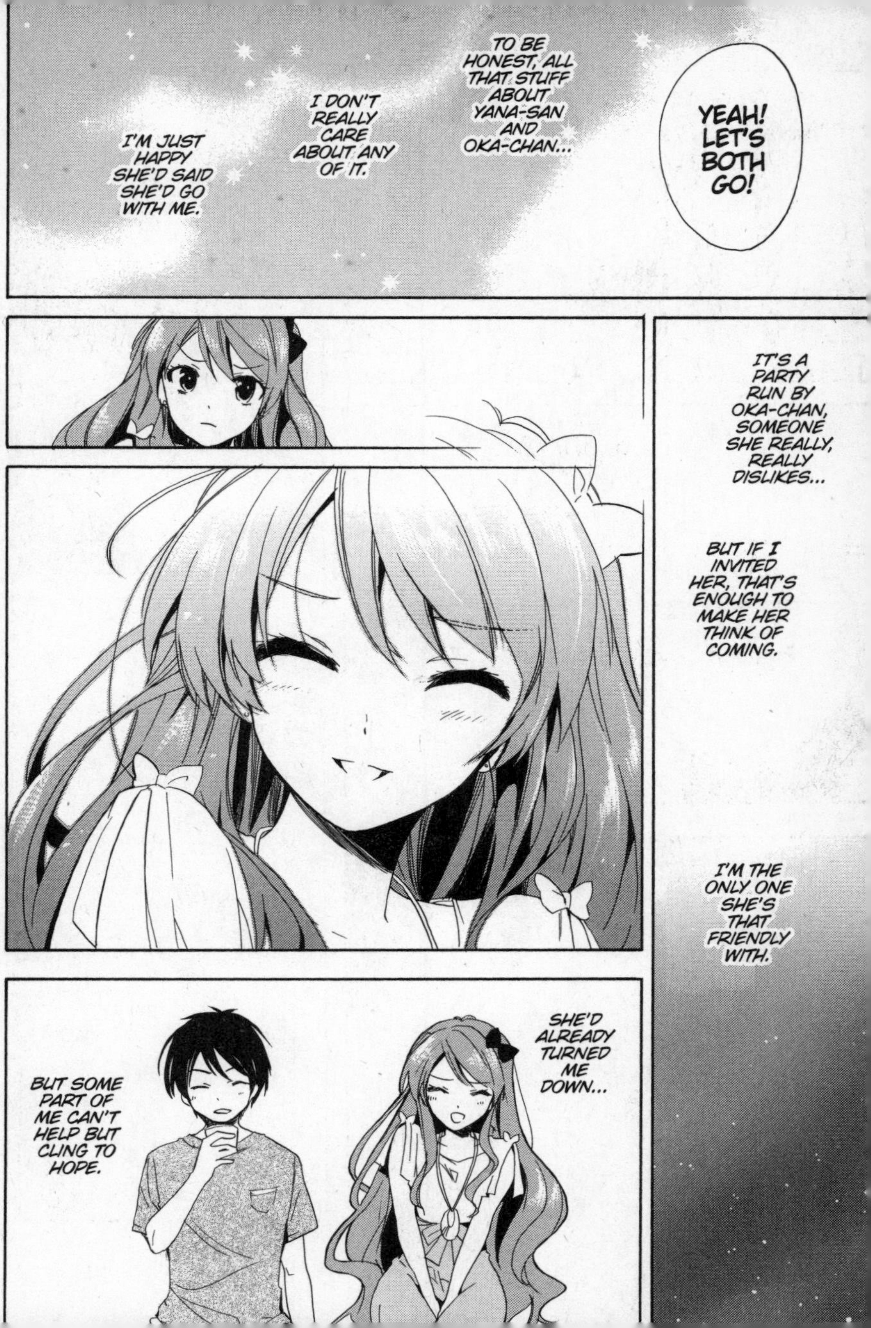
YEAH! LET'S BOTH GO!
TO BE HONEST, ALL THAT STUFF ABOUT YANA-SAN AND OKA-CHAN...
I DON'T REALLY CARE ABOUT ANY OF IT.
I'M JUST HAPPY SHE'D SAID SHE'D GO WITH ME.
IT'S A PARTY RUN BY OKA-CHAN, SOMEONE SHE REALLY, REALLY DISLIKES...
BUT IF I INVITED HER, THAT'S ENOUGH TO MAKE HER THINK OF COMING.
I'M THE ONLY ONE SHE'S THAT FRIENDLY WITH.
SHE'D ALREADY TURNED ME DOWN...
BUT SOME PART OF ME CAN'T HELP BUT CLING TO HOPE.

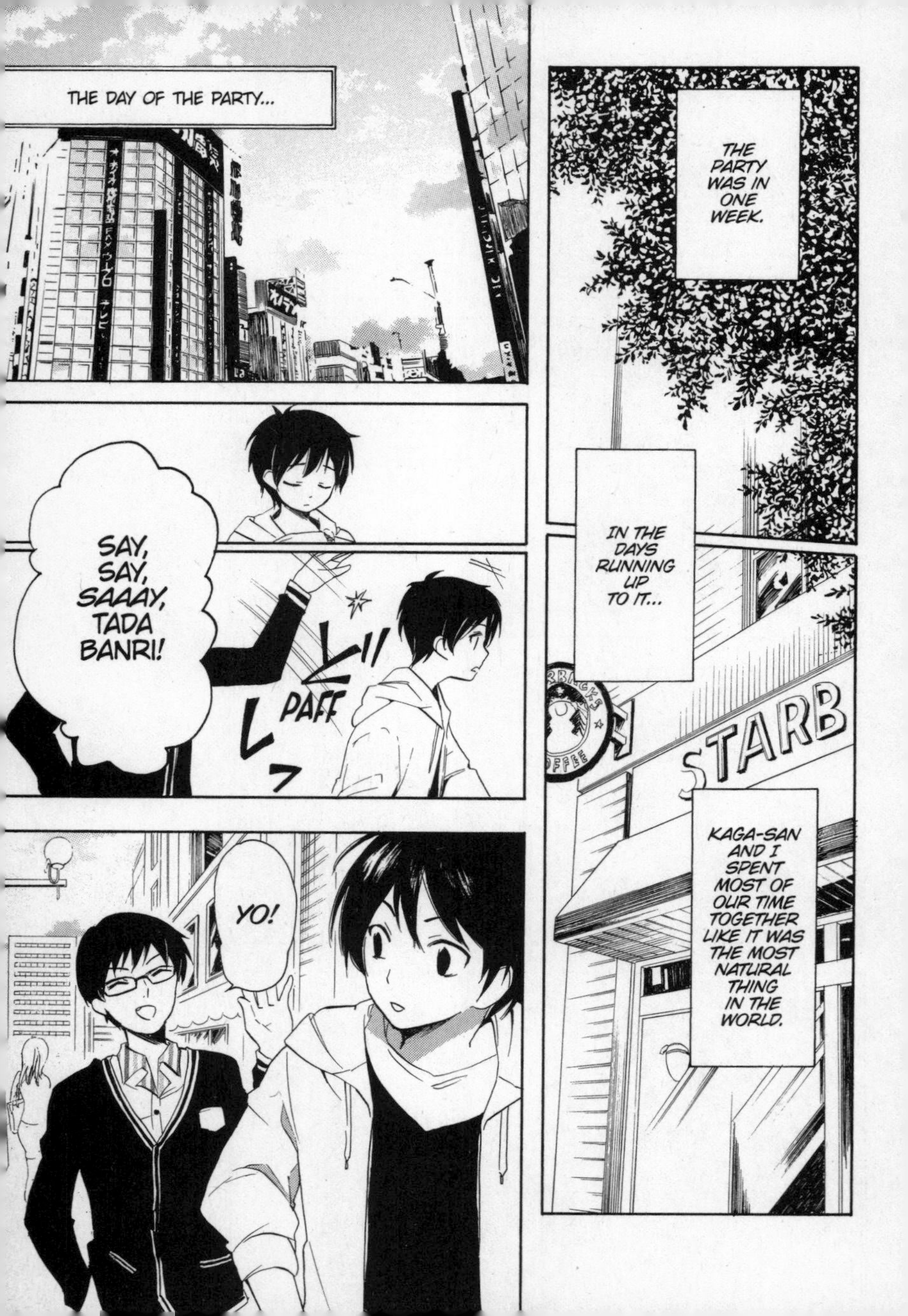
THE PARTY WAS IN ONE WEEK.
IN THE DAYS RUNNING UP TO IT...
STARB
KAGA-SAN AND I SPENT MOST OF OUR TIME TOGETHER LIKE IT WAS THE MOST NATURAL THING IN THE WORLD.
THE DAY OF THE PARTY...
SAY, SAY, SAAAY, TADA BANRI!
PAFF
YO!

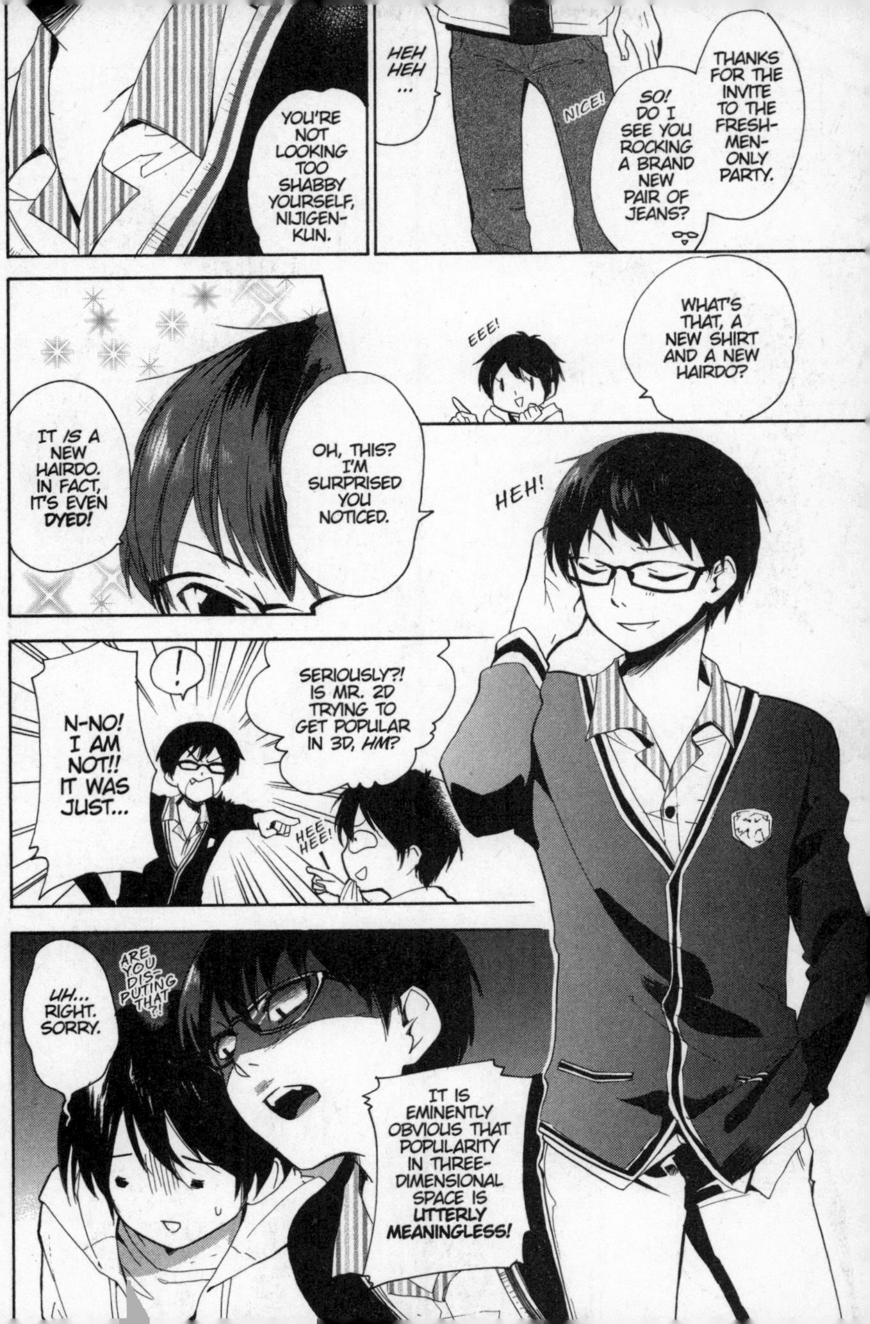

THANKS FOR THE INVITE TO THE FRESHMEN-ONLY PARTY.
SO! DO I SEE YOU ROCKING A BRAND NEW PAIR OF JEANS?
NICE!
HEH HEH ...
YOU'RE NOT LOOKING TOO SHABBY YOURSELF, NIJIGEN-KUN.
WHAT'S THAT, A NEW SHIRT AND A NEW HAIRDO?
EEE!
HEH!
OH, THIS? I'M SURPRISED YOU NOTICED.
IT *IS* A NEW HAIRDO. IN FACT, IT'S EVEN **DYED!**
SERIOUSLY?! IS MR. 2D TRYING TO GET POPULAR IN 3D, *HM?*
HEE HEE!
!
!
N-NO! I AM NOT!! IT WAS JUST...
IT IS EMINENTLY OBVIOUS THAT POPULARITY IN THREE-DIMENSIONAL SPACE IS **UTTERLY MEANINGLESS!**
ARE YOU DISPUTING THAT?!
UH... RIGHT. SORRY.

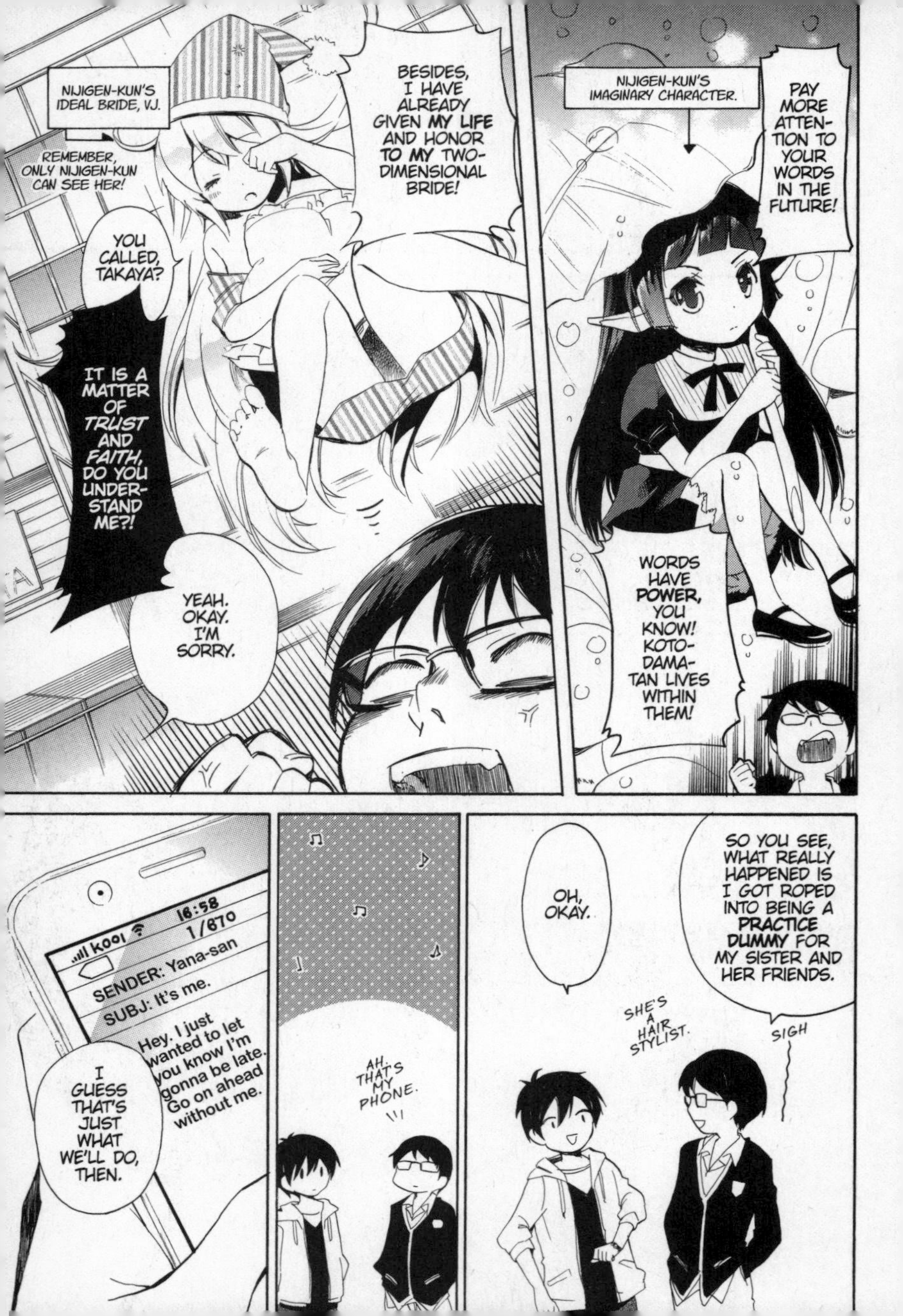
PAY MORE ATTENTION TO YOUR WORDS IN THE FUTURE!
NIJIGEN-KUN'S IMAGINARY CHARACTER.
WORDS HAVE POWER, YOU KNOW! KOTODAMA-TAN LIVES WITHIN THEM!
BESIDES, I HAVE ALREADY GIVEN MY LIFE AND HONOR TO MY TWO-DIMENSIONAL BRIDE!
NIJIGEN-KUN'S IDEAL BRIDE, VJ.
REMEMBER, ONLY NIJIGEN-KUN CAN SEE HER!
YOU CALLED, TAKAYA?
IT IS A MATTER OF TRUST AND FAITH, DO YOU UNDERSTAND ME?!
YEAH. OKAY. I'M SORRY.
SO YOU SEE, WHAT REALLY HAPPENED IS I GOT ROPED INTO BEING A PRACTICE DUMMY FOR MY SISTER AND HER FRIENDS.
OH, OKAY.
SIGH
SHE'S A HAIR STYLIST.
AH. THAT'S MY PHONE.
16:58
1/670
KOOI
SENDER: Yana-san
SUBJ: It's me.
Hey. I just wanted to let you know I'm gonna be late. Go on ahead without me.
I GUESS THAT'S JUST WHAT WE'LL DO, THEN.

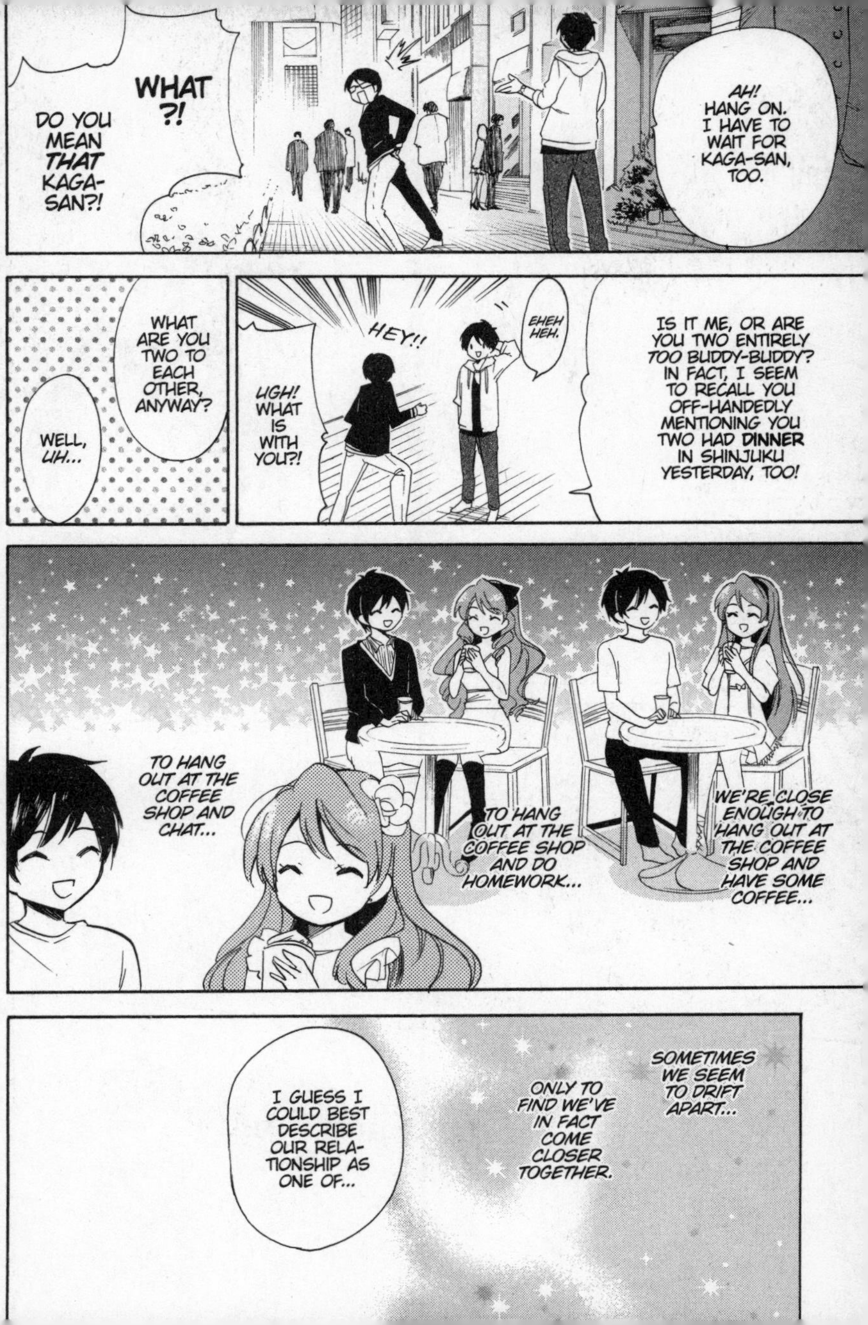
AH! HANG ON. I HAVE TO WAIT FOR KAGA-SAN, TOO.
WHAT ?!
DO YOU MEAN THAT KAGA-SAN?!
IS IT ME, OR ARE YOU TWO ENTIRELY TOO BUDDY-BUDDY? IN FACT, I SEEM TO RECALL YOU OFF-HANDEDLY MENTIONING YOU TWO HAD DINNER IN SHINJUKU YESTERDAY, TOO!
EHEH HEH.
HEY!!
UGH! WHAT IS WITH YOU?!
WHAT ARE YOU TWO TO EACH OTHER, ANYWAY?
WELL, UH...
WE'RE CLOSE ENOUGH TO HANG OUT AT THE COFFEE SHOP AND HAVE SOME COFFEE...
TO HANG OUT AT THE COFFEE SHOP AND DO HOMEWORK...
TO HANG OUT AT THE COFFEE SHOP AND CHAT...
SOMETIMES WE SEEM TO DRIFT APART...
ONLY TO FIND WE'VE IN FACT COME CLOSER TOGETHER.
I GUESS I COULD BEST DESCRIBE OUR RELATIONSHIP AS ONE OF...

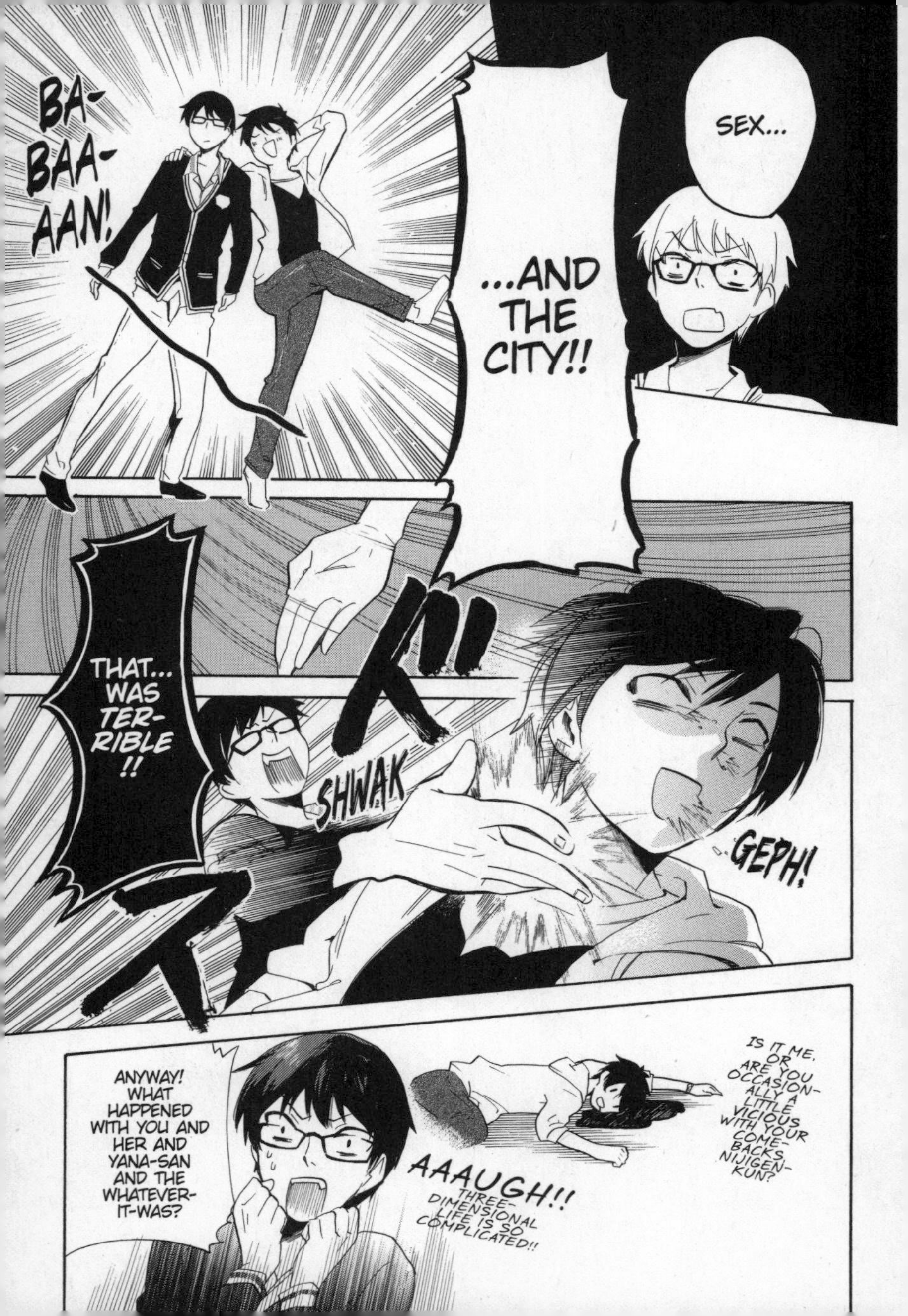
SEX...
...AND THE CITY!!
BA-BAA-AAN!
GEPH!
SHWAK
THAT... WAS TER-RIBLE!!
IS IT ME, OR ARE YOU OCCASION-ALLY A LITTLE VICIOUS WITH YOUR COME-BACKS, NIJIGEN-KUN?
AAAUGH!!
THREE-DIMENSIONAL LIFE IS SO COMPLICATED!!
ANYWAY! WHAT HAPPENED WITH YOU AND HER AND YANA-SAN AND THE WHATEVER-IT-WAS?

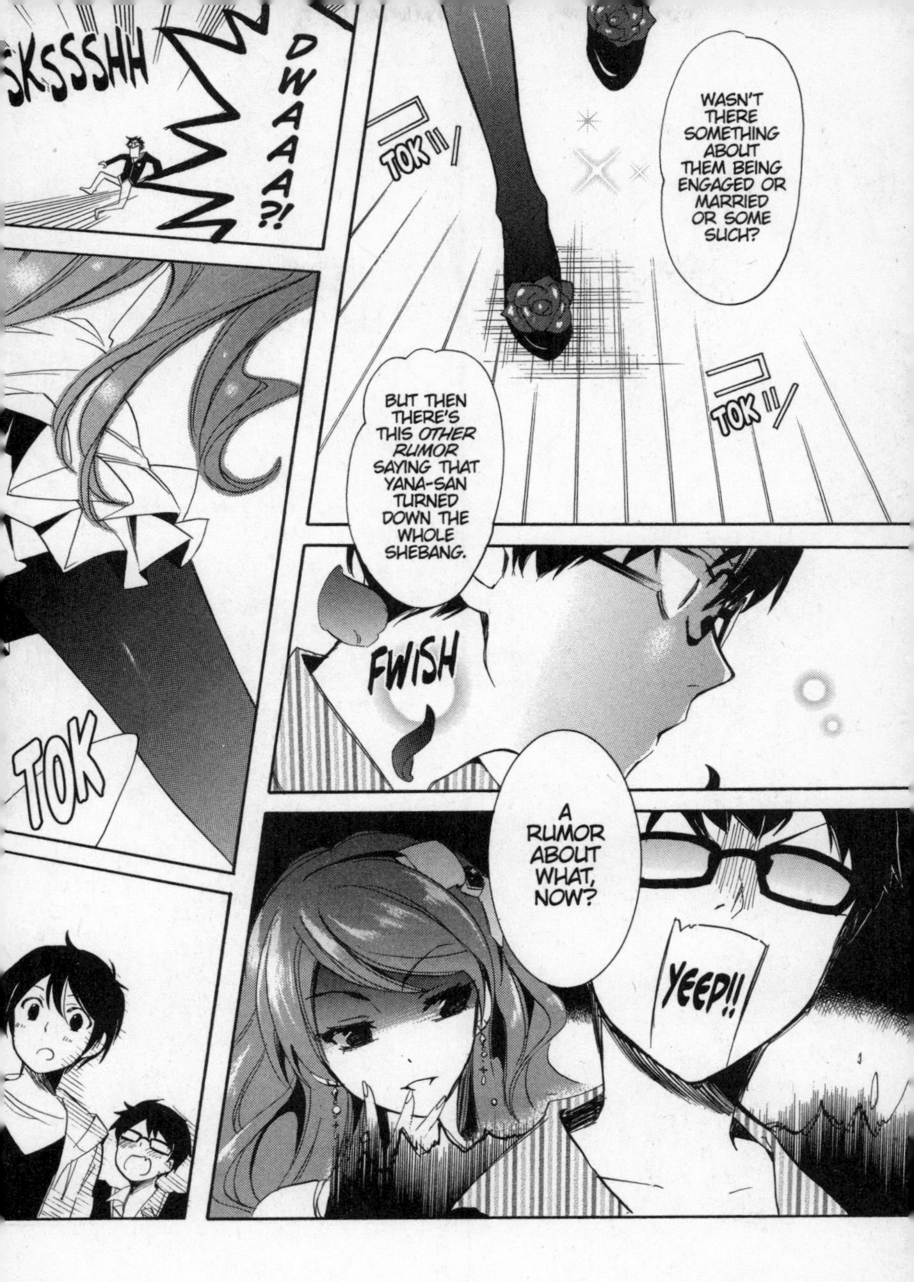
WASN'T THERE SOMETHING ABOUT THEM BEING ENGAGED OR MARRIED OR SOME SUCH?
TOK
TOK
DWAAAAA?!
SKSSSHH
BUT THEN THERE'S THIS *OTHER RUMOR* SAYING THAT YANA-SAN TURNED DOWN THE WHOLE SHEBANG.
FWISH
TOK
A RUMOR ABOUT WHAT, NOW?
YEEP!!

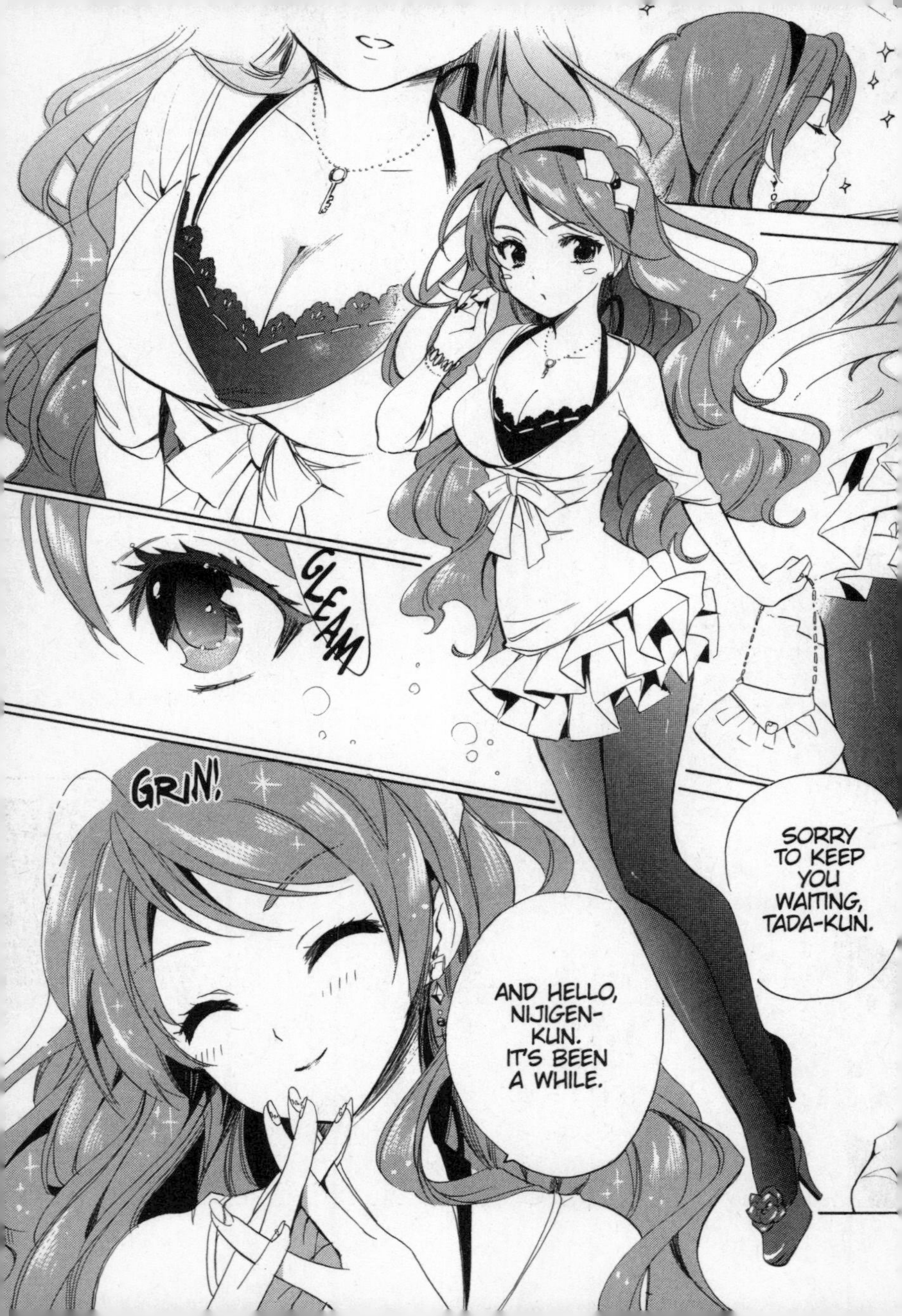
SORRY TO KEEP YOU WAITING, TADA-KUN.
GLEAM
GRIN!
AND HELLO, NIJIGEN-KUN. IT'S BEEN A WHILE.

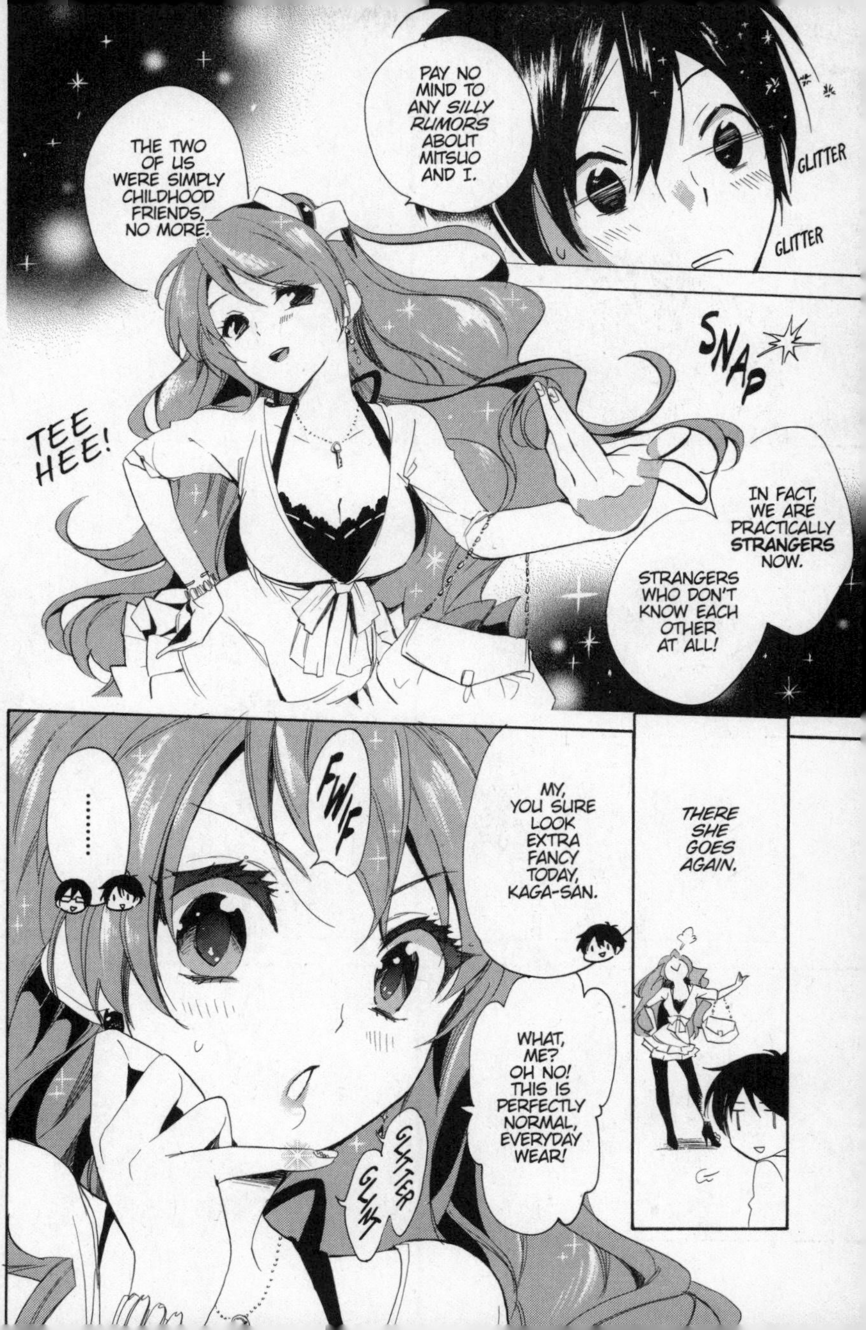
PAY NO MIND TO ANY SILLY RUMORS ABOUT MITSUO AND I.
THE TWO OF US WERE SIMPLY CHILDHOOD FRIENDS, NO MORE.
GLITTER
GLITTER
SNAP
TEE HEE!
IN FACT, WE ARE PRACTICALLY STRANGERS NOW.
STRANGERS WHO DON'T KNOW EACH OTHER AT ALL!
THERE SHE GOES AGAIN.
MY, YOU SURE LOOK EXTRA FANCY TODAY, KAGA-SAN.
FWIP
......
WHAT, ME? OH NO! THIS IS PERFECTLY NORMAL, EVERYDAY WEAR!
GLITTER
GLINT

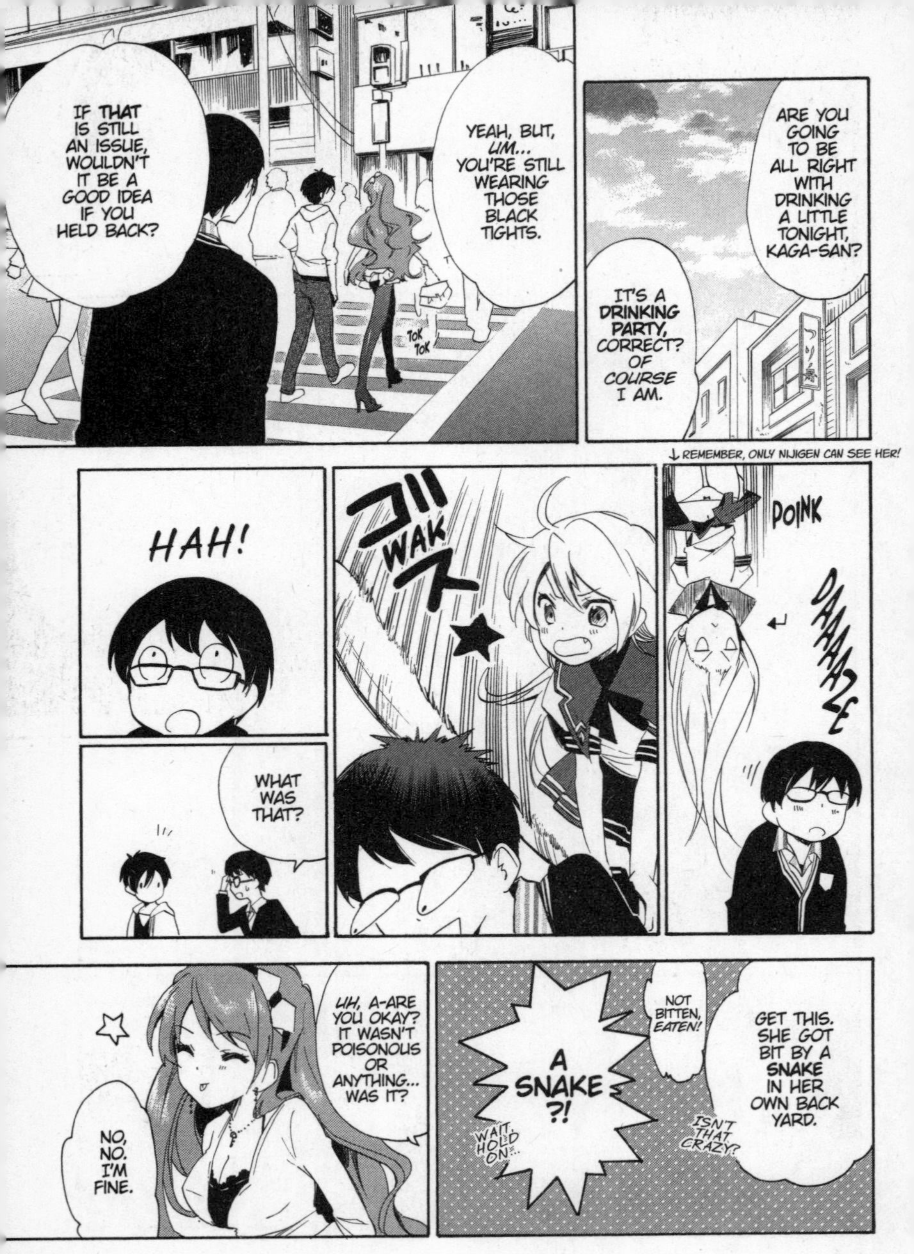
ARE YOU GOING TO BE ALL RIGHT WITH DRINKING A LITTLE TONIGHT, KAGA-SAN?
IT'S A DRINKING PARTY, CORRECT? OF COURSE I AM.
YEAH, BUT, UM... YOU'RE STILL WEARING THOSE BLACK TIGHTS.
TOK TOK
IF THAT IS STILL AN ISSUE, WOULDN'T IT BE A GOOD IDEA IF YOU HELD BACK?
↓ REMEMBER, ONLY NIJIGEN CAN SEE HER!
POINK
DAAAAAZE
WAK
HAH!
WHAT WAS THAT?
GET THIS. SHE GOT BIT BY A SNAKE IN HER OWN BACK YARD.
ISN'T THAT CRAZY?
NOT BITTEN, EATEN!
A SNAKE?!
WAIT, HOLD ON...
UH, A-ARE YOU OKAY? IT WASN'T POISONOUS OR ANYTHING... WAS IT?
NO, NO. I'M FINE.

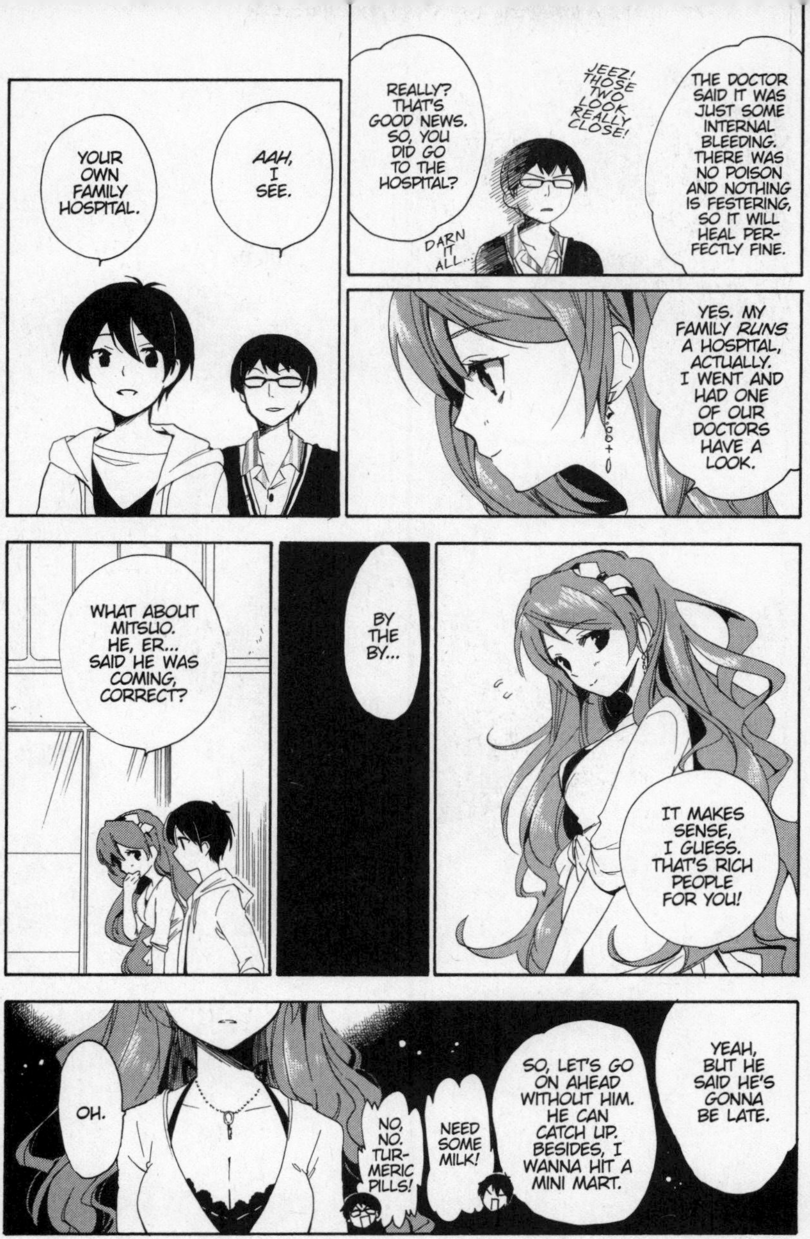
THE DOCTOR SAID IT WAS JUST SOME INTERNAL BLEEDING. THERE WAS NO POISON AND NOTHING IS FESTERING, SO IT WILL HEAL PER-FECTLY FINE.
JEEZ! THOSE TWO LOOK REALLY CLOSE!
REALLY? THAT'S GOOD NEWS. SO, YOU DID GO TO THE HOSPITAL?
DARN IT ALL...
YES. MY FAMILY *RUNS* A HOSPITAL, ACTUALLY. I WENT AND HAD ONE OF OUR DOCTORS HAVE A LOOK.
AAH, I SEE.
YOUR OWN FAMILY HOSPITAL.
IT MAKES SENSE, I GUESS. THAT'S RICH PEOPLE FOR YOU!
BY THE BY...
WHAT ABOUT MITSUO. HE, ER... SAID HE WAS COMING, CORRECT?
YEAH, BUT HE SAID HE'S GONNA BE LATE.
SO, LET'S GO ON AHEAD WITHOUT HIM. HE CAN CATCH UP. BESIDES, I WANNA HIT A MINI MART.
NEED SOME MILK!
NO, NO. TUR-MERIC PILLS!
OH.

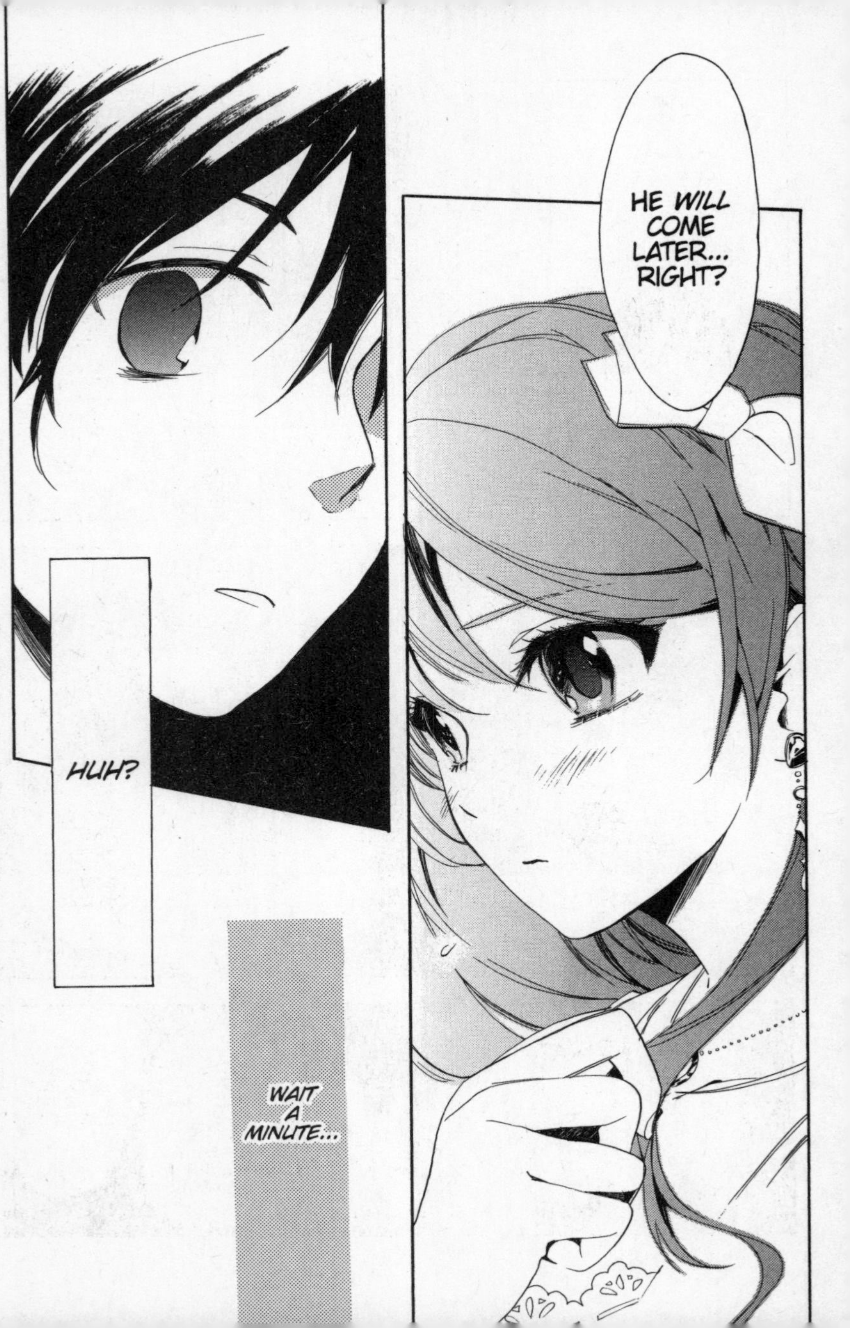
HE WILL COME LATER... RIGHT?
HUH?
WAIT A MINUTE...

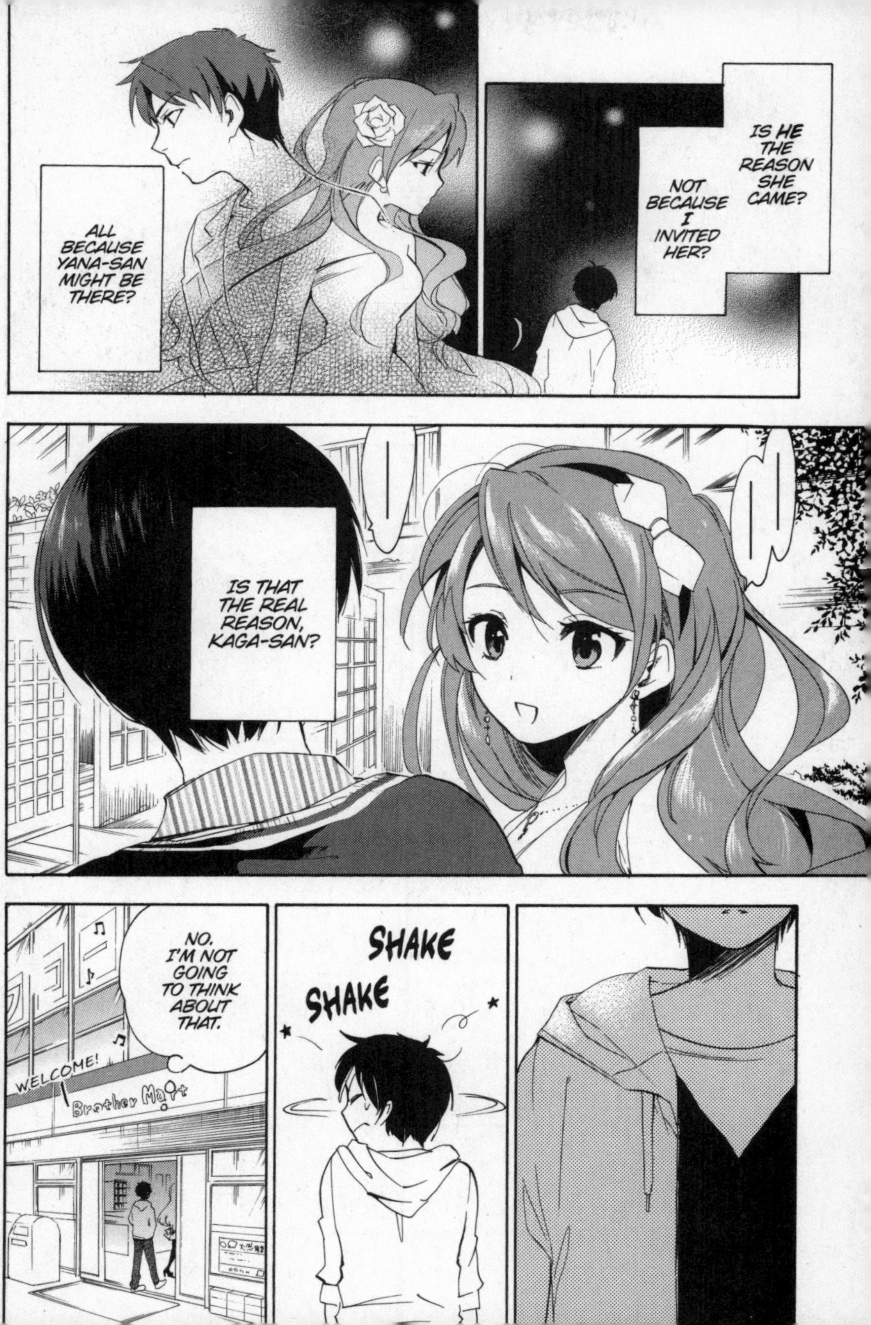
IS HE THE REASON SHE CAME?
NOT BECAUSE I INVITED HER?
ALL BECAUSE YANA-SAN MIGHT BE THERE?
IS THAT THE REAL REASON, KAGA-SAN?
SHAKE
SHAKE
NO. I'M NOT GOING TO THINK ABOUT THAT.
WELCOME!
Brother Mart

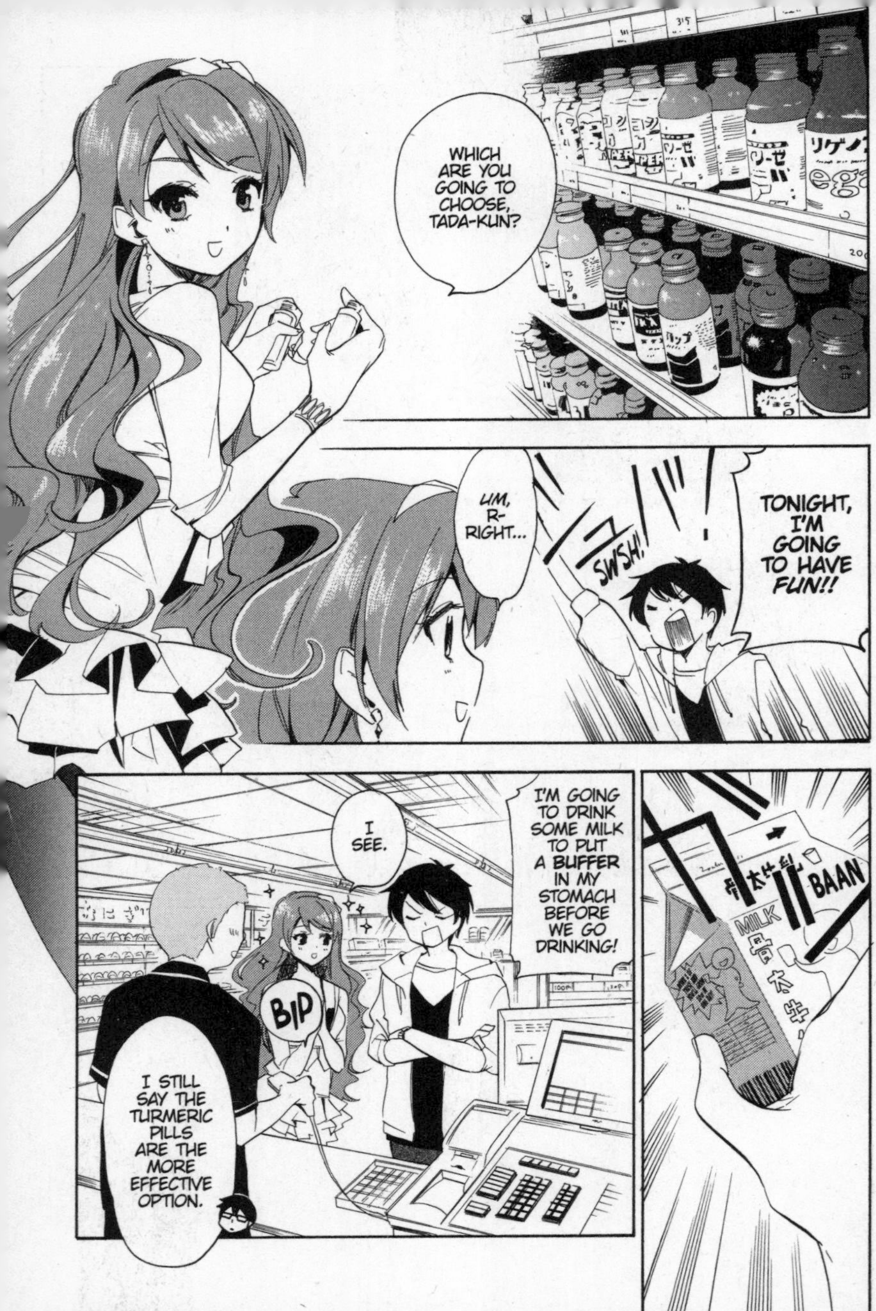
WHICH ARE YOU GOING TO CHOOSE, TADA-KUN?
TONIGHT, I'M GOING TO HAVE FUN!!
SWSH!
UM, R-RIGHT...
BAAN
MILK
I'M GOING TO DRINK SOME MILK TO PUT A BUFFER IN MY STOMACH BEFORE WE GO DRINKING!
I SEE.
BIP
I STILL SAY THE TURMERIC PILLS ARE THE MORE EFFECTIVE OPTION.

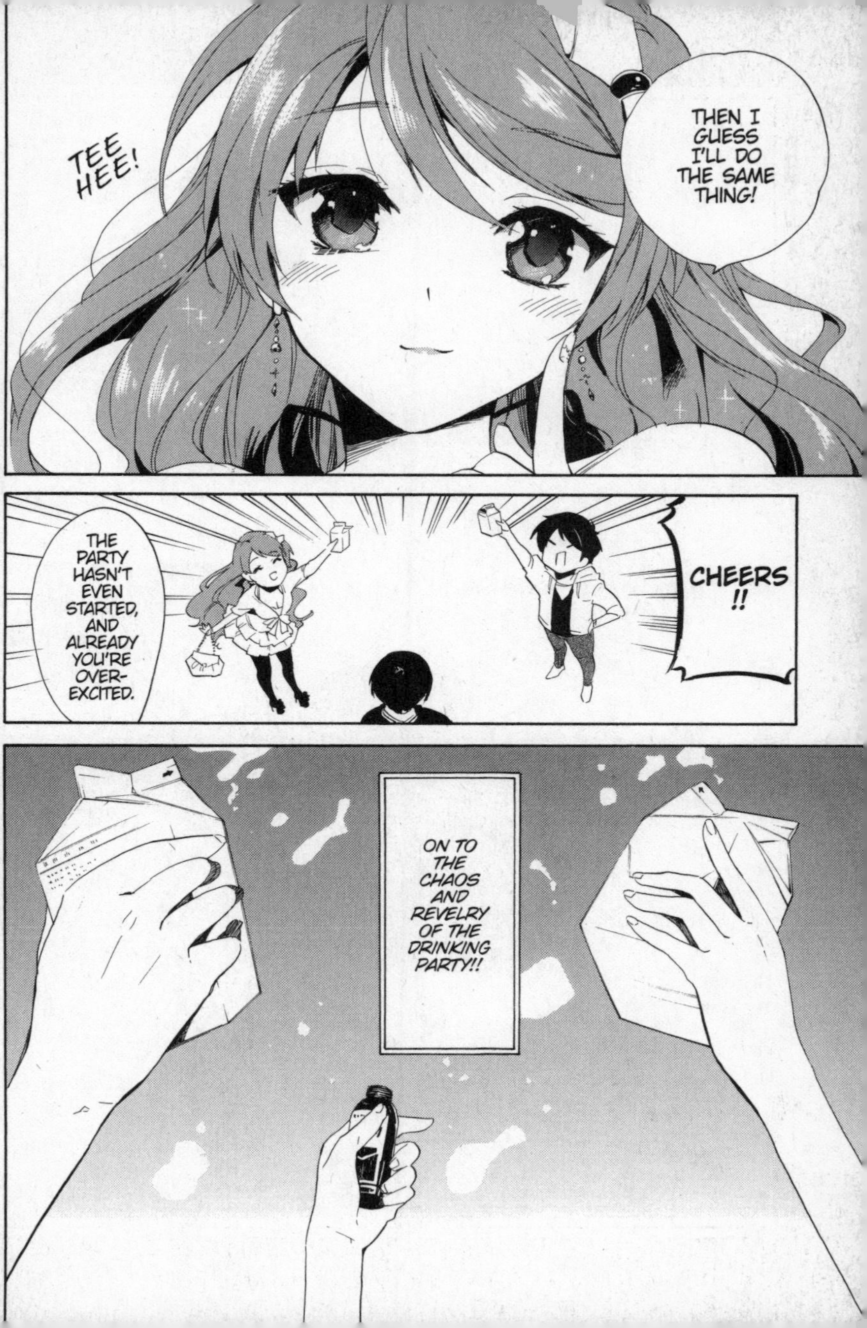
THEN I GUESS I'LL DO THE SAME THING!
TEE HEE!
CHEERS!!
THE PARTY HASN'T EVEN STARTED, AND ALREADY YOU'RE OVER-EXCITED.
ON TO THE CHAOS AND REVELRY OF THE DRINKING PARTY!!

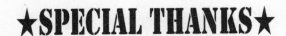

★SPECIAL THANKS★

YUYUKO TAKEMIYA-SENSEI
EIJI KOMATSU-SENSEI
IMANARI-SAN
YUASA-SAN
SOMETANI-SAN

★

TATSUYA
KAHO
MA-TSUN
TAKANI-CHAN
MOM
NACHI

★

AND ALL YOU READERS OUT THERE! ♥

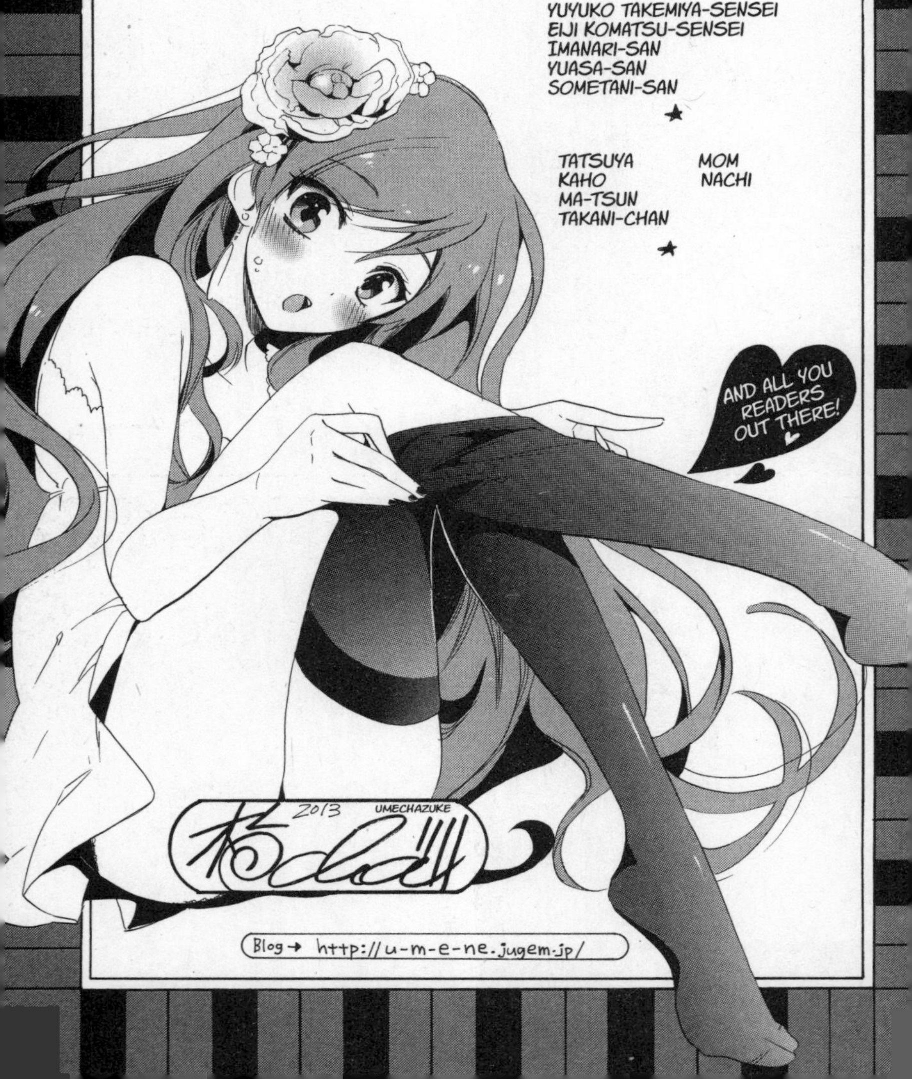

2013
UMECHAZUKE

Blog → http://u-m-e-ne.jugem.jp/

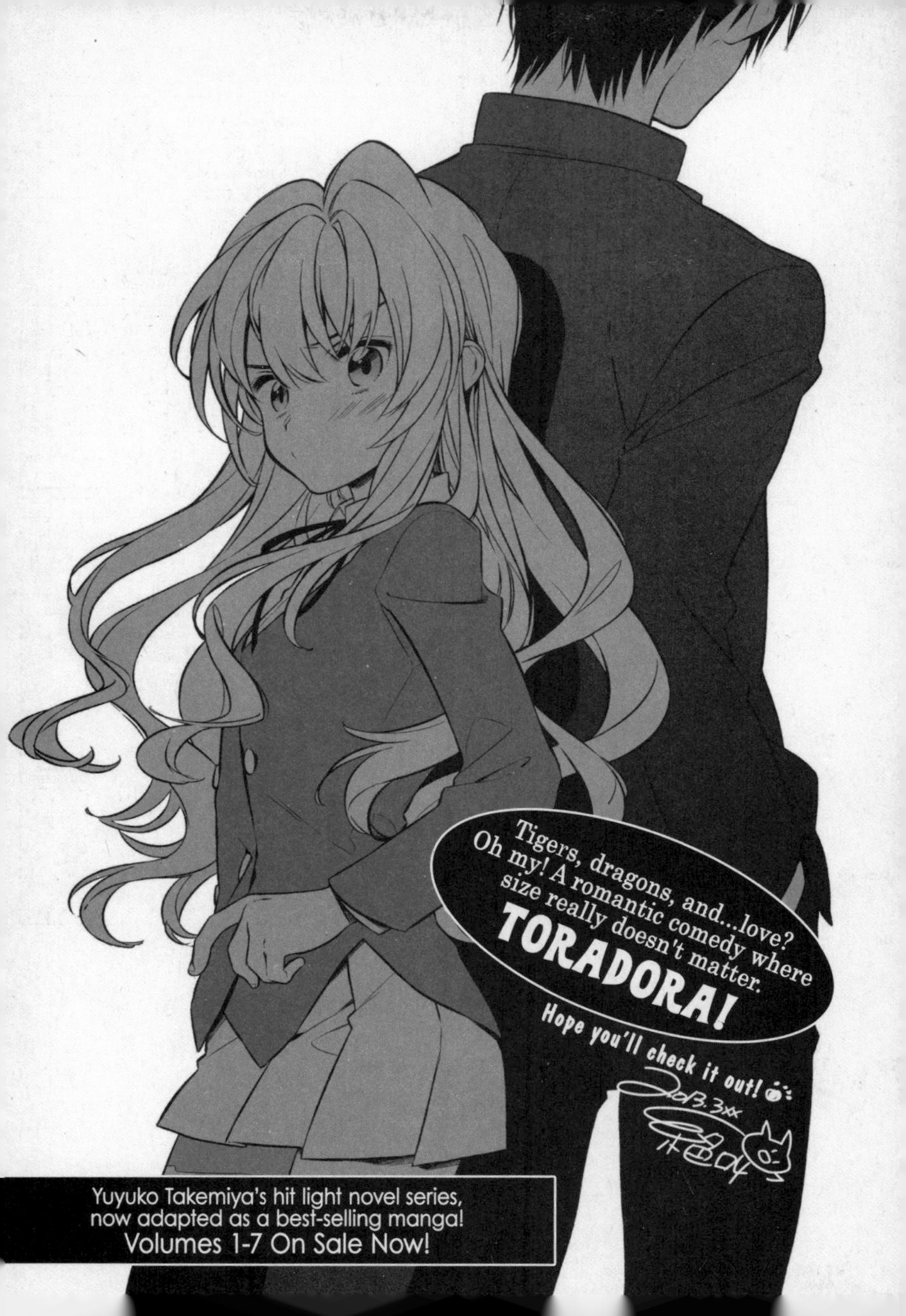

Tigers, dragons, and...love? Oh my! A romantic comedy where size really doesn't matter.
TORADORA!
Hope you'll check it out!
2013.3xx
Yuyuko Takemiya's hit light novel series, now adapted as a best-selling manga!
Volumes 1-7 On Sale Now!

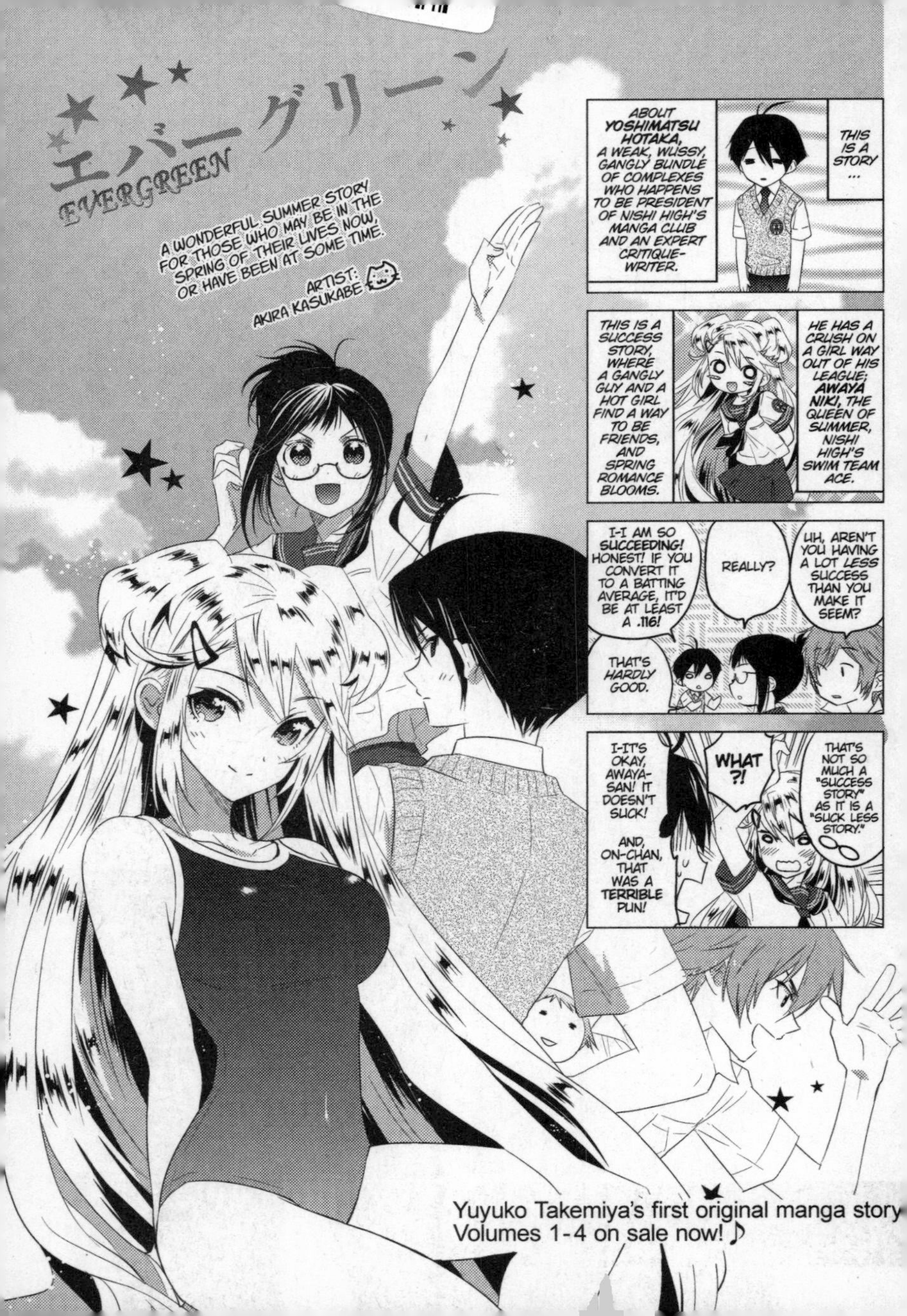
THIS IS A STORY ...
ABOUT YOSHIMATSU HOTAKA, A WEAK, WUSSY, GANGLY BUNDLE OF COMPLEXES WHO HAPPENS TO BE PRESIDENT OF NISHI HIGH'S MANGA CLUB AND AN EXPERT CRITIQUE-WRITER.
HE HAS A CRUSH ON A GIRL WAY OUT OF HIS LEAGUE; AWAYA NIKI, THE QUEEN OF SUMMER, NISHI HIGH'S SWIM TEAM ACE.
THIS IS A SUCCESS STORY, WHERE A GANGLY GUY AND A HOT GIRL FIND A WAY TO BE FRIENDS, AND SPRING ROMANCE BLOOMS.
UH, AREN'T YOU HAVING A LOT LESS SUCCESS THAN YOU MAKE IT SEEM?
REALLY?
I-I AM SO SUCCEEDING! HONEST! IF YOU CONVERT IT TO A BATTING AVERAGE, IT'D BE AT LEAST A .116!
THAT'S HARDLY GOOD.
THAT'S NOT SO MUCH A "SUCCESS STORY" AS IT IS A "SUCK LESS STORY."
WHAT?!
I-IT'S OKAY, AWAYA-SAN! IT DOESN'T SUCK!
AND, ON-CHAN, THAT WAS A TERRIBLE PUN!
エバーグリーン
EVERGREEN
A WONDERFUL SUMMER STORY FOR THOSE WHO MAY BE IN THE SPRING OF THEIR LIVES NOW, OR HAVE BEEN AT SOME TIME.
ARTIST: AKIRA KASUKABE
Yuyuko Takemiya's first original manga story
Volumes 1-4 on sale now!♪

SEVEN SEAS ENTER

GOLDEN TIME ゴールデンタイム VOL. 3

based on the novel by **YUYUKO TAKEMIYA** / art by **UMECHAZUKE** / original character design by **E-JI KOMATSU**

TRANSLATION
Adrienne Beck

ADAPTATION
Bambi Eloriaga-Amago

LETTERING
Roland Amago

LAYOUT
Mheeya Wok

COVER DESIGN
Nicky Lim

PROOFREADER
Shanti Whitesides

PRODUCTION MANAGER
Lissa Pattillo

EDITOR-IN-CHIEF
Adam Arnold

PUBLISHER
Jason DeAngelis

GOLDEN TIME VOL. 3

Edited by ASCII MEDIA WORKS.
First published in Japan in 2013 by KADOKAWA CORPORATION, Tokyo.
English translation rights arranged with KADOKAWA CORPORATION, Tokyo.

Seven Seas books may be purchased in bulk for educational, business, or promotional use. For information on bulk purchases, please contact Macmillan Corporate & Premium Sales Department at 1-800-221-7945 (ext 5442) or write specialmarkets@macmillan.com.

ISBN: 978-1-626922-56-3

Printed in Canada

First Printing: April 2016

10 9 8 7 6 5 4 3 2 1

FOLLOW US ONLINE: ***www.gomanga.com***

READING DIRECTIONS

This book reads from ***right to left***, Japanese style. If this is your first time reading manga, you start reading from the top right panel on each page and take it from there. If you get lost, just follow the numbered diagram here. It may seem backwards at first, but you'll get the hang of it! Have fun!!

1
2
3
4
5
6
7
8
9

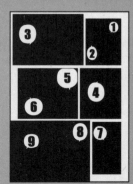